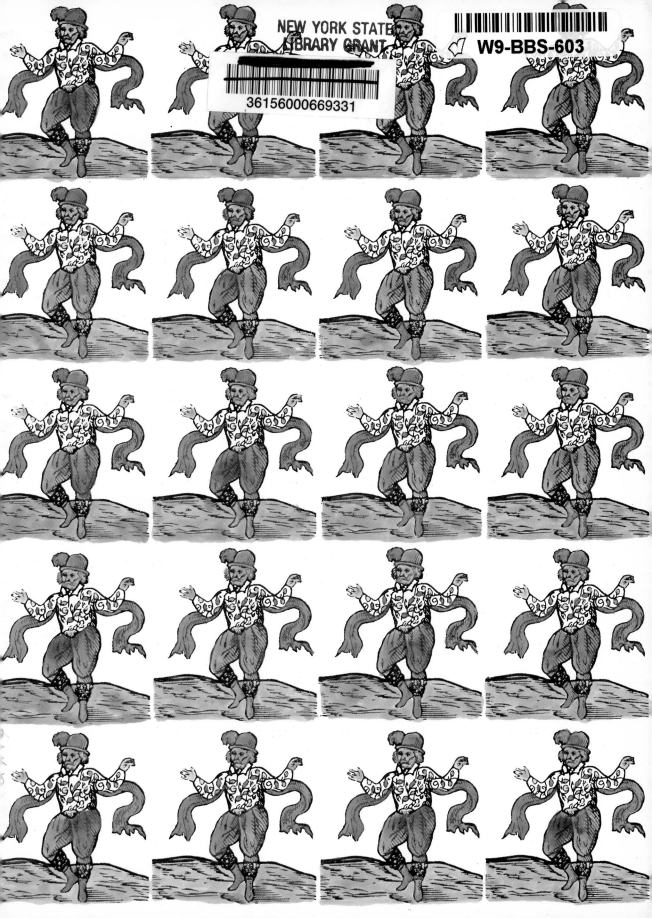

W9-BBS-603

The Customs
and Ceremonies
of Britain

CHARLES KIGHTLY

The Customs and Ceremonies of Britain

AN ENCYCLOPAEDIA OF LIVING TRADITIONS

WITH OVER 200 ILLUSTRATIONS,
12 IN COLOR

THAMES AND HUDSON

To
Martha Rhoden's Tuppenny Dish
The Shropshire Bedlams
and
The York Gentlemen

© 1986 Thames and Hudson Ltd, London

First published in the United States in 1986 by
Thames and Hudson Inc., 500 Fifth Avenue,
New York, New York 10110

Library of Congress Catalog Card Number 85-51466

Printed and bound in Spain
Artes Gráficas Toledo, S.A.
D.L. TO: 1896-85

Contents

Acknowledgments

The author would like to express his grateful thanks to the following people and organizations, who kindly provided local information on customs and ceremonies, or otherwise rendered invaluable assistance during the preparation of this book.

Ian Ball, Sarn; Anthony Barton, York; Mrs S Bastain, District Information Officer, Congleton, Cheshire; Revd M. Beaumont, Rector of Ideford, Devon; Ingrid Beeby, York; Revd P.D.S. Blake, Rector of Hartfield, East Sussex; City of Bristol Publicity and Information Dept; the British Tourist Authority; Mrs J. Brooks, Huntington, York; Brian Bugler, Company of Purbeck Marblers and Stonecutters; Revd D. Burden, Rector of Keevil, Wiltshire; Brian Buttery, Verger, St Wulfram's, Grantham, Lincolnshire; Revd C. Carter, Llansilin, Powys; Rex Clark, Assistant County Librarian, North-West Worcestershire Division; the Court Leet of the Manor of Clifton, North Yorkshire; Mr D. Coggan, Westwoodside, Haxey, Lincolnshire; Revd M. Collier, Rector of Hope, Derbyshire; R.D. Cooper, Bideford, Devon; Penny Crocker, York; Cumbria Tourist Board; J.C. Davies, Market Harborough, Leicestershire; Revd A.J.F. Dulley, Vicar of Langham, Rutland; East Midlands Tourist Board; Mrs E.M. Elson, Information Clerk, Borough of Crewe and Nantwich, Cheshire; Francis Felix OSB; Revd J.F. Finney, Vicar of Leigh, Lancashire; Mr and Mrs D. Fletcher, Ruscombe, Stroud, Gloucestershire; Gloucester Tourist Information Office; Revd M.C. Goldsmith, Rector of St Peter's, Nottingham; R.C. Goodwin, Mayor's Secretary, City of Canterbury; Revd R. Harris, Vicar of Rippingale, Lincolnshire; Mrs M. Harrison, Librarian, Buckingham Library; Hastings Borough Tourist and Information Department; E.B. Hawkes, Civic and Publicity Officer, Preston, Lancashire; Heart of England Tourist Board; Revd J. Heffer, Rector of Wingrave, Buckinghamshire; Hereford City Library; Herefordshire County Record Office; G.R. Hiatt, Divisional Librarian, Gloucester; Mr Hibbert, Sellack, Herefordshire; Richard Hillier, Assistant Librarian (Local Studies) Cambridgeshire; Revd G.Holmes, Piddinghoe, Sussex; Revd Canon R. Howe, Rural Dean of Grantham, Lincolnshire; B. Hughes, Director of Education and Arts, Bolton, Lancashire; Revd R. Hunting, Rector of Sileby, Leicestershire; Mr A.W. Hutton, Whitby; Revd D.R. Jenkins, Rector of Harlington, Middlesex; Revd M. Jenner, Vicar of Ellington, Cambridgeshire; Miss J. Jetten, Twyford, Hampshire; Revd Tony Knox, Vicar of Toddington, Bedfordshire; Knutsford Service Centre of Macclesfield Borough Council, Cheshire; Revd Adrian Leak, York; Lichfield District Council; Revd T.L. Lloyd, formerly Rector of Braughing, Hertfordshire; London Tourist Board; Sam McCarthy, Secretary, British Marbles Board of Control; J. Main, Divisional Librarian, Durham County; Mrs J. Maskell, Assistant Clerk to the Trustees, Reading Charities, Berkshire; Revd Canon D.P. Maurice, Rector of Glaven and Stiffkey, Norfolk; Mrs Margaret Metcalfe, Bainbridge, North Yorkshire; Owen Metcalfe, Askrigg, North Yorkshire; Bill Midwinter, Master of the Ringers, Newark, Nottinghamshire; F.J. Mills, Malmesbury, Wiltshire; Minehead and West Somerset Publicity Association; Revd Canon D. Naumann, Rector of Sandwich, Kent; Revd K. Newbon, Vicar of Braunstone, Leicestershire; Revd G.L. North, Vicar of Old Weston, Cambridgeshire; Northampton Tourist Centre; North West Tourist Board; Northumbria Tourist Board; Gil de Pablo; H.A. Poole, Charity Commission (Northern Office); Fr M. Reynolds, Rector of Holsworthy, Devon; Michael Riley, formerly of St Andrews; R.J. Sage, Chairman of the Trustees of St Bartholomew's Hospital, Sandwich, Kent; Fr B. Scott, Rector of Barrowden, Rutland; Scottish Tourist Board; T.P. Shanks, Chairman, Royal Burgh of Lanark Community Council; South East England Tourist Board; Southern Tourist Board; Jim Spriggs, York and Abingdon; Stroud District Council, Gloucestershire; Revd P.F. Tambling, Rector of Glenfield, Leicestershire; Thames and Chiltern Tourist Board; Revd Canon B. Thompson, Rector of St Mary's, Woodbridge, Suffolk; Rob Thomson, York; Mrs J.M. Tomlinson, Town Clerk, Clitheroe, Lancashire; G.H. Varah, Barton-on-Humber, Lincolnshire; J. Venables, Churchwarden, Burgh-le-Marsh, Lincolnshire; E.R. Venn, Tower Captain, Woodstock, Oxfordshire; M. Waring, Leigh, Lancashire; Warwick Town Council; Revd M. Watts, Vicar of Ufton Nervet, Berkshire; R. Weaver, Churchwarden, Castlemorton, Worcestershire; West Country Tourist Board; Mrs E.L. Whitnall, Broadstairs, Kent; Pat Williams, Ripon, North Yorkshire; Metropolitan Borough of Wirral; Revd J. Woolfenden, Vicar of Geddington, Northamptonshire; Norman Wright and Hodgson, Chartered Surveyors, Bourne, Lincolnshire; Yorkshire and Humberside Tourist Board; the staff of York City Library Reference Department and York Minster Library.

PHOTOGRAPHIC CREDITS

Illustrations are identified by page number and, where necessary, T = top, C = centre, B = bottom, L = left, R = right.
L.Argyle: 167; R. Armstrong: 99; BBC Hulton Picture Library: 49BR, 76, 102B, 103, 116, 140, 146, 155, 197, 202; Beamish North of England Open Air Museum: 105, 237; Birmingham Public Libraries, The Sir Benjamin Stone Collection: 42B, 43, 87, 123, 141, 213, 228, 232T; Bristol Town Hall: 78; British Library Board: 179L; Trustees of the British Museum: 102T, 111C, 120; British Tourist Authority: 42T, 62, 220; E. Brown: 232B; Cambridge Evening News: 49BL; Carluke and Lanark Gazette: 234; Christie's Ltd, London: 69; Cheltenham Museum of Art: 133; Cumbria County Council: 200; K. Ellis Collection: 56L, 83TL, 129, 135B, 151L, 179TR, 192L; Syndics of the Fitzwilliam Museum, Cambridge: 169; L. Garnade: 47, 101B; Guildhall Library, City of London: 214; E. Harris: 83TR; S. Hartley: 27; D. Harvey: 142; Hawick Museum: 86L; The Helston Packet: 122; Hove Reference Library: 119L; Leger Galleries Ltd, London: 49T; Leicestershire County Council: 143; London Museum: 15; Mansell Collection: 73, 74L, 135T, 175, 207, 211L; Manx Press Pictures: 224; E. McCabe: 181; Sam McCarthy Marbles Collection: 156; Merseyside County Council, Lady Lever Art Gallery: 163; N. Mead: 222; National Museum of Wales, Welsh Folk Museum: 157; Nottinghamshire County Library Service: 111TL, 111BL; Oldham Metropolitan Borough: 199; Oxford County Library: 153, 161T; Private Collection: 218; J. Ravilious, Beaford Archive: 81; Reading Chronicle: 65; F. Rodgers: 206; Doc Rowe: 19, 21, 25, 29, 33, 37, 39, 56R, 60, 211R, 216TL; Doc Rowe Collection: 119R; photo: Royal Academy of Arts, London: 218; Royal and Ancient Golf Club of St Andrews: 194; Royal Institution of Cornwall, Truro: 236R; University of St Andrews: 147; Scarborough Council: 208; Scotsman Publications Ltd: 179BR, 209; Scottish Tourist Board: 63, 86R, 138L, 138TR, 138BR, 225; Brian Shuel: 17, 23, 31, 35, 45, 64, 67, 112, 114, 124, 136, 165, 171C, 171B, 173L, 173R, 182, 186, 203, 210, 216TR, 216CL, 230, 236L; The Skinners' Company: 117; Edwin Smith: 40; Society of Antiquaries, London: 205; Southern Newspapers PLC: 149; S & G Press Agency Ltd: 126, 151R, 178, 184R; Homer Sykes: 52, 61, 68, 131R; C. Tait: 57, 212; Tate Gallery, London: 101T; Times Newspapers Ltd: 83B, 91L, 91TR, 91BR, 93, 94, 125, 184L, 192R, 195, 198, 221, 235; Victoria and Albert Museum, London: 74R; Wales Tourist Board: 108; J. Walton: 223; The Whitby Gazette: 187; D. Widdicombe: 111CR; D. Widdicombe Collection: 100; R. Winstone: 58, 71T, 71B, 79, 106R, 128, 171T; York Gentlemen: 216B. Calendar illustrations from: T. Bewick; R. Chambers, Book of Days, 1866; G. Cruikshank; J. Gerard, Herball 1597; C. Leighton, Four Hedges, 1935.

How to use this book

———◆———

Where the custom or festival described (e.g. Ash Wednesday; Abbots Bromley Horn Dance) warrants a separate entry, it appears under its own name: but many customs appear in groups, under a group title (e.g. Beating the Bounds). Some of the more important events within the group, however, also have cross-reference entries directing readers to the appropriate title (e.g. Dunting the Freeholder *see* BEATING THE BOUNDS). Cross references also give alternative titles (e.g. Tandering *see* TIN CAN BAND) or direct readers to groups of connected entries (e.g. Feudal Customs *see* BREAD AND CHEESE THROWING, CLAMEUR DE HARO ...). Titles in small capitals within the body of main entries (e.g. '... they may also ring at EASTER and WHITSUN ...') direct to other related or relevant entries.

Entries are in alphabetical order: and a regional gazetteer, listing all the customs mentioned under the names of the places where they occur, is on page 241. A calendar of customs, also outlining the variations in the dates of 'movable feasts', appears on page 15.

Old Style and New Style
The calendar change of 1752

———◆———

Throughout this book, references will be found to 'Old Style' and 'New Style', and to festivals called 'Old Michaelmas' and so forth. In order to explain this situation (and the fact that many customs are still celebrated eleven days or so after their 'proper' date) it is necessary to understand that, until the 16th century, both Britain and Christian Europe observed a different calendar from that used today. This 'Old Style' or 'Julian' calendar (introduced by Julius Caesar in 45 BC) was based on a calculation of the solar year at 365¼ days, the extra day being made up by four-yearly 'leap year' days. But the calculation was a slight over-estimate; and by the 16th century European astronomers had established that an eleven-day discrepancy had developed between the Julian calendar and the solar year. In 1582 therefore,

Pope Gregory XIII introduced a 'New Style' or 'Gregorian' calendar, correcting the error by missing out the eleven surplus days.

In 1582, however, a staunchly Protestant Britain was in no mood to accept changes decreed by the head of the Roman Catholic Church: and throughout most of the next two centuries Britain obstinately adhered to the old Julian calendar. During this period, therefore, Britain was eleven days 'behind' most of Europe: so that William of Orange, for instance, left Holland on 11 November 1688 (New Style), to arrive in England (after a four-day voyage) on 5 November 1688 (Old Style). To make matters worse, moreover, England and Ireland continued to maintain their old tradition of beginning the year on 25 March (Lady Day): while the 'Gregorian' nations (and Scotland after 1600, though she did not then adopt the 'New Style' calendar) began theirs on 1 January. During January, February and March, therefore, England was apparently twelve months and eleven days behind Europe, the European 11 February 1648 being regarded as 1 February 1647 in England.

This inconvenient if entertaining situation endured until the British Parliament at last fell into line with Europe in 1751: decreeing that the following 1 January should be 1 January 1752, and that the changeover to the Gregorian 'New Style' should be effected by missing out the calendar dates between 2 September and 14 September in that year. The British public, however, were outraged by this arbitrary 'theft' of part of their lives: and though the London rioters who demanded 'Give us back our eleven days' were soon quelled, at least a hundred years passed before conservative country folk could be brought to accept the change – particularly with regard to their traditional customs and ceremonies.

These, therefore, steadfastly continued to observe their festivals at their 'real' date, whatever the calendar might say. Well into the present century many insisted that the 'proper Christmas' fell on the new 6 January (Twelfth Night), while the genuine May Day fell on the new 12 May: triumphantly pointing out that the snow necessary for a real Christmas was more likely to fall in early January, while 'May blossom', which rarely appears by 1 May, is almost always in evidence eleven days later. Even now, moreover, a number of customs adhere to the 'Old Style' calendar: Burghead, for instance, still 'Burns the Clavie' on 11 January, or Old New Year's Eve; the Whalton Baal Fire still blazes on 5 July, or Old Midsummer; and Nottingham's Michaelmas Goose Fair still begins around 10 October, eleven days after the 'official' Feast of St Michael.

Introduction

The Western city dweller is perhaps the least customary human creature that ever existed. But even he eats pancakes on SHROVE TUESDAY, eggs (if only chocolate eggs) at EASTER, and specially luxurious meals at CHRISTMAS: and while this introduction was being written a national greetings-card manufacturer, reporting an upsurge in the sales of his wares, claimed to have identified a growing demand for 'more festivals to celebrate'.

Customs and festivals, however, do not merely provide a welcome variation on the daily round: they are also comfortingly fixed points and necessary anchors in a changing world. As such, the great majority have their roots in a rural and agricultural past, dominated by the rhythms of seedtime, harvest and stockrearing, and thus by the unpredictable vagaries of the seasons and elements. Custom therefore remains strong in the countryside even yet, for many tenant farmers are legally bound to cultivate their land 'according to the custom of the country', and not a few do not so much observe festivals as use them, regulating their operations by 'Michaelmas' and 'May Fair time'.

In the beginning, indeed, man may have believed that by marking and celebrating the passage of the seasons, he was somehow controlling them. But this kind of theorizing leads onto dangerous ground, and we might do best to take the advice of the Cornish Christmas wassailers' song, and

> Ask not the reason, from where it did spring
> For you know very well, it's an old ancient thing.

Since at least the 16th century, nevertheless, generations of observers have been irresistibly impelled to explain customary ceremonies according to the intellectual climate fashionable in their time. For early Protestant and Puritan commentators, then, most festivals could be dismissed as 'superstitious Popish relics' and 'heathen abuses'; while John Aubrey and his later 17th-century contemporaries, steeped in Classical education, were inclined to see shadowy Greeks and Romans behind every village maypole and garland. 'Druids' and Phoenicians subsequently joined the ranks of the alleged founders of British customs: and very seldom are the native inhabitants given credit for devising their own celebrations.

This is not to deny, however, that some continuing British observances really did begin as ancient pagan rites: indeed, it is difficult to account for practices like BURNING THE CLAVIE or dressing WELLS in any other manner. But however they originated (and in most cases we can never know for certain) the great proportion of ancient customs survived either because they became inextricably interwoven with the festivals of the Christian Church, or because they served some purpose useful to the community. They might, for instance, be necessary to establish an important demarcation line (like BEATING THE BOUNDS and COMMON RIDINGS); to preserve or regulate access to vital COMMON LAND; or (like BREAD AND CHEESE THROWING) to defend valued rights and privileges. Alternatively (like 'guys' and Christmas carol-singing) they could furnish an opportunity for legalized begging; legitimize 'by ancient custom' outbreaks of protest or letting off steam – like STREET BALL GAMES; or (like CLUB WALKS, PEACE AND GOOD NEIGHBOURHOOD FEASTS and HARVEST CUSTOMS) simply help to cement the community together.

Though such communal observances suffered considerably from Victorian 'tidying' and the trauma of the 1914-18 War (for, as Aubrey remarked of an earlier conflict, 'Warres not only extinguish Religion and Lawes, but Superstition: and no suffumen is a greater fugator of Phantosmes, than Gunpowder') a surprising number of them persist, constituting a major element in the body of authentically surviving British custom. Closely related to them are CLIPPING THE CHURCH, RUSHBEARINGS and other church-centred activities; the ancient if now transformed FAIRS and FEASTS; the various traditional village sports and races; the fascinating though little-publicized CHARITIES and other 'endowed' customs; and the better-known folklore celebrations like those on MAY DAY – though many of these last are in fact comparatively modern revivals, based on a rose-tinted vision of an Arcadian past.

Together with the seasonal festivals of the Church, from CANDLEMAS to CHRISTMAS, and the beliefs and conventions surrounding BIRTHS, WEDDINGS and FUNERALS, 'customs of the people' make up a sizeable proportion of the contents of this book. No less important a part in British tradition, however, is played by the official ceremonial of crown and state (including those most ancient and magnificent of rituals, CORONATIONS): and this too receives its due here, as do the most notable of the thousands of CIVIC CUSTOMS, ranging from the solemnity of the LORD MAYOR OF LONDON'S INSTALLATION to the cheerful WEIGHING THE MAYOR at High Wycombe; and curious relics of the feudal system like the HORSESHOE TAX and the various QUIT RENT CEREMONIES.

Some of the best-known and longest-established British sporting events are also described, as are the COMMEMORATIONS of the famous, the extra-ordinarily resilient MUMMING PLAY and dance traditions of Britain, and that remarkable piece of custom fabrication, the ORANGE GIVING at Sileby. In short, an attempt has been made to include an account of most of the traditional customs and ceremonies accessible to the public, as well as a selection of those not normally open to general view. For reasons of space, however, the essentially private customs of such institutions as colleges, schools, clubs and regiments have generally been left out, and so too have purely commercial events.

An attempt has been made to trace the way in which particular customs and ceremonies have ebbed and flowed in popularity over the centuries; to note how they have expanded or contracted their geographical range; and to judge whether they are at present flourishing or declining. For though custom is proverbially accused of possessing a dead hand, it is in fact very much a living organism: which might perhaps be compared to a perennial plant with many shoots, some of them dying while others are springing up anew. One of the most remarkable examples of this process is MOTHERING SUNDAY, the long-established mid-Lent festival which was reported to be 'virtually extinct' by the beginning of the Second World War. But a few years later that war brought to Britain a flood of American servicemen, and with them the entirely distinct transatlantic observance called Mother's Day, instituted in 1907 and celebrated on the second Sunday in May. The vigorous American custom immediately hybridized with the moribund native festival, frequently adopting the American title of Mother's Day but firmly retaining the British mid-Lent date; and since the 1950s the cross-breed has continued to thrive almost excessively, colonizing areas of Britain which the original version never penetrated.

A more recent (and at first sight a more pernicious) American import is the children's prank of 'Trick or Treating' at HALLOWEEN: which appears to have spread to Britain only during the 1980s. On closer inspection, however, this custom proves not to be an alien at all: for it is nothing but the originally Scots and northern English MISCHIEF NIGHT tradition of Halloween tricks in ghost or witch disguise, now returning home with an American accent. The jolly red-clad and white-bearded figure so eagerly awaited on Christmas Eve is yet another example of British-American (or rather British-European-American) cross-fertilization. His native title of Father Christmas, admittedly, still holds out against the intruding 'Santa Claus', and some of his characteristics derive from the Old English personification of the season, familiar since the 17th century; yet he owes much more to the chimney-haunting and reindeer-sledged 'Sinte Klaas', who was born in America of Dutch, German and Russian parentage, and who re-crossed the Atlantic only in the late-Victorian era.

A number of other seemingly immemorial British customs turn out to be not quite as ancient as they might appear: but these (to continue the botanical metaphor) are not so much hybrids as forced growths. Notable among such are HARVEST FESTIVALS, carefully nurtured by the Victorians to replace the old, riotous and socially levelling celebrations of harvest-end: and many of the church observances and processions now popular on ASCENSION DAY, ASH WEDNESDAY, EASTER and PALM SUNDAY, together with ceremonies like BLESSING THE SEAS AND FISHERIES. These latter, admittedly, are often nominally revivals of genuine medieval practices: but they are deliberately induced rather than spontaneous revivals, products of the Anglo-Catholic Oxford Movement whose clerical adherents sought to reintroduce all manner of pre-Reformation rituals into the Church of England. At first vehemently rejected as 'Popish mummeries' by public opinion, or simply laughed at as 'all smells and lace', such ceremonies even gave rise to the prosecution (and in at least one case, the imprisonment) of their sponsors. Yet by gradual degrees they became acceptable: and today 'idolatrous' Christmas cribs are commonplace even in Nonconformist chapels, while for once-a-year Anglican worshippers the favourite service is the revealingly named Christmas midnight 'mass'.

This kind of introduced ritual has probably taken root because – like the communal customs mentioned earlier – it fulfils some basic human need. Other artificially imposed customs, however, have fallen victim to the changing times: and the once very popular Empire Day (instituted in 1892 and celebrated on 24 May, Queen Victoria's birthday) could not survive the loss of Britain's overseas possessions, despite the attempt to modernize its ethos by renaming it 'Commonwealth Day' in 1958. ST GEORGE'S DAY, like-wise, is today little regarded, and in recent decades there has been a marked falling-off in the formerly universal solemnity of REMEMBRANCE SUNDAY.

Well within living memory, too, many far more ancient customs and festivals have either died out altogether or greatly diminished in popularity. Some have even been forcibly suppressed by authority – like Teddy Rowe's Band, a kind of pre-dawn TIN CAN BAND which until prohibited by the police in 1964 preceded the Pack Monday Fair at Sherborne in Dorset: and though officialdom can no longer enforce the wholesale abolition of 'unsuitable' customs on quite the Victorian scale (as witness the rout in 1954 of the attack on ABBOTSBURY GARLAND DAY) it has other, more insidious, weapons at its disposal. These are the pressures to tidy up and prettify festivals, or to elaborate them for the benefit of the tourist trade: a process which has overtaken the revived BAWMING THE THORN and the COTSWOLD OLYMPICK GAMES, to name but two of many; but from which BURNING BARTLE and other refreshingly spontaneous observances have so far escaped. Economic and social factors, meanwhile, are clearly responsible for the decline of CLUB WALKS and the like: and (aided by official disapproval) for the demise of such seasonal begging customs as St Thomas's Day 'gooding' in ADVENT and Halloween SOULING. But it is less easy to explain why MIDSUMMER is now so scantily kept (except by comic Druids and deadly serious 'eco-pagans') or why OAK APPLE DAY goes largely unnoticed: though the latter has probably been over-shadowed by the revival of May Day celebrations, as May Day itself was once threatened by Oak Apple Day.

As ARBOR DAY, the CASTLETON GARLAND and the WHALTON BAAL FIRE demonstrate, strictly local versions of both Midsummer and Oak Apple Day continue to flourish here and there: a fact which serves to illustrate the tendency of certain once-widespread customs to retreat into a small and well-defined area. Undoubtedly, too, a number of observances now boasted as absolutely and immemorially unique to one community – like the BURRY MAN, Hungerford HOCKTIDE, RAM ROASTING or SWINGING THE FIREBALLS – turn out to be, in reality, embattled survivors of a formerly more generalized tradition. Exactly why such customs endured where they do can rarely be established – though the remoteness of a village, or the presence therein of a strongly traditionalist group or family, must surely play a part in some cases: but almost invariably the custom has become truly the community's own over the centuries, so that any explanation which detracts from its uniqueness is unlikely to find local favour. And where two or more places keep up a similar but otherwise unusual ceremony – as with the MINEHEAD and the PADSTOW HOBBY HORSE – each vociferously insists that their version is the only genuine article, unscrupulously plagiarized (and of course debased) by their rival.

Such accusations are not always totally unfounded: for customs and ceremonies can and do expand as well as contract their range, and (in recent centuries at least) this process generally involves direct imitation. Thus, for instance, PUNKY NIGHT – claimed as their own by two rival Somerset villages, but very probably a local version of Halloween celebrations – has spread in recent years to a number of surrounding communities: while Common Ridings, which had survived only in a handful of Scottish border burghs, have since the Second World War re-expanded their range throughout the whole Borders region. Both these customs (to return to the metaphorical plant) have thus spread along the ground like a creeper, from one neighbouring population centre to the next; but other expanding festivals, somewhat like dandelions, have instead established scattered colonies over a wide area by means of wind-blown seeds – the wind being provided by books and newspapers and latterly by radio and television.

By such means, for example, imitations of the DUNMOW FLITCH trial and of SHROVE TUESDAY pancake races – both customs with a high entertainment value – have not only sprung up all over Britain but also spread to the USA and other parts of the English-speaking world: and the once-localized Cotswold form of MORRIS DANCING, disseminated through the medium of Cecil Sharp's writings, has become the predominant style of ceremonial dance throughout England, sometimes strangling in the process more appropriately regional dance traditions. The most extraordinary expansion of all, however, is that of HIGHLAND GAMES and the associated trappings of 'Tartanism' – the kilts, pipes, feather bonnets and be-Cairngormed weaponry of the tourist trade's 'Bonnie Scotland'. Once confined (though in a form unrecognizable to modern eyes) to the Gaelic-speaking parts of the Highlands, and seen elsewhere as the symbols of a despised culture and a feared barbarian race, the tartan ethos began its inexorable southward spread early in the 19th century: and it has since colonized all Scotland, increasingly overshadowing the ancient, proud, and quite distinct customs and traditions of the Lowlands and the Borders. Visitors therefore expect to see plaids and pipes from the moment they cross the Anglo-Scottish boundary – and, regrettably, are rarely disappointed: while in recent years tartanism has even begun to take root in England itself. That a kilted piper should recently have accompanied a mission to promote *England* in San Francisco is merely laughable: but it was sadder to see, in 1985, a fully accoutred 'Highland' piper of the West Midlands Police Pipe Band heading the Arbor Day procession in rural Shropshire.

This recent irruption of tartanism is perhaps largely attributable to the influence of television, that most universally pervasive and persuasive of all the media: and the effect of television on the future of British customs is likely to be considerable. Anchoring people in silent house-bound groups while bombarding them with packaged and frequently imported entertainment, television seems almost certain eventually to destroy communal and customary life altogether: or at least to damage irreparably the local particularism which lends British festivals and ceremonies so much of their variety and interest. We may perhaps take comfort, nevertheless, from the knowledge that similar prophecies of doom have been voiced before, being prompted in turn by the advent of radio, cinema, and the music hall; by the spread of general literacy, the Methodist revival and the Industrial Revolution; by the 1752 calendar change, the Civil Wars, and the Protestant Reformation – and very probably by the Norman Conquest, the coming of Christianity, and the invention of the wheel. All these events did indeed change British customary life to a greater or lesser extent, but they did not destroy it: and it may well be that, like the living organism it is, custom cannot survive without change and development.

Finally, an apology and the traditional word of warning. Try though he might, the author has been unable to prevent his carefully nurtured collection of illogical prejudices from insinuating themselves into this book at intervals; where detectable, these should not be regarded too seriously. And though every effort was made to establish that the observances and events described were still genuinely in being at the time of writing – not an easy task, and one which would have been impossible without the generous assistance of those mentioned in the acknowledgments – some may since have died out: while others, lamented as extinct, may since have revived.

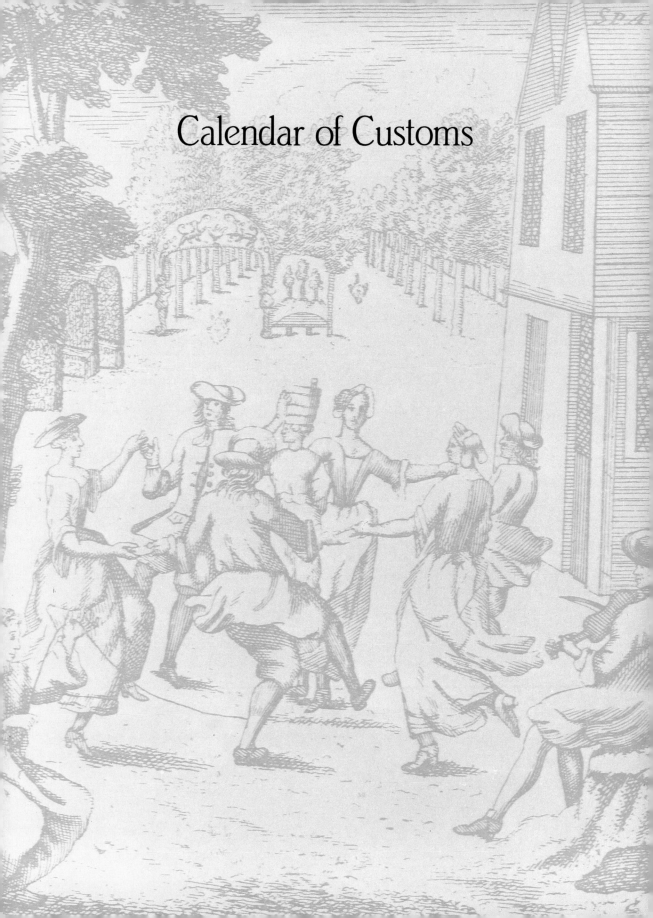

Calendar of Customs

January

1

New Year's Day:
Kirkwall Ba' Game

2

3

4

5

During the month:
Mari Lwyd
Hooden Horse
Wassailing
Wassailing the Apple Trees ·

6

Twelfth Night/Epiphany:
Epiphany Gifts Ceremony
Haxey Hood Game · Baddeley Cake

7

Straw Bear Day
Saturday before Plough Monday

8

9

Plough Monday
Monday after Epiphany:
Sword dancing

10

11

Burning the Clavie

Up-Helly-Aa
last Tuesday in January

12

Maid's Money
last Thursday in January

13

14

15

16

17

18

19

20

21

22

23

24

25

Burns Night

26

27

28

29

30

Charles I Commemoration

31

Opposite:
Haxey Hood Game

February

Left column		Right column
1		17
2		18

Candlemas · Cross quarter day
Jedburgh Ba' Games
Forty Shilling Day · Carlow's Charity

| 3 | | 19 |

Blessing the Throats

| 4 | | 20 |

| 5 | | 21 |

Duelling Sermon

Collop Monday
Monday before Shrove Tuesday

| 6 | | 22 |

| 7 | | 23 |

Shrove Tuesday/Fastern's E'en
*41 days before Easter; falls between
3 February and 9 March inclusive:*
Shrovetide Football
Skipping
Marblers' and Stonecutters' Day
Pancake Greeze
Pancake Races
Lichfield Fair
Hurling the Silver Ball

| 8 | | 24 |

| 9 | | 25 |

Ash Wednesday
40 days before Easter, beginning of Lent

| 10 | | 26 |

Kissing Friday
Friday after Ash Wednesday

| 11 | | 27 |

King's Lynn Mart
during 2 weeks after 14 February

| 12 | | 28 |

| 13 | | 29 |

| 14 | | |

Valentine's Day

| 15 | | |

| 16 | | |

March

1 St David's Day / Whuppity Stourie	**17**
2	**18**
3	**19**
4	**20**
5	**21**
6	**22**
7	**23**
8	**24**
9	**25** Lady Day / Quarter Day / Tichborne Dole
10	**26**
11 Handy Sermon	**27**
Bombshell Sermon	
12	**28**
13	**29**
14	**30**
15	**31**
16	

Clown Service
Sunday in February or March

Oxford and Cambridge boat race
Saturday in March or April

Lent
the 40 days before Easter

Mothering Sunday
4th in Lent

Passion/Carlings Sunday
5th in Lent

Palm Sunday
6th in Lent:
Pax Cakes Ceremony

Kiplingcotes Derby
3rd Thursday in March

Oranges and Lemons Service
late March

Maundy Thursday
Thursday before Easter:
Royal Maundy
Marvyn Dole
Travice Dole

Good Friday
Friday before Easter:
Skipping
Marbles Championship
Burning Judas
Widow's Bun Ceremony
Rivington Pike Fair
Butterworth Charity

Easter Saturday:
Hubbard's Hymn Charity
Britannia Coconut Dancers

Easter Sunday
*falls between 22 March and 25 April
inclusive*

Easter Monday:
Biddenden Maids' Charity
Bottle Kicking and Hare Pie Scramble
Whitebread Meadow Running Auction

Opposite:
Clown Service

April

1

April Fools' Day
Hunting the Gowk

2

Taily Day

3

4

5

John Stow Commemoration

6

7

8

9

10

11

12

13

14

15

16

Grand National
1st Saturday in April

Hocktide
*2nd Monday and Tuesday after Easter
Sunday; falls between 30-31 March
and 3-4 May inclusive:*
Randwick Wap

Spital Sermon
2nd Wednesday after Easter

Kate Kennedy Procession
Saturday in mid-April

Minehead Hobby Horse
30 April to 3 May

17

18

19

20

21

22

23

St George's Day
Shakespeare's Birthday Ceremony

24

25

26

27

28

29

30

May Eve

Opposite:
Britannia Coconut Dancers
(Easter Saturday)

May

1
May Day · Cross quarter day
Garland Dressing · May Singing
Padstow Hobby Horse · May Goslings

2

3

4

5

6

7

8

Furry Dance

9

10

11

12

Florence Nightingale Service

13

Abbotsbury Garland Day

14

15

16

During the month:
Well dressings
Opening of the General Assembly
Orange-giving Ceremony
May Fairs

Cheese Rolling
1st Sunday in May

Cup Final
Saturday in early May

Rogationtide
3 days before Ascension Day:
Beating the Bounds

Penny Hedge
day before Ascension Day

Ascension Day/Holy Thursday
*40 days after Easter Sunday; falls between
30 April and 3 June inclusive:*
Wicken Love Feast

Swearing on the Horns
Wednesday before Whit Sunday

Whit Sunday
*50 days after Easter Sunday; falls between
10 May and 13 June inclusive:*
Bread and Cheese Throwing

Whit Monday:
Corby Pole Fair (*every 20 years*)
Ram Roasting
Court of Array and Greenhill Bower
Selling the Keep of the Wether

Whit Tuesday:
Dicing for Bibles
Maypole Raising (*every 3 years*)

Cotswold Olympick Games
Friday and Saturday after Whit Monday

Coventry Crock Fair
29 May-4 June

Neville's Cross Commemoration
Saturday nearest 29 May

Weighing the Mayor
an evening in late May

17

18

19

20

21

Ceremony of the lilies and roses

22

23

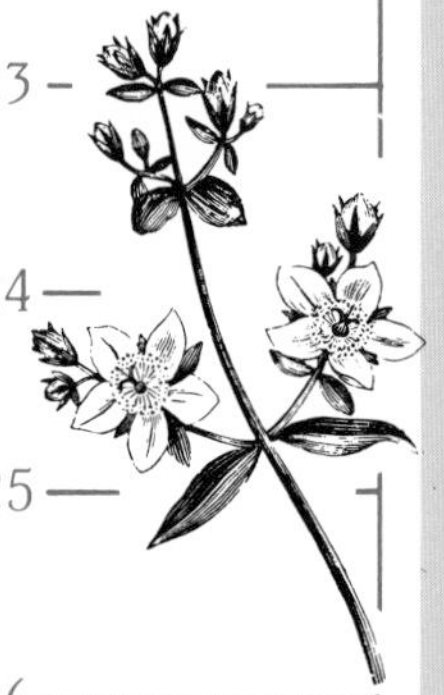

24

25

26

Pepys Commemoration

27

28

29

Oak Apple Day · Arbor Day
Castleton Garland · Grovely Rights Day

30

31

Opposite:
Abbotsbury Garland Day

June

Left column dates: 1–16

Right column dates: 17–30

During the month:
Common Ridings
Dunmow Flitch (*leap years*)
Highland Games

Trinity Sunday
Sunday after Whit Sunday, falls between
17 May and 27 June

Bubble Sermon
1st Tuesday in June

Derby Day
1st Wednesday in June

Appleby Horse Fair
early June

Trooping the Colour
2nd Saturday in June

Lanimer Day
2nd or 3rd week in June

Garter Ceremony
Monday of Royal Ascot Week

Royal Ascot
4 days in mid-June

Mayor of Ock Street
Saturday nearest 19 June

Bawming the Thorn
late June

Jankyn Smith's Charity
Thursday nearest 28 June

Lot Meadows
week after 29 June

Mary Gibson's Sermon

Barnaby Fair

Midsummer Eve

Midsummer Day
Midsummer Fairs

St Peter's Day
Rushbearing Sermon

Opposite:
Garter Ceremony, Windsor Castle

July

During the month:
Doggett's Coat and Badge Race
Common Ridings
Burrator Reservoir Ceremony
Highland Games
Blessing the Seas and Fisheries

Henley Royal Regatta
4 days in early July

Admiralty Court
1st or 2nd Saturday in July

International Musical Eisteddfod
early July

Reiver's Week
1st full week in July

Durham Miners' Gala
2nd Saturday in July

Black Cherry Fair
2nd Saturday in July

Pretty Maid's Charity
2nd Wednesday in July

Tweedmouth Feast
Sunday after 18 July

Swan Upping
Monday-Thursday, 3rd full week in July

Armada Sermon
Sunday nearest 29 July

1

2

3

4

Whalton Baal Fire

5

Midsummer Day, Old Style
Tynwald Ceremonies
Lord Mayor of Kilburn

6

7

8

9

10

11

12

13

14

15

St Swithin's Day

16

17

18

19

Little Edith's Treat

20

21

22

23

24

25

St James's Day
Ebernoe Horn Fair
John Knill's Charity *(every 5 years)*

26

27

28

29

30

31

Opposite:
Swan Upping

August

1
Lammas · Lammas Fairs
Cross quarter day

2

3

4

5
Brigg Fair

6

7

8

9

10

11

12

13

14

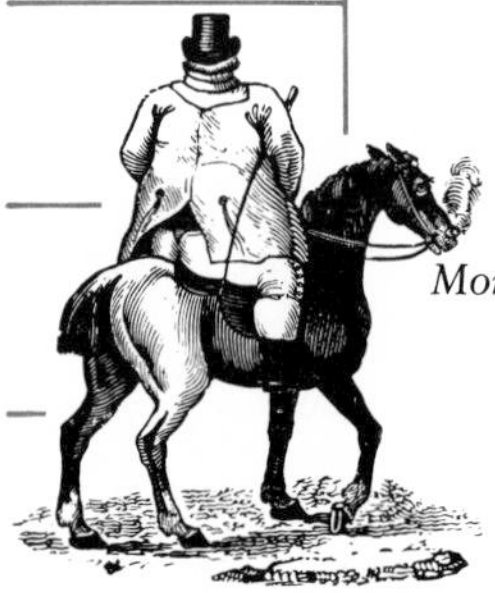

15

16

During the month:
Common Ridings
Coracle Races
Highland Games
National Eisteddfod

Knighthood of Old Green
1st Wednesday-Friday in August

St Wilfrid's Feast Procession
Saturday before 1st Monday in August

Woodmen of Arden's Grand Wardmote
1st week in August

Hat and Ribbon Race
1st Thursday in August

The Burry Man
2nd Friday in August

Marymass Fair
3rd or 4th Monday in August

Marhamchurch Revel
Monday following 12 August

Boys' Ploughing Match
mid-August

Priddy Fair
Wednesday nearest 21 August

Red Hose Race
3rd or 4th Thursday in August

Cow Head Wakes
weekend nearest 24 August

Burning Bartle
Saturday after 24 August

Bartholomew Fair
during fortnight after 24 August

Harvest Festivals
begin late August

Plague Sunday
last Sunday in August

Preston Pot Fair
last week in August

Preston Guild Merchant
Monday after 29 August (every 20 years)

17

18

19

20

21

22

23
William Wallace Commemoration

24
St Bartholomew's Day
St Bartholomew's Bun Race
Lee Gap Fair

25

26

27

28

29
Kirkby Hill Races
(every 2 years)

30

31

Opposite:
Plough Horse
at Boys' Ploughing Match

September

During the month:
Harvest Festivals
Highland Games

Swearing on the Horns
Wednesday 9 days after
Summer Bank Holiday

St Giles' Fair
Monday and Tuesday following
1st Sunday after 1 September

Sowerby Bridge Rush Cart
first Saturday and Sunday in September

Abbots Bromley Horn Dance
Monday after Sunday following
4 September

Cheese and Onion Fair
1st or 2nd Tuesday in September

Widecombe Fair
2nd Tuesday in September

Pipe Walk
a Saturday in September

Barnstaple Fair
Wednesday nearest 17 September

Pig Face Sunday
Sunday after 14 September

Clipping the Church
Sunday after 19 September

Colchester Oyster Ceremonies
late September

Bridgwater St Matthew's Fair
last Wednesday in September

1

2

3
Cromwell's Day

4

5

6

7

8
Sheriff's Ride

9

10

11

12

13

14
Holy Cross Day

15

16

17

18
Dr Johnson's Birthday

19

20

21

22

23

24

25

26

27
Hornblowing begins, Bainbridge

28

29
Michaelmas · Quarter Day
Lord Mayor of London's Installation
Mop Fairs

30
Bristol Fair
Brough Hill Fair

Opposite:
Rush Cart, Sowerby Bridge

October

1	17
2 — Old Man's Day	18
3	19
4	20 — Colchester Oyster Ceremonies
5	21
6	22
7 — Lost in the Dark Bells, Twyford	23
8	24
9	25
10 — Mop Fairs / Lost in the Dark Bells begin, Burgh-le-Marsh	26
11	27
12	28
13	29
14	30
15	31 — Halloween
16 — Lion Sermon	*Opposite:* Punky Night

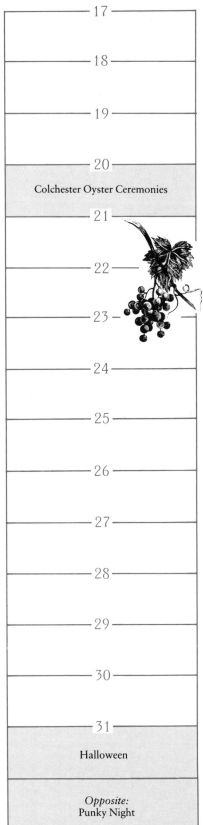

Harvest Festivals
early October

Nottingham Goose Fair
3 days beginning 1st Thursday in October

Crabapple Fair
Saturday nearest 18 October

Tavistock 'Goosey' Fair
2nd Wednesday in October

Punky Night
last week in October

November

1	**17**
All Saints Day · Cross quarter day All Hallows Day	
2	**18**
All Souls Day	
3	**19**
4	**20**
Mischief Night	
5	**21**
Guy Fawkes Night Turning the Devil's Stone Lewes Bonfire Night	
6	**22**
7	**23**
8	**24**
9	**25**
Mayor of Shammickshire	
10	**26**
11	**27**
Martinmas · Armistice Day Fenny Poppers · Wroth Silver	
12	**28**
13	**29**
14	**30**
	St Andrew's Day
15	
16	

Raisin Monday
4 weeks after beginning of university year

Souling
1st 2 weeks in November

Wild Horse of Antrobus
1st 2 weeks in November

Big Court Night
1st Monday in November

Gunpowder Plot Sermon
Sunday nearest 5 November

Bridgwater Squibbing Night
Thursday nearest 5 November

Lord Mayor of London's Show
second Saturday in November

Remembrance Sunday
Sunday after 11 November

Stir-up Sunday
Sunday before Advent Sunday

Opposite:
Lewes Bonfire Night

December

1
2
3
4
5
6 — St Nicholas's Day
7
8
9
10
11
12
13
14
15
16

Advent Sunday
*beginning of Advent – 4th Sunday before
Christmas; falls between 27 November
and 3 December inclusive*

Tin Can Band
2nd Sunday in December

During the Christmas season:
Mari Lwyd
Wassailing
Mumming plays
Longsword Dancing

17
18
19
20
21 — St Thomas's Day
22
23
24 — **Christmas Eve:**
Yule log burning
Tolling the Devil's Knell
25 — **Christmas Day:**
Kirkwall Ba' Game
26 — **Boxing/St Stephen's Day**
27
28 — **Childermas/Holy Innocents' Day**
29
30
31 — **New Year's Eve/Hogmanay:**
Allendale Tar Barrels
Burning the Old Year Out
Swinging Fireballs
Comrie Flambeaux Procession

Opposite:
Mumming play, Ripon

A

· Abbots Bromley Horn Dance ·
Abbots Bromley, Staffordshire: Monday after the Sunday following 4 September

It is fitting that this book should open with the Horn Dance of Abbots Bromley; which is not only a custom unique in Europe but also possibly the oldest surviving ceremony in Britain. The observance begins at 8.30 on the morning of 'Wakes Monday' – formerly the date of the village feast – when the performers collect their regalia from its usual resting place in the parish church, and move off for their first dance on the vicarage lawn. First come the six horn-dancers, dressed in stylized Elizabethan costume and each bearing a pair of reindeer antlers – three sets painted white with brown tips and three brown with golden tips – attached to a wooden deer's head on a short staff, which is carried so that the horns normally rest on the dancers' shoulders. Then follow 'Maid Marian', a man in 'medieval' woman's clothes, with an old wooden ladle; and a simple HOBBY HORSE, wearing a cape and skirt over a waist-level hoop, and carrying a small horse-head with snapping jaws. A boy bearing a bow with attached arrow and a Fool in conventional jester's motley make up the complement of dancers: and there are two musicians, a boy with a triangle and a man with accordion or melodeon.

As the single-file procession nears the performance area, the musicians strike up some favourite dance tune – a special Horn Dance air was said to be 'irretrievably forgotten' by 1893, and claims to have rediscovered it are rejected by Abbots Bromley – and the ten dancers break into a simple country-dance step. First the line weaves and 'heys' in and out of itself like a snake, always moving forward: and then, at the beginning of the dance proper, the hornbearers lead it into a ring, which suddenly turns inside out and sets off in the opposite direction. After making a number of such continuously alternate clockwise and anti-clockwise circles, the dancers move neatly into two opposing lines, with the bearers of the white horns facing those with the brown, the Bowman facing the Hobby Horse, and the Fool opposite Maid Marian. They are then ready to begin the second, climactic, figure of the dance.

Now the two lines advance three steps forward to meet each other, and as they do so the hornbearers swing the antlers forwards and upwards like fighting stags, only to retire and advance again three times over: while the approaching and backing Bowman snaps his arrow against his bow, the horse clacks his jaws, and Maid Marian bangs a stick into the bowl of her ladle, all in time with the music. Next the dancers meet and cross over, left shoulder to left shoulder, and then once again

meet and retreat three times, finally forming again into single file and dancing off as they processed on.

This, then, is the simple but immensely dramatic Horn Dance, which will be performed over and over again throughout Wakes Monday. After dancing at the vicarage, the company move on to repeat their ritual in the streets and market place of Abbots Bromley village, and then set off on a twenty-mile tour of the parish. By about noon – having danced outside many houses and farms along the way – they reach Blithfield Hall, ancestral home of the Bagot family, where they dance on the lawn and stop for a meal: then they continue their taxing and strenuous perambulation – for to miss out any of the parish farms would be to expose it to ill luck – eventually returning to the village and reaching the church shortly before dusk falls.

The present leader's family claim to have been 'out with the horns' for over 400 years, its women being pressed into service when not enough men were available. Most unusually, moreover, the documentary record of the dance stretches back over more than three centuries: for in 1686 it was described thus by Dr Robert Plot's *Natural History of Staffordshire*:

At Abbots, or now rather Pagets Bromley, they had also within memory, a sort of sport, which they celebrated at Christmas (on New Year and Twelfth Day) called the Hobby-horse dance, from a person that carried the image of a horse between his legs, made of thin boards: and in his hand a bow and arrow, which passing through a hole in the bow, and stopping upon a shoulder he had in it, he made a snapping noise as he drew it to and fro, keeping time with the Music. With this man danced six others, carrying on their shoulders as many Rain deers heads, three of them painted white and three red, with the Arms of the chief families (viz of Paget, Bagot and Wells) to whom the revenues of the Town chiefly belonged, depicted in the palms of them: with which they danced the Hays and other Country dances. To this Hobby-horse dance there also belonged a pot, which was kept by turns by four or five of the chief of the Town, whom they called Reeves, who provided Cakes and Ale to put in this pot. All people who had any kindness for the good intent of the Institution of the sport, gave pence apiece for themselves and families: and so foreigners too, that came to see it. With which money ... they not only repaired their Church but kept their poor too: which charges are not now perhaps, so cheerfully borne.

A contemporary of Plot's confirmed this report, and noted that the dance had been 'continued until the war' – i.e. the Civil War of 1642-6 – whereupon it presumably fell victim to Puritan prohibition. It had certainly been revived, however, well before 1725: and it was perhaps at this stage that its performance date altered from Christmastide to that of Abbots Bromley 'Wakes' – which were originally held (under a charter of 1226) around St Bartholomew's Day (24 August) but were transferred, after the calendar change of 1752, to the present date around 4 September, St Bartholomew's

Day Old Style. Since the post-Civil War revival observances to have been continuous, and during the course of time the dance acquired its 'man-woman' (first called 'Maid Marian' in 1893) – its separate character to operate the bow originally wielded by the Hobby Horse, and perhaps its Fool. It was not until the 1880s that the horn-bearers appeared in the ancestors of their present Elizabethan costumes, made by a vicar's wife and daughters and possibly based on illustrations in the family Shakespeare: until then, they had worn their own ordinary clothes, decorated with bunches of ribbon.

The essentials of the dance, nevertheless, have remained unchanged since Plot's time: by then it had apparently become – like contemporary hobby-horse customs in at least two other Staffordshire parishes – primarily a method of raising money for church funds. But the Horn Dance clearly originated as something quite different, and the keys to its origins may well be the horns themselves. These are in fact 'Rain deers'' horns, ranging in size from 29 inches wide from tip to tip, and in weight from 16¼ to 25¼ pounds a pair: they bear the traces of many successive coats of paint – red, blue, black and cream – and are attached to wooden heads apparently manufactured during the 16th century. At least one set of antlers, however, is very much older than that: for radio-carbon dating tests have shown that the deer from which they came lived at some time during a 120-year period centred on AD 1000.

Remarkable though this discovery is, it proves conclusively neither that all the antlers are as ancient, nor even that the dance is as old – or as recent – as the horns: nor is it clear how the horns came to be at Abbots Bromley, since the native English reindeer almost certainly died

Above: Bearing their ancient reindeer horns, a relaxed modern team perform the central 'stag-fight' figure of the **Abbots Bromley Horn Dance.** *Below:* Properly solemn performers at the turn of the century: among the horn-bearers (left to right) are the boy with the bow; the Fool; the moustachio'd Maid Marian; a musician; and the Hobby Horse.

out in prehistoric times. They may, of course, have been brought either from northern Scotland – where reindeer probably survived until 1000 – or from Scandinavia, perhaps by a Norse immigrant: though there is little evidence for Viking settlement in this area, and in 1000 the village was owned by the irreproachably English Wulfric 'Spot', who died fighting Danish invaders at Ringmere in Norfolk in 1010. Before his death, it is just conceivable that he took the horns as spoil from a Viking, but this is the merest speculation: and all that may reasonably be deduced from the carbon dating – though this, in itself, is startling enough – is that the Horn Dance custom probably pre-dates the Norman Conquest.

The original meaning of the custom is equally obscure: but here the significant factor is that Abbots Bromley lay on the edge of Needwood Forest, and several of its medieval inhabitants were foresters by profession. It is often stated, indeed, that the custom celebrates a charter of 1125, which granted forest hunting rights to the villagers: and though this theory lacks foundation – since the relevant charter refers to grazing privileges only – it does seem likely that the Horn Dance was in some way connected with the chase of the deer. Whether it originated as a piece of ritual magic, designed either to increase the number of stags or to afford protection to the hunters; or whether it was perhaps the dance of some foresters' guild, we shall probably never know. But the Horn Dance was plainly deep-rooted enough in the community to continue through nearly a thousand years of changes and upheavals: and to survive as one of the most fascinating – if one of the most mysterious – of all British customs.

· Abbotsbury Garland Day ·
Abbotsbury, Dorset: 13 May

On 13 May – which is MAY DAY, Old Style – pole-borne flower-garlands woven onto wire frames are carried by children about the streets of the seaside village of Abbotsbury: and at each house the bearers stop to 'show' the luck-bringing garland, collecting small sums of money which are later shared between them. Normally there are three such garlands. During the day, one made of wild and another of garden flowers are processed by the younger children, who have a school holiday for the purpose: while in the evening a third, much larger, garland is displayed by the older children who have been attending school in Weymouth. When the showing is over, all three garlands are usually laid on the village war memorial: but in recent years the 'wild garland' has sometimes been carried to the beach and ceremonially thrown into the sea, a revival of the older form of the custom.

For, up until the early years of this century, Garland Day was essentially a form of BLESSING THE SEA, which marked the opening of the mackerel season for the village's small and now-vanished fishing fleet. Each fisher family made its own garland, and when these had been 'shown' in the village they were hung on the prow of the family boat, taken out to sea and back again, and then carried to the church for a service of blessing. Thereafter the whole village danced and played games on the beach, and finally the garlands were again taken out in the boats, but this time they were solemnly cast overboard 'in the firm belief that this would bring luck to the mackerel fishery'.

Children prepare to take their garlands out to sea, on an Edwardian **Abbotsbury Garland Day.**

When the custom originated is unknown, but its celebration on Old May Day indicates that it certainly pre-dates the calendar change of 1752, and local opinion proudly insists that Garland Day is 'fully a thousand years old'. The outrage which greeted an attempt to suppress it in 1954, therefore, was very considerable. Taking the view that the 'showing' was merely a form of illegal begging, a new and zealous village policeman – a stranger to the district – prohibited the processions and confiscated the money collected by the children: but their elders at once organized a 'procession of protest', and lodged a strong complaint with the Chief Constable of Dorset. That worthy, to his credit, apologized profusely; the offending policeman was transferred; and the custom has duly continued ever since.

· Admiral of the Medway's Cruise ·
see BEATING THE BOUNDS

· Admiralty Court, Rochester ·
The pier, Rochester, Kent: first or second Saturday in July, depending on tides

Since the mid-15th century, the Mayor of Rochester has also held the office of Admiral of the River Medway: and in that capacity he not only takes part in BEATING THE BOUNDS of his jurisdiction, but also presides over an annual court for 'ordering and regulating the Fishery of the waters thereof'. Confirmed by Act of Parliament in 1727 (and then said to have taken place 'since time out of mind') it is convened on board a decorated barge moored off Rochester pier, whither the mayor and aldermen process in full regalia, accompanied by the Principal Water Bailiff with his great silver oar of office. Though most of its duties are now purely nominal, the court still swears in new water bailiffs, checks over the list of Free Fishermen, and elects from them a twelve-man jury to supervise the Medway's 'Oyster and Floating Fishery' during the following year.

· Advent ·

Advent, the season of preparation for Christ's coming (Latin: *adventus*) which opens the Church's year, is heralded by STIR-UP SUNDAY and begins on the fourth Sunday before CHRISTMAS DAY. Formerly, its great festivals were 6 December (the day of St Nicholas, patron saint of children) when cathedrals and other churches elected a chorister 'boy bishop' to rule the Christmas celebrations – a custom recently revived at Edwinstowe, Nottinghamshire and elsewhere: and St Thomas's Day (21 December) when needy women (and, by a tradition applying to this day only, even the quite well-to-do) went begging from door to door for Christmas 'goodenings'.

Nowadays, however, two recently imported Advent customs are sweeping all before them. Almost every family with small children makes (or more generally buys) an Advent Calendar, whose little windows are opened in succession on each day of the season, to reveal religious or Christmassy pictures: these were introduced from the USA during the 1950s, having originated in Germany. From Germany and Scandinavia, too, came Advent Crowns. Made from greenery and tinsel, these rings topped by semi-circular hoops carry four red candles (one to be lit on each of the four Advent Sundays) and one larger white one (for Christmas Day).

· Ale-tasting Ceremonies ·
see COURTS LEET AND BARON

· Allendale Tar Barrels ·
Allendale Town, Northumberland: 31 December

The little town of Allendale, in the wild country of the northern Pennines, is one of the few places in England to hold a BURNING THE OLD YEAR OUT ceremony. At about 9 p.m. on NEW YEAR'S EVE, fancy-dressed 'guisers' – nearly all local men, who traditionally must make their own costumes – begin their rounds of the town pubs: then, shortly before midnight, some forty or fifty of them form up in three columns outside the Dale Hotel, each carrying a blazing tar barrel on his head. These 'tar kits' are the tops or bottoms of barrels, sawn off at a height of fifteen inches and filled with tar, wood, and shavings soaked in paraffin: so they are heavy, as well as extremely hot.

The Tar-Barrellers' procession which now follows is, therefore, necessarily conducted at a brisk pace. Led by the six-man Allendale band, it loops its way around the streets and back again to the market place, where it circles a great unlit bonfire. Then, as midnight strikes, some of the kits are hurled into the pile of pine branches, setting it ablaze at once: formerly, all were thus thrown, but wooden barrels are now so scarce and expensive that some must be extinguished and saved for succeeding years. Finally, after the communal singing of 'Auld Lang Syne', many of the guisers spend the rest of the night first-footing.

This spectacular ceremony has certainly been carried on for over a century: but there is some doubt whether (as the local tourist board will have us believe) it has been in existence since 'the Dark Ages' and 'echoes a paganism as old as man himself'. It seems more probable, indeed, that the tar kits made their first appearance on a blustery New Year's Eve around 1860, when the wind continually blew out the candles lighting the sheet music of a band accompanying Wesleyan Methodist hymn singers. 'So some bright spark suggested a tar-barrel', reported an eye-witness, 'and the band played round it.'

Apparently oblivious to the flames, the 'guisers' process their **Allendale Tar Barrels** through the town on New Year's Eve.

· Apple Howling ·
see WASSAILING THE APPLE TREES

· April Fools' Day ·
1 April

The first of April, some do say
Is set apart for All Fools Day
But why the people call it so
Nor I nor they themselves do know
Poor Robin's Almanack, 1760

The origin of this laudable tradition is still wrapped in obscurity: though some claim – apparently seriously – to have traced it to the festival of an unauthenticated Celtic laughter god, or to the topsy-turvy and determinedly irreverent Roman feast of Saturnalia.

What is certain is that making fools of people on this day – also practised in other English-speaking lands, much of western Europe and India – remains one of the most flourishing of all British customs. It is, of course, best beloved by children, teachers being the favourite target: but apprentices and other novices are also likely to be sent for such mythical objects as sky-hooks, left-handed screwdrivers, striped paint, or 'a long stand' – only to be told 'you can stand there as long as you like'. Or the joke may be prolonged – especially in Scotland, where this sport is called 'Hunting the Gowk' (cuckoo). The victim is sent with a sealed message, which enjoins the receiver:

Don't you laugh and don't you smile
Hunt the gowk another mile

whereupon the 'gowk' is despatched with a similar note on some further pointless errand, and so on. In recent years, too, a sizeable proportion of the adult population has been taken in by media hoaxes like the BBC's 'spaghetti harvest' or the *Guardian*'s island of 'San Seriffe'.

Only two rules govern this annual outburst of foolery. No one is exempt until noon, but after that the joking must cease, or the hoax rebounds on the hoaxer, for

April Fools' Day's past and gone
You're the fool for making one.

In some areas, nevertheless, children refuse to let the opportunity for licensed mischief slip so soon. So in the English West Midlands, the afternoon is 'trip-up time', and in Fife, 2 April is 'Taily Day', devoted exclusively to tricks involving backs or bottoms – like the famous 'Kick me' placard. While children from North Yorkshire to the Borders, not content with making 'April Noddies' at the conventional time, also repeat their pranks to fool 'May Goslings' on the morning of MAY DAY.

· Appleby Horse Fair ·
see HORSE FAIRS

· Arbor Day ·
Aston-on-Clun, Shropshire: 29 May

The black poplar tree at the centre of Aston-on-Clun is permanently bedecked with large flags, which are ceremonially renewed each 29 May. According to village tradition, this custom began on the same date in 1786, in honour of the wedding of the local squire, whose delighted bride gave a sum of money to ensure its annual repetition. Certainly her descendants continued to do so until the sale of their estate in 1951, whereupon Hopesay parish council took over responsibility.

It may be that the custom is somewhat older: for the wedding took place (probably by design) on OAK APPLE DAY, when a village tradition of dressing the tree may already have existed. But there is no evidence whatever for the oft-repeated statement that Arbor Day must therefore be a relic of tree-worship: and still less for believing that the perfectly explicable name of 'the Bride's Tree' proves that the poplar (not three centuries old, and of a species with no particular magical properties, which may not even be native to Britain) was once a 'tree-shrine of the fertility-goddess Brigid' (who was, in any case, a water deity unconnected with trees).

Related to these nonsenses, but far more pernicious, was a comparatively recent spate of media-generated publicity about the alleged fertility-inducing powers of twigs from the tree: this resulted both in damage to the poplar and local criticism of the custom, so that it was very nearly abandoned. But it is now once more gaining strength as the centrepiece of the village fête – which also features (as if to emphasize the 18th-century origin of the tree-dressing) a re-enactment by schoolchildren of the squire's wedding.

· Archery Customs ·
see SILVER ARROW CONTESTS; WOODMEN OF ARDEN'S GRAND WARDMOTE

· Armada Sermon ·
see SERMONS

· Ascension Day ·

The celebration of Christ's Ascension into Heaven, which – in order to leave time for His many earthly appearances after His Resurrection – is deemed to have occurred forty days after EASTER, on Ascension Day or 'Holy Thursday'. Symbolized in the Middle Ages by the hoisting of a crucifix or statue of Christ up to the church roof, in the Protestant centuries after the Reformation this festival was principally marked – like Rogationtide, the days immediately before it – by the ceremony of BEATING THE BOUNDS, which is still carried on then in many parishes. Since the Anglo-Catholic revival of late-Victorian times, however, it has increasingly been once again celebrated for itself, with the floral decoration of churches and (following the Ascension theme) the singing of morning anthems from the tops of church towers. This last custom appears to have originated at St John's College, Cambridge, where it has been observed annually since 1904: and since then has become particularly popular in the Midlands, where it is still carried on (among other places) at Warwick and Wroxall, Warwickshire; and at Evesham, Malvern and Bromsgrove, Worcestershire.

The folk customs of the day are mainly concerned with water. Ascensiontide rain, if collected as it falls straight from a Heaven opened for Christ's entry, was (and perhaps still is) quite logically regarded as an infallible remedy for sore eyes. But the belief in the curative powers of water drawn from certain 'holy wells' on Ascension morning – like the practice of dropping pins and other offerings into 'wishing wells' then – is less obviously Christian than related to the ancient WELLS AND WELL DRESSING customs for which this season is also famous.

· Ashen Faggot ·
see YULE LOG

· The Ashes ·
see TEST MATCHES

· Ash Wednesday ·

The first day of LENT, when the Church calls its members to repentance and when, in the early Middle Ages, ashes were poured over the heads of sackcloth-clad penitents: in a modified version of this custom, Roman Catholic and some 'High' Anglican priests still make the sign of the cross on the foreheads of their congregations, using the ashes of last year's PALM SUNDAY palms. As a warning to the obdurate, moreover, the Church of England solemnly reads 'A Commination, or Denouncing of God's Anger and Judgements against Sinners' – a formula colloquially called 'the Cursing', whence Ash Wednesday's nickname of 'Cussing Day'.

Ash Wednesday's folk customs, however, have little connection with its Christian significance. Some, like the once-widespread burning, shooting or general maltreatment of 'Jack o' Lent' dummies, probably originated in the symbolic slaying of a pagan winter-god: and others spring from a real or affected misunderstanding of the

On top of the 180-foot-high tower of St John's College Chapel, Cambridge, a small boy grimly holds on to a music stand to prevent it being blown over during the **Ascension Day** carol service.

day's titles. Thus Yorkshire lads, wilfully confusing 'cussing' and 'kissing', acted accordingly with any girl they could corner on the following 'Kissing Friday': while Sussex and Hampshire children still occasionally carry flowering ash-tree twigs, and persecute those without them; and Somerset housewives serve minced meat on 'Hash Wednesday'. Other traditional dishes, more appropriate to this first day of the fleshless Lenten fast, include 'Hasty puddings' quickly compounded of milk, flour and syrup (English Midland counties); fritters made of fried dough (northern England); and grey peas cooked in bacon fat (Warwickshire).

B

· Baddeley Cake ·
see TWELFTH NIGHT

· Bardic Ceremonies ·
see EISTEDDFODAU

· Bawming the Thorn ·
Appleton Thorn, near Warrington, Cheshire: late June

The ceremony of 'Bawming' – from a Middle English word meaning to 'embalm' or 'anoint', and hence 'adorning' – the Thorn now takes place at a variable date in late June, when local primary-school children decorate the tree with ribbons, garlands and flags: they then dance about it in a ring, singing a Victorian 'Bawming song'. The present hawthorn tree, which stands in a railed enclosure near the centre of the village, was planted only in 1967, to replace a blown-down predecessor: but it is said to be a direct descendant of the original tree which gave Appleton Thorn its surname, and which was itself allegedly an offshoot of the Holy Thorn of Glastonbury, brought here by a 12th-century Lord of the Manor, Adam de Dutton.

The present incarnation of the ceremony – which is essentially a children's affair, followed by high tea and sports – is also of comparatively recent vintage, being a revival of a revival (during the 1930s) of an ancient custom discontinued in mid-Victorian times. This, however, was apparently a far more robust celebration, when all the village turned out each St Peter's Day (29 June) to 'pay respect to the tree by bawming and adorning it with flowers and ribbons, and holding a rural fête around it': visitors from the neighbouring towns, moreover, flocked to join them, but these eventually caused so great an annual outbreak of 'rowdyism' that the custom had to be suppressed.

How, why and when it first began are (as so often) quite unknown. Some folklorists, pointing to the hawthorn's reputation for great supernatural powers, have nevertheless hailed the ceremony as a relic of ancient tree worship (*see* ARBOR DAY): while others, noting the festival's late-June date and the tradition that it was once performed mainly by unmarried girls, interpret it as a survival of MIDSUMMER fertility rites.

· Beating Retreat ·
see ROYAL CEREMONIES

· Beating the Bounds ·

This ancient custom, once an essential part of community life throughout Britain and still flourishing here and there in various modified forms, has a long and complex history. One of its component parts, the tradition of holding processions about the fields to sing psalms and chant prayers (Latin: *rogationes*) for God's protection on crops, beasts and people, originated during a period of prolonged natural disasters in mid-5th-century France. Practised on ASCENSION DAY or the three days immediately beforehand (hence known as 'Rogationtide') by the 8th century this had spread to Britain: where it soon merged with an already long-established custom of fixing territorial boundaries by ceremonially walking them annually, preceded by a cross, banner or holy relic, on 'Cross' or 'Ganging' (Old English: 'going' or 'walking') Days. Crop blessing and boundary processing were thereafter performed during the same ceremony: but after the Reformation – when the former part of the observance fell under suspicion of being 'Popish' or merely 'superstitious' – 'walking the bounds' became much the more important element, and has generally remained so ever since.

Parish clergy, nevertheless, have always played a leading (and legitimizing) part in perambulations. At each boundary marker – be it an inscribed stone, a wall plaque or, in country districts, a stream, boulder or other natural feature – they recite a suitable passage from Scripture: often 'Cursed be he that removeth his neighbour's landmark' (Deuteronomy 27.17). At certain traditionally fixed intervals along the way, moreover, they lead the singing of Psalms (generally the 100th, 103rd and 104th) and read the Rogationtide Gospel: this being often done at ancient trees called 'Gospel Oaks', whose memory is preserved in many place-names. These, too, were frequently the scenes of 'cakes and ale' feasts, when 'Ganging beer' and 'Rammalation biscuits' (provided in some places by CHARITIES) were consumed amid much jollity by the whole company of 'processioners'.

Yet 'processioning' – widely corrupted, significantly, to 'possessioning' – was not merely a religious duty, an excuse for a junket, or a pleasant springtime walk. For it also fulfilled the vital function of ensuring that no land-hungry neighbouring village or expansionist farmer had encroached upon the bounds of the parish, thus depriving the entire community of some outlying fishpond, COMMON LAND grazing, or firewood-yielding copse essential for its welfare. Behind vicar and parish constable, therefore, marched men armed with axes and crowbars, ready to smash any 'false stones, cunningly erected', dig in new markers, or demolish 'unlicensed fences enclosing the township's grazing'. Perhaps regrettably – because the arbitrary seizure of commons is

by no means unknown today – such actions are now extremely rare, though a few parishes still religiously mend or clean their boundary markers annually. Nor do processioners from rival villages engage (as they once frequently did) in free fights at debatable points: though every third Ascension Day, when the beaters of the TOWER OF LONDON Liberty and of All Hallows-by-the-Tower parish meet at a disputed marker on Tower Hill, the Lord Mayor of London still appears to symbolically challenge the Tower's governor.

The convention that perambulators must visit and beat *all* their markers, whatever the inconvenience, has also become largely a matter of traditional pride – one boundary stone belonging to All Hallows, for instance, is now in mid-Thames, while one of St Clement Danes', London, is currently below ground level, so that in each case a choirboy must be held by the ankles while he strikes them. And so too has the necessity for processioners to follow a set and unvarying course, whatever lies in the way – which is very pleasant for the parishioners of St Michael-at-the-Northgate, Oxford, whose route lies through the bar of the Roebuck Inn, but less so for the citizens of Richmond, North Yorkshire, whose perambulation includes a wade into the River Swale, at least for the water bailiff. Once, however, the observance of such niceties was vitally important: especially in towns, where a slight deviation from the usual route could establish a disastrous precedent, losing a parish the rates and taxes of a whole crowded street or saddling it with several families of additional paupers to maintain. For Poor Law assessors were notoriously exact – in one famous case where a pauper's bed straddled a boundary line, they ruled that the parish in which his head usually rested was responsible for him.

Above all, then, it was essential for the processioners to know precisely where the boundary and its markers lay: information which – in the absence of maps, printed records, or indeed general literacy – was necessarily stored in the minds of men, and transmitted by oral tradition. So old-established residents were in demand to direct the walkers, and especial care had to be taken to ensure that their vital knowledge be passed on to their eventual successors, the village children – usually by subjecting these to some painful but memorable experience at significant points along the route. Boys were therefore bent over marker stones and beaten, thrown into boundary ponds or clumps of nettles, or upended and 'bumped' where the borderline changed direction: and were thereafter mollified (and also further 'remembered') by gifts of cakes, fruit or pennies. Nor were adults always exempt from such painful 'rememberings', especially if (like the unsuspecting curates who provided favourite victims) they were newcomers to the parish.

As perambulations became increasingly symbolic, however, and Victorian public opinion came progressively to frown on 'indecorous horse-play', this part of

Above: **Beating the Bounds** of an English parish in 1848, by Edward Rippingille. On the left, labourers gleefully prepare to demolish a bricked-up doorway blocking the processioners' path; at centre right is the liveried parish constable; and on the right (by the cross-base boundary marker) the sexton instructs bounds-beating village boys.
Below: A child is upended to 'remember' her of the parish boundary, while beating the bounds of Cottenham, Cambridgeshire in 1977. *Right:* The bannerers of Laugharne in Carmarthenshire enjoy a well-earned rest during their twenty-six-mile walk in 1948.

the custom changed. 'Remembering' by reward was preferred to 'remembering' by force, bounds instead of boys were beaten, and the wands formerly used to belabour children were instead used by them to belabour markers. These milder conventions are now general, though the older traditions are still playfully maintained here and there: at Laugharne, Carmarthenshire and Newport, Pembrokeshire, for instance, a child's failure to remember the correct names of boundary stones earns a token beating; and during the five-yearly Ascensiontide perambulation of the Manor of the Savoy (a London enclave of the Duchy of Lancaster, centred on the Strand) choirboys are upended and bumped – though a hassock is first placed beneath their heads. At Newbiggin-by-the-Sea, Northumberland, moreover, the annual inspection of the common moor – held on the Wednesday nearest 18 May, and allegedly practised since 1235 – includes a ceremony called 'Dunting the Freeholder' wherein new 'commoners' (whatever their age) are thrice bumped, bottom first, onto an ancient boundary stone.

Though parish 'walkings' have always been the most widespread type of perambulation, other kinds of community also beat their bounds regularly, often with considerable pomp and ceremony. The Dean and Chapter of Lichfield Cathedral, for example, process theirs annually on Ascension Day, bearing elm boughs and stopping in eight places to sing psalms: and so too (though not always at Rogationtide) do some COMMON LAND trustees and the COURTS LEET of a few manors, both royal and privately owned. The bounds of the Island and Royal Manor of Portland, Dorset, are beaten only on every seventh Ascension Day, while those of the manor of Spaunton, near Kirby Moorside, North Yorkshire – possibly because of the thirty-mile distance involved – are walked only when a new Lord of the Manor succeeds. But perhaps the most impressive (as well as among the lengthiest, since they take in large areas of town commons) of processionings are those of certain ancient boroughs: some of which, like the analogous COMMON RIDINGS of Scotland are carried out on horseback.

Among these is the Sheriff's Ride at Lichfield, Staffordshire (held annually, on or near 8 September, since the city elected its first sheriff under a royal charter of 1553) whose twenty-two mile route includes stops for numerous stirrup cups and a programme of HORSE RACES for participants. Berwick-upon-Tweed's ten-mile bounds, which include a section of the Anglo-Scottish border – are also ridden annually (on MAY DAY) and have been since Henry VIII's reign: and so, rather more irregularly, are those of Morpeth, Northumberland. The hardy 'common walkers' of Laugharne, Carmarthenshire, however, cover their twenty-six mile circuit on foot, setting out at 6 a.m. each Spring Bank Holiday Monday to march over hill and dale behind their mayor and two 'banners'. At Richmond, North Yorkshire, too, mayor and corporation, escorted by halberdiers

and sergeants-at-mace, lead the eighteen-mile walk every seventh September: but the lengthy processioning of Lancaster (also held septennially, on the Wednesday after Spring Bank Holiday) is now carried out only by the 'flagman' and his companion, who are met by a car-borne corporation at certain boundary markers. At least two long-established perambulations, moreover, have always been made by water. The Mayor of Rochester, Kent, in his ex-officio capacity as Admiral of the Medway, cruises that river on a day in June or July, sailing from up-stream Burham and travelling to Garrison Point, Sheerness, where its estuary meets that of the Thames: while the Mayor of Poole, Dorset, as Admiral of Poole Harbour, inspects his sea marks by boat every three years.

These, and other surviving bounds-beating ceremonies are, however, merely a tiny remnant of the vast number once performed throughout Britain. Struck a severe blow by the almost universal enclosures of the 18th and early 19th centuries – when lowland parishes were carefully charted, commons apportioned, and legal boundaries fixed – and another by the publication of Ordnance Survey maps (begun in 1801), the custom had by later Victorian times became largely a matter of civic or parochial pride rather than necessity. (Though on several occasions during recent decades, commons have again been 'perambulated' in all seriousness, as a protest against their threatened annexation by 'agribusiness'.) At almost the same time, however, the wheel of custom turned full circle, and the other, long-neglected, aspect of Rogationtide ceremonies – the blessing of crops – began to enjoy a minor revival: and since the First World War crop-blessing processions, often unrelated to boundaries, have again been held in a number of parishes, particularly in southern England. Among the more remarkable are the Blessing of the Cherry Orchards, performed each May around Newington-by-Sittingbourne, Kent; the Rogationtide crop-blessing at Llanfair Caereinion, Montgomeryshire – conducted from a train on the Welshpool and Llanfair Light Railway; and the numerous related BLESSING THE SEAS ceremonies.

· Bells and Bellringing Customs ·

Bells have been used as a summons to Christian worship since at least the 5th century. The oldest surviving British examples (often associated with Celtic missionaries like ST DAVID) are small handbells: but by the late Anglo-Saxon period church towers were being built to accommodate very much larger bells, and such have always been endowed with names and personalities – like St Paul's Cathedral's seventeen-ton 'Great Paul', the biggest bell in Britain; Westminster's 'Big Ben'; and York Minster's 'Great Peter'. Medieval bells were actually 'christened', and are frequently engraved with invocations to patron saints. After the Reformation, however, they were more likely to be inaugurated by being up-ended and filled with beer: and to be inscribed with pious, practical or belligerently Anglican slogans:

I to the church the living call
And to the grave do summon all
Gloucestershire

Arise and go to your business
St Ives, Cambridgeshire

Prosperity to the Church of England
and no encouragement to Enthusiasm
[Methodism]
Welwyn, Hertfordshire

or with the praise of bellfounder or donor:

Thomas Gardiner he did me cast
I'll sing his praise unto the last
Ickworth, Suffolk

All ye of Bath that hear me sound
Thank Lady Hopton's hundred pound.
Bath Abbey, Somerset

Today, new or recast bells are formally consecrated by a bishop.

Bells may be struck externally with a hammer (as in a clock or carillon) but are more usually sounded against an internal clapper, by means of a system of ropes and wheels. This may be done by swinging the bell from side to side, called 'tolling' a single bell or 'chiming' if several are rung in succession. In ringing proper, however, the bells are made to revolve through almost a complete circle, first in one direction and then in the other, so that the clapper strikes them on each ascent. This method is unique to Britain and the English-speaking nations, as is the practice of 'change-ringing', whereby a tuned set of five or more bells are rung in a slightly re-arranged order at each pull. Thus a ring of eight bells is capable of over 40,000 permutations, and marathon peals of over 5000 changes are frequently rung on special occasions.

The invention and development of this science made the later 17th and 18th centuries a golden age of bellringing. New and recast bells proliferated, and local ringers formed themselves into close-knit bands: jealous of their fees and privileges and tenacious of 'ancient custom' – it was, for instance, they who perpetuated CASTLETON GARLAND – they strongly resisted interference by vicar or churchwarden, and even now ringers' strikes and 'belfry lockouts' are not unknown. Among the gentry and professional classes, too, change-ringing became a popular sport, and clubs like the 'Ancient Society of College Youths' (founded 1637) continue to arrange tours of country belfries – many of which still display sets of rules, along the lines of:

If that to ring you do come here
You must ring well with hand and ear
If that you ring in spur or hat
A quart of Ale must pay for that
And if a bell you overthrow

Sixpence is due before you go
And if you curse or swear, I say
A shilling's due without delay
And if you quarrill in this place
You shall not ring in any case.
Hornsey, Middlesex

Such forfeits invariably served to fill 'ringers' jugs', like the four-gallon beer 'gotch' kept at Hadleigh church, Suffolk.

The most frequent use of church bells is, of course, to herald Sunday services. Practice varies greatly, but it is usual to end the ringing with a five-minute bell to hasten sluggards: while a few belfries maintain the custom of sounding chimes as the service closes, called 'Pudding' or 'Oven' bells because they warned cooks of churchgoers' imminent return for Sunday dinner. At the appropriate points in Mass or Communion celebrations, Catholic and 'High' Anglican churches also ring 'Sanctus' and 'Sacrament' ('Elevation') bells, a medieval custom designed to call hearers to prayer at these solemn moments.

Bells are also rung (or, if the number and enthusiasm of the ringers allows, pealed) for the Church's great festivals, CHRISTMAS and NEW YEAR'S nights being favourite occasions for ambitious change-ringing. Some churches still ring PANCAKE BELLS on SHROVE TUESDAY, but thereafter the bells conventionally keep silence during LENT (except perhaps for a muffled tolling on GOOD FRIDAY) until the EASTER morning peal: they may also ring long and loud on ASCENSION DAY, at WHITSUN, and on the feast of the church's patron saint. They mark, too, the most significant events of human life. For though they rarely now proclaim a BIRTH – to royalty or, very occasionally, to the family of a popular squire, parson, or ringer – they almost invariably celebrate WEDDINGS: and if PASSING BELLS to announce a parishioner's death are becoming unusual, tolling at FUNERALS remains general.

Church bells play their part, too, on purely secular occasions, pealing for CORONATIONS, jubilees and royal visits, and tolling on REMEMBRANCE SUNDAY. Other national anniversaries, however, are now much less widely 'rung in' than formerly. Only a few belfries, for instance, still keep OAK APPLE DAY, once the ringers' greatest festival: and fewer yet maintain the once mandatory celebration of GUY FAWKES NIGHT – among them the ringers of Harlington, Middlesex who afterwards enjoy a 'Leg o' Pork Supper' endowed by some patriotic but now unidentifiable donor.

Some towns still ring church or municipal bells to announce annual FAIRS or weekly markets, and many more to welcome incoming mayors. While a number of places (including Wallingford, Berkshire; Morpeth and Berwick-upon-Tweed, Northumberland; Richmond, North Yorkshire; Chertsey, Surrey; and Chester Cathedral) continue to toll the evening 'curfew' bells which once reminded householders to cover fires

The **Biddenden Maids' Charity** dole of bread, cheese and tea being distributed from the old workhouse window, apparently to a somewhat querulous beneficiary.

(French: *couvre-feu*) and lock up for the night: or which, as LOST IN THE DARK BELLS, guided in benighted travellers.

Bells, finally, also have their uses in emergencies. Their booming voice, feared by the demons of the air, was once thought sovereign for quelling storms and plagues, and is even now half-jokingly sounded (as during TURNING THE DEVIL'S STONE) to 'frighten off evil spirits'. And though sirens have replaced fire bells like that at Sherborne in Dorset, inscribed:

> Lord Quench This Furious Flame
> Arise, Run, Help Put Out the Same

the great carrying power of bells can still spread a vital warning. During the great East Coast floods of 1953, for instance, the church bells of Lincolnshire roused hundreds of endangered villagers from sleep, and from 1940 to 1945 the belfries of Britain stood silent, waiting to sound the alarm of invasion.

· Biddenden Maids' Charity ·
The White House, Biddenden, near Tenterden, Kent: Easter Monday

One of the most famous English CHARITIES, principally because of a picturesque story about its origins. Every EASTER MONDAY, the widows and pensioners of Biddenden are each entitled to a loaf of bread, a pound of cheese and a pound of tea, paid for with the rent of twenty acres called 'the Bread and Cheese Lands': and at the same time all present – visitors included – are given a small biscuit called a Biddenden cake. Stamped upon this are the crude figures of two women, whose bodies apparently merge: above their heads are the names Elisa and Mary Chulkhurst, and the skirt of one bears the number thirty-four, while that of the other is inscribed 'in 1100'. These, the legend relates, are the founders of the dole, who were born in 1100 joined together at the shoulders and hips. The 'Siamese twins' lived for thirty-four years, whereafter one of them died: but the other stoutly refused to be separated from the corpse, declaring that 'as we came together, we will also go together', and within a few hours she too was dead.

Whether the Chulkhurst sisters really did found the charity – and, indeed, whether they ever existed at all – is, however, very much open to doubt: for the historian Edward Hasted, writing in the 1790s, insisted that the figures (then unnamed and undated) had only appeared on the biscuits some fifty years beforehand: and, moreover, that they had not originally been intended to represent the donors, but rather the widows who benefitted from the distribution. The dole, he suggested, had really been endowed by a pair of perfectly normal maiden ladies named Preston, though at what date he could not discover. The Chulkhurst tale (which apparently first appears in an 18th-century broadside printed locally) may therefore have begun to explain the biscuits, rather than vice versa: or, like a similar story once current at Norton St Philip, Somerset, it may have been prompted by some crude monument to two ladies which once existed in Biddenden church.

How and when the charity actually originated is therefore obscure. But it was certainly well established by 1646, when William Horner, the vicar intruded by Parliament during the Civil War, attempted to annexe the Bread and Cheese Lands to his parson's perquisites: his case being dismissed by the county authorities, he appealed a decade later to Cromwell's Court of Exchequer, only to be dismissed again. So the dole survived, to weather a further threat in 1682. At that time the bread and cheese were distributed inside the church on Easter Sunday, and were supplemented by a plentiful issue of beer – which last, Vicar Hinton complained to the Archbishop of Canterbury, caused the custom 'to be observed with much disorder and indecency'. The beer dole was thereupon stopped – tea being eventually substituted in Victorian times – and the ceremony was exiled to the church porch, where it remained until the end of the 19th century. Then it moved once again, appropriately enough to the old workhouse built on the Bread and Cheese Lands, and since converted into cottages: and here the dole is still distributed, before a crowd of visitors drawn by the tale of the Biddenden Maids.

· Big Court Night ·
see CIVIC CUSTOMS

· Birth ·

It is easy to understand why a host of customs, ceremonies and beliefs have always surrounded the beginning of a new human life: and why a surprisingly large number of these are still covertly or openly observed even in this supposedly rationalist age. For, despite modern medical advances, childbirth remains (in the words of the *Book of Common Prayer*) 'a time of great pain and peril': and though the horrifying infant mortality rate of former times – in 1800, for example, a baby had scarcely a 50 per cent chance of reaching the age of five – has thankfully been very much reduced, yet the first weeks and months of existence continue to be fraught with hazards. Far from extinct, too, is the belief that things done or experienced at the beginning of life will influence the remainder of its course: or (as evidenced by the current fad for 'astrology') the conviction that the time and circumstances of birth exercise an ineradicable control over the baby's destiny.

What is altogether more difficult is to decide which of these customs and beliefs survive, and which have become extinct. For, like the closely related customs connected with those other 'rites of passage', WEDDINGS and FUNERALS, birth observances vary not only from region to region but also from family to family: to an even greater extent, moreover, they tend to be practised in private, or half-shamefacedly carried on 'just in case'. Still fairly general, at least among older folk, is the belief that an expectant mother must avoid certain actions – other than those forbidden by medicine or by common sense – which might affect the fate or appearance of her unborn child. A hare crossing her path, for instance, was once thought to engender harelip in the baby: while sudden frights during the last month of pregnancy are still sometimes held responsible for birthmarks, which may resemble the shape of the animal or object that caused the shock. In Wales, too, it is or was believed that pregnant women should not step over graves, lest the child be stillborn; touch dirty water, lest it develop 'coarse hands'; gather strongly scented flowers, in which case it might lack a sense of smell; or, more logically, tie a cord round their waist, lest the babe be 'born unlucky'.

A widespread and still-flourishing taboo also prohibits taking delivery of a pram, cot or cradle before the birth, lest 'providence' be tempted and the baby never live to lie in it: or using any second-hand object associated with a dead child. In the North of England and Scotland, however, some hold that the cradle must be paid for in advance, or the infant will grow up 'so poor that it can't pay for its own coffin'. There, too, rocking an empty cradle after the baby's birth was said to bring on its death or severe illness, though in East Anglia the same process is allegedly still employed as a charm by childless women who 'want a baby'.

The worldwide belief that some of the discomfort of pregnancy and the pain of childbirth can transfer itself to the father – particularly of a first child – may also linger here and there in Britain: certainly it flourished along the Welsh March in the early 20th century, and was stronger still in Georgian Yorkshire, where inexplicably sick bachelors sometimes fell under suspicion of having fathered bastards. Certainly, too, the position of the unborn infant is still widely held to indicate its sex, boys supposedly being 'carried high' and girls 'carried low'.

Convinced that the position of the stars at **birth** will influence the child's life, astrologers study the sky as the mother is delivered on a 'groaning stool': from the *Compleat Astrologer*, 1587.

Monday's child is fair of face
Tuesday's child is full of grace
Wednesday's child is full of woe
Thursday's child has far to go
Friday's child is loving and giving
Saturday's child works hard for a living
But the child that's born on the Sabbath day
Is bonny and blithe and good and gay.

Sunday's children, moreover, were believed to be protected for life from the wiles of witches and evil spirits, and so were those born during the Twelve Days of CHRISTMAS: while those born in Sussex at either time could never be drowned or hanged. Luckiest and most gifted of all, however, are seventh children of seventh children.

Exceedingly lucky, too, are children delivered with part of the foetal membrane – known as the 'caul' or *hallihoo* (holy hood) – clinging to their head: and if this is dried and kept the infant will remain fortunate for life, as well as becoming notably eloquent and entirely proof against rheumatism and drowning. Since the caul's powers were also transferable, they were until very recently in demand among sailors: but prices were high, for many believed that if they were lost or destroyed, the cauled baby might pine or even die. Midlands infants born with hair on their arms and hands are thought to be destined for prosperity: and so, generally, are those with dimples on their chins; but

A dimple on the cheek
Leaves a fortune to seek.

Lucky, too (at least in Lincolnshire), are large-eared babies: and the same county holds that infants born with open hands will be generous, while closed hands presage meanness. Children born with teeth, moreover, are doomed to grow up hard-bitten and grasping; and those whose eyebrows meet in the middle will inevitably become bad-tempered and peevish.

New-born babies, it was generally believed, should be 'taken up' before being 'taken down', or else they will never 'rise in the world': those delivered in an upstairs room, therefore, were often carried up a specially placed ladder before being taken downstairs. More horrifying to modern midwives, but insisted upon by their Edwardian predecessors along the Welsh border, was the custom of wrapping new arrivals in something old, preferably a red flannel petticoat: or the old Scots practice of plunging them immediately into cold water, even if the ice had to be broken first. Cotswold babies born in winter, moreover, might be taken out and rolled in the snow, in order to strengthen them and endow lifelong immunity from chilblains: and if they then showed signs of marked restlessness, might be treated to a magical jelly of hares' brains. More usually, however, the first food to pass baby's lips – a matter of great symbolic importance – was a spoonful of butter and sugar, though some Herefordshire mothers preferred a

Very much more can be ascertained, according to folk belief, from the time at which the baby finally does arrive. Children born at certain hours, for instance, were credited with the power of prophecy and the ability to see ghosts, and may still be regarded as especially lucky: though regional opinion varies as to what constitutes the magical period. East Anglians hold it to be the 'chiming hours' of three, six, nine and twelve, by day or night: while in southern and western England visionary children are those born between midnight and one on a Friday; in Yorkshire at the same period on any day; in Warwickshire on Christmas Day only; and in Wales the gift comes to all those born at night. There also the state of the moon is important, for babies born at the new moon will grow eloquent and those who arrive during its last quarter become good reasoners: generally, however, babies born during a waxing moon are said to be fortunate, while all along Britain's eastern seaboard those who arrive at ebb tide are condemned to a life of ill luck.

Best known and most widely held of all prophecies relating to the time of birth, however, is the one enshrined in some version of the following:

small quantity of bitter rue ('the herb of Grace') pounded with sugar, and those of north-western England favoured 'cinder-water', into which a red-hot coal had been dropped.

Mother, meanwhile, was doubtless enjoying a nourishing *caudle* of old ale, oatmeal, sugar and spices, preferably blended with water from a 'holy' *Caudle* or Birthing Well: and thus strengthened, she would soon be well enough to leave the house for her CHURCHING. Earlier on, especially in the English Midlands, she would have been prepared for the ordeal of childbirth with a slice or two of 'groaning cake', made from a pain-killing mixture of flour, crushed hempseed, rhubarb root, eggs, grated dandelion root, milk and gin. The rest of the cake (and, in northern England and Scotland, the 'groaning cheese') were saved for celebrations of the birth, when unmarried girls were given a slice for luck. They, and anyone else visiting the child for the first time, were and still are expected to bring it symbolic gifts, traditionally including an egg, a handful of salt, and a coal or a box of matches, as well as a piece of silver money pressed into the baby's hand. This last custom remains general, particularly in northern Britain, where old-fashioned 'real silver' threepences and sixpences are regarded as the luckiest coins.

Even these, however, are scarcely sufficient to ward off the ill effects of cutting rather than biting off a child's nails before it is a year old – in which case it will certainly grow up 'light-fingered'; permitting it to see itself reflected in a pool or mirror, lest its soul be 'taken'; or allowing a cat to 'suck its breath' and so kill it – a belief perpetuated by the still-flourishing notion that cats make a habit of sitting on infant's faces. The only sure way of safeguarding a baby's physical and spiritual health, indeed, is to hasten on its CHRISTENING.

· Blessing the Crops ·
see BEATING THE BOUNDS

· Blessing the Seas and Fisheries ·

A good many fishing communities around Britain (including some whose fishery connections are now effectively a matter of history) hold annual services of blessing on boats, nets and fisherfolk, as well as on the waters themselves. Generally celebrated on ASCENSION DAY, or during the three days of 'Rogationtide' immediately before it, such ceremonies are for the most part fairly recent in origin, being maritime versions of the crop-blessing services (*see* BEATING THE BOUNDS) revived during the present century.

Beginning in south-western England, these include the Blessing of the River Dart, delivered from both sides of its estuary at Dartmouth and Kingswear, Devon: while a few miles further east, Brixham in Devon blesses its fishing fleet in a waterside service, also at Rogationtide. At Mudeford, Hampshire, however, the vicar puts out

in a boat to bless the waters: and at Southampton (where prayers are offered for the port's great liners and cargo ships) Rogationtide services are held both at Ocean and the Town Quays, the blessing again being delivered from a small boat moored offshore. Eastward into Sussex, the lifeboat provides a pulpit for the Blessing of the Sea at Hastings: while among the numerous Kentish services are those at Folkestone (in July); Broadstairs (held on the ancient jetty during the fourth week in April); and oyster-fishing Whitstable – held at Reeves' Beach on or near St James's Day, 25 July, and older than most, since it dates from the early 19th century.

Moving into East Anglia, the pleasure-boating Norfolk Broads are blessed by the Bishop of Norwich on the first Sunday in August, at a service held amid the ruins of St Benet's Hulme Abbey, near Horning. While much further north the still-flourishing fishing town of Whitby, North Yorkshire holds a Rogationtide Blessing of the Sea: and so too do the Northumberland ports of North Shields (where choir and clergy take ship on the Tyne) and Cullercoats (where they sail round the harbour to bless the fishing boats). The most impressive of these northern services, however, is held at inland Norham on the border river Tweed, whose salmon fisheries are blessed just before midnight on 14 February: this is the actual start of the netting season, and immediately after the wintry open-air service the first hardy boatmen put out into the river, presenting their first catch to the vicar.

Certainly the most unusual of all sea blessings, nevertheless, is that held at Margate in Kent, on a January date coinciding with EPIPHANY according to the Greek Orthodox calendar. Organized by the town's sizeable Greek-Cypriot community, and usually conducted by the Orthodox Archbishop of Thyateira and Great Britain, it includes the old Greek custom of casting a flower-decked crucifix into the sea, from which it must be retrieved by a waiting swimmer. (*See* ABBOTSBURY GARLAND DAY; BURRY MAN; HARVEST FESTIVALS)

· Blessing the Throats ·
St Etheldreda's church, Ely Place, London: 3 February

On 3 February every year, hundreds of victims of throat complaints seek a cure at the Roman Catholic church of St Etheldreda, near Holborn Circus in London. After a special service, two long altar candles are blessed and tied into a X-shape with ribbons: supplicants then kneel before the altar, and a priest holds the candle-cross beneath their chins, meanwhile praying, 'May the Lord deliver you from the evil of the throat, and from every other evil'.

The ceremony (performed here for over a century, and long familiar in Catholic Europe) invokes St Blaise, the 4th-century Armenian physician-bishop whose feast day this is. On his way to martyrdom, according to

· Bottle Kicking and Hare Pie Scramble ·
Hallaton, Leicestershire: Easter Monday

This unique custom (or pair of customs) takes place at Hallaton, near Market Harborough in Leicestershire, on EASTER MONDAY. First, a locally made hare pie is blessed in the parish church, and half of it is distributed and eaten outside the churchyard gate. The remainder then heads a parade through the village, and behind it march three men holding aloft small ribbon-decked and iron-hooped barrels (or 'bottles') – two of these being full of beer and the other ('the dummy') being empty. When the procession reaches a hill called 'Hare Pie Bank', pieces are scattered about and 'scrambled for' by the crowd – though no one now attempts to eat any they manage to capture.

The scramble over, the ceremony continues with the thrice-repeated throwing up of the first full barrel: and as it hits the ground for the third time the 'bottle kicking' begins. A boisterous version of the free-for-all STREET BALL GAMES played elsewhere, this consists of an extended running brawl between a Hallaton team – of unlimited size – and another nominally from neighbouring Medbourne, though any non-Hallatonian may in practice join it. Each side attempts to kick, throw, carry, scrum or otherwise convey the bottle over their own touch-line – the Hallaton goal being a stream at one side of the bank, and the Medbourne target a hedge on the

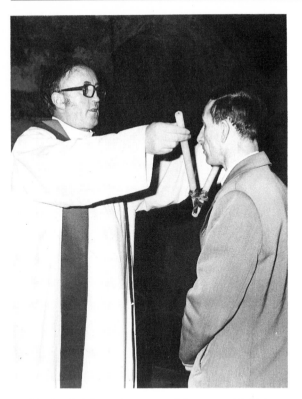

Blessing the Throats in memory of the martyred St Blaise, the priest touches them with crossed altar-candles.

legend, he miraculously saved a child from choking to death on a fishbone, thus becoming the patron saint of throat sufferers; thereafter he was torn to death with sharp iron combs, a fate which endeared him also to the woolcombers who prepared wool for spinning and, by extension, to the whole woollen trade. Until the early 19th century, therefore, many wool towns (notably Norwich, Northampton, Bury St Edmunds, Bradford, York and Aberdeen) celebrated 'Bishop Blaise Day' with elaborate and splendid pageants. Bonfires were also widely lit then, either from confusion between 'Blaise' and 'blaze' or because of the festival's proximity to CANDLEMAS.

· Boat Races ·
see CORACLE RACES; DOGGETT'S COAT AND BADGE RACE; HENLEY REGATTA; OXFORD AND CAMBRIDGE BOAT RACE

· Bombshell Sermon ·
see SERMONS

A contestant in the no-holds-barred **Bottle Kicking** at Hallaton is forced to relinquish the beer-filled and iron-hooped 'bottle.'

other – and as soon as one goal has been scored, the second full bottle is brought into play: only if this produces a draw, however, is the empty dummy used. In any case, the contest is a long and hard-fought one, which can continue for over four hours: but at its end both sides return fairly amicably to Hallaton's old Butter 'Cross' – a pyramid topped by a ball – which the winners scale to toast their victory in beer straight from the 'bottle'.

Involving as it does the 'sacred' hare, this custom has inevitably become a happy hunting ground for folklore theorists, who have variously derived it from a 'ritual battle between summer and winter'; 'a fertility sacrifice'; and 'a pre-Christian spring festival'. Its beginnings, however, are in reality quite unknown, and it may even be that the hare-pie and bottle-kicking elements were not originally connected. The only certainty, indeed, is that at some now unidentifiable date before 1770, the rectors of Hallaton were bequeathed a plot of land called Hare Crop Leys, from whose rent they had to provide 'two hare pies, a quantity of ale and two dozen penny loaves for the Easter Monday bottle-kicking'. One local explanation of this endowment tells how a Hallaton woman, having been preserved from a charging bull by a hare which suddenly rose in its path, somewhat ungratefully provided that her escape be commemorated by the eating of pies made from her saviour's relations: but the bequest may equally well have been made (*see* PAX CAKES) to perpetuate some already ancient custom, perhaps related to the ceremonial Easter Monday hare hunts once held at Leicester and at Coleshill and Wooton Wawen in Warwickshire.

However it originated, the Bottle Kicking and Hare Pie Scramble has been well defended against all attempts to change or suppress it. In 1790, for instance, when a vicar suggested diverting its funds for 'more benevolent ends', chalked messages warned him that 'No Pie' would mean 'No Parson, and a Job for the Glazier': and in 1878 a further effort to appropriate the money 'to sports ... more in character with the tastes of the age' was also roundly defeated by the outraged parishioners.

· Bower Day ·
see COURT OF ARRAY

· Boxing Day ·
see CHRISTMAS

· Boys' Ploughing Match ·
St Margaret's Hope, South Ronaldsay, Orkney: mid August

The original significance of this ancient custom is uncertain: but since it formerly took place at Easter, it may well have been connected with a spring ploughing rite. Currently, however, it takes the form of a children's version of the horse-ploughing matches still popular all over Britain. But the 'horses' are young boys and girls,

The judging at the Orkney **Boys' Ploughing Match** is taken very seriously.

dressed in elaborate and often hereditarily handed-down costumes in distinctly Scandinavian style – which is scarcely surprising, for Orkney remained under Danish rule until the late Middle Ages, and still uses many Norse dialect words. Their tall pointed hats, horse collars, jackets and fringed shorts are covered – perhaps to 'reflect away' bad luck – with gold braid, spangles, tiny mirrors and shining bells: and round their ankles are hair fringes like a plough horse's 'feathering', worn above shoes painted to resemble hooves.

Prizes are awarded for the best decorated 'animal' and the most thorough grooming of teeth, nails and hooves: but thereafter the 'horses' no longer take part in the match. This is the task of the 'ploughmen': boys only, under fifteen, and each equipped with a beautifully made miniature plough which is also frequently an heirloom. Once they ploughed a real field, but now the competition takes place on a marked-out stretch of wet beach at the Sands O' Right. There, the ordinary and championship classes turn as straight, even and un-broken a furrow as possible in a given time, the judging being carried out with considerable precision by expert adult ploughmen.

· Bread and Bun Doles ·

As the most basic and direct form of poor relief, distributions of bread were probably the commonest type of British traditional CHARITIES. Almost every parish once had its regular bread dole: and the more munificent founders aimed at weekly distributions, often conducted from the carved and painted 'charity bread shelves' still displayed in a few churches. Largely due to the ravages of inflation, however, weekly doles are now extremely rare, one of the few survivors being John Sayer's charity at Woodbridge in Suffolk. As originally endowed in 1638, this provided over eighty large 'twopenny loaves' every week: but now the fund runs only to a mere handful, which local pensioners collect each Saturday from the bread shelves in the porch of St Mary's church. Another East Anglian dole – founded in 1558 by Ralph Greenaway, a London alderman with local connections – survives in altered form at Wiveton Green, near Holt in Norfolk: initially intended to provide thirteen 'aged and indigent' parishioners with a weekly sixpence in money and sixpennyworth of bread, this now distributes £1.25 a week to thirteen pensioners, handed over in the church on the first Saturday of every month.

Annual bread distributions – sometimes in the form of GRAVESIDE DOLES – were also frequent, being normally held at appropriately charitable seasons like LENT or CHRISTMAS: at Ellington near Huntingdon, for example, twelve shillings' (60p) worth of bread is still handed out on GOOD FRIDAY, under an agreement made in 1613. At Geddington, Northamptonshire, however, the distribution takes place – unusually – on MAY DAY. Endowed in the early 17th century by a Lady Montagu of nearby Boughton House, this 'May Bread charity' was intended to ensure that poor local cottagers (who normally subsisted on low-grade rye or barley bread) should enjoy at least one 'white wheaten loaf' a year: but any parishioner who wishes may now collect a symbolic piece of white bread from the church.

Carrying symbolism yet further, a few charities have lately substituted buns or cakes for the loaves originally specified. At St Michael's-on-the-Mount, Bristol, for instance, a bread dole dating from at least 1739 is now distributed in the form of large buns called 'Twopenny Starvers': several hundred of which are consumed, mainly by children, after service on EASTER TUESDAY. George Tayler's charity, moreover, specifically requires that buns be distributed – presumably as an inducement to attend the annual sermon, 'suited to the capacity of children and young people', which he endowed in 1852 at Keevil near Trowbridge, Wiltshire. Now held on the first convenient Sunday after Easter, the 'Bun Service' ends with the gift of a small ('twopenny') bun to each Sunday-school child, and a larger ('fourpenny') one to every Sunday-school teacher. (*See also* ST BARTHOLOMEW'S BUN RACE)

The choirboys of St Michael's-on-the-Mount, Bristol, enjoying their Easter **Bread and Bun Dole** of mammoth 'Twopenny Starvers'.

· Bread and Cheese Throwing ·
St Briavels, Gloucestershire: Whit Sunday

In most places, BREAD AND BUN DOLES were conducted in a sober and respectable manner. Here and there, however, the loaves were instead hurled into a waiting crowd and 'scrambled' for – a process which, if it did little to improve the eventual condition of the bread, undoubtedly added to the general enjoyment of the event. Such scrambles were formerly held, for instance, in the churchyards of Barford St Michael, Oxfordshire; Wath-on-Dearne, West Yorkshire; and Paddington, London: but the only example to have survived – probably because it was also an assertion of a valued COMMON right – is the Bread and Cheese Throwing at St Briavels, the ancient capital of the Forest of Dean.

In its present form, the ceremony takes place after evensong on Whit Sunday (*see* WHITSUN), when several basketfuls of bread and cheese are thrown from a wall near the castle, to be scrambled for in the lane below. Held to date from the reign of King John (1199-1216), the performance of this custom is said to preserve the right of the people of St Briavels and Hewelsfield to take unlimited timber from nearby Hudnalls Wood. The woodcutting privilege, in fact, may have existed even before John's time, when the earls of Hereford were overlords of Dean Forest: for a dubious local tradition maintains that it was won from a niggardly earl by his charitable countess, who was forced as payment to ride naked through the village like Lady Godiva. Certainly the right was documented in 1282, and upheld by Act of Parliament in 1667: but the exact nature of its connection with the bread and cheese ceremony is obscure. Perhaps the most likely explanation, nevertheless, is that the dole began as a QUIT RENT – a symbolic annual duty which the St Briavels men were obliged to fulfil in return for their timber.

Some memory of this obligation, moreover, seems to have survived until 1779, when the custom was first recorded: for at that time every village householder was required to pay a penny (later doubled) towards the cost of the bread and cheese. In those days, too, the ceremony actually took place inside the church, the food being thrown to the congregation from its upper galleries. This occasioned 'as great a tumult and uproar as the amusements of a village wake', especially since the hardest cheese and stalest bread were always carefully selected – 'and it was the custom to use them as pellets, the parson coming in for his share as he left the pulpit'.

Not surprisingly, then, the Victorians thought this 'unseemly custom' 'very ill suited to a sacred edifice', and in about 1857 it was expelled to the churchyard, the dole being thrown down from the church tower. Later on it was exiled completely from holy ground, to the road outside the church gates, but still 'all the roughs of the Forest came over, and there was much drinking and fighting'. So, for a time, the custom lapsed altogether: but it was too well established as an annual foresters' gathering to disappear for long, and it was soon revived on its present site – which is, of course, yet further from 'the sacred edifice'. Some local people, nevertheless, still believe the thrown bread and cheese possesses special powers, and pieces of it are occasionally kept as lucky charms. (*See* FOREST CUSTOMS)

· Bridgwater Squibbing Night ·
see GUY FAWKES NIGHT

· Britannia Coconut Dancers ·
see MORRIS DANCING

· Brotherhood and Guestling, Court of, ·
see CINQUE PORTS CUSTOMS

· Bubble Sermon ·
see SERMONS

· Burning Bartle ·
West Witton, North Yorkshire: Saturday after 24 August

Though comparatively little-known outside its home area, the ceremony of 'Burning Bartle' is one of the most curious and interesting of surviving English customs. It takes place in the Wensleydale village of West Witton, at the foot of towering Pen Hill: where, after dark on the evening of the Saturday following St Bartholomew's Day (24 August) a guy-like effigy emerges from a house at the west end of the single street, its arms draped over the shoulders of two of its makers. This is 'Bartle', whose more than life-sized body is stuffed with rags and old fleeces soaked in paraffin, and whose shapeless head is weirdly lit by electric-bulb eyes. A crowd, mainly of locals, falls in behind him; and as he passes down West Witton's main street he halts a number of times outside the village pubs, the houses of the organizers' friends, and the homes of old and respected inhabitants. Whenever he does so, a third member of his retinue chants in a loud monotone:

> At Penhill crags he tore his rags
> At Hunter's Thorn he blew his horn
> At Capplebank Stee he had the misfortune
> to brak' his knee
> At Grassgill Beck he brak' his neck
> At Wadham's End he couldn't fend
> At Grassgill End we'll mak' his end
> Shout, boys, shout!

Whereupon the crowd gives a loud cheer, followed – after an encouraging 'Hip, Hip' – by another: those who have bottles of beer or whisky then take another swig, and the impromptu procession moves off again.

When it reaches the far end of the village, it turns into the lane called 'Grassgill End': and there Bartle 'maks

Pig thief or patron saint, West Witton's enigmatic 'Bartle' always meets a fiery end at the climax of **Burning Bartle**.

Since West Witton's ancient church is dedicated to St Bartholomew, however, it is rather too much of a coincidence that the thief (or giant) should be called Bartle, and that his death should be celebrated on St Bartholomew's feast day – as it invariably was until latterly moved 'for convenience' to the following Saturday. An alternative local theory, therefore, ingeniously suggests that Bartle represents, not the saint himself, but a plaster effigy of him kept in the church in the Middle Ages. At the Reformation, when such statues were being destroyed by Protestants, the villagers decided to save their patron by removing and concealing him; but they were pursued by the agents of the new order, and during the chase across Pen Hill various portions of the effigy were damaged – as in the chant – until at last it was captured and burnt at Grassgill End.

Perhaps the nearest approach to the truth lies in a synthesis of these two explanations. For it is quite possible that – as in many other places before the Reformation – a statue of the patron saint was borne about the parish on his feast day: possibly in connection with a ceremony of BEATING THE BOUNDS, since many of the places in the chant lie on or near the West Witton boundary. Over the centuries, however, this custom may have become confused or amalgamated with a re-enactment of the death of the legendary giant, to produce the current form of the observance.

How old this is, of course, nobody knows: and in the 1890s its beginnings were reported to be 'lost in the mists of time'. But whatever its origins, 'Burning Bartle' continues to be kept up with a great deal of vigour: and a village trust fund – which provides £3 annually to the Bartle-makers, £1 to each villager over 70, and an extra £1 to the 'oldest inhabitant' – has recently been established to ensure its survival.

his end', being first stabbed with a knife and then set on fire. Sometimes fireworks concealed inside his body explode at this point, and as he blazes the crowd sing, not a 'traditional' verse, but any current 'pops' or 'standards' that come into their heads.

The usual explanation of this lively and quite unprettified custom is that Bartle was a notorious pig thief, who lived on Pen Hill 'hundreds of years ago'. Exasperated by his depredations, the West Witton men assembled a posse to catch him: and after chasing him all over the hill – the place names in the chant are all situated there, and Capplebank Stee is steep enough to break anyone's knee – they finally cornered and slew him at Grassgill End. Nor is there any reason why this tale should not contain some element of truth – it is, at least, more entertaining than the folklorists' rigmarole about 'the survival of fertility rites' – especially since a parallel legend tells of the wicked Giant of Pen Hill, who kept a herd of prize pigs and was killed by local farmers, to lie on the hill 'in a grave big enough for ten'.

· Burning Judas ·
see GOOD FRIDAY

· Burning the Clavie ·
Burghead, Morayshire: 11 January

Scorning the calendar change of 1752, the north-eastern Scottish fishing port of Burghead still keeps its NEW YEAR'S EVE on the Old Style date of 11 January, with the ceremony of 'Burning the Clavie'. This word – probably derived from the Gaelic *cliabh* (basket) – describes a species of portable fire beacon, which is made during 'Auld Hogmanay' afternoon at a traditional site, and according to unvarying rules. Only the 'Clavie Crew', young men belonging to certain long-established local families, may have anything to do with its manufacture, and all its materials must be given or lent, never bought.

Basically, it consists of an 'Archangel tar-barrel' (or, more recently, a whisky cask) sawn into two unequal halves. The smaller bottom section is then fixed onto an

The 'Clavie King' begins his smashing of the fire-beacon, to end Burghead's **Burning the Clavie** ceremony.

eight-foot pole ('the spoke') with a single long nail specially forged by the smith: this must be driven in with a round stone, the use of metal hammers being absolutely prohibited. Next, the structure is reinforced with staves from a herring cask, their top ends fastened at intervals round the outside of the barrel and their lower parts to the spoke, leaving a gap large enough for a man's head between two of the staves. When it is finished, the clavie is filled with the unused remains of the barrel and other dried wood, piled into a pyramid and soaked in tar.

At about 6 p.m., when darkness has fallen, the 'Clavie King' ignites all this with a burning peat brought from a household fire: matches or lighters are forbidden. Then the first clavie bearer – whose sought-after post was formerly granted to the most recently married crew member – takes it on his head and shoulders and sets off at a run for the harbour, followed by a cheering crowd. Should he stumble or fall beneath his heavy, hot and tar-dripping load, calamity is sure to overtake both him

and the whole town within the twelvemonth. So at set intervals the bearers are changed, while smouldering brands from the clavie are thrown into house doors or given to selected bystanders: to obtain one brings good fortune and protection during the year, and it was once believed essential to keep a flame from the clavie burning somewhere in Burghead until the ceremony was repeated (*see* YULE LOGS).

After the clavie – following a fixed route which circles the 'old town' but ignores post-1800 extensions – has completed its half-hour circuit, it is carried sunwise round an artificial mound called 'the Doorie', where a cairn used to be annually made to receive it. Since 1809, however, its pole has been slotted into a hole in a stone pillar on the summit. Once, it would burn there all night, and the Clavie King still climbs the pillar, amid loud shouts, to refuel it with more tar. After an interval, however, he now smashes it to pieces with a hatchet, so that flaming tar and blazing wood pour down the mound-side: and the ceremony ends with a general scramble for embers, to be kept for luck or sent to Burghead people 'living away'.

The date of the custom, its numerous taboos, and the fact that Burghead ('fortress headland') was once the site of a Pictish capital, all suggest a very ancient origin for Burning the Clavie. Indeed, the records of several neighbouring ports (which once also burnt clavies) show that even in the early 18th century the custom was regarded as 'old', as well as 'superstitious, Idolatrous and sinfule' and 'an abominable Heathenish practice'. In those days, as at Burghead until about 1875, clavies were carried not only around the towns but also into each fishing boat, handfuls of grain being sprinkled on their decks to ensure plenty in the coming year. So the ceremony probably began as a pagan BLESSING THE SEAS AND THE FISHERIES, or, rather, the coastal form of a once-widespread fertility rite. For in the inland Banff-shire parish of Inveravon, 'ane act against Clavies' of 1704 reveals that these were also 'carried about Idolatrouslie sanctifieing the cornes and cattle': while a similar NEW YEAR crop-blessing custom, using a burning hawthorn bush, survived in Herefordshire until well into the present century.

· Burning the Old Year Out ·
Comrie, Perthshire; Biggar, Lanarkshire; Wick, Caithness:
31 December

One of the original purposes of the midwinter fires that once blazed all over Britain was, doubtless, to encourage the slowly returning sun. So they were all the more necessary where days are shortest, in Scotland and the Borders, and it is there that the custom still survives – though it is now kept up for luck, for fun, and to burn out the old and welcome the NEW YEAR in.

Some places do so with flaming tar barrels, 'clavies', fireballs or boats (*see* ALLENDALE TAR BARRELS; BURNING THE CLAVIE; SWINGING FIREBALLS; UP-HELLY-AA) and others with torchlit processions, as at Comrie near Crieff in Perthshire. There, towards midnight on 31 December, fantastically dressed 'guisers' congregate in the village square; and as the hour strikes they light 'flambeaux', torches of combustibles tied to six-foot poles. Led by pipers, they then parade these about the village, finally returning to the square to cast them in a blazing pile, which all present dance round until it burns out.

Elsewhere, the bonfire is the central feature. At Wick, in the far north of Scotland, a midnight-kindled blaze burns in the Bignold Park. And at Biggar in Lanarkshire, fire-building begins as early as November, on an ancient site near the now-vanished Mercat Cross. By the evening of 31 December, when it is lit, it has grown to huge proportions, for it must burn all night: and as children dance about it, red herrings – a popular local Hogmanay gift, symbolizing plenty in the coming year – are toasted by the flames and eaten. Then, after the last

Burning the Old Year Out with the 'flambeaux' procession at Comrie, Perthshire.

chime of twelve and the singing of 'Auld Lang Syne', the adults set off first footing, while the younger people play all the tricks of a MISCHIEF NIGHT.

· Burns Night ·
25 January

The birthday of Robert Burns (1759-96), 'the common man's poet'. First commemorated by 'Burns Clubs' soon after his death, it now far outshines ST ANDREW'S DAY as a Scottish patriotic festival, to be celebrated wherever Scots gather together.

The evening begins with a supper of 'hamely farin', its menu often written in the poet's 'Lallans' dialect and sometimes in rhyme. This may include such delicacies as 'Powsowdie' (sheep's head broth); 'Cabbie-claw' (wind-dried cod with horseradish and egg sauce); and 'Finnan Toasties' (smoked haddock): but pride of place goes to the haggis – minced mutton, offal, oatmeal and spices boiled in a sheep's stomach.

Preceded if possible by a piper, the haggis is ceremonially carried in by the cooks, laid before the chief guest, and solemnly 'addressed' with Burns' own verse, beginning:

> Fair fa' your honest sonsie face
> Great chieftain o' the pudden race.

The haggis, 'great chieftain o' the pudden race', is piped in to a **Burns Night** dinner.

It is then cut, traditionally by making a St Andrew's Cross-shaped incision in the 'paunch' and turning back the flaps: and the meal begins with the grace:

> Some hae meat that canna eat
> And some wad eat that want it
> But we hae meat and we can eat
> Sae let the Lord be thankit

and finishes with:

> O Lord, since we hae feasted thus,
> Whilk we sae little merit
> Let Meg noo tak' awa the flesh
> And Jock bring in the spirit.

This last is now drunk to multifarious toasts, followed by patriotic or sentimental speeches – some of which can be very trying to any non-Caledonians present. It behoves them, however, to heed the *Dictionary of National Biography's* warning, that 'Criticism of Burns is only permitted to Scotchmen of pure blood'. The celebration then continues with performances of Burns' fine narrative poems (especially 'Tam o' Shanter', which a surprising number of Scots can recite faultlessly from memory) and of his many songs: and concludes with the linked-arm singing of the most famous of them all, 'Auld Lang Syne'.

· Burrator Reservoir Ceremony ·
Burrator Reservoir, near Yelverton, Devon: a day in July

In his native Devon, the great sea captain Sir Francis Drake is remembered as a folk hero of superhuman stature, who is said to have brought drinking water to drought-stricken Plymouth by galloping from a Dartmoor spring, summoning its pure waters to follow him by magic. Drake did indeed provide Plymouth with its water supply, albeit by the more orthodox and laborious process of ordering a 'leat' or canal, some twenty-five miles long, to be cut from the River Meavy. This was completed in 1591, when Sir Francis provided the basis of the legend by riding alongside the first incoming waters, to the sound of trumpets; and for centuries afterwards a grateful corporation ceremonially commemorated his benefaction with an annual 'Survey of the Water Works and Head Weir', culminating in a toast to his memory.

This 'Leat Riding' – once necessitated by the water-diverting activities of local tin miners – has ceased, but the toast is still drunk each July at the head weir, now represented by Burrator Reservoir on the edge of Dartmoor. A goblet of reservoir water, drawn by the city engineer, is tasted first by the Lord Mayor and then by all present, each repeating the words: 'To the Pious Memory of Sir Francis Drake.' Then the City Chamberlain hands a goblet of wine to the mayor, and this is passed round with the toast: 'May the descendants of him who brought us Water never want Wine'. A 'Fyshynge Feast' of grilled lake trout, eaten in the open air by the whole company, completes the ceremony.

· The Burry Man ·
South Queensferry, West Lothian: second Friday in August

On the day before the annual Ferry Fair, an extraordinary figure parades the town of South Queensferry. It is covered from head to foot with the sticky burrs of the burdock plant, crowned with roses, and bears in each hand a flower-bedecked staff, carried at arm's length. Thus attired, it walks a seven-mile course round the boundaries of the town, guided by two attendants who support its outstretched arms and collect money at the houses along the route: and though it is generally greeted with a shout of welcome wherever it appears, the 'Burry Man' traditionally maintains complete silence throughout the day-long ritual.

Much work has gone into the preparation of the Burry Man's costume, which varies little from year to year. First, thousands of burrs are collected, and made up into forty-two small 'mats' on squares of brown paper; and the hat, a bowler covered with a net, is planted with seventy roses and one red dahlia. Next, early in the morning of the parade, the man playing the role dons woolly combinations over his clothes, ties a Union Jack about his waist, and puts over his head a back-to-front balaclava helmet with holes cut for his

Encumbered by the burrs which cover his entire body, South Queensferry's **Burry Man** needs two attendants to help him complete his seven-mile course.

eyes and mouth. His attendants then cover him entirely in burrs, laying on the mats one by one; and help prepare his staffs, which are wrapped in Union Jacks and stuck with a profusion of garden flowers. Finally, when the customary four roses have been added to his back and four to his front, he sets off on his rounds.

The nature and origins of this curious custom – which appears to have been performed in much the same manner since at least the 1740s – have been much discussed, but never satisfactorily explained. Some have interpreted it as merely a glorified BEATING THE BOUNDS of the 'burgh' by a 'burghman' or 'burleyman' (by-law man): while others declare that both it and the following day's fair commemorate the landing at Queensferry of Queen Margaret, who is supposed to have given the town its name, and whose husband King Malcolm Canmore (1057-93) is alleged to have once hidden himself from the English with a covering of burrs. What neither of these 'explanations' take into account, however, is that the Burry Man's parade was at one time the preserve of local fishermen: and, more important, that very similar customs formerly took place in at least two other eastern Scottish fishing ports.

In 1859, for example, when the herring fishing was 'very backward', the fishermen of Buckie in Banffshire dressed a cooper in a shirt 'stuck all over with burrs',

and wheeled him around the town in a barrow, 'as a charm to raise the herring'. While at nearby Fraserburgh in Aberdeenshire, during the 1860s, 'luck' was brought to the herring fishery by covering a fisherman entirely with burrs, and parading him about the streets on the shoulders of his colleagues. At Queensferry the custom appears to have been slightly different: for though the Burry Man is still believed to bring luck to the houses he visits, he seems once to have been paraded in thanksgiving for a successful fishing season rather than brought out in order to produce one.

It is most probable, then, that the Burry Man was originally a pagan figure – perhaps a representation of the sea or fish god responsible for the increase of herrings – and that the custom of parading him was kept up 'for luck' by the notoriously superstitious fishing community. Why he should be covered in burrs, clearly an essential part of his costume everywhere, remains a mystery: but one commentator has plausibly suggested that this was a piece of 'sympathetic magic', performed in the hope that the fish would be as numerous as the burrs, and would stick to the nets as firmly as the burrs stick to the Burry Man.

· Butterworth Charity ·
see GRAVESIDE DOLES

C

· Cakes and Ale Charities ·
see PAX CAKES CEREMONY; PEACE AND GOOD
NEIGHBOURHOOD FEASTS

· Caking Night ·
see SOULING

· Candle Auctions ·

The curious practice of auctioning 'by an inch of candle' consists basically of only taking bids while a candle is alight, and accepting the last offer made before it burns out. Presumably intended either to limit the duration of the proceedings, or to introduce an element of chance into the sale of property whose value was uncertain, it apparently first became popular in Britain in the mid-17th century: Pepys notes it as a novelty in 1660, and two years afterwards remarked that 'it was pleasant to see how backward men are at first to bid; and yet, when the candle is going out, how they bawl'. Though once used to sell many kinds of goods, candle auctions were particularly favoured as a fair means of settling the annual lease of grazing land, especially land bequeathed by CHARITIES for the maintenance of church or poor: and a handful still survive for this purpose.

Among the most flourishing of these customs is the auction of the 'Poors' Pasture', a sixteen-acre charity field at Hubberholme in Upper Wharfedale, North Yorkshire: which is held on the first Monday night in January at the George Inn, once the rectory. Here the bidders gather in one room, 'the House of Commons', while the vicar and churchwardens sit with the candle in another, 'the House of Lords': thus the candle is invisible to would-be buyers, who can neither see how far down it has burnt nor delay their bid (like an iron-nerved and invariably successful purchaser observed by Pepys) until the smoke descends onto the dying flame. After saying a prayer for peace and good will and ringing a bell, the vicar lights the candle: and the last bidder to 'shout through' from the Commons before it expires becomes tenant for the year, his rent – over £200 in 1982 – being used to help any parishioner 'in financial embarrassment'. Dating from the mid-18th-century enclosure of the parish, the auction is invariably accompanied by much merriment, and despite the remoteness of the place and the inclemency of the season is always well attended.

A partially invisible candle – because it is suspended above the auctioneer's table in a container with raised sides – also features in the auction of Stowell Mead,

seven-and-a-half acres of watermeadow at Tatworth, near Chard in Somerset. This is held, usually at the 'Poppe Inn', on the Tuesday after the first Saturday after 6 April – which is LADY DAY, Old Style. The date alone suggests that the custom is an old one, but its origins are unknown, for the records of Stowell COURTS LEET were burnt in 1832 after a dispute about the use of the mead, which was then COMMON LAND. Only the owners of twenty-five former common-right properties (who are called 'colts') may therefore bid for it: and the rent paid by the winner – less the cost of the bread, cheese and Stowell Mead watercress supper which precedes the auction – is divided among the unsuccessful bidders, according to the size of their holdings. Another Somerset auction, at Chedzoy near Bridgwater, more conventionally devotes its proceeds to the church: but, unusually, it takes place only every twenty-one years (e.g. 1967, 1988) when the 'Church Piece', given by a member of the Sydenham family during the 15th century, is granted on long lease to the last bidder before the candle dies. And at Leigh near Sherborne in Dorset, the 'aftergrass' of two meadows – which is to say the autumn and

Waiting for the nail to drop at Aldermaston's **Candle Auction** in 1980: the last bid before it does so will buy a lease of grazing land.

winter grazing between LAMMAS and VALENTINE'S DAY – is annually auctioned in a similar manner, a custom apparently dating from the early 17th century.

Some candle auctions, however, follow a slightly different practice. For a pin or nail is driven into the candle, an inch or so below the wick, so that it will drop out when the flame reaches it: and the last bid before it does so is the successful one. This is the practice, for instance, at Aldermaston in Berkshire, where the auction is held during every third December. Conducted by the vicar, attended by the Lord of the Manor, and enlivened by hot rum punch and churchwarden pipes, the form of the ceremony dates from at least 1801, when the common land previously auctioned was enclosed.

Common land, this time the grazing of roadside verges, is also auctioned by 'pin and candle' at Whissendine, in the old county of Rutland, now subsumed into Leicestershire: called 'Letting the Banks', the ceremony takes place at the annual village assembly during the third week in March. And in the week following, a similar auction is held at Old Bolingbroke in Lincolnshire, where the summer grazing of a six-acre playing field is leased, the rent going towards the upkeep of the village hall. In its present form, this custom dates only from the 1950s, when the field was bequeathed on condition that it must be let in this manner: the intention being to perpetuate a far older pin-and-candle auction (which ceased in 1938) whereby another piece of land called 'Poor Folks' Close' was rented to provide a pre-Christmas dole for the needy.

Wishford in Wiltshire, finally, varies the candle-auction principle by using the sun. Each Rogation Monday (see BEATING THE BOUNDS) the 'foreshare' or summer grazing of two anciently bequeathed water-meadows is auctioned in the churchyard: where, at five minutes to sunset, the parish clerk begins pacing back and forth between the church porch and the gate. While he does so, bids may be made, but as soon as the sun disappears beneath the horizon he strikes the gate with his massive church key, and the last bidder gains the 'Midsummer tithes' – the right of grazing between Rogationtide and 12 August, Old Lammas Day. (See also HOURGLASS, CROWN AND RUNNING AUCTIONS; LOT MEADOW MOWING)

· Candlemas ·
2 February

Forty days after Christmas the Virgin Mary, following Jewish custom, completed her ritual cleansing after Jesus's birth, and 'brought him to Jerusalem to present him to the Lord': so 2 February is 'the feast of the Purification of St Mary and the Presentation at the Temple'. It is also Candlemas, for the day's gospel reading (Luke 2. 22) describes Christ as 'a light to lighten the Gentiles', and from early times the Church celebrated it by blessing candles and carrying them in procession. Condemned as 'Popish and superstitious' by

Protestant theologians, such ceremonies lost favour in post-Reformation Britain: but they never quite died out (especially in Wales and northern England) and are now enjoying a revival, with blessed and lighted candles being distributed in many Anglican as well as in Roman Catholic churches. Another medieval Candlemas custom, 'Cradle Rocking', has been revived at Blidworth, Nottinghamshire, since 1923. On the Sunday nearest the feast, the most recently baptized baby boy in the parish (representing the infant Christ) is presented to the vicar by his parents, and ceremonially rocked in a cradle during the service.

In the world outside, Candlemas is the season when winter's grip starts to loosen; when days noticeably lengthen; geese should begin laying; and snowdrops – called 'February Fair Maids' in some southern counties and occasionally brought in to 'purify the house' – make their first appearance. But fine weather now may presage a second, fiercer, winter and is particularly to be feared on the feast itself, for:

> If Candlemas Day is fair and clear
> There'll be two winters in one year
> *Trad., Scotland*

and

> If Candlemas Day be sunny and warm
> Ye may mend yer auld mittens and look for a storm
> *Trad., Cumbria*

but

> If Candlemas Day be wind and rain
> Winter is gone, and won't come again.
> *Trad., Warwickshire*

Even so, a prudent husbandman should not let fodder stocks run low for

> A farmer should have, on Candlemas Day
> Half his corn, and half his hay.
> *Yorkshire*

With the change in the calendar, some Candlemas ceremonies (see BLESSING THE SEAS AND FISHERIES) have moved to VALENTINE'S DAY, but HURLING THE SILVER BALL and JEDBURGH BA' GAMES are still held on 2 February.

· Cards ·
see CHRISTMAS; VALENTINE'S DAY

· Carlings Sunday ·

> Tid, mid, miseray
> Carlings, Palm and Pace-Egg Day
> *Childrens' Lent and Easter rhyme, Durham*

The fifth Sunday in LENT, when churches begin their particular contemplation of Christ's sufferings (Latin: *passio* – hence its official title of 'Passion Sunday') and drape their altars and crosses with the purple of mourning (Middle English: *care* – hence the colloquial names 'Care', 'Caring', or 'Carling Sunday' used in northern England and Scotland and, by transference, the 'carlings' or grey peas still eaten there on this day).

The method of preparing these carlings varies somewhat from place to place. On Teesside, for instance – where carlings are sold pre-packed in local supermarkets, and appear annually both in pubs and on hospital menus – they are steeped in water over Friday night, boiled with fat bacon on Saturday evening, and on Sunday served hot or cold with salt and vinegar: while in Newcastle and Northumberland they are steeped, dried, and fried in butter, and elsewhere they may be soaked in beer instead of water, or eaten with rum and sugar.

Though dried peas must always have been an important food during the fasting and pre-refrigeration shortages of Lent, it is by no means clear why they should be ceremonially eaten on this particular day – as they once also were in many other parts of Britain. Local explanations of the practice abound, such as that it commemorates the relief of a Berwick-upon-Tweed famine by the arrival of a pea-laden ship: but a better clue may perhaps be the suspicious similarity between 'Peasen Sunday' – the festival's old West-Country title – and Passion Sunday. Like many of the folk observances of ASH WEDNESDAY, therefore, the custom may simply have originated in the misinterpretation of a word.

· Carlow's Charity ·
see GRAVESIDE DOLES

· Castleton Garland ·
Castleton, Derbyshire: 29 May

The village of Castleton, set amid the spectacular scenery and 'Blue John' caverns of the High Peak, enacts a remarkable ceremony on OAK APPLE DAY – or the day after, if 29 May is a Sunday. The ritual begins in the morning at the 'host pub' (one of six locals, acting in rotation) with the making of 'the Garland' – a hollow cone of flowers over three feet high, topped by a separate posy of especially fine blooms, called 'the Queen'. In the early evening, the 'Garland King' and his 'Lady', dressed in Stuart costume and mounted on white horses, ride round the parish boundary, and eventually to the pub: here the Garland is placed over the King's head, so that it completely envelops him to the waist. Followed by the Lady, the local band, a group of white-clad schoolgirls bearing flowers and an escort of scouts and cubs, he is then led on horseback through the village: at each of its six inns the procession halts for drinks, while the girls dance to 'the Garland tune'.

Their progress over, the King and Lady ride unaccompanied to the churchyard gate, where the 'Queen' is removed from the Garland: the Garland itself is then hauled to the top of the tower and fixed to one of eight

Enveloped by the hollow **Castleton Garland** itself, the 'Garland King' prepares to set out on his traditional Oak Apple Day progress round the Derbyshire village.

pinnacles, the rest being already decorated with oak boughs. Finally, the King places the 'Queen' on the war memorial, the Last Post is sounded, and the children and many of the adult villagers (wearing oak sprigs) dance back to the host pub. Some of the older inhabitants still sing an obscure and 'unofficial' song, apparently abusing the neighbouring village of Bradwell: but this part of the custom is rapidly fading away.

Garland Day has, indeed, undergone many changes, even within living memory. Until 1897, all dancing was done by the organizing bellringers; and until 1916 the Queen posy was the prize of an honoured female visitor: the 'Cavalier' dress is still more recent (the King's previous costume, a red coachman's coat, is displayed at Castleton Museum) while before 1955 the Lady was always played by a man in womens' clothes. But these developments do not entirely obscure the custom's ancient origins. For while the date and the oak leaves identify it with post-1660 celebrations of OAK APPLE DAY, yet the 'man-woman', the Garland, and above all the flower-decked Garland King – once, perhaps, a sacrificial victim – may well perpetuate pagan MAY DAY rites. Like WELLS AND WELL-DRESSING CUSTOMS and other traditions of this once remote and conservative region, Castleton Garland probably began as a compromise between magic and Christianity.

· Changing the Guard ·
Buckingham Palace, St James's Palace, the Tower of London, and Whitehall, London; Windsor Castle, Berkshire

One of the most popular of all London's tourist attractions, the Changing of the Queen's personal Guard is best seen when she is officially 'in residence': at other times, however, it continues on a reduced scale. The favourite viewpoint is Buckingham Palace where (as at the TOWER) the ceremony takes place at 11.30 a.m., daily in the summer and on alternate days in winter: and where the personnel is usually provided by whichever of the five regiments of Foot Guards is then on duty.

At 11 a.m., the St James's Palace detachment of the retiring guard – the senior party, since St James's is the longer-established royal residence, and therefore the bearers of the regimental Colour – marches down the Mall behind its drums, to join the Buckingham Palace detachment drawn up for inspection on the palace forecourt. Meanwhile, the New Guard is marching with its band from Wellington barracks, and on its arrival at 11.30 a.m. it advances across the forecourt to the appropriate regimental slow march. The retiring guard commander then ceremonially hands over the palace keys, and new sentries are posted with much stamping and barking of orders, while the band plays. Finally, the Old Guard returns to barracks, while a detachment of the New marches off to St James's. Bearskins and scarlet dress tunics are worn, but in winter the latter are covered by grey greatcoats.

The Foot Guard is similarly changed at Windsor Castle, at 11 a.m. on Monday to Saturday, or daily if the Queen is resident there. And at 11 a.m. daily (10 a.m. on Sundays) the mounted Guard of Household Cavalry – either the red-tunicked Life Guards or the blue-clad Blues and Royals – is ceremonially changed at Whitehall.

· Charities ·

The best-known modern charities – massive organizations like the Red Cross, the RSPCA and Oxfam – very properly concern themselves with national and international problems: but until the present century the overwhelming majority of charitable foundations operated on a smaller, more personal and (literally) more parochial scale. Virtually every parish in Britain formerly possessed at least one such foundation, endowed by some local philanthropist for the purpose of providing

'a weekly loaf to thirteen poor village widows', financing the apprenticeships of 'honest but decayed weavers' sons', or maintaining the nightly tolling of LOST IN THE DARK BELLS. Overtaken by inflation or changes in land law, or extinguished by a squire's parsimony or a parson's indifference, many of these unique institutions are now extinct. Yet a surprising number of ancient parish charities quietly continue to flourish: and to these are connected some of the oldest continuously performed (if, as a class, the least publicized) of British traditional ceremonies, as well as some of the most curious.

There seems little doubt, indeed, that some donors (like the founders of JOHN KNILL'S CHARITY or OLD MAN'S DAY) deliberately attached eccentric conditions to their charity, in order to be the better remembered: while others, for much the same purpose, ordained that

John Sayer's 17th-century foundation at Woodbridge in Suffolk is one of the few surviving **charities** which still provide a weekly bread dole, collected by parish pensioners from the bread shelves in St Mary's church.

The Poor Law Guardians discuss an application for bread: painting by Charles West Cope, 1841. **Charity** was dispensed only to the 'deserving' poor.

their largesse be distributed at their tombs (*see* GRAVESIDE DOLES) and many more fixed the distribution date at the anniversary of their death. By such means, too, medieval founders hoped to encourage the recipients of charity to pray for their benefactor's soul – a practice officially discountenanced as 'Popish' at the Protestant Reformation, when the memorial Masses attached to charities like JANKYN SMITH'S were transmogrified into SERMONS, and when endowed sermons themselves became a popular form of 'charity'. But whatever the motive for the foundation – whether the perpetuation of the donor's memory, the purchase of an eternal insurance policy, or, as in most cases, pure philanthropy – the method of endowment was much the same: land, property or money was bequeathed to the parish, and the annual rent or interest arising was devoted to fulfilling the founder's specified charitable ends.

These were many and varied, and among the 'purposes of sundry well-disposed persons' listed by the Elizabethan Statute of Charitable Uses (still a mainstay of charity law) are 'the relief of aged, impotent and poor people ... the maintenance of sick and maimed soldiers

and mariners, schools of learning and scholars at universities ... the repair of bridges, ports, havens, causeways, churches, seabanks and highways ... the relief and redemption of prisoners', and the financing of 'the marriages of poor maidens' (*see* MARRIAGE PORTION CHARITIES). Charitable funds still exist in several places, moreover, for the encouragement of faithful domestic servants (MAIDS' MONEY) or village bellringers; the provision of WAYFARERS' DOLES to poor travellers; and the maintenance of such community-cementing activities as BEATING THE BOUNDS; PEACE AND GOOD NEIGHBOURHOOD FEASTS; and RUSHBEARINGS. While other thoughtful donors (whose foundations are, alas, now extinct) hoped to combine charity with utility by paying paupers to hold the parson's horse while he preached (Yapham, East Yorkshire); to awaken those who nodded off during his sermon (Claverley, Shropshire); or to drive out any stray dogs which ventured into church (Chislet, Kent, where the charity land is still called 'Dogwhipper's Marsh'). Some of its 'beneficiaries', nevertheless, may have doubted the usefulness of Robert Dowe's 'charity': which financed the ringing of a handbell (still to be seen in St Sepulchre's,

Holborn, London) outside the cells of condemned Newgate felons, while a sexton exhorted them to repentance.

By far the largest proportion of charities, however, have always concentrated on distributing physical relief to the poor, either in the form of cash or of basic foodstuffs. Indeed a few ancient foundations – like the TICHBORNE DOLE – still hand out flour, the most elementary form of sustenance: but more frequently this is baked into loaves or even (especially where distributions are now purely symbolic) into cakes and buns (*see* BREAD AND BUN DOLES). Some donors, too, added butter and cheese (*see* BREAD AND CHEESE THROWING) and others (like the BIDDENDEN MAIDS) also provided beer and cider to wash it down – though disapproving later generations frequently substituted tea. Such inexpensive fare might be offered as often as once a week, but a few donors preferred to ensure that their beneficiaries enjoyed one really substantial meal a year – generally beef and plum pudding at CHRISTMAS; though one vanished Oxfordshire charity stipulated EASTER veal pies, and others up and down the country doled out LENT peas and red herrings. Christmas, too, is the usual time for charity fuel distributions, and also for gifts of warm clothing – or, in the case of foundations like the MARVYN DOLE, of lengths of cloth for the paupers to 'make up' themselves. Two eccentric Derbyshire gentlemen called Gray and Greene, incidentally, insisted that the colours of the garments distributed should always match their surnames.

The problem of exactly how such largesse should be distributed also greatly exercised the minds of donors. For few indeed were as generously indiscriminate as Thomas Moseley, who decreed that a penny be paid to every soul in the Staffordshire town of Walsall – casual visitors included – on EPIPHANY EVE: a distribution which took three men several days to perform, but which was unsportingly suppressed as 'very useless' by the Charity Commissioners in 1825. More often, founders were most specific about the destination of their relief: laying down, for instance, that it should be paid to 'six poor widows of drowned men' (Dover); 'to the two oldest bachelors in the parish of Bowes' (North Yorkshire); or 'to poor persons of the name of Nicholson' – but only if they were English and Protestant. Some, too, ordained that candidates for their charity must qualify by passing a certain test (e.g. FORTY SHILLING DAY) or by emerging the victor in a solemnly performed game of chance (DICING FOR BIBLES; MAIDS' MONEY): while others, doubtless holding with the Book of Proverbs (18.18) that 'The Lot causeth contention to cease', extended the principle of divinely guided chance to the selection of charity trustees (e.g. KIRKBY HILL RACES) or the renting-out of charity lands (CANDLE AUCTIONS).

In general, however, alms were simply directed to the poor of a particular parish, or rather to its 'deserving poor' – a category all too often interpreted as those who had offended neither squire nor parson, and who displayed the proper degree of humility and gratitude. Such attitudes gave 'charity' a bad name, and many expressed themselves ready to starve rather than accept it: the stigma, moreover, persists, and probably contributes (at least as much as the alleged 'abolition of poverty') to the reported decline in applicants for surviving parish doles. It may well be that such foundations have outlived their usefulness: yet those that remain serve as a memorial to our ancestors' genuine good intentions as well as their eccentricity, and their final disappearance would greatly diminish the store of British traditional customs and ceremonies.

· Charles I Commemoration ·
see COMMEMORATIONS

· Cheese Rolling ·
Cooper's Hill, Brockworth, near Gloucester:
Spring Bank Holiday Monday;
Randwick, near Stroud, Gloucestershire: first Sunday in May

The ancient and lively sport of cheese rolling – or, more precisely, 'cheese racing' – takes place on a steep slope of Cooper's Hill, Brockworth, where the Cotswolds drop precipitously into the Vale of Severn. The cheeses used are specially made and disc-shaped 'Double Gloucesters' (the modern version, since the mahogany-and-white Gloucester cattle which produced the true cheese are now very rare indeed) encased in strong wooden frames to protect them as they roll and bounce down the hill. At 6 p.m., the first of these is handed to the Starter – some honoured local personality – by the white-coated and ribbon-toppered Master of Ceremonies, and on the count of three it is launched down the one-in-three incline, followed headlong on the count of four by the competitors. Anyone may enter the race, but it is emphatically not for the faint-hearted, since progress is generally by means of 'tumbling, sliding, and flying head-over-heels': the first to the bottom of the hill – usually a skillful racer who has managed to keep his feet throughout – wins the cheese. Five or six similar but subsidiary contests then follow, normally including several for boys, one for girls, and one for 'ladies'.

Formerly held on WHITSUN MONDAY, the Cooper's Hill cheese rolling was once the centrepiece of a famous 'Wake' – which also included sports like 'grinning for the cake', 'jumping in the bag', and 'chattering for a bladder of snuff by old women': and though the Wake itself was suppressed as 'rowdy' in late-Victorian times, the cheese rolling continued without a break – even during the rationing of the Second World War, when a small morsel of precious cheese was rolled in a wooden dummy. Exactly how and when the custom originated is uncertain. Some local folklore enthusiasts claim to trace it from a ritual introduced by prehistoric Phoenician traders in honour of the god Baal: but a far more general

Above: Supervised by the top-hatted Master of Ceremonies, the cheese is launched down Cooper's Hill during a 1950s **Cheese Rolling.** *Right:* 'Tumbling, sliding and flying head-over-heels', the competitors chase their prize down the one-in-three slope.

(and indeed far more probable) tradition declares it to be a 'ceremony of record' – related both to BEATING THE BOUNDS and QUIT RENTS – whose annual performance is necessary to preserve ancient rights of access to COMMON LAND grazing on Cooper's Hill.

Similar cheese-rolling races were held during the 18th century at Uffington in Berkshire, in connection with the communal 'scouring' of the hillside 'White Horse' there: while a rather different form of the custom has lately been revived at Randwick, not far from Brockworth, on the first Sunday in May. There, three flower-decked Double Gloucesters are ceremonially borne to the churchyard, blessed, and then solemnly rolled three times anti-clockwise round the church. One is afterwards cut up and distributed, while the other two are put aside for a week, to be rolled down a slope at the opening of 'Randwick Wap' – which is described under MOCK MAYORS.

· Childermas (Holy Innocents' Day) ·
see CHRISTMAS

· Christening ·

Christening, the usual English term for baptism, is the ceremony at which a person is incorporated into the Church and (in the case of infants) at the same time given their 'Christian names'. Some sects, notably the Baptists, reject the christening of infants, and baptize adults by total immersion in a river or specially constructed pool: but the standard practice is for babies to be brought to church and christened at the font, either at a special ceremony or, increasingly, during the course of a family service or parish Communion. Having required the godparents to renounce 'the World, the Flesh and the Devil' and make certain promises on the infant's behalf, the priest asks them what name it is to be given. Then, 'if they shall certify him that the Child may well endure it', he may 'dip it in the Water discreetly and warily': but more often he simply sprinkles holy water over it, meanwhile baptizing it in the name of the Father, Son and Holy Ghost and thereafter completing the rite by making the sign of the Cross on its forehead.

The Anglican *Book of Common Prayer* requires that a baby be christened within a week or so of its BIRTH; provides for the baptism at home of infants too sickly for the journey to church; and in extreme cases when no priest is available, allows the rite to be performed by a lay person. All these provisions are intended to shorten the perilous period during which the infant remains unbaptized, and above all to obviate the appalling risk – disregarded by the modern parents who leave long delays before arranging the ceremony – that it might perish unchristened. Such chances were rarely taken by followers of traditional folk beliefs, which held not only that christening infallibly strengthened the health of an ailing child, but also that unbaptized babies were the favourite prey of witches, fairies and evil spirits – who could, however, be frustrated by placing salt and iron near the cradle, and laying a bible among its bedclothes. According to strict Christian doctrine, moreover, unbaptized infants cannot enter Heaven, and various opinions existed about their fate after death. Some Roman Catholics, for instance, still maintain the medieval belief that they dwell in a painless borderland of Heaven called limbo (Latin: *limbus*, a fringe): but folklore, more pessimistic, held that their souls were bound to earth in the form of will o' the wisps, butterflies, or the moths that fluttered about lamps; or that they joined the Wild Hunt which pursued the damned among storm clouds. Neither might their bodies rest in consecrated ground, and in much of England and Scotland their lonely graves were avoided as unlucky or accursed: though in south-west England and Wales a kindlier tradition covertly buried them in already open graves, as a sure passport to Heaven for the next person interred there.

To christen, therefore, is clearly advisable: but even then care must be taken, for the conduct of the ceremony is governed by many traditional rites, and it may produce omens concerning the child's future. Many parents, for example, still refuse to reveal or use the infant's name before baptism, and some remain wary of calling it after a recently dead friend or relation, lest it be soon summoned away by its namesake. Much thought, too, needs to be expended on choosing the godparents, if only because they are responsible both for the child's spiritual upbringing and – at least morally – for its physical welfare should the parents die: along the Welsh March, however, their appearance is also important, for if one looks into the font during the ceremony the child will come to resemble them. Two of the same, and one of the opposite sex to the baby are traditional, and in Wales it was thought luckier if each hailed from a separate parish. At a Yorkshire multiple baptism, moreover, it was held essential for boys to be christened before girls, lest the former fail to grow beards and the latter sprout them.

The baby's own behaviour at the christening is also highly significant, the universal and still-flourishing belief being that it should cry out at the touch of the holy water. This demonstrates that the 'Old Adam' of original sin, or even the Devil himself, has been driven out, and in some churches the north or 'Devil's door' is left ajar to speed his exit. Children who cry especially loudly are, quite logically, expected to become good singers, but those who remain silent are thought 'too good for this world', and will soon leave it: covert pokes and pinches were (and perhaps still are) therefore employed to ensure the appropriate response. In Wales, too, babies who held up their heads throughout the ceremony were certain to obtain a great age, while those who persistently let them loll would not survive long.

The holy water of baptism – most efficacious if (as for royal christenings) it is brought from the river Jordan, where Christ Himself was baptized – should not, of course, be wiped off after the ceremony: and any left in the font was sometimes begged from the vicar for use as a remedy if the child fell sick. Powerful for good, it could also be perilous in the wrong hands – like those of witches, who coveted it for their blasphemous rites: hence the elaborate, lockable, font covers still seen in many ancient churches.

· Christmas ·
25 December – 6 January

Easily the most popular and best-beloved of festivals throughout most of Britain, Christmas rightly remains primarily the celebration of Christ's Nativity – in Latin, His *dies natalis*, whence the Welsh *Nadolig* and Scots Gaelic *Nollaig*. Yet there is no reason to believe that this event occurred in midwinter (in fact, biblical evidence rather suggests the contrary) and it was not commemorated at that season until the 4th century – when Christianity, after becoming the state religion of Rome, adapted aspects of popular pagan cults. These kept 25

'The Gate of the Old English Gentleman' by Seymour, 1836. The deserving poor, though relieved with **Christmas** charity, are kept firmly at a distance by the guardian footmen.

December (the Roman winter solstice) as the 'birthday of the Unconquered Sun', an anniversary painlessly appropriated to Christ as 'Sun of Righteousness': and the preceding week as 'Saturnalia', whose merrymaking, reconciliations and social levelling were (though never effectively shorn of their accompanying debauchery) equally well suited to the joyful celebration of Jesus' birth. In Britain and northern Europe, the new festival subsequently acquired a great many more customs from the heathen Germanic midwinter feast of 'Yule': and by the mid-11th century (when the name was first used by the Anglo-Saxon Chronicle) the Nativity, Roman and Yule elements were fast synthesizing into a recognizable 'Christ's Mass'.

Some of the quasi-pagan ceremonies of this composite medieval Christmas still survive (*see* MARI LWYD; MUMMING PLAYS; SWORD DANCING; WASSAILING; WASS- AILING THE APPLE TREES; YULE LOGS): but most such were understandably (if regrettably) condemned as 'superstitious' by the Protestant Reformation. In Low- land Scotland, indeed, the Calvinist Kirk suppressed *all* public celebrations of Christmas so long and deter- minedly that secular NEW YEAR festivities have largely taken their place. And though a brief Puritan abolition after the Civil War had less effect on English jollifica- tions, these undoubtedly declined in fervour during the Georgian era. In the 1840s, however, Prince Albert and Charles Dickens spearheaded the great upsurge of sentimentality, traditionalism and 'Christian Socialism' which produced the 'Victorian Christmas' – the immedi- ate prototype of the modern festival.

The preparations for this start long before 25 December (and often before the beginning of ADVENT) and among its earliest heralds are Christmas cards. The first specifically produced for sale was published by Sir Henry Cole (of the South Kensington Museum, London) in 1846: but it was not until the 1870s that cheaper colour lithography combined with a special postage rate to initiate their meteoric rise in popularity. Over a thousand million cards are currently sent in Britain annually, and since the 1950s a growing proportion of these have been sold in aid of charities. Even greater outlay (and worry) is expended at this time on presents, whose general exchange also dates from mid-Victorian times: for though Christmas gifts to servants, tenants and children had long previously been customary, up until then the usual season for present-giving to equals had been NEW YEAR or TWELFTH NIGHT.

Christmas decorations also appear well in advance of the feast, though some still hold it unlucky to erect them before Christmas Eve. This belief applies particularly to evergreens, whose links with midwinter rites long pre-date Christianity: the most favoured are holly, ivy and mistletoe, all magical plants bearing fruit in a dead season. The berries of the 'male' holly (also powerful against witches) are said to represent Christ's blood, and

Left: Victoria and Albert, the leading exponents of the Victorian 'childrens' **Christmas'**, with one of the German Christmas trees they did so much to popularize. From the *Illustrated London News*, 1848. *Above:* The earliest printed Christmas card, designed by John Calcott for Sir Henry Cole and first sold in 1846. The festive middle-class family are carefully insulated by rustic foliage from the poor in the side-panels.

its prickles His Crown of Thorns, while the clinging 'female' ivy symbolizes immortality. No such respectable mythology, however, attaches to mistletoe, whose pagan associations are still so strong that no church decorator will tolerate it – except at York Minster, which by a tradition of obscure origin places a piece on its High Altar. And though the purely English custom of kissing beneath it (properly, only one kiss is allowed for each berry, which must then be removed) has ensured its continued inclusion among home decorations, these no longer focus on an elaborately bedizened mistletoe bough.

Instead, pride of place goes to the Christmas tree popularized by Prince Albert, who introduced one from his native Germany in 1840 – whereupon it immediately became the symbol of the Victorian family-centred Christmas tradition which still continues (and whose less attractive features include the decline of communal celebrations and the exclusion of 'outsiders'). In recent times, however, 'fairy-lighted' trees are increasingly also seen in town centres (a notable example, given annually by Oslo in Norway, has since 1947 been erected in London's Trafalgar Square) and in the roadside windows and gardens of public-spirited householders. Along with all other Christmas decorations, these must be removed on Twelfth Night (6 January). To do so before or after is thought most unlucky, as is their casual

disposal: some hold that they should be left to rot naturally, and others think they should be burnt at once: while in Wales and some western English counties they were formerly left up until CANDLEMAS, and thereafter kept to kindle the oven for SHROVE TUESDAY pancakes.

For most people, the festival proper begins on Christmas Eve, when churches are crowded with worshippers (many making their one annual visit) for Midnight Mass. This service, only in general use since the Second World War, is Roman Catholic in origin, and so too is the crib then prominently displayed. Such representations of the Bethlehem stable scene, however, now appear not only in churches of most persuasions, but also in schools – where they figure in the universally popular Nativity plays – homes, shops and public places. Other churchgoers may prefer the more traditionally Protestant Christmas morning service, accompanied by triumphant peals of BELLS (*see* TOLLING THE DEVIL'S KNELL), or a 'Festival' of nine appropriate scriptural lessons, interspersed with carols.

These originated around the 13th century as popular songs (not specifically connected with Nativity or religious themes) to accompany round dances – hence their repeated choruses. The majority of those most familiar today, however (e.g. 'O Come All Ye Faithful'; 'Hark the Herald Angels'; 'Once in Royal David's City'; 'Good King Wenceslas'; 'O Little Town of Bethlehem') were written or set to music in Victorian times. Local carols and tunes, mainly from earlier Nonconformist sources, can nevertheless still be heard in certain south-west Yorkshire pubs (notably the Fountain at Ingbirchworth; the Black Bull at Ecclesfield and the

Royal at Dungworth) between Sheffield and Huddersfield. And unaccompanied carol singing in Welsh continues at the candlelit 'Plygain' services now regaining ground in northern mid-Wales, the best known being at Llanfihangel-yng-Ngwnfa, near Llanfyllin, Powys: originally held at cock-crow (*plygain*) on Christmas morning, plygeiniau are now distributed throughout the season.

Christians returning from late-night services need have no fear of evil spirits, which are powerless during this holy time: so ghost stories may safely be told, though the custom may originally have stemmed from the pagan belief that sinister entities were particularly dangerous at midwinter. One supernatural being welcomed by all, however, is Father Christmas, alias Santa Claus. Known as a vague personification of the season since at least the 15th century, the English Old Father Christmas figures in early MUMMING PLAYS and appears in approximately his modern garb in a woodcut of 1653: but 'Santa's' Christmas Eve visits, his habit of descending chimneys to fill stockings (or, more ambitiously, pillow cases) and his reindeer-drawn sleigh all derive from that melting pot of traditions, the USA. His character there was blended from European legends about the 4th-century St Nicholas of Myra (who saved three maidens from prostitution by a surreptitious midnight gift of dowry money, and who as *Sinte Klaas* filled the shoes of Dutch-American children on 6 December, his feast day); the German-American *Krisskringle* (who rewarded good and punished bad children); and Scandinavian or Russian tales about North-Pole-dwelling wizards. After crystallization in a popular poem, 'The Night Before Christmas' (1823), this composite American Santa quietly recrossed the Atlantic during the 1870s: since when, his reputation apparently undamaged by numerous commercial impersonators, he has increasingly provided a purely secular focus for 'the children's Christmas'.

An earlier American import, the turkey, is now the conventional centrepiece of the Christmas fare: but though well established as a seasonal dish by Elizabethan times, it has only recently wrested supremacy from the goose, the chicken, and the joint of roast beef. Long since vanquished, however – except at The Queen's College, Oxford and certain GUILDS' feasts – is the once indispensable boar's head, along with its poor relation the Christmas brawn: and the stupendous Yorkshire Christmas pies filled with hecatombs of whole geese, hares and wildfowl. Another old English favourite, the thick 'plum porridge' of beef, raisins, and prunes, had solidified by the early 19th century into the still ubiquitous Christmas pudding, customarily prepared on STIR-UP SUNDAY and containing lucky silver coins or charms. Mince pies, too, have a long and surprisingly controversial history. Originally eaten before the meal, and made with real 'mincemeat' (generally fat mutton) baked with fruit and spices into cases representing Christ's manger, they were thus regarded by Puritans as especially 'idolatrous': later, however, they were justified as 'solidly Protestant', despite the fact that many of their ingredients came (like the oranges, figs and dates relished since late medieval times) from Catholic countries. Each one made by a different cook brings a lucky month in the coming year; so mince pies are still exchanged between households, or sent to absent friends.

Having eaten all this, and pulled their crackers (invented in 1846 by a London baker, who got the idea from a crackling Christmas fire) many families settle down to the sovereign's Christmas message, first broadcast (by George V) in 1932 and televised since 1956. Thereafter, however, the remainder of the season all too often degenerates into dyspeptic gloom, unenlivened by the many customary and religious observances which once marked the Twelve Days after Christmas. Few, for instance, now emulate Wenceslas by treating their poor neighbours 'on the feast of St Stephen', better known as Boxing Day from the Christmas boxes which postmen, dustmen and others have virtually ceased to collect: neither, fortunately, do wrens, squirrels and other small creatures continue to be hunted then. Some misguided employers, moreover, demand a return to work on 'Childermas' (28 December) though this commemoration of the 'Holy Innocents' slaughtered by Herod is notoriously the unluckiest day of the year, especially for beginning things. But for most the holiday season is now generally prolonged until after the New Year festivities, if rarely until its traditional end on TWELFTH NIGHT (6 January) or the following PLOUGH MONDAY.

· Churching of Women ·

The short service of 'Thanksgiving after Childbirth, commonly called the Churching of Women' is still performed on request in many Anglican churches, especially in rural areas. Consisting of a psalm, some prayers and a Communion celebration, it is designed exclusively to offer thanks for a safe delivery from 'the great pain and peril of childbirth' (*see* BIRTH): and makes no reference whatever to the ancient belief that a woman who has recently borne a child is somehow 'unclean' and thus in need of ritual purification (*see* CANDLEMAS). For many centuries, nevertheless, 'churching' has been popularly regarded as just such a ritual purification: and among older country people – particularly in northern and western England and in Wales – an unchurched mother is still viewed as at least very 'unlucky'. Until she goes to attend the ceremony, therefore, tradition holds that a newly delivered woman should preferably not leave her house at all – still less enter the homes of others, lest she leave ill fortune there. Neither may she cross any road or running water, lest these spread her bad luck far and wide: and above all she must not visit, touch, or even speak to a pregnant woman, or dire misfortune will overtake the unborn child.

A meeting of the Court of Brotherhood and Guestling, one of the surviving **Cinque Ports Ceremonies,** at the Maison Dieu in Dover in 1953.

· Cinque Ports Ceremonies ·

From the time of Edward the Confessor, certain ports in Kent and Sussex furnished the Kings of England with ships for defence and transport, receiving in return privileges which made them virtually a self-governing state. Called the 'Cinque Ports' – from the French word for 'five', invariably pronounced 'sink' in the English manner – after the five 'head ports' of Hastings, Sandwich, Dover, Romney and Hythe, the confederacy reached the zenith of its power in the 13th century, following its victory over a French invasion fleet off Sandwich on St Bartholomew's Day 1217 (*see* ST BARTHOLOMEW'S BUN RACE). By that time its members included two associated 'Ancient Towns', Rye and Winchelsea, and a number of lesser harbours, which operated as 'Limbs' or subsidiaries of one of the head ports: and between them these not only controlled the entire coastline from Pevensey to Chatham, but also claimed sweeping 'rights of Admiralty' over the English Channel and the outer Thames Estuary.

Ruthless and piratical in their dealings both with foreign enemies and English rivals – in 1297, for instance, their fleet attacked and sank thirty-two ships from Yarmouth – the Cinque Ports nevertheless began to lose their influence during the later Middle Ages. Damaging French counter-raids and the increasing prosperity of non-confederate ports like Southampton both contributed to their decline: but the main factor was the rapid and catastrophic change in coastal geography which, by Elizabethan times, had silted up many of the Ports and left others stranded well inland, so that only Dover now retains anything like its former importance.

Their increasing decline into insignificance, however, only made the Cinque Ports all the more determined to maintain their ancient customs and privileges. Sandwich, for example, is now over two miles from the sea, and had ceased to provide vessels for royal service by the 17th century: yet it still collects 'ship-money' contributions from certain of its 'Limbs', namely 3s 4d (17p) from Fordwich near Canterbury (now a small village, six miles from the nearest navigable waterway) and 10s (50p) from Brightlingsea in Essex, the only member of the confederacy outside Kent and Sussex. Both places, therefore, continue annually to elect a 'mayor deputy', who carries the levy to the Mayor of Sandwich, receiving a chain of office in return: and a similar chain is likewise given to the 'chief citizen' of Sarre near Ramsgate, now a tiny inland hamlet, even though this

Limb of Sandwich has paid no ship money for more than four centuries.

The Cinque Ports also claim the right to hold their own special courts, though the functions of these are now largely ceremonial. Nominally the most important is the Court of Shepway, which dates from the 12th century and was formerly convened in the open air, at a site now marked by the Shepway Cross between Hythe and Lympne. Once the only outside legal authority recognized by the Ports, it dealt not only with serious crimes like murder and treason – for which the penalties might be drowning or burial alive – but also with external complaints against the confederation (though these had scant chance of redress, since the portmen themselves made up the jury). It was and is, however, presided over by a royal official, who bears the titles of 'Judge Supreme of the Court of Shepway, Constable of Dover Castle, and Lord Warden of the Cinque Ports', and who once had the unenviable task of controlling the worst excesses of the portmen while at the same time defending their privileges. But the post has long been an honorary one, given on their retirement to great statesmen like William Pitt, the Duke of Wellington and Sir Winston Churchill: and the swearing in and installation of new lords warden is now virtually the Court of Shepway's only role.

The Court of Brotherhood and Guestling, which meets rather more frequently (generally at Romney or Hythe) now fulfils the function of a Cinque Ports PARLIAMENT, complete with a Speaker and immunity from arrest for members while it is in session. Originally, however, the Brotherhood supervised the portmen's much-disputed right to monopolize the rich herring-fishing grounds off distant Yarmouth, and even to manage that long-suffering town's Michaelmas Herring FAIRS. The principal foundation of the murderous feud between Yarmouth and the Ports, this practice lapsed in 1663: but by that time the Brotherhood court had merged with 'the Guestling', first held in the Sussex hamlet of that name as a joint court for Hastings, Rye and Winchelsea. Subsequently expanded to include all the main ports and many of the limbs, the Court of Brotherhood and Guestling ceremonially assembles whenever the privileges of the confederation are felt to be threatened – as by local government changes – or to arrange the exercise of those privileges at CORONATIONS.

The right to bear canopies over the heads of the king and queen during the coronation procession, and afterwards to dine at the royal banquetting table, are the oldest and most valued of Cinque Ports privileges: all the more so, indeed, because the bearers were allowed to keep for themselves the costly purple and gold silk canopies, and the still more precious silver-gilt poles on which they were borne. Granted to the 'barons' – or leading citizens – of the confederacy in acknowledgment of their vital role in national defence, these 'Honours at Court' were already being exercised 'by ancient custom' at Richard I's crowning in 1189, and were thereafter performed at every coronation until that of George IV in 1821 – though not always without unseemly squabbles. At Charles II's Coronation (1661), for instance, the bearers – still obstinately clutching the canopy poles – were dragged up and down the banquetting hall by a band of rapacious royal footmen: and at George IV's they had to seek sanctuary from determined souvenir-hunters by hiding with their prize in the House of Lords. After the latter incident, therefore, the bearing of canopies was discontinued, and for a while the confederacies' representatives were excluded altogether from coronations. But when Edward VII was crowned they reasserted their privileges, and since then eighteen selected barons – always including the mayors of the five original Cinque Ports – have again taken part in the ceremony: at the Coronation of Queen Elizabeth II, they had charge of the banners of the Commonwealth.

· Civic Customs ·

A very large proportion of Britain's oldest surviving customs and ceremonies – so many, in fact, that a complete account of them would fill many volumes – are connected with towns and cities, and inextricably bound up with their long and complex history. Speaking generally (for each place's history is as unique as its customs) our most ancient towns date their continuous history from the late Anglo-Saxon period, when they began as merchant communities gathered amid the ruins of Roman cities, on new sites fortified against the Vikings, or simply at convenient route-centres. Known as 'ports' (irrespective of whether they were near the sea) or 'burhs' (later 'boroughs') these fortified market communities generally contained a royal mint and an important church, and were administered by a royal official called a 'portreeve'. This ancient title is still borne by the chief citizens of a handful of places, including Hungerford in Berkshire (see HOCKTIDE) and Laugharne in Pembrokeshire, where the portreeve is elected annually on 'Big Court Night' (first Monday in November) being thereafter presented with his official chain of golden cockle-shells and carried three times round the town hall on the shoulders of his constables.

As towns grew larger and more prosperous – a process hastened by the firm rule of the 12th- and 13th-century Angevin kings – they began to seek the right to administer their own justice, collect their own taxes, and generally to conduct their own affairs without interference from neighbouring barons or the King's rapacious sheriffs and bailiffs. For such concessions, embodied in a royal charter, they were prepared to pay a high price, and many of our oldest municipalities owe their independence to the pressing financial needs of Richard I (1189-99) and John (1199-1216). To set the seal on their hard-won freedom, the citizens at once elected their own governor, known as the 'mayor', from the Latin *maior* – greater: London had done so by 1191,

'Swearing in the Mayor', still the most symbolically important of **civic customs**, is here depicted in the frontispiece of the Bristol 'Maire's Kalendar' of 1474. The sword and mace of civic authority are prominently displayed.

and York its holder was so powerful that he was customarily addressed as 'My Lord the Mayor', or simply 'Lord Mayor', a title also accorded since 1888 to the chief citizens of most larger or 'county' boroughs. Before that time, however, the grant of 'county' status to a town was a mark of unusual distinction: conceded to London during the 12th century, to Bristol in 1373 and to York in 1396, it is symbolized by the bearing of a sword as well as a mace before the mayor, and splendidly bedecked swords are the pride of those cities' regalia. Bristol possesses four of them, each suited to a particular type of occasion – the State, Pearl, Mourning and Lent Swords: and London no less than five – the City Sword, the Mourning Sword, the Sword of Justice which hangs at the Old Bailey, the Justice Room Sword at the Mansion House, and Queen Elizabeth I's Pearl Sword, which is ceremonially surrendered whenever a monarch enters the city in state. The senior of York's two swords – once the property of the Holy Roman Emperor Sigismund – is however borne even in the sovereign's presence, though it is then carried point downwards instead of, as usual, erect.

County (or 'shire') status also allowed a town to elect its own 'shire-reeves', originally legal officers who represented the crown in the same manner as the 'high sheriffs' of rural counties. Now generally restricted to a ceremonial role, sheriffs are usually regarded as deputies to the mayor, and chosen by him from senior councillors: but in some places, like Lichfield, they retain distinctive duties of their own (*see* BEATING THE BOUNDS). While in London, the two sheriffs are still formally elected by the liverymen of the City GUILDS on MIDSUMMER DAY, at a private ceremony in the ancient Guildhall: and ceremonially 'admitted' there on 28 September – which is the day before the Lord Mayor's election, a reminder of the fact that in London, unusually, their office is older than his. So too is that of the aldermen, whose name derives from the Anglo-Saxon *ealdormen* who ruled shires and provinces before the Norman Conquest, but who in towns represented 'wards' or divisions of the community, and who together made up an inner council called 'the mayor's brethen'. Known alternatively in some places as 'portmen' or 'jurats', their office is now (outside London) a purely honorary one, marked only by specially elaborate robes: but the 25 London aldermen still form – with 136 'common councilmen' – a distinct element of the 'Common Council', the local authority for the square mile of the City, which ceremonially meets at the Guildhall on alternate Thursdays.

and York and a dozen other leading towns by 1216, and soon the existence of a mayor became the very symbol of the much-valued privilege of urban self-government.

The dignity of the mayor, then, was and is the dignity of the town or city, and the pomp which still surrounds him is the embodiment of civic pride. Until very recently, moreover, the mayor's position was by no means purely symbolic. For the ceremonial mace traditionally borne before him – an emblem of power whose origins go back at least to Anglo-Saxon times – signified his authority as the King's lieutenant in the town as well as its chief magistrate: while the bodyguard of halberdiers which in some places still accompanies him on state occasions recalls the fact that his person was sacrosanct, so that even to verbally insult (let alone physically assault) him was to court banishment from the town, if not imprisonment for life. In some towns, too, the office carries with it additional dignities – like the Mayor of Rochester's Admiralty of the Medway (*see* ADMIRALTY COURT) or the CINQUE PORTS mayors' right to attend CORONATIONS – and in great cities like London

Apart from their mayor, sheriffs and councillors, most older towns also have a variety of other elected or appointed officials of ancient lineage, though many of these now perform only vestigial and ceremonial duties. Among them are chamberlains, who dealt with finance; marshals, constables, bailiffs and sergeants-at-mace, once responsible for public order, and still employed as debt-collectors in some places; bridgemasters, gatekeepers, and clerks of the market, to gather tolls and supervise FAIRS; and watermen or water bailiffs, whose badge of office at Rochester and Bristol is a silver oar. Formerly, too, many corporations had their own musicians or 'Waits', who sometimes doubled as night-watchmen: at Bristol their ceremonial chains of silver roses and pomegranates, dating from the reign of Queen Mary, are still worn by the city trumpeters, and York's Elizabethan Waits' chains now adorn the swordbearer and the macebearer. That city, nevertheless, has recently revived its musical Waits, who play at civic events in their scarlet livery gowns. Both York and London once also possessed an official called 'The Common Hunt', whose duty was to provide game for corporation feasts: while the Lord Mayor of London's official Fool was expected to jump fully-clad into a cauldron of custard at his master's inaugural banquet.

Such feastings, and indeed most forms of civic ceremonial, seem to have enjoyed their heyday between the late 17th and early 19th centuries, when the civil wars were over and the cold winds of democratization and local government 'reform' had not yet begun to chill Britain's town halls. It is probably no accident, there-fore, that the ceremonial dress of this period – cocked or tricorne hats, elaborate open gowns and knee-breeches – has continued to be almost universally worn on formal civic occasions. Many of the most extravagant man-ifestations of civic pride likewise originated in those palmy days: among them the mayoral coaches of London and Bristol; the specially built Mansion Houses or official mayoral residences; and the great accum-ulations of magnificent regalia and massy silver plate which still adorn mayoral tables. In 1835, however, the Municipal Corporations Act opened the attack on civic privilege by substituting a uniform system of ratepayer-elected councils for the heterogeneous collection of self-perpetuating oligarchies which had hitherto gov-erned British towns: and since then a series of centraliz-ing measures – including the major local government reorganization of 1974 – have progressively robbed many ancient corporations of all but a shadow of their former power.

Fortunately for lovers of tradition, however, the outward show of civic pomp has generally survived the withering away of civic authority, being most often expressed in the ceremonies of electing and installing the mayor. The most ancient and magnificent of such ceremonies, appropriately enough, are those surround-ing the LORD MAYOR OF LONDON: but many other towns also maintain the time-honoured customs of their 'Mayoring Days', which since 1948 have everywhere taken place during May. Almost invariably, the cor-poration processes through the streets in full state on the day itself: and it frequently repeats the process on the 'Mayor's Sunday' following, when the newly elected chief citizen formally attends service at his town's principal church. At Durham, Rye, and elsewhere, moreover, the new mayor still throws hot pennies to be

The town crier is an indispensable feature of civic customs in many places. Mr C. Bethell, crier of Corsham in Wiltshire, wears the traditional 18th-century livery universally popular among such officials.

'scrambled for' by schoolchildren; and at High Wycombe in Buckinghamshire he is expected to submit to the custom of WEIGHING THE MAYOR: while at Canterbury in Kent the ancient Burghmote Horn, dating from around 1200, is ceremonially blown before his inaugural speech; and at Sandwich in the same county – where he still wears a black gown, in remembrance of a predecessor killed by French pirates in 1457 – he is presented with a new blackthorn staff, whose purpose is allegedly to ward off the evil spells of witches.

· La Clameur de Haro ·
Channel Islands

The Channel Islands – principally Jersey, Guernsey, Alderney and Sark – have been part of the Duchy of Normandy since 933: and have been attached to the English crown since 1066, when the Dukes of Norman-dy became Kings of England. When the rest of Normandy fell to the French in 1204, moreover, the islanders remained under English rule, though not strictly part of England: for to the islanders the monarch is still 'The Queen, Our Duke', and they still maintain their own distinctive and basically Norman laws, among them the custom called 'La Clameur de Haro'.

This custom – which for a few centuries after 1066, also obtained in England and Normandy – preserves the right of all Normans to appeal directly for justice to their Duke. To invoke this, the claimant must kneel before witnesses: and cry out in a loud voice – 'Haro! Haro! Haro!; a l'aide, mon Prince, on me fait tort' (Haro! Haro! Haro! To my aid, my Prince, I am being wronged). In Jersey this alone is sufficient, but in Guernsey and Alderney the plaintiff and witnesses must then repeat the Lord's Prayer in French, and on Sark the words following the Haro are somewhat different. On all the islands, however, the person complained against must at once cease the allegedly wrongful action, while the plaintiff must report the cause of complaint to the appropriate court as soon as is practicable. If 'La Clameur' is then judged to have been raised with good reason, the defendant is fined accordingly: but if the complaint is not upheld by the court, the raiser of the Clameur will themselves be fined.

On Guernsey, both those that continued an offence after 'La Clameur' and those that raised it wrongfully were formerly imprisoned in the deepest dungeon of Castle Cornet: and though punishments are no longer so Draconian, the Clameur is still taken very seriously indeed. For the past few centuries, however, it has generally been employed against real or alleged encroachments on land or possessions: in which case it must be raised as near as possible to the disputed property. On a famous occasion in 1870, for example, it was raised at St Helier Station, in an unsuccessful attempt to stop the running of the first train of the Jersey Railway: and in 1974 a Clameur made in a Jersey potato field resulted in a fine for the encroaching farmer, who had also to return both the misappropriated land and the potatoes he had grown on it. A decision made admits of no appeal whatever to a higher court.

The respect paid to the Clameur is frequently but erroneously said to stem from its origin as an appeal ('Ha Rou') to Rou or Rollo, also known as Rolf the Ganger, the Norse Viking leader who became the first Duke of Normandy. But though Rolf was indeed notorious for dispensing summary justice, and may well have been called on in this way, the cry of 'Haro' – meaning 'Help', 'Alas', or even 'Watch Out' – was in fact a common interjection of distress throughout medieval England and France. In Chaucer's Miller's Tale, for instance, the hard-pressed Alison cries out:

> Why lat be, lat be Nicholas
> Or I wol crie, 'out, harrow' and 'alas'
> Do wey your handes, for youre curteisye

while in modern French to 'cry haro' on someone still means 'to raise the hue and cry' or, more colloquially, to express extreme disapproval.

· Clipping the Church ·
Painswick, Gloucestershire: Sunday after 19 September; elsewhere on various dates

On 19 September, the feast of the Nativity of St Mary, Old Style, the famous yews surrounding St Mary's church at Painswick are given their annual trim: and on the following 'Feast Sunday' the church itself is 'clipped' – in modern terms 'hugged' or 'embraced'. Led by choir and clergy, flower-wearing village children process about the churchyard, singing hymns to the music of the local band: then, while the special 'Clipping Hymn' is sung, they link hands in one continuous chain around the church, rush forward all together to kick it, and retire without breaking the circle. After this has been repeated three times, the whole company process to the tower, whence the 'Clipping Sermon' is preached from the belfry door.

Despite the kicking – apparently a recent addition, probably by the children themselves – the clipping ceremony is said to symbolize the people's love for their parish church. Until late Victorian times, a similar custom was widespread throughout the most westerly English counties – especially Somerset, Wiltshire and Shropshire – where it usually occurred either on SHROVE TUESDAY or (as in Birmingham) EASTER MONDAY: and in recent decades it has been revived at such places as All Saints', Hastings (on MOTHERING SUNDAY); Radley, near Oxford (Easter Sunday); Burbage, near Buxton, Derbyshire (late July); and St Oswald's, Guiseley, West Yorkshire (on the patronal festival, 5 August).

The Painswick version (performed annually since its revival, after a lapse, in 1897) coincides with the village feast once notorious both for its riotousness and its 'Puppy-dog pies'. One authority somewhat implausibly traces these to a Roman dog sacrifice, but the usual story tells how a local publican, desperate for meat to feed the visiting crowds, filled his pies with a litter of baked puppies – thus saddling his fellow villagers with the nickname of 'Painswick bow-wows', an insult which can still lead to free fights. Yet Painswick clearly takes a perverse pride in the tale, and continues to perpetuate it by baking small china dogs into the pies and cakes sold on Clipping Day.

· Clown Service ·
see COMMEMORATIONS OF FAMOUS PEOPLE

· Club Walks ·

Village 'sharing-out' or 'sick clubs' provided a rudimentary form of social security for their subscribers, who could claim small benefits when they were ill or otherwise unable to work. With the encouragement of parson, squire and farmers – who saw them not only as a praiseworthy example of thrifty self-help, but also as a means of reducing charges on the Poor Rate – they reached a peak of popularity in the mid-Victorian

Led by the vital band and banner, Iddesleigh in Devon's Friendly Society sets out on its annual **club walk**.

period, when their annual feasts or 'walking days' were often the most important event in the village calendar.

Generally timed to coincide with WHITSUN, OAK APPLE DAY or some other established summer festival (whose observances they partly incorporated and partly supplanted) the centrepiece of these celebrations was a procession through the village streets to a special club service in church, often returning via the houses of the squire and other wealthy sponsors. Led by a band, by the beribboned and garlanded club standards and regalia, and sometimes by the bearer of 'the money box', the marching members wore gaily coloured sashes over their Sunday best, and carried wands or staffs topped by elaborate club devices: and exiled sons of the village came from far and wide to join the 'walking', the subsequent afternoon sports, and the all-important 'dinner and drinking' in the evening.

Having been effectively made redundant in 1913 by Lloyd George's National Insurance scheme, and further disrupted by the cataclysm of the 1914-18 war, village

'friendly societies' and their associated 'feasts' thereafter went into rapid decline. But a few places still keep up club walks, if only for 'old times' sake'. In Devon, for example, Chawleigh Friendly Society still processes on the first Saturday in June, and that of Iddesleigh on the Saturday nearest MAY DAY; while in Somerset the Long Sutton club walks at a varying summertime date, and that of Langport and Huish on the Saturday nearest Oak Apple Day (29 May) – as does the 'Hearts of Oak' Friendly Society of Fownhope in Herefordshire. Further north, the Female Friendly Society of Neston in the Cheshire Wirral (as they have done since 1817) march from the church to the market cross on the first Thursday in June, carrying white wands garlanded with flowers and ribbons. And on the same day Askrigg Club in Wensleydale, North Yorkshire 'walks' behind its banner 'depicting the Eye of God looking down on a scene of Peace and Repose' – a condition which the members are said locally to lapse into after the evening's 'dinner and booze-up'.

· Colchester Oyster Ceremonies ·
Colchester, Essex: late September and around 20 October

Colchester 'native' oysters – or, to be more precise, the oysters of the nearby Colne estuary – were apparently being exploited even before the Romans came: and during the 1st century AD they were exported to Rome itself, where the writer Pliny tasted them with approval. Nor did their popularity diminish in the Middle Ages, and the Colne Fishery rights bestowed on Colchester by Richard I in 1196 were (and are) a valuable commodity indeed: the corporation still owns them, and asserts the fact every September, when the mayor and councillors ceremonially open the oyster-dredging season. After travelling to Brightlingsea, the party dons full regalia and sails by fishing boat to the oyster-fattening beds in Pyefleet Creek: where the town clerk reads a proclamation of 1256, declaring that the rights have belonged to Colchester 'from time beyond which memory runneth not to the contrary'. The company then drink the 'Loyal Toast' in gin and eat gingerbread, whereafter the mayor lowers the first oyster-dredge of the season: by custom, he must eat the first oyster brought up, just as it comes from the water.

A great many more oysters – up to 12,000 of them – are consumed about a month later at the famous Oyster Feast in Colchester Moot Hall. Already a well-established custom by the 17th century, this has apparently always been held on or about 20 October – the eve of St Dennis' Day, Old Style, and the first day of St Dennis' FAIR, which dates from 1319. Though briefly abolished under the Municipal Reform Act of 1835, the feast was soon revived as a private mayoral function, and it is currently attended by about 400 invited guests, often including a member of the royal family.

· Collop Monday ·
see SHROVE TUESDAY

· Commemorations of Famous People ·

Over the centuries, many people – notable and otherwise – have taken immense care that their memories shall be kept fresh after their deaths: the most effective method being the endowment of CHARITIES, SERMONS, or better still institutions like schools and hospitals, with their annual FOUNDERS' DAYS. Others are remembered without such efforts, in connection with particular customs and events (for instance, the BURRATOR RESERVOIR CEREMONY, or the WIDOW'S BUN): and a few simply for themselves, with commemoration ceremonies which are frequently attended by many who have no connection with the famous dead, other than a desire to honour them.

Among these last is King Charles I, whose cause still finds impassioned supporters more than four centuries after his execution on 30 January 1649. On its anniversary, members of the Royal Stuart Society and similar organizations hold services in various churches, and lay wreaths at the King's statue in Whitehall, London: on the last Sunday in January, moreover, hundreds of members of the 'King's Army' – the Royalist wing of the battle re-enacting English Civil War Society – march in the full panoply of 17th-century warfare from the statue to the King's place of execution outside the Banqueting House, where a wreath-laying ceremony and drum-head service are held. Not to be outfaced, the equally convinced partisans of Oliver Cromwell attend a service at his statue (appropriately placed outside the Houses of Parliament) on 3 September – the anniversary of the Protector's great victories at Dunbar (1650) and Worcester (1651) and also of his death in 1658 – when a speech is made by a prominent historian of the period. The Roundhead Association – rivals of the King's Army – also march with musket and pike to the statue, on a Sunday near this date.

Another 17th-century figure, the well-loved diarist Samuel Pepys, is remembered at his parish church and burial place, St Olave's, Hart Street, London EC3, on a date near the anniversary of his death on 26 May 1703. During the service a laurel wreath is laid on his grave by the Lord Mayor of London, and music of Pepys' time is used throughout, sometimes including a song composed by the diarist himself. The Lord Mayor also attends the commemoration service for John Stow, the great London historian and antiquarian who died on 5 April 1605: held as near as possible to this anniversary at St Andrew Undershaft, Leadenhall Street, London EC3, its central feature is the mayor's annual replacement of the real quill pen in the stone hand of Stow's memorial effigy.

Not all famous literary men, however, lived in London. The most renowned of all, William Shakespeare, is commemorated in his native Stratford-upon-Avon, Warwickshire, on 23 April – which is both his birthday and ST GEORGE'S DAY. A procession marches through the town to lay a wreath on his tomb at the parish church; and flags of all nations, symbolizing his international appeal, are unfurled in Bridge Street. That somewhat more insular figure, Dr Samuel Johnson – 'Dictionary Johnson' – was born on 18 September 1700 at Lichfield, Staffordshire, where he is remembered on the Saturday nearest the anniversary. At noon, the mayor and corporation, accompanied by Johnson Society officials and pupils of the Doctor's old school, ceremonially place a wreath on his statue, while the cathedral choir sing hymns and the Johnson Anthem. The party then visit his birthplace, and in the evening a private Johnson supper (invariably including his favourite dishes, steak and kidney pie and apple tart with cream) is held in the Guildhall. On the following Monday, Uttoxeter in the same county adds its own Johnson tribute, laying a wreath at the spot in the market place where he stood to do penance – fifty years after the offence – for disobeying his father there. The

Above left: In memory of the London historian John Stow, a new quill pen is annually placed in the stone hand of his effigy (left) at St Andrew Undershaft by the Lord Mayor of London. *Above:* The 'Clown Service' at Holy Trinity, Dalston, attended by the international Circus Clowns Club, is a **commemoration** of their famous colleague Joseph Grimaldi. *Left:* The musketeers of the 'King's Army' (including female recruits) march down Whitehall in 1985, during their annual commemoration of Charles I's execution in 1649.

anniversaries of two great Scots writers, Sir Walter Scott and Robert Burns, are also widely commemorated in their homeland – the former mainly in its Borders region, and the latter all over the country (and beyond) on BURNS NIGHT: while a more martial Scots hero, William Wallace, is remembered annually at his birthplace – Elderslie, near Glasgow – on or near 23 August, the anniversary of his execution in 1305.

Among the many other people honoured by services and wreath layings, finally, two others with widely differing talents must be mentioned. One is Florence Nightingale, remembered on or near her birthday – 12 May – at Westminster Abbey: attended by Chelsea Pensioners (representing the wounded soldiers for whom she worked in the Crimea) and by nurses and nursing trainees, the ceremony includes the placing on the High Altar of her famous attribute – a lamp. The other is Joseph Grimaldi (1779-1837), the 'Prince of Clowns' and allegedly the creator of the clown character and outfit as it is now known. He is therefore commemorated by an annual 'Clown Service', held on a Sunday in February or March at Holy Trinity, Dalston, London E8, the church of the International Circus Clowns Club: many members of this arrive – and read the lessons – in full costume and make-up, and a free clown show is afterwards held in the church hall.

· Common Land ·

Common land, around which so many traditional customs revolve, was once vital to the livelihood of every local community in Britain. Contrary to popular opinion, however, common land is not and never was open to the general public; being simply a tract of ground which two or more people have the right to use 'in common', but which is not in any way physically divided up between them. Such commons normally originated as the unenclosed and uncultivated 'waste' on the fringes of the farmland round a village, which the whole community used as a source of firewood, of building timber, and above all of grazing for animals. Farmland resting 'fallow' from crops might also be used for this last purpose, and so too – outside the hay-growing season – might low-lying watermeadows (see LOT MEADOWS): but these alone were not sufficient for the year-round sustenance of the oxen and horses which ploughed the all-important cornland, or the sheep and cows which manured it; and without the common waste the village would have starved.

In Anglo-Saxon times, therefore, 'waste' appears to have been regarded as the joint possession of all the villagers; and even after the Norman Conquest had made it (along with all other land on the manor) the property of the feudal lord, a right to use the common was automatically granted to every one of his tenants. The precise nature of such rights, however, varied with MANORIAL CUSTOM. For the common could only maintain a finite quantity of grazing animals throughout the year: and in many places the number of beasts a tenant might pasture there was strictly graded (or 'stinted') according to the size of his smallholding. Neither could the waste produce limitless amounts of fuel, timber, and fish: so that the local COURTS LEET AND BARON had also to carefully regulate such rights as 'turbary' (the cutting of peat for fuel), 'piscary' (fishing) and 'estovers' – from the Old French word for 'necessities', a term which included the taking of wood for burning ('fire-bote'), for house-building and repairs ('house-bote'), for making implements ('plough-bote and cart-bote') and for repairing fences or hedges ('hay-bote'). The general rule in all these cases being that material could be taken only for the immediate use of the tenant himself, and not for sale.

A far greater threat to commons than over-use, nevertheless, was actual loss of land by seizure: whence the importance of BEATING THE BOUNDS and COMMON RIDINGS to prevent encroachments by neighbouring villages or individual farmers. Annexations of the waste by the lord of the manor himself, however, were harder to resist: for while laws dating from the 13th century decreed that such appropriations must leave sufficient pasture to maintain the village community, landlords clearly had the advantage in disputes about the definition of 'sufficient'. The total 'enclosures' of commons which gathered momentum under the Tudors, moreover, frequently disregarded both law and commoners'

rights altogether: and though during the peak period of enclosures (which occurred between 1760 and 1860, under the twin pressures of improved farming methods and the need to provide food for a rapidly expanding population) individual Acts of Parliament were supposed to apportion extra land to farmers in compensation for their lost common rights, the landless poor still suffered considerable hardship from the disappearance of their only source of grazing and fuel. Thus a bitter rhyme commented:

> The law locks up a man or woman
> Who steals the goose from off the common
> But leaves the greater villain loose
> Who steals the common from the goose

and protests were widespread, sometimes taking the form of enclosure riots disguised as STREET BALL GAMES: so too were appeals to ancient customs, designed (like CHEESE ROLLING) to preserve access to threatened commons or (like BREAD AND CHEESE THROWING, Hungerford HOCKTIDE or GROVELY RIGHTS DAY) to emphasize that common rights were guaranteed by long-standing traditions and immemorial grants.

Such protests, however, could not prevent the loss of the great majority of the commons of lowland England: but in upland Britain the story was somewhat different. For there the poorer land is unsuitable for corn-growing, and there large tracts of rough moorland grazing are still shared in common between the sheep farmers of a village or estate, generally under the supervision of a court leet or similar body. On the fringes of Dartmoor, for instance, the vast 'Commons of Devon' stretch from Okehampton to near Plymouth, including the greater part of no less than twenty-seven parishes: while much of the Pennine moorlands of northern England and the mountain pastures of Scotland and Wales also remain common grazing.

Even there, however, common land is under threat from developers, 'modern farmers' and 'agribusiness'. For though legal opinion – led by the Commons Preservation Society – had begun by late-Victorian times to favour public access to commons near towns for 'air and exercise'; and though ecologists now recognize the pressing need to preserve the disappearing waste and wetland habitats found only on uncultivated land; yet commons are still fast disappearing beneath the plough, generally to produce unwanted grain for quick profit. Neither has the well-meaning but inept Commons Registration Act of 1965 done much to improve matters: for it contained the fatal proviso that any common not registered by January 1970 would thus cease to be common, and it contains so many loopholes that means have been found to misappropriate even those commons which were so registered. Local protests – sometimes including the revival of customs like beating the bounds – have beaten off the encroachers in some places: but further legislation is urgently required if Britain's commons are not to vanish altogether.

· Common Ridings ·

Scotland, especially the border region: June, July or August

'Common Ridings', or 'Ridings of the Marches' – which is to say the boundaries – are basically the Scottish version of the ceremonies known in England as BEATING THE BOUNDS: and similarly originated with the need to carry out a regular inspection of the community's boundary lines and markers, thus protecting its territory against unlawful encroachments. For several historical reasons, however, the Scots custom differs considerably in form and atmosphere from the average English 'processioning'. Firstly (as the title implies) the boundaries concerned are those of the often very extensive tracts of COMMON LAND grazing and peat moor surrounding Scottish 'burghs' or chartered towns: which, being much lengthier than their English counterparts, are necessarily ridden rather than walked. Secondly, the ridings are essentially civic and secular rather than quasi-religious ceremonies: for the Scots Kirk, with its Calvinist suspicion of all ceremonies, never gave the custom the sanction it received from the English Church. So their central figure is not the parson, but the young man – generally called the 'Cornet', after the junior officers who carried cavalry standards – chosen to bear the burgh banner, head the cavalcade of horsemen, and lead the 'Cornet's Gallop' which frequently ends the ride. All these factors, then, make the ridings – held, not at Rogationtide, but generally to coincide with the less 'churchified' MIDSUMMER festival – far more dashing and exciting events than their literally pedestrian English equivalents.

Towns all over Scotland once perambulated their bounds annually as a matter of course, but only a few in the northern and central parts of the country still do so: notably Aberdeen, which has revived the ancient 'Riding of the March Stones' – delineating common land given by King Robert Bruce in 1319 – during two days in mid-June; Linlithgow, West Lothian (once effectively the capital of Scotland) whose carriage-borne procession, held since at least 1541 on the first Tuesday after the second Thursday in June, is led by the magnificently clad town herald, halberdiers, provost and bailies; and the Midlothian burghs of Musselburgh (mid-July) and Penicuik (second week in June) where revived ceremonial rides are headed respectively by the 'Honest Lad' – Musselburgh's motto is 'Honesty' – and the 'Huntsman'.

The home of the classic Common Riding, however, is the region immediately north of the Anglo-Scottish border. In this notoriously lawless land, boundaries needed to be continually and vigorously defended both against English incursions and unruly Scots neighbours – for savage feuds were endemic here until the 17th century and beyond, and the words 'rider' and 'raider' were virtually synonymous. Here, then, the traditional form of Riding the Marches survived longest: and here too a strong sense of history and community (not to mention the growth of tourism) has given rise to widespread revivals or new institutions of the custom, especially since the Second World War. Nearly every border burgh, therefore, now organizes a 'summer riding' – even if it no longer has common lands to perambulate, and so sends its horsemen on a ceremonial ride to places of historical significance – and this is generally the centrepiece of a week of festivities, invariably including the crowning of a schoolgirl 'Summer Queen'.

Perhaps the best known of the old-established border ridings is that of Selkirk, which has been held for at least four centuries on the Friday after the second Monday in June. Two months beforehand, a special meeting of the burgh council selects the Standard Bearer, invariably a popular local bachelor and a practised March rider: who, on the Sunday before the event is ceremonially 'kirked' at a church service. Then, on the Thursday evening, the burgh officer parades through the town with fifes and drums, 'Crying the Burley' to summon the 'burleymen' (bylawmen or 'common right heritors') to prepare for the morning's perambulation of their bounds. During the same evening, too, the banners of Selkirk's four 'Incorporations' (or GUILDS), together with those of the ex-soldiers and colonials societies, are formally 'bussed' by being decked with bunches of brightly coloured ribbon.

The Riding-day ceremonies begin soon after dawn, when bands play in the streets before leading a procession of 'Souters' – shoemakers, the local nickname for Selkirkians – to the 'bussing' of the burgh flag by the provost's lady. This is now given into the care of the Standard Bearer, and to cries of 'Safe Oot, Safe In', he leads his cavalcade out to begin their four-hour Riding of the boundaries. After tracing the line through woods and crags, splashing through streams, and at times pounding along roads, they eventually ford the Ettrick water and gallop back into town for a custom unique to Selkirk. Called 'the Casting of the Colours', it commemorates the disastrous Scots defeat at Flodden in 1513, when the sole survivor of the eighty-strong Selkirk contingent mutely cast down a tattered standard at the feet of a horrified provost. Now, however, the resplendent burgh flag is whirled and swung about the Standard Bearer's head before a silent crowd; and so, afterwards, are those of the Incorporations and societies, until the ceremony concludes with the Flodden lament, 'The Flowers of the Forest'. Then follow two traditional features of Common Ridings throughout the borders, the afternoon horse race and the Standard Bearer's evening ball, when the town's champion leads the dancing.

Nearby Hawick's Common Riding, usually held the week before Selkirk's, takes much the same basic form – though its leader is called the 'Cornet' and here (as elsewhere) is supported by Right and Left-hand Men, the two previous office holders. Preceded by five practice 'ride-outs', and itself spread over two days, the

Above: Resplendent in the height of early Victorian fashion, the Hawick Cornet and his Right and Left-hand Men before the Common Riding of 1857. *Right:* Bearing the Galashiels banner, the Standard Bearer and lass ford the Gala Water as part of the 'Braw Lad's Gathering'.

Hawick Ride's climax is the 'Cornet's Dash' up Vertish Hill, said to commemorate a victory over English raiders at Hornshole in 1514. Throughout the ceremonies, moreover, the town's own song, 'Teribus, ye Teri Odin', is frequently and loudly sung. Langholm in Dumfriesshire (at the western and once still wilder end of the border) also incorporates a number of distinctive features in its Riding, held on the last Friday in July. Among these are the Hound Race which starts the day, the annual adoption of Riding colours following those of the DERBY winner – said to have originated when a Langholm horse won that 'classic' – and the 'Crying of the FAIR'. Most notable, however, are the four 'Emblems' carried on poles at the head of the procession – a flowery crown, a giant thistle, a heather-decked spade for the symbolic cutting of peats, and a huge 'Barley Bannock', nailed with a salt herring across it to a wooden platter. This may represent either the burgh's right to collect food-market tolls or, more simply, the whim of those who founded the Riding in 1816. Far older (and indeed allegedly the oldest of all surviving Scots ridings) is that of Lanark, called Lanimer (landmark) Day and held during the second or third week in June. Perhaps because of this seniority, or because of its Royal Burgh status, Lanark aspires to a 'Lord Cornet': but the Monday perambulation here is now somewhat overshadowed by the carnival procession and 'Queen' crowning on Lanimer Thursday. During that afternoon, however, the ancient race for the 'Burgh Spurs' is still contested by a field strictly confined to march riders and visiting Cornets.

'New' or revived riding ceremonies, along broadly similar lines, also take place at a dozen or so other border burghs. At Annan on the Solway, walking and sailing perambulations precede the Ride, which occurs on the first Saturday in July and includes the thrusting of a boy through a hedge to 'beat' a boundary mark. Coldstream in Berwickshire, lacking commons, rides behind its 'Coldstreamer' to Flodden Field on the first Thursday in August; while Duns in the same county's 'Reiver's Week' (the first in July) includes a Common Riding, a 'Hand Ba'' game, and a service commemorating the signing of the Presbyterian National Covenant of 1639 on Duns Law. Dumfries's 'Guid Nychburris Day' Ride – during the last week in June – boasts not only a Cornet but also a 'Pursuivant' (representing the crown) and four 'Lynors', who mark the boundaries with posts and flags: and Galashiels in Selkirkshire, during the same week, holds an immensely popular 'Braw Lad's Gathering' with Rides commemorating a number of local incidents, including the defeat of an English raiding party in a plum grove which originated the town's motto, 'Soor plums'.

Similar Rides – notably one re-enacting the 'Raid of Reidswire' in 1575 – also take place at the ancient Roxburghshire town of Jedburgh in early July, under the direction of the 'Callant': while Kelso in the same county, under the 'Kelso Laddie', holds its Yetholm and Whipman's Rides a week later. Lauder in Berwickshire perambulates its 1700-acre commons on the first Saturday in August, when the Cornet ceremonially adds a stone to the Burgess Cairn, symbolizing the once-annual repair of landmarks: and the Cornet of Locker-bie, Dumfriesshire, during his Ride on the second Saturday in June, collects a turf in token of the burgh's right to 'cast, win, and carry away Fewell' from its common peat bogs. Melrose in Roxburghshire (most unusually for this area) holds a 'Common Walk' rather than a Ride during the last week in June: but the Peebles March Riding on Midsummer Eve (revived as early as 1897) is very much a horseman's festival, whose highlight is the 'Cornet's Canter' to Neidpath Castle.

· Comrie Flambeaux Procession ·
see BURNING THE OLD YEAR OUT

· Coracle Races ·
Cilgerran, Cardiganshire, Dyfed: during a week in August

As archaeological evidence proves, coracles (Welsh: *cwrwgl*) have been used on British rivers since at least the Bronze Age. Calico waterproofed with pitch has replaced the untanned animal skins formerly stretched over a framework of hazel or willow withies, but otherwise these portable one-man boats remain much as they were described by Gerald of Wales in the 1190s. So too does the method of salmon fishing from them, by means of a weighted net stretched between two coracles: but this now survives only on two western Welsh rivers, the Teifi and the Tywi.

The very considerable skill needed to handle these tricky craft is displayed each August at Cilgerran near Cardigan, where the Teifi cascades through a spectacular gorge. In a week-long programme of races, local fishermen negotiate rocks, shallows and whirlpools at remarkable speeds: and the principal event is a race between the Teifi coracle-men and their rivals from the Tywi, each encouraged by a crowd of vociferous supporters.

· Corby Pole Fair ·
Corby, Northamptonshire: Whit Monday, every twenty years (e.g. 1982, 2002)

According to local legend, Queen Elizabeth's grant of a charter to Corby in 1585 was a reward to the villagers who rescued her from a nearby bog, into which she had accidentally fallen: and though the charter gives no permission for a fair, a fair to celebrate it has nevertheless been held every twenty years since the grant was confirmed by Charles II in 1682. Called 'the Pole Fair', it features a curious custom of unknown origin, whereby 'miscreants' are lifted bodily on a pole (if male) or a chair (if female) and carried through the streets, to be placed in one of the town's three surviving sets of stocks. This penalty may be incurred by anyone who refuses to pay a toll at the barriers set across all the roads into the town at dawn on WHITSUN MONDAY: or indeed anyone at all – regardless of age, sex, or social position – who declines to give due ransom to the pole-bearers on fair day. The custom is, moreover, rigidly enforced: and even if some victims prefer a pole ride to submission, they must still pay to escape from the stocks.

Cheerful male 'offenders' are carried to the stocks on poles, while lady 'miscreants' enjoy a more comfortable chair ride: **Corby Pole Fair** in 1902.

· Coronations ·

Coronations, without rival the most magnificent of all British ceremonies – or indeed of ceremonies anywhere in the world – are nevertheless far from being merely splendid pageants. They are, rather, rituals in the truest sense, which must be correct in every detail in order to be valid: so that their essentials cannot be changed, and in fact have not been changed – despite numerous alterations of dynasty, a major religious upheaval, and a radical revision of the powers of the monarchy – since the Coronation of King Edgar in 973. For by that time coronations had already acquired their principal elements: the Christian rite of anointing the sovereign with holy oil (probably derived from the example of the Frankish Emperor Charlemagne, and first used in England at the consecration of King Ecgferth of Mercia in 787) and the performance by churchmen of the ancestral Saxon customs of enthroning the monarch and investing him with the insignia of power, including the ceremonial helmet which later became a crown. The crown proper probably did not appear in Britain until the Norman Conquest: and even now the actual crowning is only one part of a ritual which must also include the recognition of the sovereign by the people; the oath to rule well; the vital anointment; and the homage of the magnates.

Following the maxim 'The King is Dead, Long Live the King', the process leading to a coronation begins immediately after the death of the previous monarch: when the Accession Council is at once summoned to draft and sign the successor's Proclamation. Currently composed of Privy Councillors, peers and members of the royal family, this body is the direct descendant of the Anglo-Saxon 'Witan' and the Norman 'Great Council', which enjoyed and sometimes exercised the right to 'elect' the new king – or usually to select the most suitable candidate from the existing royal house. For many centuries now, however, the succession has been established in advance by law, and since the 18th century the new monarch's reign has legally begun at the moment of their predecessor's demise. Normally, then, the ceremonial Proclamation is read out by Garter King of Arms (the principal English herald) as soon as possible after that event, first outside St James's Palace and then in Whitehall and elsewhere in London: and since the advent of modern communications Proclamation ceremonies have simultaneously taken place in towns and cities throughout Britain and the Commonwealth – though Scotland preserves the custom of delaying the Proclamation for a week, supposedly the time taken for the news to arrive. Before being proclaimed, however, the sovereign must first sign a declaration of resolve to take the Coronation Oath and (following the Act of Union with Scotland in 1707) also swear to preserve the Scots Presbyterian Kirk: and because the present Queen (upon whose Coronation this account is based) was abroad when her father died in February 1952, her Proclamation therefore had to be delayed until her return.

Sixteen months then elapsed before her Coronation on 2 June 1953. Such a delay would have been unthinkable in the medieval period, when a sovereign's reign was not deemed to begin until his coronation rites had been carried out: and so vital and urgent was the ceremony that Henry II attempted to assure the succession by crowning his son in his own lifetime; while the nine-year-old Henry III, on the sudden death of his father King John, was at once crowned with a makeshift diadem to forestall the consecration of a rival candidate by rebellious barons. In 1953, however, ample time could safely be allowed for the prodigious amount of preparation work carried out under the direction of the Earl Marshal, the Duke of Norfolk (whose ancestors have held the office since the first Duke was granted it for supporting the usurpation of Richard III in 1483) before the ceremony took place at Westminster Abbey, the customary crowning-place of English monarchs since 1066.

For Queen Elizabeth II, the ceremony was to last nearly two-and-a-half hours. It was, nevertheless, short by comparison with past coronations, whose preliminaries had begun two days beforehand at the Tower of London, where the monarch customarily lived (doubtless for reasons of security) between his accession and his consecration. There, in medieval times, the sovereign took a ritually purifying bath on the night before the ceremony – as did the young men thereafter created 'Knights of the Bath' (see ORDERS OF CHIVALRY): and thence the royal procession (including every nobleman in England) set out for Westminster, a procession which alone lasted five hours at the Coronation of Charles II in 1661, after which it was discontinued. Even in 1953, moreover, the Coronation service had already been in progress for almost an hour before the Queen entered the Abbey choir at 11.10 a.m., to a great shout of 'Vivat Regina. ['Long Live the Queen'] Vivat Regina Elizabetha. Vivat! Vivat! Vivat!'

After kneeling by her 'Chair of Estate' for a brief private prayer, the Queen moved forward to stand near the coronation throne or 'King Edward's Chair', made by Walter of Durham in 1296 to house the 'Stone of Scone' taken as a trophy during Edward I's conquest of Scotland. Upon this stone Scottish kings had been consecrated since at least the 10th century – though (largely because of English claims to overlordship of their realm) the papacy did not permit them to use the rituals of anointment and crowning until 1329, when King Robert Bruce had finally established independence: and tradition relates that it is far older, having been brought from Ireland in about 500 by Fergus Mac Erca, first King of Scots. Earlier still, moreover, the stone is said to have been used as a pillow by the Patriarch Jacob when he dreamt of 'Jacob's Ladder' at Bethel (Genesis 28.10–22). In sober fact the boulder at Westminster is composed of the red-grey sandstone commonly found around the consecration-place at Scone in Perthshire, and some Scots have asserted that it is not therefore the genuine article at all, but merely a lump of local rock palmed off on the unsuspecting Edward. Other Scots patriots, more convinced of its authenticity, daringly spirited it away from the Abbey on Christmas Day 1950: but it was later deposited at Arbroath and returned in good time for the Coronation of Queen Elizabeth II – or, according to Scots computation, Queen Elizabeth I.

Whatever the truth about the stone, the first of the ceremonies performed as the monarch stands by it is undoubtedly of considerable antiquity. The mitred Archbishop of Canterbury, bearing his Metropolitan Cross and backed by the four Great Officers of State – the Lord Chancellor, Lord Great Chamberlain, Lord High Constable and Earl Marshal – faced to the east and demanded in a loud voice: 'Sirs, I here present unto you Queen Elizabeth, your undoubted Queen, where-fore all you who are come this day to do your homage and service. Are you willing to do the same?' Whereup-on the section of the congregation before him responded 'God Save Queen Elizabeth!', and the trumpets rang out. Then the Archbishop turned successively (and in the lucky clockwise direction) to face south, west, and north, while the Queen also turned towards those quarters of the Abbey: and in each quarter the question and thunderous answer was repeated.

Such is the 'Collaudatio' or 'Recognition' of the monarch's 'election', which may well have originated in the Germanic custom of appointing new rulers by acclamation, but which seems not to have been custom-ary in England until the Coronation of William the Conqueror, when it was introduced to reinforce his claim to the throne by battle. On that occasion, however, it caused a near-disaster, for the guards outside the Abbey misinterpreted the shouts within as rioting, and promptly began burning the surrounding houses: at which many of those within rushed out, and the King and Archbishop were left standing almost alone until calm was restored and the Coronation continued. Then, as later, the consent of the people was assumed to be forthcoming: and as the idea of succes-sion by hereditary right totally replaced that of election the phrase 'undoubted monarch' appeared in the question, while the answer became simply a formal promise to obey. But the question must still be asked, and in 1953 the Archbishop declared that the 'willing assent of the people' was still necessary before the Coronation could proceed.

This given, the Queen returned to her Chair of Estate, which was flanked by the Bishops of Durham and of Bath and Wells: whose predecessors in office, since at least the Coronation of Richard I in 1189, have 'supported' sovereigns throughout the ceremony – in the cases of the infant Richard II and the gouty Queen Anne, quite literally so. Now the time had come for her to swear the Coronation Oath which binds the monarch

to rule within certain set limits: both the oath and the limits, however, have varied throughout the centuries, as powerful rulers expanded their powers and weaker or more constitutional ones had them circumscribed by barons and later by parliaments. Thus, in 1953, Queen Elizabeth not only promised to govern the peoples of Britain, the Commonwealth and the Empire 'according to their respective laws and customs'; and to 'cause Law and Justice in Mercy' to be executed in all her judgments; but also 'to maintain in the United Kingdom the Protestant Reformed Religion established by Law'. This, substantially, is the form of oath devised for the Coronation in 1689 of William and Mary, the Protes-tant 'constitutional' monarchs appointed by Parliament after the 'Glorious Revolution' which expelled the Roman Catholic James II. At their Coronation, too, the Protestant custom of presenting a bible to the sovereign also began: and in 1953, for the first time, this was done by the Moderator of the Scots Presbyterian Kirk, immediately after the Queen had affirmed her Oath with her hand upon the Gospels placed on the altar.

But though the Coronation Oath of 1689 ensured that no Catholic could ever again rule Britain, neither the Protestant Reformation nor the Glorious Revolution altered the religious elements of the coronation service. For this remains essentially an English translation of the special coronation Mass laid down – like so many other continuing features of the ceremony – by the *Liber Regalis* (*Royal Book*) compiled in about 1377 by Abbot Nicholas Lytlington of Westminster: and this itself draws on earlier forms of service going back to Anglo-Saxon times. The service, therefore, now con-tinued with the introit; the prayers for the sovereign; the Epistle ('Fear God, Honour the King' I. Peter 2.17); the Gospel ('Render unto Caesar' Matthew 22.16); the Creed; and the anthem 'Zadok the Priest', whose music was composed by Handel for George II's Coronation but whose words have been used at every ceremony since that of King Edgar. Taken from the First Book of Kings, these tell how 'Zadok the priest and Nathan the prophet anointed Solomon king; and all the people rejoiced and said; "God Save the King, Long Live the King, May the King Live for Ever..."': and as they were sung the Queen – having been recognized by her people and having sworn to rule them justly – prepared for the central and most sacred ritual of the Coronation, the Anointment.

The Anointment with holy oil, far more than the actual crowning, is indeed the element which sets the monarch apart from and above his or her subjects: for many of these (like the peers and heralds at coronations) also wear crowns, but the monarch alone is anointed. Resembling the anointment of Catholic priests and bishops, which is likewise said to confer the gifts of the Holy Spirit, the ritual makes the sovereign both priest and layman and, as some asserted, superior in status to both: and it was as the 'Vicar of God' and the 'Lord's

Anointed' that the Stuart monarchs disastrously claimed the 'Divine Right of Kings' to do as God directed – or as they liked. It is also, of course, the most ancient element of the coronation ceremony, used (as the anthem recalls) by the biblical prophets to consecrate the divinely chosen Kings of Israel: and Anglo-Saxon rulers were consecrated by anointment at least two centuries before they were ever crowned.

From the earliest times, too, the mystic importance of the anointment has been emphasized by contrasting the extreme simplicity of its ritual with the splendours of the coronation. First, therefore, the Queen was divested of her jewelled diadem, her crimson royal robe, and her collar of the Order of the Garter, while her embroidered dress was covered by an unadorned white garment: and thus bareheaded and plainly clad, she moved to King Edward's chair. Then, to hide the sacred ceremony from public view – the television cameras being also turned aside at this point – four Knights of the Garter held above her head a magnificent cloth-of-gold canopy on silver poles, while the assisting bishops closed round her to further shield her with their voluminous copes. Next, the Dean of Westminster bore from the altar the eagle-shaped Ampulla containing the holy oil, which he poured into the Anointing Spoon: and the Archbishop of Canterbury, taking the oil on his fingers, anointed the sovereign with the sign of the cross on the hands, breast and head, saying meanwhile the ancient consecration prayer – 'be thou anointed, blessed and consecrated Queen over the Peoples, whom the Lord thy God hath given thee to rule and govern'. He then blessed her, and the most vital act of the 'great solemnity of coronation' was complete.

Until the time of William and Mary, monarchs were also anointed on the back and the insides of the elbows: but since then – apart from Queen Victoria, who omitted the breast anointment 'for decency's sake' – they have been anointed thrice. At one time, moreover, the unction used was allegedly of miraculous origin. For, not to be outdone by their arch-rivals the Kings of France (who boasted of consecration with oil provided by an angel for the baptism of the Frankish ruler Clovis) the 14th-century sovereigns of England fostered the legend of a phial of ointment given to St Thomas Becket by no less than the Blessed Virgin herself. In 1399, therefore, Henry IV bolstered a somewhat shaky claim to the throne by having himself anointed with this oil (which had conveniently come to light in the Tower): and subsequent monarchs followed suit – though the forthright Queen Elizabeth I declared it 'a nasty grease, and smelt ill' – until the supply was exhausted by James I. Thereafter new and sweeter-smelling unctions were produced as necessary, and that used in 1953 was concocted from Charles I's recipe by a Bond Street chemist.

Next the Queen was invested with the robes of royalty which can only be worn by an anointed monarch – and then only once in a lifetime, during the climax of the coronation service. Probably based originally on the ceremonial garb of the Emperors of Constantinople, these so much resemble ecclesiastical vestments – thus reinforcing the high-priestly role of the consecrated sovereign – that one medieval commentator called them simply 'bysshopps gere'. First she put on the white *colobium sindonis* – literally a 'sleeveless muslin undergarment' – and next the shining gold *Supertunica* or dalmatic, fastened at the waist with a golden sword-belt. Then the great gold spurs of knighthood were brought forward by Lords Hastings and Churton, descendants of the baronial family of Grey of Ruthin who have performed this service for centuries, and the Queen touched them in token of acceptance before they were returned to the altar. At the coronation of a King, they would have been fastened briefly on his heels, and a King would also have been girded with the 'Sword for the Offering'. In 1953, however, this sword was first blessed on the altar and then placed upright in her hands by the Archbishop, with the knightly injunction that it must be used to do justice, to defend the Church and widows and orphans, and 'punish and reform what is amiss': then, carrying the sword horizontally with outstretched arms, the sovereign bore it back to the altar and laid it there as an offering. But since this sword is traditionally the monarch's personal property, the Lord Great Chamberlain immediately stepped forward to 'redeem' it for the sum of a hundred freshly minted shillings in an embroidered bag: and he thereupon drew it and carried it unsheathed beside the Queen during the rest of the ceremony – as the sheathed Swords of State, of Mercy (the blunted 'Curtana'), of Spiritual and of Temporal Justice are also carried.

Now the investiture continued with the putting on of the gold bracelets – ancient emblems of power worn both by the Kings of Israel and by Anglo-Saxon and Scandinavian rulers, but reintroduced in 1953 (as a gift from the Commonwealth) for the first time since the Coronation of the first Elizabeth: and of the quasi-priestly Stole, a strip of embroidered silk hung around the Queen's neck and tied to her arms above the elbows. And then, last and most magnificent robe of all, came the great Pallium or 'mantle royal' of pure cloth-of-gold, embossed and embroidered with Tudor roses, thistles, leeks, shamrocks and the Imperial Eagles of Byzantium, the symbol of imperial rule over many lands.

Thus hieratically clad all in gold, the Queen was ready to receive the 'Regalia' or insignia of royalty, also called 'the Crown Jewels'. Valued at some twenty million pounds in 1953, but better described as literally priceless, the present regalia is not nevertheless of great antiquity. For, apart from the Anointing Spoon, part of the Ampulla, and some re-set jewels, the whole collection was made for Charles II's Coronation in 1661: the earlier regalia having been 'totally broken, defaced and sold' in 1649, by order of the Parliament which executed Charles I and abolished the monarchy as 'useless, burdensome and dangerous to England'. From

Above: The mystic rite of Anointment is a vital preliminary to **Coronation**. Here the Queen, bare-headed and simply dressed, awaits the holy oil beneath a cloth-of-gold canopy borne by Knights of the Garter. *Above right:* Now anointed and clad in gold, but still uncrowned, the Queen holds the Sword for the Offering. Flanking her are the supporting Bishops of Durham and of Bath and Wells, and in the background stand the Ladies-in-Waiting and the tabarded Heralds. *Right:* The investiture with the Regalia. The Archbishop of Canterbury presents the Orb, watched by the ermine-robed Great Officers of State.

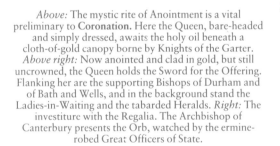

an inventory made before this was done, however, it is known that the old regalia included 'King Alfred's Crowne of gould wyerworke sett with slight stones and two little bells' (possibly the consular coronet given him by the Pope in 853): but the Parliamentary commissioners were disappointed to discover that some of the articles 'formerly thought to be all gould' turned out to be merely gilded iron, wood or horn, hence perhaps the low value of £2,647 they put on the whole collection. The new regalia which Charles II ordered 'to retain their old names and fashion', however, really was 'all gold', and cost £32,000. There is also, of course, a separate (and considerably older) Scots regalia, known as the 'Honours of Scotland' and displayed in Edinburgh Castle (*see* ROYAL CEREMONIES).

The first 'ornament' to be placed in the Queen's right hand was the Orb (Latin: *orbis*, 'world'), a jewelled gold globe six-and-a-half inches in diameter and weighing three pounds, topped by a cross. Used as a symbol of universal dominion by Roman emperors, this was delivered with the Archbishop's reminder that, as the cross overtops the Orb, so the whole world is subject to the rule of Christ. The Orb being removed (to appear again later in the ceremony), the Ring set with a sapphire and ruby cross was put on the fourth finger of the monarch's right hand, as 'a sign of kingly dignity and the seal of the Catholic church'. Also called the 'wedding ring of England', tradition holds that the closer it fits, the longer and more successful will be the sovereign's reign: a belief that was certainly true of

Queen Victoria, whose Coronation ring was forced by mistake onto the wrong finger, and thus fitted so tightly as to cause her considerable pain. Next came the 'Rich Glove' for the right hand, presented for many centuries as a QUIT RENT for the manor of Farnham Royal in Buckinghamshire, and later for that of Worksop in Nottinghamshire. But shortly before 1953 the lordship of Worksop had been taken over by a commercial property company, whose claim to perform the service was disallowed, and the Rich Glove was presented instead by the Chancellor of the Duchy of Lancaster: he was not, however, called upon to carry out the second part of the Worksop feudal service, the duty of supporting the monarch's right arm while she held the next item of the regalia, the weighty 'Sceptre with the Cross'.

This sceptre, 'the ensign of kingly power and justice', is a three-foot-long golden rod: into whose head, below the cross, is set the most perfect diamond in the world – the 530-carat 'Star of Africa', cut from the Cullinan diamond, the largest ever discovered. As it was placed in the Queen's right hand, so the 'Sceptre with the Dove' – 'the Rod of Equity and Mercy' – was set in her left, as a token that royal justice must always be tempered with mercy. Topped by a white enamel dove, the symbol of the Holy Ghost and the badge of the sainted King Edward the Confessor, such sceptres have been the special emblems of the English monarchy since at least the 12th century: and sceptres in general are an older attribute of power even than the crown, one having been found among the regalia of Raedwald, King of the East Anglia (d. 625), in the famous Sutton Hoo treasure-ship. Until the time of William and Mary, therefore, the sceptres were presented only to a crowned monarch: but since then the crown has become the focal point of the investiture, and as the Queen sat stiffly on the ancient throne, holding the two sceptres upright, this was blessed and brought from the altar.

Like her father and grandfather before her – but unlike several earlier sovereigns, who thought it too awkward and heavy – Queen Elizabeth had chosen to be crowned with 'St Edward's Crown', which is used only at coronations: rather than the 'Imperial State Crown' she would wear later in the ceremony, and subsequently on great occasions like the Opening of PARLIAMENT. Made for Charles II to the pattern of the destroyed crown worn by Tudor sovereigns, St Edward's is a solid gold coronet decorated with alternate crosses and fleurs-de-lis, set with some 440 jewels and surmounted by two arches in the form of a cross: these arches are slightly depressed at their junction (supposedly to indicate that this is the crown of a kingdom, and not a 'Crown Imperial') and above them rises the over-topping orb and cross. Within the crown, forming a lining, is the ermine-trimmed purple velvet 'cap of maintenance', apparently adopted by Edward III in token of his claim to the Duchies of Normandy and Aquitaine: and a similar cap is worn within the

'Imperial State Crown' made for the Coronation of Queen Victoria. Much the same in form – save that its arches are not depressed – this Imperial crown has a much lighter and more delicate framework of platinum, completely covered by 2,700 diamonds and hundreds of other jewels, including a number saved by Royalist sympathizers from the break-up of the old regalia. These include the sapphire of Edward the Confessor, the first Elizabeth's pearl earrings, and the great rough-cut ruby of the Black Prince, worn by Henry V at Agincourt: which with the second 'Star of Africa' diamond make this the most magnificent and valuable piece of jewellery in the world.

It was the older crown of St Edward, however, which the Archbishop of Canterbury, standing before the throne, raised high over the head of the seated and motionless Queen: and which he then slowly brought down to crown Elizabeth, the fortieth monarch of England since the Conquest and the seventeenth sovereign of the conjoint realm of Great Britain. As he did so, all the peers and peeresses put on their coronets, the heralds donned their crowns, and the clergy their caps and mitres. Then a thunderous shout of 'God Save the Queen' burst out from the whole congregation, mingling with fanfares of trumpets and the pealing of the Abbey bells: while at the Tower and Hyde Park the radio-alerted artillery began their 101-gun coronation ROYAL SALUTES.

When the tumult of acclamation had died down, the Archbishop intoned the prayer 'Coronet te Deus' – 'God crown you with a crown of glory and righteousness': and the choirs sang the Anthem 'Be strong and of good courage', both used at coronations since the 11th century. Then, after a Blessing, the crowned Queen left King Edward's Chair and walked slowly to the Throne, which was set on a raised dais with five steps: on each step stood a bishop, with a peer of one of the five degrees – dukes, marquises, earls, viscounts and barons – and as she mounted the dais these symbolically stretched out their hands to lift her into 'the possession and seisin' of her throne and realm. This ceremony of 'Elevation' or 'Enthronement', until Tudor times, was carried out immediately before the coronation, and by the nobles alone: who physically lifted the monarch onto the seat of justice called 'King's Bench' (still the name of a High Court division) in Westminster Hall. It was thus entirely separate from the Christian service, and is indeed a distant echo of the pagan Germanic and late-Roman custom of raising a new ruler on a shield, only subsumed into the religious Abbey ceremonial at the Coronation of Charles I.

The next – and final – act of the coronation once also took place separately, largely because of the considerable length of time it originally took to perform. This was the swearing of 'fealty', by which both bishops and peers promised to keep faith (Latin: *fidelitatem*) with the newly crowned monarch: and of 'homage', by which each of the peers became the sovereign's liege man

The climax of the **Coronation.** The Queen is crowned by Archbishop Fisher of Canterbury.

(French: *homme*, hence 'hommage') and undertook to support her against all enemies. A vital factor in the governance of the feudal kingdom – since one who had done homage and fealty could only rebel at the risk of life, property and immortal soul – such oaths had to be sworn individually and publicly, so that none could afterwards deny having taken them: and in Richard I's time this process lasted all day. Only after the feudal system had begun to break down, therefore, could the oaths be sworn in groups: and even as late as Queen Victoria's Coronation every single member of a sizeable aristocracy symbolically touched the crown, a ceremony lasting nearly an hour. While this was going on, however, the Treasurer of the Household somewhat relieved the monotony by 'throwing among the People Medals of Gold and Silver, as the Queen's Princely Largesse or Donative'.

'Princely donatives' have since been replaced by the coronation medals presented as 'personal souvenirs' to selected people, and the 'general pardon' for criminals once also proclaimed at this point ceased after the Coronation of George II: but the shorter homage ceremony performed in 1953 retained all the original forms – the oath of fealty having changed little, and that of homage not at all, since early medieval times. First to swear, by immemorial right, was the Archbishop of Canterbury. Kneeling bareheaded before the Queen, he placed his joined hands between hers in the ancient gesture of submission, and promised:

I Geoffrey, Archbishop of Canterbury, will be faithful and true, and faith and truth will bear unto you, our Sovereign Lady, Queen of this Realm and Defender of the Faith, and unto your heirs and successors according to law. So help me God.

'Elevated' to the raised Throne after her **Coronation**, the Queen receives the homage of the Duke of Edinburgh: all around stand the representatives of each degree of the peerage, in their distinctive coronets.

While all the bishops, kneeling in their places, repeated the words of fealty after him, substituting their names and those of their dioceses.

Then came the turn of the peers, headed by the Queen's husband, Prince Philip. Laying aside his coronet, he too knelt, placed his hands between those of his wife and sovereign, and swore the oath of homage:

I Philip, Duke of Edinburgh, do become your liege man of life and limb and of earthly worship; and faith and truth will I bear to you, to live and die, against all manner of folks. So help me God.

Rising to his feet, he then touched the crown on the Queen's head and kissed her on the cheek – being privileged, as her husband and a royal Duke, to bestow there the kiss of feudal homage which all other peers, since the Coronation of Queen Victoria, have placed instead on the sovereign's right hand. Homage was then sworn by the two other royal dukes, of Gloucester and Kent: and thereafter by the senior nobleman of each degree – the Duke of Norfolk, the Marquis of Huntly, the Earl of Shrewsbury, Viscount Arbuthnot and Baron Mowbray – who came in turn to swear the oath, its words being repeated by the other peers of their order; to touch the crown ('as promising by Way of Ceremony, ever to be ready to support it with all their power'); and to kiss the Queen's hand.

Thus, with the homage of the barons, the ceremonies of the coronation proper drew to a close: and once again the drums and trumpets mingled with a final acclamation:

God save Queen Elizabeth
Long live Queen Elizabeth
May the Queen live forever.

The Communion service in which the coronation rites are set, however, was still to reach its climax: and as the whole congregation sang the 'Old Hundredth' Psalm – this being the first time that the familiar 'All people that on earth do dwell' had ever been heard at a coronation, and the first occasion for many centuries when congregation rather than choirs were permitted to sing at all – the Queen descended from her throne, divested herself of crown and sceptres, and stood bareheaded before the altar. There she made the traditional royal offerings of the bread and wine for the Communion, of a golden altarcloth, and of a wedge of solid gold, 'being a pound's weight': and, kneeling down, she was at last joined by her husband for the Communion prayers and the taking of the sanctified bread and wine – during which private devotions the television cameras, as at the Anointment, were again turned aside. And finally she resumed the crown and sceptres, returned to the throne, and sat motionless through the singing of the 'Gloria' and the 'Te Deum' – the great celebratory hymn heard at every coronation since Anglo-Saxon times.

This completed the service, and the Queen thereafter moved in state to the privacy of St Edward's Chapel: there to take off the weighty crown, and to exchange the golden consecration vestments for an immense cloak of gold-embroidered and ermine-trimmed royal purple – a colour traditionally worn only after the crowning – so long that no less than six ladies-in-waiting were needed as train-bearers. Then, wearing now the diamond-studded Imperial State Crown and bearing the Orb and the Sceptre with the Cross, she re-appeared to the sound of the national anthem, and processed through the Abbey into the annexe – outside which the great Coronation parade was preparing to set out for Buckingham Palace.

The head of this parade had already travelled nearly two miles before the Queen – assuming the position of honour at its end – finally left the Abbey in the golden state coach, hauled by four pairs of matched Windsor Greys. Taking more than forty-five minutes to pass any given point, it was composed of some 13,000 troops – including contingents from the then still relatively far-flung British Empire – twenty-nine bands, and twenty-seven horse-drawn coaches and carriages: among the best-remembered being that of the mountainous Queen Salote of Tonga, who greatly endeared herself to the crowds by refusing to raise its hood against the driving rain, and smiling broadly if wetly throughout.

For the lover of customs, however, neither all this pomp, nor the fly-past, nor even the Queen's repeated appearances on Buckingham Palace balcony (which ended only at midnight) could compensate for the loss of the traditional coronation banquet. This disappeared at the notoriously stingy 'penny Coronation' in 1831 of William IV – the 'Sailor King' who hated court etiquette as much as he loathed extravagance, and who eventually consented to be crowned only on condition that every expense was spared – and it has never since been revived. With it vanished the performance of a whole range of ancient feudal services and quit rents, by which the lords of many manors had long held their lands. At the last coronation banquet in 1821, for instance, the Lord of the Isle of Man presented George IV with a pair of falcons; the squire of Nether Bilsington in Kent produced three maple cups, which were then handed to the Mayor of Oxford as a reward for serving the King with a bowl of wine; and the owner of 'half the manor' of Heydon in Essex performed his traditional duty of holding a towel when the sovereign washed his hands before dinner.

Perhaps the strangest service, however, was performed by the manor lord of Addington in Surrey, once held by William the Conqueror's cook: for he had to make and serve 'the mess called "dilligrout" or, if fat be added, "malpigernout"', apparently a kind of gruel. While easily the most impressive was that of the lords of Scrivelsby in Lincolnshire, who have acted as 'King's Champion' since at least the 13th century. This officer's task, performed by members of the Dymoke family since the Coronation of Richard II, was to ride fully armoured into the banqueting hall, thrice challenge anyone who disputed the royal title to instant battle, and three times cast down his gauntlet. If none took up gauntlet or challenge (and, not surprisingly, none ever apparently did) the Champion was sent a gold cup of wine, drank the King's health with it, and then rode off with it as his fee. Though his service could no longer be performed, the current Champion was granted the right to bear the Union Standard at the 1953 Coronation: at which the now-redundant 'barons' of the CINQUE PORTS were also found places. Thus was custom and tradition preserved, in this richest and least changed of all British ceremonies; whose complex structure weaves together traces of all the various elements – Roman, Saxon, Christian, Feudal, Reformation and Constitutional – which make up the history of the nation; and which has outlasted all its European rivals to remain the envy of the world.

· Cotswold Olympick Games ·
Chipping Campden, Gloucestershire:
Friday and Saturday after Spring Bank Holiday

Founded in about 1604 by a wealthy attorney named 'Captain' Robert Dover, these renowned country sports were originally held throughout WHITSUN week in the open country around Dover's Hill near Chipping Campden. As a gesture of defiance against Puritan attempts to ban 'sinful games', they enjoyed from the first the enthusiastic support of courtiers like Endymion Porter – who suggested their 'Olympick' title and obtained the suit of King James I's clothes which Dover wore to direct them: while country gentry and village champions alike flocked to compete for handsome money prizes and the Captain's coveted yellow rosettes. Wrestling, leap-frog, hammer throwing, hare coursing and horse races figured prominently among their attractions, but they were most famous for cudgel fights and shin-kicking contests – whose exponents wore iron-tipped boots, and frequently limped for the rest of their lives.

Suspended during the Civil War years following Dover's death in 1641, they were revived under Charles II, and their fame – or notoriety – spread far and wide during the early 19th century – when 'the scum and refuse of the nearest factory towns' bivouacked in thousands around Campden, and 'armed bands of Birmingham yahoos swilled unlimited beer from unlimited booths'. In 1852, therefore, the games were prohibited by Act of Parliament: but in recent decades a determinedly more genteel version has once again been organized. The Friday games now include motor-cycle displays and Scottish dancing as well as tugs-of-war and greasy-pole competions, and end with a torchlight

Engraving from an early 17th-century pamphlet promoting the **Cotswold Olympick Games.**

'arrayed in arms' for inspection by the King's Commissioners of Array, who during times of crisis would conscript the best men for service in the royal army. When Lichfield received its Charter in 1553, its High Constables and bailiffs gained the right to supervise their own inspections: and the city's pride in this privilege has perpetuated the local Court of Array for many centuries after the legal requirement to hold it ceased under Charles I.

The ST GEORGE'S DAY Court Leet, therefore, still elects two 'Dozeners' – or local inspectors of weapons and armour – for every ward of the city: and when the Court of Array convenes at the Guildhall these present formal reports to the High Constable, who reports in turn to the Lord of the Manor, alias the Mayor of Lichfield. The whole court then joins the 'Bower Day' procession to Greenhill, where ancient suits of armour – survivors of the city's own statutory contribution to its defence force – are displayed and inspected.

The Greenhill mound, allegedly the site of a pagan temple, was also the traditional scene of the Whitsun 'Bower' celebration; so called, presumably, because bowers of branches and greenery were built to cover its stalls and booths. The beginnings of this festival are lost in the mists of antiquity, though some declare it to date from the 7th century and others from pre-Christian times: during the Middle Ages, however, it was certainly marked by a procession of city GUILDS with flowery garlands, and it still continues as a carnival parade and pleasure fair, followed by a huge sports meeting in Beacon Park.

procession from Dover's Hill to Campden: while the highlight of 'Scuttlebrook Wake', held on the following day, is a fancy-dress parade and procession of decorated floats. Robert Dover may well be turning in his grave.

· Court of Array and Greenhill Bower ·
Lichfield, Staffordshire: Spring Bank Holiday Monday

The city of Lichfield, proudly tenacious of its ancient ceremonies (*see also* BEATING THE BOUNDS and COURTS LEET) has for many centuries celebrated two of them on the same day – formerly WHITSUN MONDAY, and now Spring Bank Holiday Monday. Originally, however, the two customs were unconnected. The first, the Court of Array, is the sole surviving relic of the medieval English system of raising 'territorial' forces, as laid down by the Assize of Arms (1176) and the Statute of Winchester (1285). These bound every free man between fourteen and sixty to provide himself with weapons and armour proper to his station in life – ranging from the costly panoply and warhorse of a knight to the simple bow and arrows of a poor peasant: and, on demand, to appear

· Courts Leet and Baron ·

Still obstinately continuing to operate in a very few places, these ancient manorial courts are among the oldest legal and local government bodies in Britain. Their origins date from the period of the Norman Conquest, when most of England was divided up into manors, each with its own lord and its own particular MANORIAL CUSTOMS – which might differ greatly from those of the neighbouring manors and which constituted, in effect, a separate system of bye-laws for each estate. Every manor therefore held its fortnightly 'court baron', presided over by the lord or his steward and compulsorily attended by all free tenants. Applying the rules of local custom, this dealt with such matters as the management of COMMON LAND; the inheritance of smallholdings; the cleansing of drainage dykes; and the control of straying beasts: and also settled disputes between landlord and tenant or between villager and villager.

In a number of manors, too, the lord also claimed the right of jurisdiction over petty criminal cases – exercised elsewhere by the King's sheriff – and the 'view' or supervision of the policing system called 'frankpledge', whereby every free man had to be a member of a 'tithing' of ten or a dozen people, who were collectively responsible for each others' good conduct. This local 'police-court' business was transacted by an annual or bi-annual 'court leet' – from the old French *eslite* (elected) – probably so called because it also elected a jury and chose the manorial officials: among these were the bailiff, the constable, the pindar or hayward who dealt with grazing animals, and sometimes the ale-tasters and bread-weighers who maintained quality control over the basic forms of nourishment.

With the decline of feudalism and the growth of a unified national legal system, the powers of such courts were progressively eroded: and though survivors still bear the proud title of 'Court Leet, Court Baron and View of Frankpledge', these institutions merged in practice into a single manorial court. As the enclosures of the 18th and 19th centuries destroyed the ancient forms of land holding and common grazing, moreover, many local courts disappeared altogether, and law reforms in 1867 and 1925 reduced their number still further, until by the mid-1970s only about thirty-five remained active. Then, in 1977, a quite unnecessary piece of 'tidying-up' legislation removed all legal jurisdiction even from these, thereby robbing them of the power to enforce their enactments. But ancient tradition was not to be so easily or arbitrarily overturned, and the survivors not only continue to sit but also (in many cases) to levy small fines – which, if no longer directly enforceable by law, are still paid according to custom.

The one exception made by the 1977 legislation, and thus the only remaining manorial court with 'official' legal powers, is the court leet of Laxton in Nottinghamshire. This owes its special position to the fact that the land around the village is (uniquely) still farmed by the medieval 'open-field system', whereby tenanted strips of arable alternate with unfenced sections of commonly held meadow grassland. Towards the end of every November, therefore, a jury elected by the court tours the open fields, carefully inspecting the drainage dykes and the boundaries between cornland and common strips. Blockages in the former and encroachments on the latter are recorded on a 'presentment paper', and when the full leet assembles in early December the perpetrators are fined small amounts, as are any of the Laxton tenants who fail to attend, thereby 'forfeiting their ensoig' of twopence a head. These financial 'pains' are then divided in two, half going to the Lord of the Manor – in this case the Ministry of Agriculture – and half towards the refreshment of next year's 'field jury', whom the court now elects and swears in.

Similar customs – the taking of 'presentments', the nominal fining of offenders, and the election of officials, at meetings frequently held in pubs – are followed in some form by most other surviving courts leet: but the scope of their activities varies widely, as does the energy with which these are carried out. Among the most active and flourishing are those in upland areas, which perform the vital function of managing vast tracts of common sheep-grazing, shared unequally between a number of right holders. At Danby in the north-east Yorkshire moorlands, for instance, the leet jury meets once a month, and makes a thorough inspection of the 11,000-acre manor every October, fining on the spot those found guilty of dumping rubbish or of exceeding the number of sheep their grazing right allows. These fines are then retrospectively confirmed by the full court meeting in the hall of Danby Castle – where an ancient muniment chest, its six keys distributed between five local families and the clerk of the court, safeguards the leet records. Courts with similar duties also survive in the neighbouring moorland manors of Whitby Laithes, Spaunton – whose leet takes part in BEATING THE BOUNDS, involving a thirty-mile walk, when a new lord succeeds; and Fyling – whose bailiff blows the horn after the planting of the PENNY HEDGE. And they operate too in the upland manors of Bowes, County Durham; Mickley, Northumberland; and Spitchwick, on the borders of Dartmoor in Devon: while the commons of the Preseli Hills in northern Pembrokeshire are managed by the courts leet of the Barony of Cemaes and the manor of Mynachlogddu.

Common land (though generally much smaller in area) also preoccupies a handful of continuing courts leet in rural lowland England – those of the manors of Bucklebury near Newbury in Berkshire; Croyland in Lincolnshire; Dorney-with-Boveney in Buckinghamshire; Dunstone near Plymouth in Devon; East Horndon in Essex; Eton-cum-Stockdales near Coleorton in Leicestershire; and of the Island and Royal Manor of Portland in Dorset, which meets every November and perambulates its bounds every seven years: as well as those of a few ancient Wessex towns with commons of their own. Probably the best-known of these town leets – because of its HOCKTIDE celebrations – is that of Hungerford in Berkshire, but courts also exist at Cricklade in Wiltshire; Stockbridge in Hampshire – which still has nominally separate courts leet and baron, whose members graze their cattle on the Borough Marsh; and Wareham in Dorset, where the court also cares for the town's Anglo-Saxon ramparts.

The principal 'business' of the Wareham leet, however, is the regulation of the borough's pubs and hotels. Accompanied by their ale-tasters, bread-weighers and chimney-sweeps, the manor officers tour these during a week in November and, much to the enjoyment of all, invariably declare the beer to be watered, the bread too heavy (usually because it is stuffed with a bottle of gin) and the chimneys too dirty. The ale-tasters of Ashburton in Devon, conversely, reward sellers of 'satisfactory' beer with a sprig of evergreen for their pub door. This ceremony takes place in July, when two loaves of bread from each baker's shop are also tested: while the Ashburton leet itself assembles on the fourth Tuesday in November at St Lawrence's Chapel (where it has met for more than six centuries) to hear its grand jury report on matters of local interest. Alcester in Warwickshire, whose court dates from 1276, likewise has active ale-tasters, who operate throughout June: but the ale-tasters of the Warwick and Henley-in-Arden leets, in the same county, are now purely honorary, as are their butter-weighers, fish and flesh-tasters, and 'brook-lookers'. At Clifton, near York, however, the 'byelaw-men' and leet jury still conduct a serious inspection of the manor's watercourses on the second Wednesday in October, whereafter the court's 'affeerors' levy fines on landowners who have allowed these to become obstructed.

The court leet of Bromsgrove in Worcestershire, which meets on the Saturday nearest MIDSUMMER DAY after a procession through the streets, has the ceremonial duty of proclaiming the ancient Midsummer Fair: which it performs by 'declaring' the town's charter of 1199, and reading out the Assize of Bread, Ale and Leather. While that of Lichfield in Staffordshire, held on ST GEORGE'S DAY (23 April) now has few real duties at all, though absentees still need to produce a convincing (or amusing) excuse to avoid the 'groat' non-attendance fine. But both the manor court of Bideford in Devon (which was instituted in 1880, when the corporation took over the manor lordship, and which meets on the Saturday after Easter) and the far older leet of Southampton (held on the Tuesday after MICHAELMAS) continue to perform one of the most important functions of the original courts: for they provide an opportunity to discuss and settle the grievances and complaints of local people. (*See* FOREST CUSTOMS)

· Cow Head Wakes ·
Westhoughton, near Wigan, Lancashire: weekend nearest 24 August

Westhoughton Cow Head Wakes – or, in local parlance 'Howfen Keaw Yed Wakes' – were once famous throughout industrial Lancashire: but only one pub (the Victoria in Market Street) now displays in its bar the symbol of the custom – a real or stuffed cow's head poking through a gate, with a saw poised ready to cut it off. This illustrates the 'Howfen legend', which tells how:

> Long years ago a cow got its head
> Fast in a gate, like this, it is said
> And the Farmer, who in a bit of a doubt
> Sawed off its head to get it out.

Up to the Second World War, most Westhoughton pubs sported similar 'exhibits': and for at least a century and a half cows and cows' heads played a prominent part in the celebration of the town's annual 'Wakes' or holiday weekend. Until late-Victorian times, heads or skulls used to be carried about on poles by rival 'Bone Clubs' – who frequently fought for possession of each other's trophies – and afterwards the 'head-meat' was either made into broth and distributed to the poor, or baked into pasties decorated with the cow and gate symbol, such as are still served with 'mushy peas' at the

Victoria. Sometimes, too, bullocks or cows were roasted whole in the streets, and the entire head was cooked in pastry as a huge 'keaw yed pie'. Westhoughton people, therefore, were insultingly called 'cow heads' by the folk of the surrounding communities, who may also have concocted the tale about the gate as a hit at the alleged stupidity of the township's farmers: but the Westhoughtonians turned the insult into a proud title, and – as with the 'Puppy-dog pies' story at Painswick (*see* CLIPPING THE CHURCH) – adopted the legend as their own.

Why Westhoughton first chose cows' heads as the dish for its FEASTS – the equivalent of Eccles' cakes or Avening's PIG FACES – nevertheless remains uncertain. But some hold that the custom began in 1815, when crowds carried off the head of a cow roasted to celebrate the Battle of Waterloo: while the earnest researchers who investigated the Wakes for 'Mass Observation' in 1938 – steeped as they were in Freud and fashionable anthropology – thought it a clear case of 'totemism', wherein Westhoughtonians killed and ate their sacred 'totem' animal. Perhaps a more plausible explanation, however, is that the custom was originally connected with St Bartholomew, to whom Westhoughton's parish church is dedicated and in honour of whose name-day (24 August) the town's festival was initiated during the Middle Ages. For since the saint was traditionally martyred by being flayed (or skinned) alive, he is also the patron saint of butchers: and the eating of severed cows' heads would thus be an appropiate manner of celebrating his feast.

· Crabapple Fair ·
Egremont, near Whitehaven, Cumbria: Saturday nearest 18 October

Held continuously (except during the two world wars) since it was established by charter in 1267, Egremont's Crabapple FAIRS are famous for a number of traditional customs: the one from which it takes its name being the distribution of free apples, from a lorry which tours the village soon after noon. In recent years ordinary eating apples have been thrown to the crowd, but formerly wild crabs were distributed: and since these are still particularly hard, sharp-tasting and generally unpalatable in October, they were more often employed as ammunition in a free-for-all apple fight than eaten.

The fair begins at dawn, when a thirty-foot-high 'greasy pole', well smeared with fat and soap, is erected in the main street. The prize for scaling it – which can rarely be achieved except by the combined efforts of a 'human ladder' – used to be the half sheep's carcase at the top, but current climbers make do with the pound note now fastened there. Children's sports, and a scramble for coppers, take place in the morning, and two long-established men's street races in the afternoon, together with WRESTLING (Cumberland-style), terrier racing and hound trails. The most unusual events,

A champion 'gurner' at Egremont's **Crabapple Fair**.

however, are reserved for the fair evening. These include a pipe-smoking match – the winner being the smoker who can keep his pipe burning longest without relighting it – contests for the best 'sentimental' and the best hunting song and, the main attraction, the 'World Champion Gurning Competition'. This features the ancient sport of 'gurning through a braffin' – or making the most grotesque possible face through a horse-collar – of which Egremont claims to provide the last surviving exhibition. Quite amazing facial distortions are achieved by top-class gurners (who can, for instance, readily cover the end of their nose with their lower lip) and those with few or removable teeth appear to have a distinct advantage.

· Cradle Rocking ·
see CANDLEMAS

· Cream of the Well ·
see NEW YEAR

· Cromwell's Day ·
see COMMEMORATIONS

· Cross Quarter Days ·
see QUARTER DAYS

· Cup Final ·
Wembley Stadium, London: usually a Saturday in early May

The Football Association's Challenge Cup competition, known colloquially as 'The Cup', annually commands more public attention than any other sporting event. Its immense appeal is partly due to the fact that it is a 'knockout' competition: one which offers the smaller, less fashionable clubs a chance to take on some of the most powerful teams. In fact, teams from the lower echelons of the Football League, (and even from outside the league) have a good record of eliminating top clubs in the early rounds.

The competition was instituted in 1871 and the first final, held at Kennington Oval in April of the following year, was won by the Wanderers who beat the Royal Engineers 1-0. The crowd was estimated to be a little more than 2,000. In those days the players were all amateurs and only one early club, Crystal Palace, bore a name that was to become established in the league. In 1895, the Cup Final was transferred to Crystal Palace, but professionalism had caused something of a revolution in the sport; and the northern teams, following a trail blazed by Blackburn Rovers, seemed to hold a monopoly on the Cup. Northern rule was interrupted, but not ended, by Tottenham Hotspur in 1901, and it was not until 1927 that there was an all-southern final. On that occasion, Cardiff City beat Arsenal 1-0.

The Cup competition was more than an annual excuse for frenzied partizanship. It brought a number of benefits to the whole game, including neutral referees and firm rules on free kicks and penalties. It was also responsible for the length of a match being fixed at ninety minutes. The Cup Final reached its present home, Wembley Stadium, in 1923. Bolton Wanderers beat Huddersfield Town in front of 125,000 spectators. The official programme claimed that Wembley was 'incontestably the finest sports ground in the world ... the largest in the world, the most comfortable, the best equipped. . . . In area it equals the Biblical City, Jericho.' The comparison with Jericho may perhaps have been a little unfortunate. For at that first Wembley final some 200,000 prospective spectators attempted to get inside the massive walls of the stadium, and the chaotic crowd scenes outside were certainly of biblical proportions.

Today, accommodation at Wembley is limited to 100,000 – most of whom can watch the match in reasonable comfort. Tickets are always very difficult to get and are sold out long before the day of the Cup Final. A great sense of occasion is built up for several hours before the match with the help of military bands and the firmly established tradition of community singing. The event is usually held in early May and, unusually for football, is often graced by warm spring sunshine.

· Cussing Day ·
see ASH WEDNESDAY

Still steaming, the mighty **Denby Dale Pie** of 1928 is carefully unloaded from its lorry.

D

· Dean, Forest of ·

see BREAD AND CHEESE THROWING; FOREST CUSTOMS

· Deathbed Customs ·

see FUNERALS

· Denby Dale Pie ·
Denby Dale, West Yorkshire

Outside the 'Pie Hall', in the West Yorkshire Pennine town of Denby Dale, stands a great steel dish, eighteen feet long by six feet wide and eighteen inches deep: which awaits the making of the next Denby Dale Pie. The last, baked in 1964 to commemorate four royal births in one year, contained three tons of beef, one and a half tons of potatoes, and over half a ton of gravy and seasoning: some 30,000 people tasted a portion, and the proceeds paid for the construction of the Pie Hall community centre. It was, moreover, the eighth gargantuan pie manufactured here. The first, made in 1788, celebrated King George III's recovery from 'his terrible mental affliction'; the second marked the victory of Waterloo; and the third – which needed thirteen horses to pull it through the town – gave thanks for the repeal of the Corn Laws in 1846. The most notorious, however, was the Great Jubilee Pie of 1887: which, when opened, 'emitted such an intolerable stench that a number of persons were injured in the stampede to escape'. When the smell died down, it was hurriedly buried in quicklime, and shortly afterwards a more successful 'Resurrection Pie' was baked as a substitute.

· The Derby ·
Epsom Downs, Surrey: first Wednesday in June

The bare facts about the Derby – that it is a race for three-year-old colts and fillies, run at Epsom over one mile and four furlongs – do little to explain why it is one of the world's most famous annual events. For beyond this simple explanation the Derby is quite unique: a searching test of the thoroughbred racehorse, a great social occasion for Londoners and a commemoration of a man who did much to set the pattern of modern racing.

Until the late 18th century, most horse races had consisted of several heats, with the winners slogging it out in a deciding race on the same day. These events were often very gruelling, and a final of six miles following a heat of four miles could never be a test of quality rather than raw stamina. Sir Charles Bunbury and the Earl of Derby, both leading figures in the early days of the Jockey Club, set out to reform the system of racing by instituting contests that were designed to test the best of the breed. These were to become the most important of the events now called the 'classics'. In 1779, a race for three-year-old fillies was run at Epsom Downs. Named 'The Oaks', after Lord Derby's house, this race preceded the Derby by one year. The first Derby was run over one mile, and was not extended to one-and-a-half miles until 1784.

It is always said that the naming of the race, whether it should be the 'Bunbury' or the 'Derby', depended upon the tossing of a coin. If this was so, justice was well distributed, because the first winner was Diomed – owned by Sir Charles Bunbury.

The Derby's other great claim to fame – as the 'Greatest Free Show on Earth' – is due to the fact that some three-quarters of a million people can crowd onto Epsom Downs to witness the event, all without paying a penny of admission money. In Victorian and Edwardian times, Derby Day was an unofficial holiday, and the *Illustrated London News* was moved to describe Epsom Downs on race day as 'the most astonishing, the most varied, the most picturesque and the most glorious spectacle that ever was, or ever can be, under any circumstances, visible to mortal eyes'. Even allowing for the deep-purple hue of Victorian prose, it has to be admitted that the first Wednesday in June on Epsom Downs presents an impressive sight. The great mass of people, the traditional fair and the gathering of open-topped omnibuses almost overwhelm the race. But to the bloodstock industry the event is of paramount

The attractions of **Derby** day at the height of its Victorian popularity, painted by William Powell Frith, 1858.

importance. The winner of the Derby rarely fails to win other top-class races, and his value as a stallion is somewhere between ten and twenty million pounds.

· Dicing for Bibles ·
All Saints' church, St Ives, Cambridgeshire: Whit Tuesday

Making his will in August 1678, Dr Robert Wilde left £50 to be invested in land, whose rent was to pay for the annual purchase of six bibles. On WHITSUN TUESDAY (then the date of the great St Ives cattle FAIRS) these were to be contested for by 'six males and six females such as are of good report, all born in the parish, each above the age of twelve years ... and able to read the Bible': and in order to decide the competition, every candidate was to 'throw three dice in a sawcer' on the altar of All Saints' church. Supported by the rent of 'Bible Orchard', the custom survived unchanged until 1880, when a disapproving Bishop ordered the transfer of the dicing to a table in the church aisle: and there (after a period of removal to the nearby school) it still takes place, the participants now being six Church of England and six Nonconformist schoolchildren.

If the juxtaposition of dicing and bibles appears eccentric, it accords well with the contradictory character of the charity's founder. For Dr Wilde, though a Puritan minister by calling, was also a popular Restoration poet, famous for his witty satires and 'licentious' comedies: and though this 'fat jolly man' was ejected from office and persecuted for his obdurate Nonconformity, he always remained the most ardent of Royalists.

The vicar of St Ives, Huntingdonshire, oversees the curious custom of **Dicing for Bibles.**

Above: **Doggett's Coat and Badge Race** nears its finish at Chelsea: mid-19th-century wash and ink drawing by Thomas Rowlandson. *Left:* Past winners of the race wearing their prize livery coats and silver Hanoverian badges: seen in 1952 with the megaphoned Bargemaster of the Fishmongers' Guild.

· Doggett's Coat and Badge Race ·
London Bridge to Cadogan Pier, Chelsea: normally in July

This famous Thames sculling race has been held for more than two-and-a-half centuries, and claims to be the oldest continuously contested boat race in the world – for though it was suspended during the two world wars, the 1915-19 competitions were rowed consecutively in 1920, and those of 1940-46 in 1947. It was founded in 1715 by Thomas Doggett, an Irish-born actor-manager who was 'a staunch Revolution Whig' and supporter of the newly established House of Hanover. His inspiration, it is said, was the courage of a young oarsman who rowed him home to Chelsea on an exceptionally stormy night: and his purpose was certainly to celebrate the anniversary of George I's accession, and thus to cock a snook at the then-impending threat of Jacobite rebellion. So the race was to be contested, on 1 August, by six Thames watermen 'just out of their apprenticeship', who were to row against the tide from London Bridge to Chelsea: and the prize was a coat in the orange livery colour of the Whigs, together with a silver 'Badge representing Liberty' – pointedly symbolized by the running horse emblem of Hanover.

In order that his race 'be continued annually on the same day for ever', Doggett bequeathed money to the London Fishmongers' Company, who still organize it.

Over the years, however, a few changes have necessarily taken place. Tidal conditions on the Thames vary considerably, so that the contest cannot often be held precisely on 1 August, and must be transferred to the nearest suitable date – generally in late July: light racing craft, moreover, have replaced the cumbersome passenger 'wherries' of Doggett's time, and these are now rowed *with* instead of *against* the tide. Even so, the race remains an exceedingly testing one, for it still covers the original distance of over four-and-a-half miles, and involves negotiating no less than ten bridges, few of which existed in 1715. And since far more entrants apply than the number prescribed by Doggett, the six final contestants – formerly selected by haphazard lot-drawing – must first have qualified via a series of gruelling heats.

Doggett's Coat (nowadays made in scarlet rather than orange, but still retaining its long-skirted 18th-century cut) and great silver Badge are, therefore, 'the marks of a really top-class rough water oarsman'. Many of their winners, indeed, are invited to join the élite ranks (only twenty-two strong) of the Royal Watermen: or to wear their coveted trophies at QUIT RENT CEREMONIES and other ROYAL and CIVIC occasions.

· Dr Johnson's Birthday ·
see COMMEMORATIONS

· Dowry Customs ·
see MAID'S MONEY; MARRIAGE PORTION CHARITIES

· Drunkenness Sermon ·
see SERMONS

· Duelling Sermon ·
see SERMONS

· Dunmow Flitch ·
Great Dunmow, Essex: held every leap year (e.g. 1984, 1988) in June

The famous 'custom of Dunmow', whereby a 'flitch' (or side) of bacon is presented to married couples who can prove that they have never repented of their union during a period of at least a year and a day after the wedding, was already well-known by the late 14th century. For Chaucer's Wife of Bath, boasting of the hard times she had given her five husbands, declared that:

> The bacon was not fetched for them, I trow
> That some men have in Essex at Dunmow

and Langland's 'Piers Plowman', a decade or two earlier, remarked that couples who lived in 'Jealousy joyless, and jangling in bed' would never get 'the flicche of Donemowe' unless they forswore themselves. According to tradition, the custom dates from the early

1200s, when Robert FitzWalter made the bacon presentation a condition of a grant of land to Little Dunmow Priory: and certainly the priory records – which show that either a flitch or a smaller 'gammon' was won in 1445, 1467 and 1510 – indicate that it was always given 'according to the form of the charter of donation'.

This laid down that 'the party or pilgrim for bacon was to take his oath before prior and convent and the whole town, humbly kneeling in the churchyard upon two hard pointed stones ... and his oath was administered with such long process, and such solemn singing over him, that doubtless must make his pilgrimage painfull. After, he was taken up upon men's shoulders, and carried first about the priory churchyard and after through the town, with all the friars and brethren and all the townsfolk young and old following him with shouts and acclamations, with his bacon borne before him, and in such manner was sent home with his bacon.'

The reason why the duty of flitch-giving was originally laid on the priory, however, is a mystery – unless perhaps the first donor intended thus to commemorate his own happy marriage. For the link between bacon and successful unions seems once to have been well understood, and in places as far apart as Vienna and Brittany contented husbands could claim similar prizes. The medieval lord of Wychnor in Staffordshire, moreover, also held his manor by the QUIT RENT of presenting

Mr and Mrs Samuels, proud and nattily dressed winners of a **'Dunmow Flitch'** presented at Ilford, Essex, in 1922.

flitches, not only to loving couples, but also to priests who had passed a year and a day without once regretting their profession: though the custom there apparently began only in the mid-14th century, and may thus have been simply an imitation of the Dunmow observance.

Whyever it originated, the Dunmow Flitch custom came to a temporary halt with the dissolution of Little Dunmow Priory at the Reformation, and by 1640 it was regarded as a thing of the past. But in 1701 it was revived in something like the old form by the priory's lay successor as Lord of the Manor, whose COURTS LEET AND BARON rewarded William and Jane Barley of Great Easton with a gammon for 'their quiet, peaceable and loving cohabitation during the space of three years'. Apparently for the first time, however, a jury of spinsters – four daughters of the squire and one of the steward – were called in to judge the couple: and the form of oath taken while kneeling on the 'hard pointed stones' also has a suspiciously 18th-century ring:

> You shall swear by custom of confession
> If ever you made nuptial transgression
> Be you either married man or wife
> If you have brawls or contentious strife;
> Or otherwise at bed or board
> Offended each other in deed or word:
> Or since the parish clerk said Amen
> You wished yourself unmarried again;
> Or in a twelvemonth and a day
> Repented not in thought any way;
> But continued true in thought and desire
> As when you joined hands in the quire:
> If to these conditions without all fear
> Of your own accord you will freely swear
> A whole gammon of bacon you shall receive
> And bear it hence with love and good leave:
> For this is our custom at Dunmow well known
> Though the pleasure be ours, the bacon's your own.

It was perhaps now, too, that the practice of carrying the triumphant couple in the 'Flitch Chair' first began: for this double seat – which is still to be seen in Little Dunmow church – is made up of pieces of 13th-century choir stalls, most probably taken from the section of the priory demolished after the Reformation.

The flitch – or rather the gammon, which doubtless conveyed the innuendo that any claims to married contentment must necessarily be 'all gammon', or nonsense – was again presented in 1751, when a jury of six bachelors and six spinsters awarded it to Thomas and Ann Shakeshaft of Wethersfield, and a 'tremendous concourse' of people turned out to chair them round the village. So large and riotous were the crowds, however, that subsequent squires of Little Dunmow resolutely declined to allow the custom to be repeated – though tradition has it that the flitch was offered to Queen Victoria, but politely refused, after the first year of her marriage to Prince Albert – and by 1768 the 'hard pointed stones' had disappeared from the churchyard.

The second 'revival' of the custom, therefore, began at Great rather than Little Dunmow in 1885, largely due to the efforts of the historical novelist William Harrison Ainsworth: and since then observances have taken place at more or less regular intervals, prompting imitations both in other parts of Britain and in the USA. The modern 'Flitch Trial', moreover, differs considerably from its original: for it takes the form of a mock court, with a 'judge', a 'counsel for the bacon' and another for the claimants, and witnesses as well as a jury. But the hilarity surrounding the proceedings – and the nature of the accompanying jokes – have probably changed little since Chaucer's time: and the most convincing claimants to married bliss still receive a flitch, while another is divided up between any other couples brave enough to 'stand trial'.

· Dunting the Freeholder ·
see BEATING THE BOUNDS

· Durham Miners' Gala ·
Durham: second Saturday in July

Commonly known as 'the Big Meeting', the great annual gathering of County Durham miners in Durham city began in 1871 as a demonstration of solidarity and of support for the newly formed county union: and by the 1920s it had developed into the biggest trade-union celebration in Europe, with nearly a quarter of a million pitmen and their families attending. Each local lodge (or branch) of the Durham union marches from the outskirts of the city behind its own colliery band and its own massive fringed banner – which is supported between two poles, stayed against the wind with ropes, and beautifully painted with scenes from union history, portraits of pitmens' heroes, or sometimes with pictures of the miners' welfare homes provided from the branch funds. Should any of those who marched behind it in the previous year have died, however, or any disaster occurred at the pit, the banner is customarily draped with black ribbons.

When the procession reaches Durham's old racecourse by the river Wear, the crowds are addressed by national miners' leaders and prominent Labour politicians – Jimmy Maxton, Wee Ellen Wilkinson and Aneurin Bevan being well-remembered speakers – before dispersing to enjoy the Gala fun-fair. And towards the end of the afternoon the procession reforms, the younger branch members dancing arm in arm beneath the banners as they return through the streets. But though the Gala is still both an important political occasion and a kind of immense community party – for which Durham pitmen who have moved to other mining areas frequently return – the great days of the Big Meeting are over. For pit closures have struck the Durham coalfield particularly hard, and where once over 300 bands and banners paraded through the streets, scarcely a score do so now.

The splendid trades union banner of Hylton lodge – depicting Hylton Castle – in the **Durham Miners' Gala** procession.

E

· Easter ·

This greatest of all Christian festivals celebrates the Resurrection of Christ from the dead, which occurred during the Jewish spring feast of Passover or *Pesach* – hence its Latin, Scots and Welsh names, respectively *Pascha*, *Pasch* or *Pesse*, and *Pasg*. Because the date of Passover is variable, being dependent on the phases of the moon, Easter is thus also a movable feast. Long and bitter were the disputes about the proper way to calculate its date – indeed, this was the principal point at issue between the Celtic churches of Ireland, Scotland and Wales and the Latin church established in England – but eventually the Roman view triumphed in Western Europe: and Easter is now celebrated (in the words of the *Book of Common Prayer*) on 'the first Sunday after the full moon which happens on or next following the twenty-first of March the Spring Equinox: and if the full moon happens upon a Sunday, Easter-day is the Sunday following'. In short, it may fall on any of the thirty-five days between 22 March and 25 April: and its varying date decides those of many other great Christian celebrations throughout the year, notably SHROVE TUES-

DAY; LENT; GOOD FRIDAY; ASCENSION DAY; and WHIT-SUN.

Whenever it is celebrated, this 'Queen of Festivals' is a 'holy day of obligation', when all Roman Catholic and Anglican Christians are obliged to attend church and receive Communion. Joyous peals of BELLS are rung, and churches everywhere are lavishly decorated. A few still keep up the old tradition of using evergreens – symbolic of eternal life – and biblical texts embroidered in red on white, or woven in straw: but most now prefer displays of flowers in the spring colours of green, yellow and white, focussed on the 'Easter lilies' decking the altar. In many places, too, 'Easter gardens' depict the cross and empty tomb amid a setting of flowers, mosses and pebbles:and the seasonal theme of Resurrection is increasingly being echoed by the floral decoration of family graves – a custom which seems to have spread (*see* PALM SUNDAY) from Wales. By long tradition, moreover, it is almost obligatory (or at least lucky) for churchgoers to wear some bright new piece of clothing – an Easter bonnet, if not a complete new outfit – on this great day: a practice which may have its origins in the new garments worn at baptism – for which Easter was once the customary time – and which is certainly the basis for the modern, secular Easter Parade.

Celebrations of spring renewal, of course, long pre-date Christianity: and according to the 8th-century historian, Bede, the English name for Easter itself derives from a pagan festival of the goddess Eostra, an

Above: Victims of **Easter** 'lifting' or 'heaving' were not always as enthusiastic as this gentleman in Hone's *Every-Day Book* of 1826. *Right:* 'Egg-shackling' at Shepton Beauchamp, Somerset. Each egg is marked with a child's name, and the one which survives uncracked longest in the shaken sieve is the winner.

obscure spring and dawn deity whose name is cognate with the East, (Germanic *Ost*) where the sun rises. Several of the folk customs popular at Easter, indeed, may have been essentially pagan in origin, though long since provided with a Christian gloss. One such was the practice of ascending some high hill before dawn on Easter Sunday, in order to see the rising sun dancing 'for joy at Christ's Resurrection': this survived longest in northern and western England and Wales, and has recently been revived in a few places there (for instance, at Bishop's Castle, Shropshire) usually in connection with a short religious service. More boisterous, but also connected (at least in theory) with the 'raising' of Christ from the dead, was the custom of 'lifting' or 'heaving' persons of the opposite sex high into the air three times – with or without the aid of a chair: the victim was then forcibly kissed by all present, and only released on paying a 'reward'. This apparently dated from at least the 13th century (when Edward I was 'heaved' by court ladies) but by early-Victorian times was confined to the north-western English and Welsh border counties, where women heaved men on Easter Monday, and men the women on Easter Tuesday, or vice versa (*see also* HOCKTIDE): but by then this 'rude, undecent and dangerous diversion' – particularly offensive to visiting clergymen and other unsuspecting outsiders seized by the lifting gangs – was 'practised chiefly by the lower orders', and by the 1890s it had virtually disappeared.

Many other traditional Easter customs and ceremonies, however, still survive – notably STREET BALL GAMES, MORRIS DANCING and CHARITIES distributions: as do various purely local observations like the BOTTLE KICKING AND HARE PIE SCRAMBLE. (This last is sometimes connected with the 'Easter hare', an animal dubiously alleged to have been sacred to Eostra, but more certainly the ancestor of the 'Easter bunnies' which have latterly spearheaded efforts to secularize an essentially religious festival.) Coming as it did after the long LENT fast, Easter was also a season of feasting: favourite dishes being spring lamb followed by early rhubarb (southern England); stuffed veal (northern and midland England); decorated *Pasch* chicken pies (Scotland); cheesecakes (west Midlands); custards (Yorkshire and East Anglia); and puddings flavoured with tansy or – still popular in Cumbria – with the plant variously called bistort, 'Easter Ledges', and 'Passion Dock'.

But the classic Easter food, the focus of the best-known Easter games, and indeed the most familiar emblem of the festival itself, is the Easter egg. As apparently lifeless objects which nevertheless contain the source of new life, eggs are an ancient and universal symbol of spring re-awakening, early adopted by Christians to signify also the Resurrection and thus firmly attached to Easter. During the Middle Ages (and in a few places very much later) large numbers were collected as a customary Easter tithe or rent to the parish priest, some of these being then ceremonially blessed and distributed as holy or 'lucky' gifts. After the Reformation, however, Protestants abandoned such ceremonies as 'Popish and superstitious' – a label until recently applied to all Easter-egg customs in parts of Presbyterian Scotland – but the giving of eggs continued, and so too did Easter-egg games.

To obtain eggs for these – or simply to eat – children spent the days before Easter touring their neighbours' houses, usually chanting some traditional doggerel rhyme. In north Wales and Anglesey, this was called egg clapping (*clepian wyau*), because the clappers normally used for bird scaring were rattled to attract attention: sometimes, however, householders would retort with some phrase like 'the cat hasn't laid yet'. 'Paste' (*Pasch*: Easter) or 'Pace Egging' was also popular throughout northern England and Scotland, and particularly in Lancashire and Cheshire, where it survived until at least the Second World War; one Cheshire chant ran:

Here comes three jovie lads all in a row
We've come a pace eggin', we hope you'll prove kind
Prove kind, prove kind, with your eggs and small beer
We hope you'll remember it's pace eggin' time.

In earlier generations, this would have been sung by young men – doubtless more interested in money and 'small beer' than eggs – as part of a Pace-Egg Play, a regional variant of the MUMMING PLAY: similar plays were also much acted in West Yorkshire, where revived local versions can be seen on GOOD FRIDAY at Mytholmroyd, Midgley, Brighouse and elsewhere in the Halifax area.

Once collected (or, in recent times, bought) 'real' Easter eggs are still often painted, decorated or dyed – either by boiling in a coloured cloth or with some natural dye like onion skins (for a golden-brown egg); furze-blossom (yellow); 'Pasque flower' (bright green) or cochineal (for the favourite red). Then (if not eaten for breakfast) they may be concealed about the garden for an egg hunt: or, especially in northern Britain, hard-boiled for egg rolling down a hill or slope – the winner being, according to local preference, the one which rolls furthest, survives most rolls, or is successfully aimed between two pegs. In many places this ancient sport – inevitably declared to be 'a solar rite' by some folklorists, but also said to symbolize the rolling away of the stone from Christ's tomb – takes place on Easter Monday at a site fixed by long tradition. Such include Arthur's Seat in Edinburgh; the castle moat at Penrith, Cumbria; Bunker's Hill, Derby; and, best publicized of all, Avenham Park at Preston, Lancashire, where tens of thousands roll and then eat both eggs and (latterly) oranges.

Alternatively, the eggs may be 'dumped' (another northern habit) by being clasped firmly in the hand and smashed against that of an opponent until one or other breaks: or (as in parts of south-western England) a number may be marked and 'shackled' (shaken) together in a sieve, the last to crack being the winner. All such old egg customs, however, are now in acute danger from the 20th century's principal contribution to the Easter canon, namely the chocolate Easter egg.

· Ebernoe Horn Fair ·
Ebernoe, near Petworth, West Sussex: 25 July

The horns at Ebernoe Horn Fair are those of a black ram, provided annually by Lord Egremont and roasted on a spit during the cricket match between the village and one of its neighbours. When it is done, it provides a mutton dinner for the two teams, while the decapitated head and horns – which have carefully been kept clear of the fire – are presented to the man who has scored most runs for the winning side.

This custom, which takes place annually on St James's Day (25 July) is said to date back at least five centuries, but in its present form it was deliberately revived in 1864, after 'a lapse of a great number of years'. According to a local folk song, rich in sexual double meanings, the earlier incarnation of the fair may moreover have been somewhat different in character:

If you would see Horn Fair you must walk on your way
I will not let you ride on my grey mare today
You'd rumple all my muslin and uncurl my hair
And leave me all distressed to be seen at Horn Fair.

Oh fairest of damsels, how can you say No?
With you I intend to Horn Fair for to go
We'll join the finest company when we do go there
With horns on their heads, boys, the finest at the Fair.

It is not entirely clear, however, whether the horns were once worn – in distinctly pagan fashion – on the heads of visitors to the fair, or whether they were supposedly borne (in invisible form) by the husbands cuckolded there: but the old fair's attractions seem certainly to have been unlike those of the present cricket match.

· Egg Games ·
see EASTER

· Eisteddfodau ·

Eisteddfodau – assemblies of Welsh poets and musicians, to compete for an 'eisteddfa' or bardic chair – have a long but somewhat chequered history. As early as the 6th century, the bards of Wales – who were harpers, genealogists and soothsayers as well as court poets and storytellers – are reported engaging in acrimonious disputes; and by the 10th their special status was recognized by law: so that formal competitions must certainly have taken place long before the first recorded eisteddfod at Cardigan in 1176, when the Lord Rhys presented chairs to the winning poet and the best performer on harp, pipe or *crwth* (a species of fiddle). Such assemblies continued to be held throughout the Middle Ages, during which the bards played a leading role in politics as well as culture: while as late as 1568 eisteddfodau were still being held for the 'licensed bards' who were thus carefully distinguished from 'travelling minstrels and sturdy vagabonds'. Thereafter, however,

Surrounded by his curiously dressed colleagues, the 'Arch Druid' chairs the victorious Chief Bard of the hard-fought National Eisteddfod of 1984.

the credit of both the Welsh language and of Welsh culture declined rapidly among the Anglicized gentry of Wales: and bardic contests took place (if they took place at all) at a local and unofficial level in taverns and alehouses.

Poetry and music nevertheless remained the focus of popular culture in Wales, and during the Romantic Revival of the late 18th century the idea of the eisteddfod was enthusiastically seized upon by the 'patriotic societies' of London Welshmen who combined sentimental nationalism with a somewhat lukewarm sympathy for the ideals of the French Revolution. Under their auspices, therefore, the first competition of modern type was organized at Corwen in Denbighshire in 1789. But this revival unfortunately coincided with a craze for the 'Ancient British Priesthood' or 'Druids' – about whom, in fact, scarcely anything is reliably known – its leading exponent being the self-styled 'Bard of Liberty' Edward Williams, generally called 'Iolo Morganwg'. This engaging charlatan claimed to have rediscovered the secret poetic rules and practices of the Druids, which had allegedly been passed on in unbroken succession by the bards of his native Glamorgan. In 1792, therefore, he organized the first Gorsedd (enthronement) of a

'Druidic Bard' on Primrose Hill in London: and by the 1820s the picturesque but almost entirely spurious trappings of 'Druidism' were being grafted onto eisteddfodau throughout Wales.

At first these took place on a regional basis – as they still do in the Welsh-speaking counties of the north-west and south-west, notably at Cardigan in early July and Lampeter in early August, and at various places in Caernarvonshire and Merionethshire. But the International Musical Eisteddfod at Llangollen in Denbighshire during early July attracts thousands of competitors (especially folk-dancers) from all over the world: and since 1880 a National Eisteddfod for the whole of Wales has been held during August at varying venues, alternating between the north and south of the principality. Following the custom observed for the Cardigan eisteddfod of 1176, this is proclaimed with considerable ceremony a year and a day in advance, and its proceedings are conducted entirely in Welsh. It is presided over by the 'Arch Druid of the Gorsedd' in his oak-leaf coronet and 'prehistoric' copper breast plate, who opens the contest by half-unsheathing his ritual sword and demanding 'A oes Heddwch?' (Is there peace?'), to which the assembly replies 'Heddwch', thus establishing that all acrimony must be abandoned during the eisteddfod. Leaving aside this and other Druidic fantasies, however, the Eisteddfod plays a vital part in keeping alive the Welsh language and encouraging and preserving Welsh culture: and though many aspects of the arts are now represented there, the place of honour is still reserved for poetry. Candidates must compose verses on set subjects – which are generally topical and even controversial rather than romantic and backward-looking – in the several strict and taxing forms of Welsh metre: and to be 'chaired' as the year's 'Chief Bard' at the close of the Eisteddfod represents a very considerable achievement.

· Ellington Bread Dole ·
see BREAD AND BUN DOLES

· Epiphany ·
see TWELFTH NIGHT

· Epiphany Gifts Ceremony ·
St James's Palace, London: 6 January

According to St Matthew's Gospel, 'Wise Men from the East' visited the infant Christ, bearing gifts of gold (symbolizing kingship); frankincense (symbolizing divinity); and myrrh – a substance used in embalming, and hence prefiguring death and resurrection. Conventionally three in number, a passage in the Psalms (72.10) led to their interpretation as 'Kings' as well as 'Magi' (Greek: 'sages') and since at least the 11th century the monarchs of Britain have annually re-enacted their gift-bringing on the feast of the Epiphany (*see* TWELFTH NIGHT). Until the madness of George III made this impracticable, they did so in person: but since then this ancient royal ceremony had been continued by proxy.

It now takes place in the Chapel Royal of St James's Palace: where, at 11.30 a.m., the 'Gentlemen and Children of the' Chapel Royal' – clad in the cassocks whose particular shade of scarlet is their jealously guarded privilege – begin singing a solemn Communion service. As the anthem commences, two Gentleman Ushers of the Royal Household in ceremonial uniform are led in at the west door by the Serjeant of the Vestry. Bearing the Queen's offerings on silver salvers, and escorted by Yeomen of the Guard (who also line the aisle) they then process slowly towards the altar, stopping three times on the way to bow reverently. The gifts are received and dedicated by the Dean of the Chapel Royal (the Bishop of London) who places them on the altar: and while an offertory hymn is sung the ushers retire, once again bowing thrice in memory of the 'Three Kings'.

The frankincense and myrrh for the ceremony are provided by the Apothecary of the Royal Household: while the gold takes the form of twenty-five sovereigns, whose considerably higher equivalent in modern currency is subsequently donated to charity.

F

· Faggot and Horseshoe Rents ·
see QUIT RENT CEREMONIES

· Fairs ·

The 7000 or so fairs still held annually in Britain are now, for the most part, purely and simply occasions for merrymaking. No doubt they have always had this association, for their name derives from the Latin *feria* – a celebration, holiday, or feast – and from the first they normally coincided with one of the religious festivals of the Church. Until the 19th century, however, the majority of fairs were at least as much concerned with business as they were with pleasure; being primarily great periodic markets of goods, animals and human labour, profitable and necessary alike for buyer, vendor and 'owner'. For the buyer, in the days when only the very largest towns had 'shops' in the modern sense, they furnished a rare chance to stock up with goods unknown at the normal weekly market – as well as to meet old friends, go a-courting, or gape at unaccustomed entertainments. To the vendor – from the large-scale stockbreeder to the village cheesewife – they brought an influx of outside purchasers for merchandise which (until the coming of the railways) it was difficult or impossible to distribute beyond the immediate area of production: while for the labourer, they gave a welcome opportunity to change his master and, if possible, to better his wages. And for the owner – the lord, church institution or town corporation on whose land they took place – fairs provided a rich harvest of income from the tolls and taxes levied on traders.

Many fairs, indeed, originated as a means of raising profits for their holders. Thus, when King Henry I's jester Rahere founded St Bartholomew's Hospital in the early 12th century in London's Smithfield, he obtained from his royal master the right to hold an annual fair during the fortnight following the feast day of its patron saint: and from this concession, whose dues maintained the hospital's inmates, developed the famous and now-revived Bartholomew Fair. For the establishment of a fair required a special royal charter, a valuable commodity which in most cases had to be bought from the crown at a swingeing price: so that it is probably no accident that most of our oldest surviving fairs – including King's Lynn Mart (held in the fortnight following VALENTINE'S DAY); Nottingham Goose Fair (three days beginning the first Thursday in October); and Cambridge Midsummer Fair – date from the reigns of the perenially impecunious Angevin monarchs of the 12th and 13th centuries, notably Richard I and John.

Though revenue from fairs has now generally dwindled to the rent charge on a field for 'rides' and 'amusements', the former economic importance of the event is still perpetuated in many places by CIVIC ceremonial. At Barnstaple in Devon, for instance, the mayor and corporation open the fair – which begins on the Wednesday nearest 17 September and claims to date from the time of King Athelstan (925-40) – by solemnly drinking to its success in special spiced ale, brewed by the Senior Beadle. At Bromsgrove in Worcestershire the Court Leet reads King John's charter of 1199 to inaugurate the Midsummer Fair: and the May Fair at Berwick-upon-Tweed – founded in 1302 and held on the last Friday in the month – begins only when the mayor and corporation ceremonially 'Walk the Fair'. While at Southwold in Suffolk (whose Trinity Fair has been held since 1485 on the second Monday after WHITSUN) the corporation has adapted to modern circumstances by proclaiming its charter from the steps of a merry-go-round, and taking the first ride on this themselves. Here and there, moreover, the ceremonial proclamation of the fair has outlived the fair itself. All that remains of a week-long cattle fair at Seamer in North Yorkshire, for example, is the procession which reads a 14th-century charter at various points in the village on St Swithin's Day (15 July), whereafter the Lord of the Manor throws coins to schoolchildren.

By their very nature, nevertheless, fairs brought – and still bring – upheaval as well as profit to a town. For the normal guild monopoly of local trade (and, indeed, virtually all normal business) had to be suspended for their duration, a fact still symbolized by the GLOVE IS UP custom at West Country fairs: while the many inevitable disputes between stallholder and customer, or between resident and visitor, necessitated the holding of a special fair court. Often called Courts of 'Piepowder' because of the 'dusty feet' (Old French: *pieds puldreux*) of the itinerant traders with whom they dealt, such tribunals are still proclaimed – though they now have no jurisdiction – at the Lichfield SHROVE TUESDAY FAIR, and for the Bristol Fairs on 30 September annually.

A number of fairs, however, managed very well without charters, courts, or indeed any official sanction at all. Many such unlicensed events began as village FEASTS, held to celebrate the local saint's day: attracting at first a handful of gingerbread or ribbon stalls and a travelling pedlar or two, these sometimes developed into full-scale fairs, which came to outshine and eventually to outlive the chartered functions of neighbouring towns. Most notable among them is St Giles' Fair at Oxford, held on the Monday and Tuesday after the first Sunday following 1 September, the feast of St Giles: originating in medieval times as the parish wake of Walton, then just outside the Oxford boundaries, it had become a considerable trading market by the Elizabethan period, and remains one of the largest and most important pleasure fairs in southern England. Further north, particularly in Lancashire and West Yorkshire, hitherto insignificant village festivities expanded to fairlike proportions with the influx of new population

brought by the Industrial Revolution: and here, too, totally new but immensely popular 'fairs' – like Rivington Pike Fair, still held on GOOD FRIDAY near Bolton in Lancashire – sprang up from nowhere on the moorland around the growing manufacturing towns.

Whatever their origins, many fairs developed special characteristics of their own, largely determined by the time of year at which they were held. Some – like Nottingham Goose Fair and Tavistock 'Goosey' Fair in Devon, both held around MICHAELMAS, Old Style, in early October – were chiefly famous for the sale of particular kinds of livestock, a function now largely usurped by regular auctions on commercial premises. But sheep are still sold in large numbers at Welsh border May fairs like those of Knighton, Radnorshire, and Hay-on-Wye, Breconshire, and at such autumn gatherings as Findon Great Sheep Fair in West Sussex (September) and Priddy Fair in Somerset (Wednesday nearest 21 August): while a number of sizeable HORSE FAIRS also continue to operate.

No longer, however, do certain fairs act as labour exchanges for young farm labourers and maidservants, who flocked there to strike the best possible bargain with the employers who would accommodate as well as pay them during the following twelve months. Prospective shepherds carried their crooks, horsemen their whips, and maids their brooms and mops – whence the name 'Mop Fairs' given to such 'hirings' in the Midlands and the West Country, where they customarily occurred at Michaelmas or Old Michaelmas (10 October). Marlborough in Wiltshire, nevertheless, still holds a nominal 'Mop' on the former date, while around the latter time 'Mops' take place in Gloucestershire at Cirencester and Tewkesbury (which dates from the 11th century, and is thus one of the oldest fairs in Britain); and at Warwick and Stratford-upon-Avon in Warwickshire – which also holds a 'Runaway Mop' a week later, where those who disliked their initial situation could try for better luck. In Wales and the north – where they continued active until the 1920s or 30s – the customary dates for hiring fairs were different: in Wales, and in Lincolnshire, they took place around MAY DAY, Old Style (13 or 14 May); in Yorkshire and northern England, at MARTINMAS, Old Style (23 or 24 November); while in Scotland, LAMMAS fairs were the occasion both for 'feeing' and for trial or 'handfast' marriages.

Other fairs were known for – and even named after – their particular regional and seasonal produce. Some such, like the Cheese and Onion Fair at Newton Abbot, Devon (first or second Tuesday in September) and the Black Cherry Fair at Chertsey, Surrey (second Saturday in July) are now simply 'fun fairs': but the eponymous delicacies can still be enjoyed at Marldon Apple Pie Fair in Devon (August Bank Holiday Saturday); Wisbech Strawberry Fair in Cambridgeshire (late July); and Bolton New Year or CARLINGS FAIR in Lancashire. Pottery and china, moreover, remain a principal attraction at Preston Pot Fair in Lancashire (last week in

Left: The transformation of British **fairs.** In early Victorian times, Nottingham Goose Fair was still mainly devoted to trading, though simple side-shows like the boxing match (left) are already in evidence.

Below left: One of the earliest purely 'pleasure' fairs, London's Bartholomew Fair (seen here in 1721) was founded in the 12th century as a trading mart, but was already famous for its side-shows by Elizabethan times.

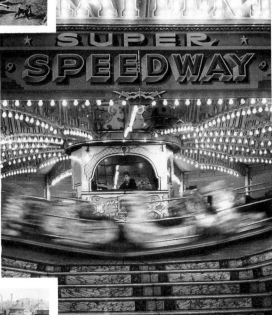

Above: The exciting, exuberantly painted and brilliantly lit 'ride' (seen here at Addlestone Fair in Surrey) continues to make fairs an unrivalled attraction.

Left: By the turn of the century, the new steam-powered 'rides' had completely taken over Nottingham Goose Fair, turning it into a purely pleasure event.

August); Coventry Crock Fair (29 May–4 June) and also at Cambridge Midsummer Fair. Yet other fairs again, finally, are or were famous for some special game or custom. In Scotland, the showpiece is often a traditional race for men, like the run for the Kilmarnock Bonnet at Eaglesham Fair near Glasgow (held every other year in mid May), the HAT AND RIBBON RACE at Inverkeithing, and Carnwath's RED HOSE RACE: or for horses, as at MARYMASS FAIR. Cumbrian 'gurning' contests, moreover, still continue at the CRABAPPLE FAIR, and so too do the ancient customs of CORBY POLE FAIR and EBERNOE HORN FAIR.

Individualizing features like these provide a welcome exception to the general rule that one fair is now very much like another, for all are basically 'fun fairs'. In some cases – as at Bartholomew Fair – shows and plays had already ousted business by the 16th century, but by and large the great transformation of fairs from partly practical to purely 'pleasure' events resulted from an interlinked series of events in mid-Victorian times. Firstly, the growth of improved communications – and particularly the spread of railways – gave all but the very poorest easy access to permanent sources of supply in market towns, which could themselves be readily supplied by rail with goods from all over the country: while an increasingly sophisticated public came to prefer the now available urban delights of theatre and music

hall to the comparatively simple games and amusements provided by contemporary travelling fairs. At the same time, 'respectable' opposition to fairs – always regarded in some quarters as potential centres of riot and disorder as well as debauchery – came to a head in measures like the Fairs Act of 1871, which gave governments the right to abolish them as 'unnecessary ... the cause of grievous immorality ... and very injurious to the inhabitants of the towns where they are held'.

For a time, therefore, it seemed probable that fairs would disappear altogether, and a number did in fact peter out. But then the showmen began to fight back, using the same steam technology that had revolutionized communications to drive (and, by means of traction engines, to transport) a series of impressive and exciting mechanical 'rides'. Accompanied by braying, exuberantly painted steam organs, and lit by brilliant gas or carbon-arc lamps, attractions like 'the Gallopers', 'the Razzle-Dazzle' and the 'Mont Blanc' proved a match for anything the music hall could offer: and their constantly developing diesel and electric powered successors – 'the Dodgems', 'the Jets', and 'the Astronaut' – still form the mainstay of the modern fairground. With the assistance of their sheer physical presence, and the unrivalled excitement they continue to generate, the transformed fair seems likely to hold its own for many years to come.

The distribution of **Farthing Bundles**, seen here in its old setting outside Miss Clara Grant's original (but now demolished) 'Settlement' at 38 Fern Street, Bromley-by-Bow.

· Farthing Bundles ·

Fern Street Settlement, Spanby Road, London E3: first Monday or Saturday of each month

This imaginative custom began in 1907, when Miss Clara Grant founded the Fern Street Settlement to help the people of Bromley-by-Bow, then as now one of the poorest parts of London. Particularly distressed by the local children's lack of playthings, she appealed to friends and supporters for toys or 'odds and ends'. To give these away as charity would, however, have offended both her own self-help principles and the pride of the East Enders: so she wrapped them into newspaper bundles and sold these each Saturday for a farthing (0.125p), then the smallest coin in use. And in order to control the great demand (over 500 applicants used to assemble outside 38 Fern Street each Saturday) she limited eligibility to children small enough to pass, without stooping, through a four-foot-high wooden arch bearing the words:

> Enter all ye children small
> None can come who are too tall.

Children too old (or too lanky) to do so had to pay a penny (0.5p) for their toys.

The sale of Farthing Bundles has continued ever since, weathering a number of changes – some of which would no doubt have gladdened Miss Grant's heart. Taller and healthier children have necessitated adding four inches to the arch's height, and decimalization has pushed the price of packets up to 1p. Falling demand, meanwhile, decreased the distributions from weekly to fortnightly and now monthly: and a few years ago the demolition of Fern Street itself transferred them to the settlement's new premises nearby, where about twenty children still buy their bundles of toys and trinkets.

· Fastern's E'en ·

see SHROVE TUESDAY

· Feasts, Revels and Wakes ·

Every village in Britain has or had its own special yearly festival, generally celebrated on or about the feast day of the patron saint to whom its parish church is dedicated. This is known as 'the Feast' in north-eastern England, Yorkshire, and the south and east Midlands; as 'the Revel' in parts of the south-west; and in the north-west and the north and west Midlands as 'the Wake' – from the medieval custom of 'waking' or keeping vigil at the church on the night before the great day. Such festivals have a very long history, dateable at least from a wise and humane letter sent by Pope Gregory the Great to St Augustine of Canterbury in AD 601, a few years after the first conversions of the southern English to Christianity. In order to make the transition from paganism easier, the Pope advised, heathen temples should not be destroyed, but rather cleansed of idols and converted into churches, '... so that flocking more readily to their usual places of worship, the people may come to know and worship the true God. And since they have a custom of sacrificing many oxen to devils [i.e. pagan gods] let some other solemnity be substituted in its place, such as a day of the Dedication or a festival of the Holy Martyrs whose relics are enshrined in the church. On such festivals they might well make bowers of branches for themselves around the churches that were formerly temples, and celebrate the observance with devout feasting.'

This, in fact, was very much the manner in which feasts, revels and wakes were celebrated throughout the Middle Ages, when images of the patron saint might also be borne in procession round the parish – a custom recalled by ST WILFRID'S FEAST at Ripon and possibly by the ceremony of BURNING BARTLE. But at the Protestant Reformation such activities came to be regarded as 'savouring too much of heathenism and idolatry', and in 1560 the Calvinist Kirk of Scotland judged the keeping of all feasts 'utterly to be abolished from this Realm' – a prohibition which it eventually succeeded in enforcing. In England, meanwhile, a more moderate decree of 1536 had ordered that every parish must hold its wake on the first Sunday in October, regardless of the date of the patronal festival. Striking as it did at the essential uniqueness of each village celebration, however, this enactment was simply ignored in most places: and though many of their more obviously Catholic trappings disappeared, English feasts obstinately stuck as close as possible to the proper saint's day, even (or indeed especially) if the saint commemorated was an obscure and local one.

At Marhamchurch in Cornwall, for instance, the 'Revel' is still held on the Monday following 12 August, the feast of St Maerwynn or Morwenna who brought Christianity to the village in the 6th century: and though the 18th-century church of Tweedmouth in northern Northumberland is dedicated to St Bartholomew, the ancient feast there nevertheless still begins on the Sunday after 18 July, the name-day of the Anglo-Saxon St Boisil who was the original patron of the parish. At Tweedmouth, unusually, the celebrations still last for a whole week; but by the early 19th century the wake festivities were generally concentrated into a single day, usually the 'Feast Sunday' after the patronal festival or, to avoid 'profaning the Sabbath', the Monday after that. Villages whose saints' days fell during the depths of winter, moreover, had by then often transferred their feasts to some summer holiday period – WHITSUN being the favourite – or else to a convenient date during the slack post-harvest month of September.

This move away from the actual saint's day – further exacerbated by the 1752 calendar change, whereafter the feast often stood its ground at the 'old' date, now eleven or twelve days after the 'new style' patronal festival – meant that the saints themselves were increasingly forgotten. Many places, however, still kept (and keep) up church-centred events like CLIPPING THE CHURCH, RUSHBEARINGS or dressing WELLS at their wake: while others prided themselves on unique forms of celebration which, if they had little to do with either church or patron, certainly marked out their feast from those of the surrounding area (*see* ABBOTS BROMLEY HORN DANCE; FENNY POPPERS; FURRY DANCE; MOCK MAYORS; RAM ROASTING; TIN CAN BAND).

Even in villages which boasted no such distinctive customs – or where the custom had already died out – 'the Feast' remained until late-Victorian times the great social event of the year. Exiled inhabitants and children working away flocked home, long-lost friends and relatives appeared on visits, and the younger folk of neighbouring communities poured in to watch the CLUB WALKS, take part in the afternoon 'Sports' (the name still often given to wakes along the Welsh border) and perhaps attend the hearty 'Feast dinner' in the evening. At this, and throughout the day, many places served their own special feast dish – like the famous 'Eccles cakes' of Eccles in Lancashire, the baked warden pears of Bedford, the 'Puppy-dog pies' of Painswick or the eponymous delicacies eaten at COW HEAD WAKES and on PIG FACE SUNDAY.

Unable to compete with the more modern attractions of the now accessible towns, the majority of rural wakes petered out soon after the First World War, though some survived in the form of small agricultural shows or 'fêtes' as genteel as their name. Other feasts, nevertheless, had long since developed along different lines, some growing into official or unofficial FAIRS while others – particularly in Lancashire, West Yorkshire and the Potteries – expanded to vast proportions with the influx of new population at the Industrial Revolution: factory owners therefore arranged their annual shut-downs to coincide with them, and until very recently the 'Wakes Weeks' of Accrington or Rochdale were awaited with keen anticipation by the seaside landladies of Blackpool, Skegness and the Isle of Man. In earlier times, however, such industrial wakes holidays had been vigorously enjoyed at home, allegedly amid such scenes of 'excess, riot and profligacy' that church leaders felt bound to organize rival events, generally in the form of 'processions of witness' or 'Walking Days'. Hence arose the famous Manchester Whit Walks, now usually held on Spring Bank Holiday Monday, and the equally renowned Walking Day of Warrington in Cheshire, originated in 1832 as a counterblast to a local race meeting and now held on the 'Wakes Friday' nearest 30 June': thirty churches of all denominations take part, and many of the female walkers still wear the traditional white dresses.

· Fenny Poppers ·
Fenny Stratford, Bucks.: 11 November

Three times during 11 November, St Martin's Day, six small cannon called the 'Fenny Poppers' are taken to Leon recreation ground, where they are rammed full of gunpowder, laid on the ground, and fired off in turn with a red-hot iron rod.

Ramming down the gunpowder to load the **Fenny Poppers**, whose resemblance to medieval cannon 'chambers' is clearly visible: wooden rammers are used to avoid causing a spark, and later the 'poppers' will be fired with a red-hot iron.

This cheerful custom commemorates the building, in 1730, of Fenny Stratford's first parish church – largely due to the then Lord of the Manor, Dr Browne Willis, who contributed most of the cost himself and raised the rest by selling ceiling space for the heraldic arms of donors, which are still to be seen. A notable scholar, eccentric and philanthropist (his many charities 'so ruined his fine estate that towards the end of his days he was obliged to dress meanly and live in squalor ... being often taken for a beggar') Willis dedicated the church to the memory of his thriftier grandfather Thomas, who had bought the manor, and who died in St Martin's Lane, London on St Martin's Day 1675. So St Martins church it became, and its builder left money to encourage the proper celebration of MARTINMAS, with a parish dinner, sermon and 'entertainment'.

Whether he also instituted the 'Fenny Poppers' is uncertain: but they were undoubtedly being fired not long after his death in 1760. Normally kept in the church, they are locally believed to be very old, and are shaped like quart-sized iron tankards – or the detachable chambers used for firing medieval breech-loading cannon: those in present use were recast in 1859 but, given Browne Willis's antique-collecting propensities, the originals may have been just that.

· Feudal Customs ·
see BREAD AND CHEESE DOLE; CLAMEUR DE HARO; COMMON LAND; CORONATIONS; COURTS LEET AND BARON; HAXEY HOOD GAME; MANORIAL CUSTOMS; PENNY HEDGE; QUIT RENT CEREMONIES; RED HOSE RACE; WROTH SILVER

· Fig Sunday ·
see PALM SUNDAY

· Fire Festivals ·
see BURNING BARTLE; BURNING THE CLAVIE; BURNING THE OLD YEAR OUT; GUY FAWKES NIGHT; HALLOWEEN; MIDSUMMER; SWINGING FIREBALLS; WHALTON BAAL FIRE

· First Footing ·
see NEW YEAR

· Fisheries Customs ·
see ABBOTSBURY GARLAND DAY; ADMIRALTY COURT; BLESSING THE SEAS AND FISHERIES; COLCHESTER OYSTER CEREMONIES; HARVEST FESTIVALS

· Five Kings' Feast ·
see SWAN UPPING

· Floral Dance ·
see FURRY DANCE

· Florence Nightingale Service ·
see COMMEMORATIONS

· Flowering Sunday ·
see PALM SUNDAY

· Forest Customs ·

At the beginning of the 13th century, nearly a quarter of the land area of England – including the whole of Essex and much of Huntingdonshire, Northamptonshire, Wiltshire and Hampshire – was occupied by the great royal hunting preserves called 'royal forests'. Generally though not necessarily wooded (the huge 'forest' of Exmoor, for example, was virtually treeless) these preserves were subject to special forest laws, designed to protect both the King's 'venison' (which included wild boar as well as deer) and the 'vert' or greenwood which sheltered them: laws whose strictness was one of the principal grievances remembered by the Anglo-Saxon Chronicle against their inventor, William the Conqueror.

> He made great preserves for the game and imposed laws concerning them
> That whosoever slew hart or hind should be blinded
> He forbade the killing of boars even as the killing of harts
> For he loved the stags as dearly, as though he had been their father
> Hares also he decreed should go unharmed
> Powerful men complained of it and the poor lamented it
> But so fierce was he that he cared not for the rancour of them all.

Though the 'powerful men' eventually forced William's successors – by the terms of Magna Carta (1215) and the subsequent Charter of the Forest (1217) – to somewhat reduce both the area of royal forest and the savagery of the forest laws, yet the code continued to be rigorously enforced throughout the Middle Ages. Under it, forest-dwellers were not only forbidden to harm or disturb game, but were even prohibited from driving deer off their own crops; neither might they fell their own timber without royal licence; while any large dogs they possessed had to be 'expeditated' or 'lawed' by cutting three claws from each forefoot, so that they could not chase the King's vension. Dogs small enough to creep through a narrow measure, however, were exempt from mutilation: and 'William Rufus's Stirrup', which still hangs in the Verderer's Hall at Lyndhurst in Hampshire – traditionally a relic of that King's mysterious murder in the New Forest in 1100 – is in fact such a measure. Ten-and-a-half inches wide by seven-and-a-half inches deep, it would have admitted no dog larger than a small terrier.

From the Tudor periods onwards, however, both royal forests and forest laws declined – though Charles I

A continuing **forest custom,** the New Forest Court of Swainmote and Attachment, here seen convening at Lyndhurst in 1930. An Agister raises his hand to open the court, and behind him stand some of the Verderers: on the wall above the fireplace hangs 'William Rufus's Stirrup', once used for measuring dogs.

made a highly unpopular attempt to revive and extend them as a source of extra-Parliamentary revenue – and after the Civil War the laws became virtually a dead letter. By the beginning of the 20th century, moreover, the great majority of royal forests had been 'dis-afforested' and turned over to agriculture, leaving the 67,000-acre New Forest in Hampshire and the 22,000-acre Forest of Dean in Gloucestershire as the only sizeable crown preserves remaining: and in 1971 the forest laws were finally abolished altogether – with the vital exception that all COMMON LAND rights enjoyed in connection with them were specifically continued in being. These common rights were also freed at last from the ancient restrictions of the 'fence-month' – the thirty days centred on MIDSUMMER, when all forest commons were closed to prevent disturbance to the calving hinds – and the 'winter heyning', the period between MARTIN-MAS and ST GEORGE'S DAY when common livestock were excluded from competing for pasture with the royal deer.

Subject to these restrictions, common rights of graz-ing, turf cutting, 'pannage' (the collection of acorns and beech nuts for pig food) and firewood gathering (*see* BREAD AND CHEESE THROWING; GROVELY RIGHTS DAY) have been claimed by forest-dwellers since the Middle Ages: and in the two surviving royal forests such rights continue to be managed and protected by officials called Verderers, whose office dates from Norman times and whose powers remain undiminished by recent COURTS LEET and commons legislation. So called because they are responsible for the 'vert' or green foliage of the preserve, the Verderers of the New Forest (which was

'new' only in 1079) are ten in number: one being elected by the commoners for each of the nine divisions or 'bailiwicks' of the forest (where he must own at least seventy-five acres of land) and one, the Chief or 'Official Verderer' being appointed by the Crown.

Together with their four green-uniformed 'Agisters', paid full-time officials who still perform their traditional task of collecting 'agistments' or grazing fees, the Verderers carry out frequent patrols of the forest by car or on horseback; during which they note unmarked or unlicensed livestock on the pastures, supervise the welfare of the deer and New Forest ponies, and also deal with the more modern problems related to tourists and picnickers. These and other similar matters, moreover, receive a public airing on the third Monday of every second month, beginning in January: when the 'Verder-ers' Court of Swainmote and Attachment' convenes at the Queen's House in Lyndhurst, the ancient adminis-trative capital of the forest. One of the oldest surviving courts in Britain, this also acts as a magistrates' court to enforce local bye-laws, but during its open sessions any forester may express an opinion or air a grievance, and complex disputes between commoners, Forestry Com-mission and members of the public are fairly frequent.

Still more complex are the disputes which fall to the jurisdiction of the Verderers' Court of the Forest of Dean in Gloucestershire, whose official headquarters are the 17th-century Speech House at West Dean near Coleford, but which frequently meets elsewhere. For in 'the Dean' – which is as old as the New Forest and which long provided much of the timber to build British fleets – the exact nature of the common grazing rights remains far from clear, despite centuries of official enactments, numerous riots and uprisings, and several Acts of Parliament. Many of the notoriously independent common graziers, moreover, also retain their ancient rights as 'Free Miners', which date from at least the 14th century and allow them to work small private coal-pits, as their ancestors formerly dug and smelted iron ore – using, of course, the King's trees as fuel. And though private smelting has ceased, mining continues, so that it is all the more difficult to disentangle the conflicting demands of industry, forestry, sheep and – since Dean became a 'Forest Park' – public access. Such problems (though to a lesser extent) also occupy the Verderers elected by the common-right holders of Epping Forest: whose 5,500 acres, now publicly owned, represent the last surviving remnant of the royal forest which once covered the entire county of Essex.

· Forty Shilling Day ·
Wotton, near Dorking, Surrey: generally on 2 February

This unusual form of GRAVESIDE DOLE was devised by William Glanville the Younger, a Treasury official under William III and the nephew of the diarist John Evelyn – who disliked him intensely.

Making his will on the last day of 1717, he bequeathed an annual 40s (£2) each to five poor boys of his home parish of Wotton: in order to qualify for this then princely sum, however, each year's candidates were required to fulfil very specific conditions on the anniversary of his death. First, with both hands laid on his tombstone in the churchyard, they must recite by heart the Lord's Prayer, the Apostles' Creed and the Ten Commandments; then, taking up a bible, they must read aloud the fifteenth chapter of the First Epistle to the Corinthians, which proclaims the doctrine of the Resurrection and forms part of the Anglican burial service; and finally they must write out two verses of this chapter 'in a legible hand'.

Glanville's wishes are still faithfully carried out annually, and normally the boys (who must be under sixteen) are chosen from Wotton itself: but if this small village cannot produce enough eligible candidates – a situation the founder foresaw – the trustees are authorized to draw on the six neighbouring parishes of Westcot, Abinger, Shere, Ashtead, Epsom and Cheam. What Glanville did not foresee, however, is that his death anniversary would fall on 2 February, which is not always an ideal time for outdoor ceremonial: in some years, therefore, a tent has to be erected over his grave: and in exceptionally hard winters the dole is postponed until a date in late spring.

· Founders' Days ·

Thousands of these specialized COMMEMORATIONS, observed by institutions such as schools, almshouses and hospitals in honour of their benefactors, take place

On one of their **Founders' Days**, Tudor-uniformed boys of Christ's Hospital School lead the London Skinners' Company's election-day procession home to Skinners' hall.

annually all over Britain: and only a few of the more ancient or remarkable of them can be detailed here.

Those two inveterate royal founders of educational establishments, Henry VI (1422-71) and Edward VI (1547-53) are much commemorated; the former notably by the Lilies and Roses Ceremony at the TOWER OF LONDON, and the latter by his many grammar-school foundations as well as his two great London institutions 'for necessitous children'. One of these, Christ's Hospital – now a pair of prestigious public schools, for boys at Horsham, Sussex, and for girls at Hertford – sends 300 representatives to St Sepulchre's–without–Newgate, London EC1 (near the site of the first foundation) on or about St Matthew's Day (21 September) each year. After a commemorative service, these then march behind Christ's Hospital Band – clad, like the rest of the boys, in the original Tudor uniform of blue cassock, yellow stockings, white bands and buckled shoes – to the Mansion House, where each receives a gift of new-minted coins from the Lord Mayor of London. Because of the support given to the school by the London Skinners' Company, uniformed boys also attend the guild's annual elections at Skinners' Hall, Dowgate EC4, on Corpus Christi Day (the second Thursday after WHITSUN): and thereafter lead the procession – every member of which carries a posy – to St Mary Aldermary church.

King Edward's second City foundation, the Bridewell school – which moved to Witley in Surrey in 1860, after centuries of uneasily sharing premises with a notorious workhouse-cum-prison – also returns to London for its commemorative service, held at St Bride's, Fleet Street,

EC4 on the second Tuesday in March: and Charles II's Royal Chelsea Hospital for old soldiers honours its merrier patron with much ceremony on OAK APPLE DAY.

Churchmen, too, figure prominently in the list of honoured founders. William of Wykeham (1324-1404), Bishop of Winchester, for instance, is remembered both at Winchester College and New College, Oxford on 27 September, the anniversary of his death: Bishop Kennedy of St Andrews – or rather his apocryphal niece – on KATE KENNEDY DAY: while Archbishop Whitgift of Canterbury (1530-1604), who endowed both a school and an almshouse at Croydon, Surrey, is commemorated there by members of both institutions each 22 March, when a wreath is laid on his tomb.

Few founders' days, however, can match the macabre symbolism of the ceremony held at St Botolph's–without–Aldgate, London EC3, on or near 20 March. This was the birthday of Sir John Cass, sheriff and MP for London, who founded the nearby school which bears his name in 1710, and increased its endowment by a deathbed will: but as he was struggling for strength to sign this an artery burst, soaking his quill with blood. The staff and pupils who attend his commemoration, therefore, each wear a scarlet feather in their hat or lapel.

· Friendly Societies ·
see CLUB WALKS

· Funerals ·

The chief object of present-day funerals – and especially the cremations which are increasingly replacing burials – seems to be the disposal of the body with the minimum of fuss, delay, or even thought: a state of affairs which may partly be a reaction against the morbid Victorian celebration of death and partly a product of the current embarrassment when faced by 'religion', but which is principally the outcome of the modern practice of 'leaving everything to the undertaker'. Funeral customs, therefore, are apparently on the wane: and, now that so many people die in hospitals or institutions and are taken thence straight to 'Chapels of Rest', so too are the rituals of the deathbed and the traditions concerning the unburied corpse. Until very recently, however, every step in the process of death and burial was surrounded by a whole range of customary observances, designed not only to assist the deceased's smooth passage from the world but also to protect the living against being either 'drawn after' the dead or troubled by their spirits. Many of these customs and beliefs, moreover, may well survive to a surprising degree – particularly in country districts, among older people, and among those who practise them 'just in case': but their essentially private nature renders it difficult to judge what continues and what does not.

Certainly belief persists in some of the many general omens of death – like dogs howling, white lilac or hawthorn in the house, or portraits of the sick suddenly falling down: if not in the assorted spectral drummers, bloody hands and White Ladies which are the private death-portents of particular families. All along the eastern coastline, too, some half-believe that the sick – particularly if they are seafarers or fishermen – are more likely to die at ebb-tide: but it is doubtful whether any still hold that the feathers of pigeons or game-birds in a mattress will lengthen the pangs of death, and that the dying ought therefore to be laid on the bare floor, preferably parallel with the floorboards.

As soon as death has actually occurred, however, it is still the general practice to draw the house-blinds, and some families also extinguish fires and stop clocks, while mirrors may be covered to prevent the spirit from being 'caught' in them, and subsequently appearing over the shoulder of a living user. At this point a few parishes still toll the PASSING BELLS, and in some places bees may be formally 'told' of a death in the family, lest they themselves die or fly away. Frequently, too, doors and windows are opened, 'to let the spirit go', and it is considered unwise ever to lock the door of the room where the corpse lies. Ideally, the body should never be left alone for a moment during the period between death and burial, and must at least be 'watched' at night, in the North of England traditionally by relays of paired relations and strangers. It was formerly the custom throughout Britain, moreover, for all the deceased's friends and neighbours to 'wake' the corpse: and though prayers and scripture readings were the usual activities on these occasions, in parts of Highland Scotland – as in Ireland – they may also become something of a 'send-off party' for the dead, with the men drinking and playing cards while the women pray.

During the interval between death and burial – even in these days of universal electricity – candles are sometimes kept burning by the corpse, and in many areas a plate of salt was once customarily placed on its chest: the purpose was supposedly to delay corruption, but originally the salt (like the candles) was doubtless designed to ward off evil spirits. In parts of Wales, visitors to the house during this period were formerly called upon to take token food and drink in the presence of the corpse – perhaps a relic of the custom of 'sin-eating' (*see* GRAVESIDE DOLES): while until very recently it was everywhere considered the height of bad manners if even casual callers did not at least view the body, and in northern England and Scotland they might also be expected to lay a hand on it. Interpreted as showing goodwill towards the dead, this custom probably arose from the belief that a corpse would bleed at its murderer's touch: and in addition to dispelling any suspicion, laying hands on the body would infallibly prevent its spirit from haunting the visitor.

All this while the corpse would be lying in an open coffin – in the Cotswolds, measurements for this would never be taken 'by numbers', but only with knotted string – which would not be sealed until immediately

Below: Attired in **funeral** mourning, an Edwardian Sussex woman 'tells the bees' of a death in the family, and trims their hive with black ribbon: if this courtesy was not done them, it was believed, the offended bees would die or depart.

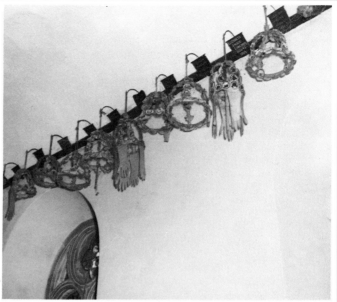

Above: Virgin's crowns and white coffin-bearers' gloves, used at the **funerals** of girls or bachelors 'of unspotted reputation', hang in the church of Abbot's Ann, Hampshire, where the custom is still maintained.

prior to the funeral. Before closing the lid, it is still not unusual to place coins over the eyes or in the hand of the body, an ancient custom originally intended as payment for the ferryman of the river of death, or perhaps for St Peter. Until the turn of the century, moreover, south-country shepherds might be buried with a crook or a hank of wool – to 'explain' their frequently necessary absences from church – while the coffins of the pious might contain a bible or Sunday-school certificate, and the bodies of priests, members of religious orders and servicemen are still buried in their vestments or uniforms. Wedding rings, too, are now generally left on, but in West Yorkshire this practice was once considered highly improper. Nor did the very poor invariably possess even coffins of their own: and well within living memory some parishes kept re-usable 'paupers' coffins' with detachable bottoms, the superstructure being drawn out of the grave as soon as the body had been laid in it.

Hearses, now generally provided by the undertaker, were formerly also the communal property of the parish, and freely available to all its inhabitants: while the coffin-bearers now usually furnished by the 'funeral director' were invariably drawn from the friends and neighbours of the deceased, to refuse this last service being regarded as a serious affront both to the dead and the bereaved. Normally they would be black-clad men, but until as recently as the 1930s it was the usual custom for the coffins of young boys and girls to be carried to the grave by their contemporaries, whose sashes, gloves or armbands would be white, the colour of purity and innocence. In some (mainly southern English) parishes, moreover, the funeral of an unmarried girl or bachelor of good reputation would be preceded by a 'maiden's garland' or 'virgin's crown' of real or artificial white flowers, which rested on the coffin during the service and was thereafter hung in the church, with the white gloves of the bearers attached. Such can still be seen in places like Minsterley in Shropshire and Bacton in Herefordshire; and at Abbots Ann in Hampshire the custom is (uniquely) still kept up. There the crowns are traditionally hung from the church gallery for three consecutive Sundays after the funeral, and if no objection is raised they are permanently fixed alongside the forty or so other garlands after a special dedication service on St Faith's Day (6 October).

Coffins are, of course, always carried with the feet of the body first – a custom which was doubtless originally meant to discourage the spirit from returning to the house: and in remote districts it was sometimes necessary to bear them over miles of rough country before reaching a road, let alone the distant parish church of a scattered community. Bearers were therefore fortified with food and drink before starting their journey, and carried the coffin in relays, resting it along the way at traditionally fixed stopping places like wayside crosses.

Nineteenth-century **funeral** pomp at its most lugubrious: the funeral of Sir Thomas Lawrence, 1830, by Turner.

Before setting off again, the coffin would then be borne three times round the stopping place in a sunwise (or clockwise) direction, and care would likewise be taken to circle the church so as to approach it from the east, for the dead must never be 'carried against the sun'. It was also considered vital for funerals to follow a set and customary path – the 'Lyke [corpse] Wake Walk' across the North Yorkshire moors between Osmotherly and Whitby being one such – even if this was by no means the shortest route: for a widespread but legally ground-less belief held that if a coffin was carried across private land, its passage would automatically create a perma-nent right of way.

In Lincolnshire it used to be believed that the sex of the first person a funeral encountered foretold the sex of the next person in the parish to die, and to meet a funeral head-on is still everywhere thought unlucky: but the omen may be averted by stopping and allowing the procession to pass or, better still, by turning to follow it for a step or two. But on no account must the funeral itself be overtaken, since the overtakers will then be hurrying towards their own deaths: and normally no-one would venture in front of the coffin until the parson met it at the churchyard lych ('corpse') gate and led it to the grave.

Nowadays graveside and coffin will probably be covered with 'floral tributes', but until about the 1860s these were considered 'heathenish': instead, mourners were often given sprigs of box, yew or (most commonly) rosemary, which they might keep 'for remembrance' or cast into the open grave; and sometimes both this and the coffin itself would also be lined with hyssop, rue and wormwood, the herbs of repentance. Graves, however, should not be prepared too far in advance, or left open too long after the burial, lest they gape for fresh victims: and in the English west Midlands it was held that a grave left open over Sunday would inevitably result in more deaths within a month, a man's grave claiming two women and vice versa.

Bodies are customarily laid in the grave facing east – the direction of the rising sun and of Jerusalem – though clergy are still sometimes buried the other way round, so as to be ready to preach to their congregation at the General Resurrection. This, it was believed, would begin at the eastern end of the graveyard (which was hence the most favoured place for burial) and continue in a sunwise direction to finish on the north (or Devil's) side, which in many parishes was thus abandoned to stran-gers, criminals and suicides – if indeed, these last were admitted at all to consecrated ground, and not buried at crossroads to confuse their vengeful ghosts. One respectable parishioner of Epworth in Lincolnshire, therefore, thought it necessary to justify his presence there with a tombstone inscription expressing a hope for a few minutes extra 'lie-in' at the Last Judgment.

> And that I might longer undisturbed abide
> I choosed to be laid on this northern side.

During the funeral service, at the words 'ashes to ashes, dust to dust', it is still usual for the principal mourners to cast some earth onto the coffin, as ordained by the Anglican *Book of Common Prayer*: and some think it proper for all present to follow suit as they leave the graveside. In northern and eastern England, too, bargains and promises – including engagements to marry – were regarded as utterly binding if sealed by clasping hands over the open grave, for the breaker of such an oath would speedily fall victim to the vengeance of the dead. An odd number of mourners at a funeral, moreover, was likely to result in the imminent death of one of them, as the dead called for a companion: and this was perhaps one reason for the rigid convention which until recently governed attendance at the ceremony. Those summoned by the 'bidders' – who in the north-east were invariably men, but rarely relatives of the deceased – were infallibly bound to be present, while to arrive unbidden was considered a serious breach of etiquette.

After the funeral, mourners can still expect a substantial repast, customarily including ham: and to be 'buried with ham' remains almost a synonym for the 'decent' funeral by which many older people still set much store, frequently keeping a best outfit (or sometimes the wedding dress) specifically to be 'laid out' in. In parts of Wales and the Marches, the mourners also keep up the tradition of attending a special commemorative service on the first Sunday after the funeral, before which it is unlucky or improper for the bereaved family to leave their home: while in northern England and southern Scotland clergy were often requested to bless the 'death house' as soon as possible after the ceremony, perhaps as a rudimentary form of exorcism.

One original purpose of mourning clothes – and particularly of the veils still occasionally worn by widows – may indeed have been to prevent the wearer being 'recognized' and claimed by the departed spirit. But by mid-Victorian times mourning dress had become an elaborate (and expensive) code of social convention, requiring widows and close female relations to wear 'deep mourning' of unadorned black for a year and a day, and thence proceed via a further eighteen months of 'second' and 'third' mourning to 'half mourning', when trimmings of grey or deep purple might gradually be introduced. Yet many older widows never 'put on colours' again – save perhaps for family WEDDINGS, when dark red was an acceptable substitute for the unlucky black. Black mourning is now rarely seen except at the funeral, and is not always worn even then.

· Furry Dance ·
Helston, Cornwall: 8 May, or the previous Saturday if 8 May falls on a Sunday

One of the most famous of all traditional British festivals is that known politely as 'Floral' or 'Flora Day', but locally and more correctly as 'the Furry' – a word most probably deriving from the Cornish 'fer' (Latin *feria*), a fair, rejoicing, or 'holy-day'. The date on which it takes place, indeed, is the feast of the Apparition of St Michael the Archangel, Helston's patron saint: and legend relates that the first Furry was danced to celebrate his deliverance from a great boulder hurled at him by Satan during a battle between the two celestial adversaries (*see* TURNING THE DEVIL'S STONE). But the 'Hell's Stone' – which is also said to have given the town its name, more soberly 'henliston' or 'old court town' – missed its mark, to land harmlessly near the Angel Inn, where part of it may still be seen embedded in a wall.

It is clear, however, that the patronal feast soon became inextricably intermingled with the celebration of MAY DAY. For one of its essential elements (now somewhat half-heartedly revived) was the maying procession called the 'Hal-an-Tow', disparagingly described thus by the *Gentleman's Magazine* of 1790:

In the morning, very early, some troublesome rogues go round the streets with drums or other noisy instruments, disturbing their sober neighbours and singing parts of a song, the whole of which nobody now recollects, and of which I know no more than that there is a mention in it of the grey goose quill and of going to the 'green wood to bring home the summer and the May-O': and, accordingly, hawthorn flowering branches are worn in hats.

The first verse of the song in fact runs as follows:

> Robin Hood and Little John, they both are
> gone to Fair-O
> And we will to the merry greenwood, to see
> what they do there-O
> And for to chase-O, to chase the buck and doe
> Hal-an-Tow, jolly Rumbelow
> And we were up, as soon as any day-O
> And for to fetch the Summer home
> The Summer and the May-O
> For Summer is a-come-O
> And Winter is-a-go-O

while subsequent verses bring in St George and a mysterious 'Aunt Mary Moses, with all her power and might-O', who may perhaps have begun either as the Virgin Mary or as Maid Marian, since 'mowse' is Cornish for 'virgin' and 'maid'. The 'Hal-an-Tow' chorus is also supposed to be in Cornish, but similar lines:

> Haile and Howe, Rumbylowe
> Steer well the good ship and let the wind blowe

appear in a sea-shanty from 15th-century Bristol, and the whole song seems to be a local version – and a rare

None but correctly dressed residents may take part in the principal **Furry Dance** of
the day, here winding its way down Helston's main street.

survivor – of those which accompanied the 'Robin Hood' May Games once played from Cornwall to southern Scotland.

In the modern revival of the 'Hal-an-Tow' (which begins at 8.30 on Furry Day morning) all the characters mentioned in the verses – plus, of course, St Michael – lead the bough-bearing mayers as they process round Helston, stopping at intervals to sing the song. Until the early 19th century, however, the mayers danced (or 'faddied') rather than walked both to and from the woods, and then through the streets, and this custom is almost certainly the origin of the great event of the day, the 'Furry' or 'Floral Dance'.

This is performed to its own famous tune, which has no connection with that of the 'Hal-an-Tow' and no special words – though a local children's doggerel is sung to it, and it formed the basis of the Edwardian ditty about 'the quaint old Cornish town' – and which is traditionally played by the Helston town band without benefit of scores. The tune is in two parts, and during the first the dancers 'trip on in couples, forming a long string, the gentleman leading his partner by the right hand. At the second part of the tune, the first gentleman turns, with both hands, the lady behind, and her partner turns the same way with the first lady; then the gentleman in the same manner with his own partner; then they trip on as before, each part of the tune being repeated.' The long lines of couples are thus performing

a very simple processional MORRIS dance, and the Furry is, indeed, so described in 1790.

At that time there were two distinct dances, one around noon for the common 'Hal-an-Towers' and another in the afternoon for the 'gentility' and their white-muslin-clad ladies: by early Victorian times, moreover, an even greater degree of social stratification had set in, with separate dances for gentry, tradesmen, servants and 'others'; and by the 1880s only 'ladies and gentlemen' were permitted to perform. Nowadays there are four dances, whose participants are distinguished by age rather than social position. The first, which begins at 7.00 a.m. and winds round the town to finish at the Guildhall at about 8.30 a.m., is for young couples: and the next, beginning at 10.15 a.m., is for schoolchildren, who are clad all in white, to match the universally worn buttonholes of the lily-of-the-valley, a symbol of the Virgin which in Helston (as in France) is the special flower of May Day.

The great and principal dance of 'the Furry', however, begins at noon: and for this the ladies wear long dresses and summer hats, while their partners must appear in grey toppers and morning coats – an inflexible rule which is doubtless a relic of the 'gentry-only' period. Led by the mayor in his chain of office, the 150 or so couples not only dance through all the greenery-decked streets, but also weave their way through any houses, gardens, or shops whose doors are left open for them, if possible entering by one way and leaving by another. Once, the dancers claimed an absolute right to do so, whether or not the doors were left open: but objections were rare, since their passage was and is believed to bring good luck to the household.

The last dance, at five in the afternoon, is headed by the young couples who danced the first: and in this (and this alone) spectators may and generally do join. By never-varied tradition, however, only those actually born in the town may lead a dance. For, despite its fame as a tourist attraction, the Furry remains very firmly Helston's own May festival. Already well-established by 1602, it is certainly far more ancient in origin; and except in times of war and disaster it has been performed without a break for centuries. (*See also* MINEHEAD and PADSTOW HOBBY HORSES)

G

· Ganging Days ·
see BEATING THE BOUNDS

· Garland Dressing ·
Charlton-on-Otmoor, Oxfordshire: 1 May or thereabouts

Locally known as 'the Garland', the wooden cross which surmounts the rood-screen of Charlton-on-Otmoor church is kept permanently decked with yew and box leaves: and twice a year, on MAY DAY and on the dedication festival on 19 September, it is taken down to be re-dressed with flowers and fresh greenery. On May Day, moreover (or the nearest school day to it) local children process to the church bearing a long rope-garland of leaves and flowers, and each also carries a small home-made flower cross: after singing the May Garland song and attending a short service, they hang the rope-garland on the screen, while the two best flower crosses are placed above the church door, whereafter the children dance in the street outside the churchyard gate.

Such is the current manner of observing a custom which dates from the Middle Ages, but which has altered significantly over the centuries. Before the Reformation, as was then usual, the cross (or 'rood') on the rood-screen was flanked by images of the Virgin Mary and St John, the chief witnesses to the Crucifixion: and on each May Day the Charlton Virgin's statue was ceremonially borne across Ot Moor for a blessing by the monks of Studley Priory. When Protestant reformers removed the images as 'superstitious idols', the conservative villagers insisted on replacing them with a pair of green garlands, which appear to have been more or less image-shaped: and until the mid-19th century they continued to process the 'Virgin' garland to the priory (even though this had long since become a private

Yew and box leaves are used for the image-shaped garland dressing in Charlton-on-Otmoor church.

house) while the second garland was carried about the village by women and children. Such processions ceased in 1857, and by 1900 the last of the 'image' garlands had disappeared: but the May Day dressing of the cross itself – sometimes known as 'My Lady' – continued, as did the children's custom of carrying their small crosses from house to house while begging for pennies. In recent years, however, this last has also died out, and only the 'Garland Cross' dressing and the 'official' children's observance remain.

· The Glove is Up ·

Until the 17th century, commerce in towns was tightly controlled by the local merchants' GUILDS, and any outsider attempting to do business there was liable to immediate expulsion or arrest. Only during FAIRS was this monopoly relaxed, the symbol of free trade being (especially in the West Country) the display of an emblematic open hand – usually in the form of a decorated glove – throughout the duration of the fair. So long as 'the glove was up' therefore, any visiting merchant or pedlar could not only buy and sell without hindrance, but could also claim the protection of the town authorities, for he was covered by 'the King's special Peace of the Fair'.

Such trading restrictions have long since passed away, but a few West Country towns still keep up the old glove

Even without the town-crier's proclamation, echoed by schoolchildren, there can be no doubt that Honiton's **Glove is up,** and its annual fair has begun.

performance of the ceremony, and thereafter erected at the White Lion – near the old horse-fair site – until being finally 'taken down'.

The same cry is used to proclaim the Exeter LAMMAS FAIR (Tuesday before the third Wednesday in July) though the fair itself no longer operates. A white stuffed glove, however, is still carried through the streets and fixed in front of the Guildhall, whereafter a civic procession reads the fair charter at each of the city's old market sites. At Barnstaple, too, a glove on a garlanded staff hangs from a Guildhall window during the still-active St Giles's Fair (Wednesday nearest 17 September until the following Saturday) – a custom recorded since at least 1569: and a fourth Devon town, Kingsbridge, also displays a white glove during its late-July fair, established by charter in 1461.

· Goathland Plough Stots ·
see PLOUGH MONDAY; SWORD DANCING

· Golfing Customs ·
see ROYAL AND ANCIENT GOLF CLUB CUSTOMS

· Good Friday ·

Good Friday – 'God's Friday' – when the Crucifixion of Christ is commemorated, is the most solemn day in the Christian calendar. Churches are stripped bare of all adornment – except, in a few traditionalist places, for the yew of mourning; BELLS are silent, or toll as if for a funeral; and in pre-Reformation times a crucifix, consecrated 'host', or image of Christ was symbolically 'buried' in an 'EASTER sepulchre', and reverently 'watched' until its 'resurrection' on Easter Day. Currently, however, the principal Good Friday service in most churches is the three hours' devotion, from noon until 3 p.m. – the period during which Jesus is said to have suffered on the cross before His death; this is spent in prayer and meditation, interspersed with scriptural readings, addresses and the singing of seasonal hymns, such as 'There is a green hill far away'. In recent decades ecumenical 'processions of witness' have also become increasingly popular: full-sized crosses are borne through the streets of towns and villages, to be erected in some public place or at the summit of a prominent hill.

Though rightly considered an appropriate day for distributing CHARITIES to the poor – especially in the form of BREAD AND BUN DOLES and GRAVESIDE DOLES – Good Friday was mainly a time of fasting and mortification: in Victorian times, penitential dinners of boiled cod were eaten behind drawn blinds, and all amusements (including traditional games like MARBLES and top spinning) were forbidden. Light-hearted customs are therefore few, and the majority even of these are connected – at least in theory – with symbolic punishments of Judas, Christ's betrayer. Thus children

custom. Best known among them is Honiton in Devon, whose three-day charter fair, dating from 1221, begins on the first Tuesday after St Margaret's Eve (19 July). At noon on that day, the town crier appears outside the old Pannier Market – now a department store – carrying a gilded leather glove atop a twelve-foot pole garlanded with flowers. Surrounded by schoolchildren, who repeat each phrase after him, he chants out:

Oyez, Oyez, Oyez
The Glove is Up
The Fair has begun
No man shall be arrested until the Glove is taken down
God Save the Queen.

Whereupon a shower of hot coppers is thrown from the upper window of the Angel Hotel, to be 'scrambled for' by the children in the street below. The whole process is then repeated at the King's Arms, upon whose balcony the Glove is displayed until midday on Thursday, when it is carried to the other end of the town for a third in parts of Liverpool's dockland still publicly burn effigies of the arch-villain on Good Friday morning – an essentially alien tradition, learnt from the crews of visiting Spanish and Portuguese ships: while Devonshire people used deliberately to break pieces of pottery, in the belief that the sharp fragments would cut his flesh. The Sussex custom of mass skipping on this 'Long Rope Day' (still observed at Alciston near Lewes and South Heighton near Newhaven) is also linked with Judas, via the rope he used to hang himself: some folklorists, however, more plausibly derive it from the once far more widespread practice of Good Friday skipping on prehistoric burial mounds, in order 'to raise the spring crops'.

Such associations with fertility – or perhaps the day's Christian holiness – may also explain the belief, still widespread throughout southern and midland England, that this is the best possible time for planting garden produce, especially potatoes and parsley. In parts of northern England and Wales, conversely, it was thought disastrously unlucky to disturb the soil in any way whatsoever, even by wearing shoes to walk to church. By and large, Good Friday is notoriously ill-omened for work of any kind, particularly in hazardous trades like mining and sea fishing. Nor, because of their use in the crucifixion, would any smith make or drive a nail then, or any prudent housewife wash even a single garment,

lest she wash away the life of one of her family: for Christ himself was said to have cursed a heartless woman who threw a bowl of water over Him on His way to Calvary.

On the same occasion, however, He blessed her more kindly neighbour for the gift of a loaf. Thus – according to one theory -- originated the tradition that bread baked on Good Friday would never go mouldy: and that, if kept and dried, it would prove a sovereign remedy for any stomach ailment of man or beast, and even preserve the house from fire. These properties once also attached to the hot cross buns still eaten on Good Friday in most British homes – though they are now rarely baked there (or even on the day itself) and are more likely to appear at teatime than, as formerly, at breakfast. The belief that they are somehow 'lucky', moreover, still survives: and is reflected in customs like the WIDOW'S BUN CEREMONY and the distribution of free buns to the children of Sidmouth in Devon – which began in 1898, when local bakers went on strike, and supplies were rushed from a neighbouring village to avert any possible misfortune.

The quasi-magical powers attributed to hot cross buns have led to much speculation about their origin. Some, for instance, claim that they are descended from the cakes offered to the pagan gods of spring; and others

By the terms of the Butterworth Charity, hot cross buns are distributed to 'poor widows' each **Good Friday** from a tombstone at St Bartholomew the Great, Smithfield, London.

that they derive from the cross-marked Communion wafers consecrated on Good Friday, which Anglo-Saxon priests are known to have kept as medicine for the sick: others again assert that they were invented by a St Albans monk during the 14th century. All that seems certain is that they are an essentially English dish, apparently unknown in Scotland and most of Wales until quite recently: and that they have provided welcome relief from Good Friday austerity since at least the 18th century.

· The Grand National ·
Aintree racecourse, Liverpool: first Saturday in April

Few sporting events have captured worldwide imagination so completely as the Grand National, a race which compels the attention not only of all horse-racing enthusiasts, but also of many who normally take no interest whatever in this form of sport. It is not altogether easy to explain why this should be so, for though the 'National' is a valuable enough race to the winning owner, it generally attracts a fair number of contestants of only moderate ability, and it is run at a somewhat unattractive course in the suburbs of Liverpool. It nevertheless possesses several unique characteristics – not the least of which is its gruelling length of over four miles, interspersed with thirty formidable fences – and the winning of it requires a special combination of a brave mount and expert horsemanship.

Another of the elements which makes the race so universally exciting is the fact that horses of very humble origins can, and frequently do, score a surprise win: very few of the winners have been top-class horses, the most notable exceptions being Golden Miller (1934), Reynoldstown (1935 and 1936) and L'Escargot (1975) – all of whom were champions before their National victories. But the race breeds its own heroes, and it is improbable that any will ever surpass Red Rum, the extraordinary steeplechaser who won three Grand Nationals – one of them while carrying top weight – and was placed in two others. His performances elsewhere were never bad, but they revealed little of his remarkable National prowess, which did so much to enhance the reputation of the race.

Though by no means the most formidable of the **Grand National's** thirty notorious jumps, the 'chair fence' (here being taken by the leaders in 1968) clearly demonstrates the arduous character of this famous race.

The National grew out of a series of races run in the Liverpool area during the 1830s: but its direct ancestor is generally held to be the 'Grand Liverpool Steeplechase' first run at Aintree in 1839. The winner, appropriately, was 'Lottery', but the best-remembered feature of the first race was the manner in which a certain Captain Becher – by plunging headlong into it – gave his name to the most feared obstacle in British steeplechasing, the water-jump called 'Becher's Brook'. Since then, despite many threats both to the course and the race itself, Aintree and the National have remained inseparable: and the crowds which flock annually to view this prestigious and hazardous steeplechase show no signs of abating.

· Graveside Doles ·

Annual distributions of alms at the site of the donors' tombs, still continued in a few places, were once fairly frequent forms of CHARITIES. Some such graveside doles, doubtless, were intended to be regular (if scaled-down) re-enactments of the lavish alms-dispersals customary at the FUNERALS of the wealthy: and were thus designed to perpetuate the benefits believed to derive therefrom, whether by topping-up the supply of paupers' prayers for the donor's soul or – after the Protestant Reformation had pronounced these 'superstitions' – in some less clearly defined manner. Where food is served from (or over) a tombstone, however, some relic of the shadowy practice called 'sin eating' may perhaps also survive. According to John Aubrey, who described it as flourishing in the Welsh borders during the mid-17th century, this involved the passing of food, drink and money over a corpse awaiting burial: these were then consumed by a specially chosen (and invariably shunned) pauper, 'in consideration whereof he took upon him (ipso facto) all the Sinnes of the Defunct, and freed him (or her) from walking after they were dead'.

Other donors, conversely, may have half-believed that graveside ceremonies would allow them a posthumous role in overseeing their charity: while others again (more prosaically) seem to have viewed them as the best means of keeping their graves tended and their bones undisturbed – or simply as the most cost-effective method of purchasing remembrance.

Whatever their motives, founders shared a common determination to have their alms distributed as near as possible to their actual burial place: a condition which surviving charities strive hard to fulfil. At Leigh near Manchester, for example, a Victorian church now covers the older building in which Henry Travice was buried in 1626: but the original memorial brass marks the approximate position of his tomb, where the Travice Dole of ten pounds is still distributed each Maundy Thursday. And though 'practicality dictates' that the fund should now be divided between far fewer people than the forty stipulated by his will, recipients must still walk the length of a pew – as they were once required to

pace the length of his grave – before collecting their share.

The surroundings of George Carlow's tomb, at Woodbridge in Suffolk, have altered still more dramatically: for the yard of the Bull Hotel now occupies the site of the back garden where this religious eccentric chose to be buried in 1738. Perhaps realizing the potential vulnerability of his tomb, he had inscribed upon it a warning to despoilers:

> Blessed be he that spares these stones
> Cursed be he that moves my bones

and willed the rent-charge on his house (now the Bull annexe) towards its upkeep. As a further guarantee of eternal rest, moreover, he bequeathed 'twenty shillings' worth of bread to be given on this stone on the second of February forever': and while this sum now no longer runs to the 120 'twopenny loaves' originally envisaged, a dozen loaves are still distributed there each CANDLEMAS by the rector and churchwardens of St Mary's parish church.

The Butterworth charity is also served from a tombstone, in the churchyard of St Bartholomew the Great, Smithfield, London EC1. Every GOOD FRIDAY morning, twenty-one piles of six new pence and the like number of hot cross buns are laid upon it, and until very recently twenty-one 'poor widows of the parish' first knelt by the stone to receive a share of the coins, and then stepped across it to take a hot cross bun and an additional half-crown (12½p): in recent years the money has been given to children instead, and the buns shared among the congregation. The tombstone used, however, has no connection with the charity's original donor – whose identity is quite unknown, as is the actual position of his or her grave. Records of the foundation are usually said to have perished in the Great Fire of London: but the only certainties are that the custom was established by 1686, and that it was re-endowed two centuries later by a Mr Butterworth, whence its present title.

The founder of another Good Friday graveside dole has, by contrast, become the hero of a local legend. This relates how Nicholas Smith, a wealthy squire in search of a home among good neighbours, roamed the Wealden country disguised as a beggar: village after village spurned him, until at last the people of Hartfield in East Sussex received him kindly – whereupon he revealed his true identity, settled down in the parish at Crotchford Manor, and cared for its poor up to and beyond his death in 1634. Thus is 'explained' the bequest of £10 which Smith certainly did order to be divided annually among forty poor Hartfield widows at the site of his tomb, and which is still distributed there – although the number of claimants is (as usual) now far smaller, and their individual shares consequently greater.

Like most such charities, Nicholas Smith's is accompanied only by a comparatively simple ceremony: but a few benefactors (see JOHN KNILL'S CHARITY; OLD MAN'S

DAY) preferred to leave detailed instructions for the distribution of their graveside alms, or attach specific conditions to their dispersal (*see* FORTY SHILLING DAY). Among these last was William Hubbard, a music-loving grocer from Market Harborough in Leicestershire, who died in 1774 and was buried in St Mary-in-Arden churchyard. Round his grave there, each EASTER SATURDAY, the choir still sing the hymn which earns them the annual guinea stipulated by his will.

· Greenaway's Dole ·
see BREAD AND BUN DOLES

· Grovely Rights Day ·
Great Wishford and Salisbury Cathedral, Wiltshire: 29 May

The villagers of Great Wishford, near Salisbury, (who also keep up a type of CANDLE AUCTION) possess the COMMON right to gather 'all kinde of deade snapping woode, Boughes and Stickes' – once very necessary for fuel – in the neighbouring and formerly royal FOREST of Grovely. But in order to preserve their privilege (which had already existed 'ever by auntient custome and tyme out of mind' when recorded in 1603) they must formally claim it annually: and since the Restoration they have done so on OAK APPLE DAY, many of whose customs are mingled with the current ceremonies.

These begin well before dawn on 29 May, when a raucous TIN CAN BAND rouses the villagers, who then go into the forest to cut green boughs, generally but not necessarily from oak trees: they must be brought back 'by strength of people', so that neither horse nor motor transport can be used, though bicycles (after some controversy) are allowed. Some are at once used to decorate village houses, and a particularly fine specimen ('the Marriage Bough') is adorned with ribbons and hauled to the top of the church tower, to bring luck to all couples married that year (*see* ARBOR DAY; CASTLETON GARLAND).

Others are carried during the most important event of the day, the claiming ceremony at Salisbury Cathedral. At one time, the villagers used to dance the entire six miles there, but since this part of the custom was revived in 1951 (after a long interval during which the claim was made at Wishford Rectory) they have travelled by coach. On arrival, four Victorian-costumed women bearing oak sprays dance first on the cathedral green and then, followed by the whole company, into the church and up to the high altar, where the sprigs are presented to the Dean; this done, the villagers raise the traditional shout of 'Grovely! Grovely! Grovely! and all Grovely!', and the right is safe for another year.

But the festivities of this crowded morning are not yet over, for the grand celebratory procession through Wishford must still be made. It is led by the same women, now carrying symbolic 'nitches' (bundles) of dry firewood; and by the Oak Apple Club's banner, with its proud motto 'Grovely! Grovely! Grovely! and all Grovely! Unity is Strength'.

Led by their sloganned banner and by women whose bundles of kindling symbolize an immemorial right to gather firewood in Grovely Forest, the Oak Apple Club parades through Great Wishford on **Grovely Rights Day.**

Opposite: The Vintners, one of the most influential of London **guilds and companies,** process to St James Garlickhythe on their election day: their path is swept by wine porters, and their barge-master and beadles carry posies to ward off infection.

· Guilds and Companies ·

Guilds (or 'gilds') originated in Anglo-Saxon times as voluntary clubs for mutual support, which cared for sick members, maintained their widows and orphans and (just as important in medieval eyes) arranged prayers for their souls after death: social and religious functions which they always retained, and to a certain extent retain still. By the 12th century, however, many places had developed 'guilds merchant' (*see* PRESTON GUILD) whose primary purpose was both to regulate (or indeed monopolize) trade within the borough and effectively to act as a town council: and during the next 200 years emphasis shifted again to the individual guilds formed by each separate trade and craft. These supervised the training of apprentices, regulated the price and quality of goods produced, and fixed wages and holidays within the craft or 'mystery' (i.e. 'mastery' or 'metier'), as well as making sure that none but accredited members might practise it: and in many cases they not only maintained special chapels or altars for their guildsmen, but also organized elaborate processions and produced annual 'Mystery plays' on religious themes.

Between them, therefore, guilds from the Basket-makers and Bowyers to the Waxchandlers and Wire-drawers controlled every aspect of the trade and industry of medieval Britain. Richest and most powerful, however, were the 'Great Guilds' of merchants and wholesalers – like the Mercers, Grocers, Fishmongers, Merchant Taylors and Vintners – and most influential of all were the merchant guilds of London, which included royalty and noblemen among their members and frequently played a significant part in national politics during the 14th and 15th centuries. By that time, moreover, many of them had been granted royal charters confirming their powers: thus becoming 'Livery Companies' with the coveted right to distinctive 'liveries' or robes, like the blue furred gowns still worn on ceremonial occasions by the London Haberdashers or the blue and yellow of the Drapers.

Guilds in general declined after the 17th century, abandoning their religious role at the Reformation and gradually losing their monopolistic control over trade with the disappearance of apprenticeship and the rise of 'private enterprise' capitalism. But the Livery Companies of London still dominate the business life of the City, even though many of their members now have scant connection with their nominal craft, and several of the crafts have themselves faded away. The Goldsmiths, however, still regulate the quality of gold and silver articles at the Assay Office in their Hall (hence 'hallmark', their seal of approval); the Gunmakers retain the monopoly on testing and proofing firearms; and the Apothecaries and the Spectacle-makers continue to award professional qualifications: while most London guilds and companies keep up their charitable traditions by maintaining schools and institutions.

All eighty-one London companies, moreover, steadfastly uphold their ancient customs and ceremonies, and guard no less carefully their position in the order of precedence established during the 15th century: this is headed by the 'Twelve Great Companies' – the Mercers, Grocers, Drapers, Fishmongers, Goldsmiths; the Merchant Taylors and the Skinners (who in 1484 settled a long-standing feud by agreeing to take sixth and seventh places in alternate years); the Haberdashers, Salters, Ironmongers, Vintners and Clothworkers. In this order the liverymen (or senior members) of the companies cast their votes at the 'election' of the LORD MAYOR OF LONDON in the significantly named 'Guildhall' on Michaelmas Day, while the liveried and mace-bearing 'beadles' of the guilds stand sentinel outside the doors of the hall.

Every year, too, each company elects its own officials – generally three or four wardens, presided over by a master, prime warden or bailiff – and on 'Installation Day' most walk in full state from their Hall to a service in their traditional guild church. At about noon on the second Thursday in July, for instance, the Vintners process from their Hall in Upper Thames Street to St James Garlickhythe: and according to ancient custom they are always preceded by wine porters in top hats and white smocks, who sweep their path with 'full besoms ... that the Master and his Wardens and Brethren ... slip not on any foulness of our streets'. Behind these come the company's beadle, stavesmen, swan markers and barge master – a reminder that the Vintners share with the Dyers the ownership of all non-royal swans on

the Thames (*see* SWAN UPPING): and then follow the master and officials, each carrying a nosegay of strong-smelling flowers and herbs, 'that their nostrils be not offended by any noxious flavours or other ill vapours'. The Skinners, whose installation procession to St Mary Aldermary on the second Thursday after Whitsun is led by Christ's Hospital Boys (*see* FOUNDERS' DAY), also carry posies with a similar purpose: while on 10 July the Grocers walk to St Stephen Wallbrook, and on the last Wednesday in October the Basketmakers go in state to St Margaret Pattens, Eastcheap.

Nor are guild processions and services confined to election days. For every ASH WEDNESDAY the Stationers process to St Faith's Chapel in St Paul's Cathedral for a service endowed by John Norton in 1612, afterwards returning to their Hall for a PEACE AND GOOD NEIGH-BOURHOOD FEAST of 'cakes and ale': and on the first Tuesday in June they attend the 'Bubble SERMONS' at St Martin's-within-Ludgate. While at various times of the year certain companies solemnly proceed to the Mansion House with traditional gifts for the Lord Mayor: thus the Butchers present him with a boar's head in January; the Gardeners with flowers and vegetables on or near 29 June; and the Fruiterers with a magnificent display of their goods in November – a custom which originated in 1748, as thanksgiving for the abolition of a City fruit-toll. Liveried officials of the Fishmongers Company, moreover, supervise DOGGETT'S COAT AND BADGE RACE in August, and those of the Watermen and Lightermen attend the Knollys Rose QUIT RENT ceremony at Midsummer.

Much the most ancient and magnificent ceremonials of the London guilds and companies, however, take place at their annual banquets: but since these are private affairs they can only be touched upon here. Many companies, for example, retain the medieval banquet custom of crowning newly installed officials with garlands or chaplets – generally elaborate silver-gilt and embroidered crowns dating from the 16th or 17th centuries. Many, too, possess precious gold or silver 'Loving Cups' of similar vintage, which they pass round according to a somewhat paranoid ritual which is dubiously alleged to stem from the murder in 978 of King Edward the Martyr, stabbed while his hands were busy with a stirrup-cup. As the Loving Cup approaches, therefore, three guildsmen rise together – one to hold the cover of the vessel, one using both hands to drink from it, and a third to stand back to back with the drinker, thus guarding him against treachery.

London, of course, is not the only place where guilds survive: for those of many provincial towns continue to function, if only as ceremonial and social institutions. Among the most ancient are the Companies of Merchant Adventurers and of Merchant Taylors of York – where other guilds are also enjoying a revival – which both maintain medieval halls: and the Worshipful Company of Smiths at Lichfield, which continues to hold its annual court every August.

· Gunpowder Plot Sermon ·
see SERMONS

· Gurning Competition ·
see CRABAPPLE FAIR

· Guy Fawkes Night ·
5 November

One of the most widespread and flourishing of all British celebrations and one of the few decreed by Act of Parliament – a Parliament saved from 'being all destroyed and blowen upp at once' when Guy Fawkes was arrested in its cellars in the early hours of 5 November 1605. Concealed there were thirty-six barrels of gunpowder, which Fawkes planned to ignite during James I's opening of Parliament later that same day, thus obliterating the entire government of England and clearing the way for a Roman Catholic coup. Whether or not (as some now claim) this 'Gunpowder Plot' was covertly encouraged by an administration anxious to discredit its Catholic opponents, its discovery certainly sparked off a nationwide explosion of patriotism and Protestant fervour, later given added force by the landing of William III – England's deliverer from the unpopular Catholic James II – on 5 November 1688.

Few, therefore, were content merely with the thanksgiving service which, until 1859, all parish churches were bound to hold on 5 November: and people eagerly seized on the opportunity for a jollification which not even the most enthusiastic Puritan could censure as 'pagan' or 'Popish'. BELLS were pealed (as they still are in some places), cannon fired, and beer flowed freely: but the most essential element has always been the lighting of bonfires – a custom which may have owed something to the old HALLOWEEN fires traditionally burned a few days earlier, and now (like MISCHIEF NIGHT) totally absorbed into the newer festival.

Except in a few places like St Peter's school, York (where Fawkes was educated) and Scotton, North Yorkshire (where he once lived), 'guys' are also vital. Ranging from elaborate effigies in period costume to shapeless bundles of old clothes, they appear days or even weeks before Bonfire Night, accompanied by bands of children collecting firework money. Recently the usual begging rhyme has been:

> Please to remember the fifth of November
> Gunpowder treason and plot
> I see no reason why gunpowder treason
> Should ever be forgot

and few recall additions like:

> A rope, a rope, to hang the Pope
> A piece of cheese to choke him
> A barrel of beer to drink his health
> And a right good fire to roast him.
> *Cambridgeshire*

Right: The daring 'tar-barrellers' of Ottery St Mary run through the streets with their blazing burdens on **Guy Fawkes Night.**

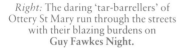

Left: Well-remembered – though not as they would have wished – the Gunpowder Plotters of 1605, with **Guy Fawkes** himself at centre right. From a contemporary German engraving.

While many are content with a simple 'Penny for the Guy', and a final, heartless:

> Guy, guy, guy
> Poke him in the eye
> Put him on the bonfire
> And there let him die.

No longer, however, are guys filled with live cats, to make their death-throes more realistic. Instead, sausages are toasted on the bonfire, and potatoes baked in its embers; while more specifically seasonal foods like 'Bonfire Parkin' (a heavy cake made with oatmeal, molasses and ginger) and 'Plot Toffee' are still very popular in Yorkshire.

Fireworks, of course, are universal: though there is an increasing (and lamentable) tendency to banish them from back gardens to the organized displays now held in most towns and villages. These can be desperately dull affairs; and only comparatively few places keep up elements of the lively (if at times riotous and dangerous) communal celebrations which once marked Guy Fawkes Night.

Among these is Lewes in Sussex, where seventeen townsmen were burnt for Protestantism under Bloody Mary. So the ceremonies here retain an anti-Catholic bias fortunately forgotten elsewhere, and among the giant effigies carried by costumed and torchlit processions of the six town bonfire societies is always one of the Pope. After a sermon from a mock bishop, this is then exploded, to cheers of 'No Popery'.

Bridgwater in Somerset's zeal for Guy Fawkes celebrations – held on the Thursday nearest the 5th – also stems from memories of Catholic-inspired persecution, after Monmouth's Rebellion in 1685. But here the high point (which follows a grand carnival procession) is the display of 'Bridgwater Squibs', spectacular fireworks specially made for the occasion.

Ottery St Mary, Devon, is unique in preserving two hazardous Guy Fawkes customs: the firing throughout the day of hand-held 'rock cannons'; and 'tar-barrel rolling' – allegedly begun to celebrate William III's landing in 1688. Nine barrels (the largest an immense sixty-five gallon hogshead) are thickly coated with bitumen, and carried blazing on the shoulders of running men: when the heat becomes too great for one 'roller' – minimum protective clothing is worn – he passes it to another, until it disintegrates.

Tar barrels also feature in Hatherleigh in Devon's Fire Festival, held on the Wednesday after 5 November. Here, however, they are piled on sledges and dragged through the town at a gallop, to ignite a final bonfire. (*See also* ALLENDALE TAR BARRELS)

H

· Halloween ·
31 October

The last night of October was the eve of Samhain, when the Celtic peoples celebrated 'Winter's Eve' and the beginning of their New Year: so it was a kind of crack in time, through which the dead returned to their old haunts, and all kinds of other supernatural beings – many of them dangerously powerful – swarmed to plague the living. In an attempt to Christianize this pagan festival (and perhaps also to protect its flock) the Church therefore adopted 1 November as the feast of All Saints (or All Hallows): and 2 November became All Souls' Day, when prayers are made for the departed.

Except for a few remnants of SOULING, All Hallows' Even has now lost most of its associations with the Returning Dead. All over northern and western Britain, however, witches and supernatural beings are still remembered (and impersonated) by the bands of disguised children who roam the streets with turnip lanterns (see PUNKY NIGHT) knocking on doors to beg for sweets or pennies. In recent years, too, they sometimes threaten 'Trick or Treat', an American custom which originated in Britain (see MISCHIEF NIGHT) and is now being reintroduced even into south-east England, where the celebration of Halloween had either been almost forgotten or – like the bonfires once burned to keep off evil spirits – transferred to GUY FAWKES NIGHT.

As a hiatus in the natural order, Halloween is also a good time to seek glimpses into the future: and though it is doubtful whether anyone now watches for the spirits of next year's dead processing through the midnight churchyard, many other 'divination rites' are still unwittingly or half-jokingly played out in Halloween party games. The most popular is 'bob-apple', where apples are either floated in water or hung by a string, to be seized with the player's teeth alone: they should then be peeled in one unbroken strip which, when thrown over the left shoulder, will form the initial of a true lover. Alternatively, two nuts or apple pips, representing a pair of lovers, are placed side by side on the fire: in Scotland and northern England, their burning quietly together presages marriage, but if they 'spit and fly' the couple will soon part. In southern England, conversely:

> If he loves me, pop and fly
> If he hates me, lie and die.

For a more generalized prophecy, Scots conceal charms in a bowl of 'champit tatties' (mashed potatoes): everyone takes a spoonful, and the charm it contains – coin for wealth, thimble for spinsterhood, wishbone for the heart's desire – shows their fortune in the coming year.

· Handy Sermon ·
see SERMONS

· Hare Pie Scramble ·
see BOTTLE KICKING

· Hartfield Dole ·
see GRAVESIDE DOLES

· Harvest Customs ·

The immemorial harvest-field customs and ceremonies of Britain have now effectively passed into history: yet they are so closely woven into the fabric of the traditional calendar that they must at least be summarized here. In their fullest form, such customs belong to the period – beginning in the mists of prehistory and enduring into the present century on some small or remote farms – when the entire process of converting standing corn to garnered grain was carried out exclusively with hand-tools. First, the corn had to be reaped with sickles or (latterly) mown with scythes, and then tied into sheaves – often by women or older men – using cornstalk 'bands' generally made by children. Next, the sheaves must be piled into stooks or 'shocks' to finish ripening, before being carted and stored in stacks or ricks, which were frequently thatched to protect them from the weather. Even when the last sheaf was pitchforked onto the last stack at 'harvest home', moreover, the work was far from over; for the grain still had to be separated from the straw and chaff by threshing with flails and winnowing with sieves or shovels, a task so lengthy that it occupied much of the 'slack' winter period.

Each step in this vital process had its own customs and conventions, which varied not only from county to county but also from parish to parish and even from farm to farm – as well as fluctuating with the passage of time. Generally speaking, however, the harvest work was preceded by the choosing of a a 'harvest lord' or 'King of the Mowers', an outstanding reaper who had also to be trusted and respected by his fellows. For it was he who negotiated harvest wages and conditions with the farmer, and his word was law in the harvest field, where he regulated the pace of work, disciplined slackers, and called the halts for tool-sharpening, meals, or the harvest beer and cider which the landowner was expected to provide. And it was he, too, who demanded the customary 'largesse' from passers-by, casual visitors or neighbouring householders – followed, if the contribution was satisfactory, by the 'hollering of largesse' with loud shouts, the blowing of harvest horns, and the throwing of sickles into the air.

As the reaping of a farm's corn drew to an end, harvesters all over Britain – but more particularly in the north and west – observed the ritual of gathering the last sheaf. In many places, the stalks of this last remnant of standing corn were tied together below the ears, and the

'The Country round Dixton Manor' in Gloucestershire, c. 1730, shows many of the hand-harvesting processes which gave rise to **harvest customs,** as well as the large number of harvest workers needed. Left of centre is a gang of mowers, and in the right foreground morris dancers follow the 'Last Load' home.

company then threw their sickles at it until one cut it down: hereupon (in Devon) he cried out 'I have un', to which his fellows replied 'What have ee?', and then all shouted 'A neck! A neck!' In Shropshire, alternatively, the last sheaf was 'the Gonder's [gander's] Neck'; in Herefordshire and elsewhere it was 'the Mare'; in Wales the *Caseg Fedi* (harvest mare); in Kent 'the Ivy Girl'; in northern England and southern Scotland 'the Kern Baby'; and in other parts of Scotland – where its gathering was sometimes reserved for the prettiest unmarried girl harvester – it was 'the Maiden' or the *Cailleach* (old woman), depending on whether the harvest was early or late. But whatever its name, the last sheaf cut was almost invariably treated with reverence, being plaited into 'corn dollies' – a custom still kept up on a few farms, even in these days of 'combines' – or dressed in women's clothes and set to preside over the harvest supper before being kept 'for luck' until the next harvest. In parts of Wales, however, some of its grain might be mixed with the seed corn, 'to teach it to grow'; while in Scotland it was sometimes ceremonially fed to the farm horses at the start of the succeeding year's ploughing.

The honours shown to the last sheaf may well have been a relic of the pagan belief that the Corn Spirit dwelt there, and it has been suggested that the sickle-throwing game originated as an attempt to diffuse or deflect the ill luck (or worse) entailed in 'killing' her. In more recent centuries, however, the custom of 'Crying the Neck' was simply a method of loudly proclaiming to all that the harvest was over, and it was often accompanied by an ironic offer to send a mare – or even 'the Mare' herself – to help out a tardier neighbouring farmer and his harvest gang. Such derisive proposals were generally made from a distance (or a galloping horse) for they

were likely to be greeted by a shower of stones, and woe betide the man the laggard harvesters caught.

In other parts of the country, especially southern and midland England, the harvest-end customs centred instead around the last (or 'Hockey') load of corn carted from the harvest field. Adorned with flags, boughs and flowers, sometimes crowned with the last sheaf, and drawn by elaborately bedecked horses, this frequently made a triumphant tour of the parish before returning to the farm, surrounded by shouting and singing harvesters: and in some places it was the custom to shower both these and the last load with buckets of water, either in token that the long-feared rain was now welcome or 'just for fun'.

The principal reason why such customs have now ceased is not far to seek. For the increasing mechanization of arable farming – beginning with the advent of mechanical threshers in the 1830s and proceeding via horse-drawn reaping and binding machines to the 'combine harvester', which converts standing corn to grain and straw in a single operation – has not only swept away all the old harvesting methods, but also banished the harvesters themselves from the fields. To gather the harvest of an average-sized farm by hand, for instance, might require as many as a hundred labourers, including gypsies, 'Irishmen' and other itinerant 'harvest gangs'; but reaping machines and steam threshers reduced this number to about twenty, and the same task can now be performed by two or three men and a 'combine'. It is notable, too, that forms of 'harvest' which remained comparatively labour-intensive – sheep-shearing and hop-picking for instance – preserved their ancient customs far longer, and in some cases retain them yet. Thus (on the Welsh border at least) a visitor to a shearing shed may still be asked for 'largesse' in the form of 'shearing cider'; while in the hop gardens of Kent and Herefordshire the 'farm bailiff' or some other notable is still occasionally plunged headfirst into a hop bin on the last day of picking.

The mechanization of farming, however, was not the only reason why the customs of the corn harvest came to an end, and many were already in decline well before the final triumph of the machine. For social and 'moral' pressures, and the increase of class-consciousness, also contributed to the downfall of the old ways: and this process is nowhere better observed than in the transformation of the farm-based 'harvest home dinner' – once the crown of the agricultural year – into the modern HARVEST FESTIVALS.

· Harvest Festivals ·

With its farm produce piled round the altar and pulpit; its familiar hymns – 'We Plough the Fields and Scatter' and 'Come Ye Thankful People, Come'; its sermon on gratitude and its packed congregation of occasional worshippers, the familiar Harvest Festival service has long since acquired the patina of an 'ancient and traditional custom'. In fact, however, harvest festivals of this kind are of comparatively recent origin, and before the mid-19th century the universal harvest-end celebration was the 'Horkey' (eastern England) 'Mell Supper' (northern England) 'Kirn-Feast' (Scotland) or 'Harvest Frolic' (West Country) – a gargantuan meal provided by the farmer for all his employees.

> In harvest time, harvest-folk, servants and all
> Should make all together good cheer in thy hall
> Once ended thy harvest, let none be beguiled
> Please such as did help thee, man woman and child

advised Thomas Tusser in 1570: and one essential feature of such farm-based rejoicings was that the master and his family should mix freely with his labourers, 'with no distinction of persons ... but in the most easy familiarity'. He might, however, choose to slip away before the end of the evening, for another vital feature of the proceedings was the copious beer and cider provided to wash down the goose, roast beef and plum pudding: some thoughtful farmers, therefore, 'laid clean, loose straw outside the barn, for those requiring temporary rest and meditation'. But before this point was reached, it was customary for the oldest harvester present to toast the farmer with some such words as:

> Here's a health unto our master, the founder of
>   the feast
> We pray to God his soul may rest, where all is love
>   and peace
> While here it is our duty, to consider his demands
> And take it as a pleasure, to bow to his command.
> *Somerset*

while in many parts of the country the feasters might play a traditional harvest-home game like the Sussex 'Turn the Cup Over'. A horn cup full of beer was set on the crown of a top hat, which the player held by the brim with both hands: by this means he raised the cup to his lips, and attempted to drink the contents without spilling a drop, while the bystanders sang:

> Over and over and over and over
> Drink up yur liquor and turn the cup over
> Over and over and over and over
> The liquor's drink'd up and the cup is turned over.

If he succeeded, he flicked the cup up and caught it in the hat; but if a drop remained, he had to start all over again.

By the beginning of Queen Victoria's reign, however, this type of harvest celebration had already begun to attract the disapproval of middle-class moralists and temperance reformers, who regarded it (not without some justification) as 'merely a disorderly, drunken rout': while a number of social-climbing farmers had come to dislike the notion of sharing a table with mere harvesters and labourers. So when two West Country rectors of the 1840s (George Denison of East Brent, Somerset, and R.S. Hawker of Morwenstow in Cornwall) simultaneously introduced a special 'harvest festival' service, followed by a tea for all the parish's harvesters (though not necessarily its farmers) the idea at once gained currency – at least among a majority of the 'governing classes'. Within a decade, such 'respectable and morally sound' celebrations, and especially the decoration of churches, had received the blessing of the Queen herself: and by 1889 one rector could declare that: 'The old harvest home is no more. We have instead "harvest festivals", tea and cake at sixpence a head in the schoolroom, and a choral service and sermon in the church.' A few traditionalist farmers nevertheless kept up the old farm-centred 'horkeys' well into the present century: and a handful do so still, even though the number of people directly concerned with the harvest has now dwindled so greatly that even parochial 'harvest suppers' are becoming rare.

Harvest festival services, conversely, continue to be universally popular and well attended, even in town churches whose congregations have little or no connection with agriculture; and many towns hold special Civic Harvest Thanksgivings. Market fruit traders, of course, remain especially affected by the abundance or otherwise of the crop: and the London costermongers called 'Pearly Kings and Queens' (whose elaborately pearl-buttoned dress is supposed to derive from Cockney enthusiasm for a sold-off cargo of Mexican costumes) hold a harvest festival of their own at St Martin's-in-the-Fields, Trafalgar Square, on the first Sunday in October. At Richmond in North Yorkshire, moreover, where the mayor also holds the office of Clerk of the Market, an ancient First Fruits of the Harvest ceremony is held annually on a Saturday in September. After a full-dress civic procession to the market place, the first local farmer to produce 'a

respectable sample of the new season's corn is presented with two bottles of wine: one he opens immediately, so that the company may drink the mayor's health, and the other he retains for his own table.

Communities connected with fishing likewise hold special thanksgiving services for the 'Harvest of the Sea', generally during October. At Flamborough in East Yorkshire; Yarmouth in Norfolk; and Mudeford in Hampshire, churches are hung with fishermen's nets for the occasion: while at St Mary-at-Hill, the parish church of London's old Billingsgate fish market, every available kind of fish is laid out on a vast slab in the porch – thirty-nine varieties used to be the traditional number, in honour of the Thirty-Nine Articles of the Church of England. After the service, as is now customary at all harvest festivals, the produce will be sent to hospitals and other charitable institutions.

· Hat and Ribbon Race ·
Inverkeithing, near Dunfermline, Fife: first Thursday in August

The annual three-day FAIRS at Inverkeithing, held at LAMMAS since early medieval times, open with a running race originally instituted for the 'herd laddies' (or young agricultural labourers) who once flocked there to 'fee' (hire) themselves out for the coming year. It is run through the streets, over an out and back distance of just under half a mile, and the double prize is a new 'lum' (top) hat for the lad himself, with a bunch of ribbons for his girl. Borne aloft on the halberd of the Burgh Officer, these are carried to the finishing line at the head of a civic procession, and presented to the winner by the Provost.

Displaying the correct mixture of patriotism and gratitude, picturesque yokels take part in an organized mid-Victorian **harvest festival** at Swallowfield in Berkshire.

A bishop and other dignitaries stand by the pile of fish (traditionally thirty-nine varieties) laid out for the **harvest festival** in St Mary-at-Hill parish church.

· Hatherleigh Fire Festival ·
see GUY FAWKES NIGHT

· The Haxey Hood Game ·
Haxey, Lincolnshire: 6 January, or the previous day if 6 January is a Sunday

On the afternoon of the Twelfth Day after CHRISTMAS – which is also Christmas Day, Old Style – the bells of Haxey church in north Lincolnshire ring out to welcome the Hood procession, as it marches up the village street singing the Hood song, 'Drink Old England Dry'. At its head walks the Fool, with blackened face, red shirt and colourfully patched trousers, bearing the Hood itself, a two-foot-long leather cylinder: and with him is the Lord of the Hood in his scarlet hunting coat and flower-decked top hat, bearing his official wand of thirteen willow rods bound round thirteen times. Behind them march the Chief Boggan, dressed like the Lord, and his twelve Boggans, athletic young men in red football shirts.

Mounted on the Mowbray Stone and holding the Hood itself, the Fool begins the **Haxey Hood Game** with his speech. Beside him stands the Lord of the Hood, with his wand of thirteen willow rods bound thirteen times.

When the procession nears the church, the Fool makes a bid to escape, but the Boggans soon recapture him, and mount him on the ancient 'Mowbray Stone' outside the churchyard wall. There, holding the Hood aloft, he makes a speech of welcome to the company: and though some of the Boggans are meanwhile 'smoking the Fool' by lighting a damp straw fire under his feet, he usually manages to finish with a reminder that the Hood game is to be played:

> Hoose agin' hoose, toon agin' toon
> If tha' meets a man, knock 'im doon
> But don't 'urt 'im.

This done, the Lord leads the way to a nearby ploughed field, on a piece of rising land roughly equidistant from the two townships of Haxey and Westwoodside. When the Boggans have ranged themselves into a wide ring round its edges, the first of twelve sacking rolls called 'Dummies' or 'Youngsters' Hoods' is thrown up: as it hits the ground, children and teenagers struggle for its possession, and eventually the winner breaks away with the prize for the field boundary – where one of the Boggans generally tackles him to the ground, and the next Dummy is thrown into play. Sometimes, however, an impromptu team manages to evade the red-shirted guardians by passing a Dummy from one to another, whereupon they carry it to a local pub for a reward of fifty pence.

After about an hour of this, the Hood proper is thrown up for the serious business of the day – 'the Sway', a scrum of anything up to a hundred men, which will eventually push and shove the Hood either to the King's Arms at Haxey or the Carpenter's Arms at Westwoodside, depending on the strength and stamina of the respective hostelries' supporters. (Until recently a third local pub also used to take part, but this has lately dropped out after a dispute about muddy carpets.) Strict rules dictate that the leather Hood may neither be run with, thrown, or kicked: and the Sway may take as long as three hours to reach its destination, generally well after darkness has fallen. For though the team which gets the scrum moving down its own side of the hill has a distinct advantage, the opposition will not give up until the Sway reaches the very doors of their opponents' pub. And while the scrummage frequently halts as its centre collapses into a heap of writhing, mud-covered bodies, nothing else will stop it: crops – hereabouts still planted medieval style, in unfenced 'open-field' strips belonging to multifarious small farmers – are cheerfully trampled underfoot, and bystanders may be unceremoniously drawn in if they fail to avoid a sudden sideways lurch of the Sway. But in the end the Hood reaches one or other pub – though during the Second World War, it was once concealed down a 'broken-legged' soldier's trousers, and spirited away to his regiment's camp – where drinks are on the house, and an evening's jollification follows. There the trophy will remain until the following New Year's Eve – curious strangers asking what it is are liable to 'buy a round' – when the Boggans collect it for a week-long tour of neighbouring inns, singing and drumming up support for the next event.

'The Hood', as this custom is invariably known locally, has been carried on in essentially the same manner for at least a century and a half, though some aspects of it were formerly conducted in an even more robust fashion than at present. The Fool, for example, was at one time 'smoked' by suspending him on a rope from a tree, and swinging him backwards and forwards over a fire – a practice which ceased after a near fatality: while 'the Sway' was, well within living memory, regarded as a very dangerous proceeding indeed, the Fool's injunction 'don't hurt him' having apparently been introduced only in about 1914.

Local tradition insists that the origins of the game date from the 13th century, when a certain Lady Mowbray – whose family were overlords of Haxey and the surrounding Isle of Axholme from around 1100 until 1481 – happened to be riding across the high land between Haxey and Westwoodside on Christmas Day. At this point a strong wind caught her red hood and blew it away, but thirteen local smallholders (or 'boggans') gave chase, and after pursuing it all over the field they finally caught it and returned it to her. So charmed and amused was she by their rustic gallantry, the tale continues, that she granted them and their descendants thirteen half-acre 'selions' of land, with the proviso that the chase must be annually re-enacted as a kind of QUIT RENT. And though the deeds to the land disappeared long ago, this has accordingly been done ever since, the thirteen original smallholders being commemorated by the thirteen rods in the Lord's wand and by the Fool and twelve Boggans, whose red clothing recalls the colour of the original Hood.

Needless to say, alternative explanations of the custom abound. Some have maintained that it is simply a local version of a PLOUGH MONDAY custom, with the Boggans taking the place of the usual Lincolnshire 'plough bullocks' – an assertion indignantly rejected by local opinion, as is the suggestion that the Hood game is merely a type of STREET BALL GAME or SHROVETIDE FOOTBALL, with a legend tacked on to lend it individuality. Similar games once played in the neighbouring villages of Epworth and Belton, the locals also insist, were only copies of the Haxey observance. The theory currently favoured by many folklorists, almost inevitably, is that the game perpetuates a pre-Christian fertility rite. Pointing to the fact that the captured Hood used once to be roasted on a spit before the victors' inn fire, and to a rural chestnut formerly included in the Fool's speech – 'We've killed a bullock and a half: the other half's still running about afield' – they believe that 'the Hood' was originally 'the head' of a sacrificial beast, ritually striven over by rival villages who coveted its fertility-inducing powers. A variant on this theory, that the game developed from the 'running' or 'baiting'

of a Christmas bull donated by the Mowbrays (as beasts were also provided by local noblemen for the bull-runnings at Stamford in Lincolnshire and Tutbury in Staffordshire) seems altogether more plausible – if not so much so as Haxey's own explanation. But whatever its origins, the Hood game is kept up with a commendable absence of commercialization or prettification, and with an admirable vigour which shows no signs of diminishing.

· Henley Royal Regatta ·
Henley-on-Thames, Oxfordshire: four days in early July

The first OXFORD AND CAMBRIDGE BOAT RACE was rowed at Henley in 1829, and ten years later a regular 'regatta' – a name originally applied to a Venetian gondola race – began there. At first a purely local event, which received its 'Royal' suffix when Prince Albert became its patron in 1855, it retains a distinctive character of its own, and has remarkably little in common with other international rowing events. Races are rowed against the stream – because stands could not be erected near the finish if they were rowed in the usual direction; the course, at 1 mile 570 yards, does not correspond to any internationally recognized distance; and the spirit and principles of amateurism are maintained, with aloof disregard for modern trends in sport. After a century and a half of coping with huge crowds, moreover, the regatta still has no permanent grandstand or spectator facilities.

In spite of its anomalies, the Henley regatta is the most respected and imitated of all rowing events, and there are 'Henley regattas' in Canada, Australia and the USA. Just as at ROYAL ASCOT, it is important to dress correctly for the occasion. At Henley, this means white trousers, striped blazers and rowing caps – a uniform much worn by people who have never rowed in their lives, and nowadays even affected by women. The chief race of the event is the Grand Thames Challenge Cup for eights. This was first contested in 1893, and has always attracted overseas competitors; many of whom (including the Russians) have carried off the trophy. The Stewards' Cup, for fours, dates from 1841: but the most publicized event today is the Diamond Sculls, so called from the diamond-studded scarf pin originally awarded as the prize. The fourth principal race is the Ladies' Plate; which is, of course, not rowed by ladies. For many spectators, however, the ambience of the regatta – one of the most elegant events of the London season – is probably quite as important as the sport.

· Highland Games ·

Though many Highland clans had long held annual gatherings which included traditional sports and games, it was not until the first decades of the 19th century that 'Highland Games' in their modern form first became established. By one of the great ironies of British history,

Above: Tossing the caber, which must describe a perfect semi-circle in the air, is both the most difficult and the most characteristic of **Highland Games** sports. *Above right:* 'Tartan romanticism' is at its most rampant during the Games, and is well exemplified by the totally anomalous men's kilts worn by female highland dancers. *Right:* This competitor 'throwing the hammer' answers once and for all the question of what is worn beneath the kilt.

however, this occurred only after the wearing of genuine Highland dress (prohibited by law between the Battle of Culloden in 1746 and 1782) had virtually come to an end: and at the very moment when thousands of Highlanders were being forced to emigrate by the systematic 'Clearances' of their ancestral lands for use as sheep pastures, a practice at least as popular among the clan chiefs themselves as among Lowland or English proprietors. Only after their customs and way of life had been all but destroyed, therefore, did the people once abominated as 'uncouth and dangerous savages' begin to be seen through rose-tinted spectacles: and the tide of Tartan Romanticism unleashed by George IV's visit to Scotland in 1822 – when the portly King donned a kilt

of a specially invented 'Royal Stuart' tartan, but insisted upon wearing pink tights beneath it – reached full flood under the influence of Queen Victoria's devotion to Balmoral and her 'beloved Highlands'.

The great popularity of Highland Games, indeed, really dates from Queen Victoria's patronage of them, which began in 1848 and has been continued ever since by her royal descendants, who frequently attend the famous gathering held at Braemar in Aberdeenshire during early September. There, as at most other Games, the most spectacular event is the great opening march-past of kilted, bonneted and be-sworded clansmen, led by the local 'clan of the land' and preceded by a brave show of pipers. At the mid-August Games at Cowal in

Argyllshire as many as a thousand pipers take part in the parade, and the majority of Games and gatherings include hard-contested championships for solo bag-pipers. Many, too, feature competitions and displays of Highland dancing – principally the 'Gille Callum' or Highland sword dance, the Highland Fling, and the *Seann Triuthas* (Old Trousers) whose name is supposed-ly a scornful reference to the garments worn during the ban on the kilt.

Athletic events at Highland Games usually include hurdle and running races – easily the most strenuous being the gruelling thirteen-mile marathon up and down the 4,406 feet of Ben Nevis, held since 1899 at the mid-July Fort William Games: as well as 'Putting the Stone'; throwing the fifty-six pound 'Weight'; 'Throw-ing the Hammer' – an iron ball on a chain; and of course 'Tossing the Caber'. Said to have originated as a means of heaving felled tree-trunks over ravines or burns, this involves tossing a long and unwieldy pole (the Braemar Caber is 19 feet long and weighs 120 pounds) so that it revolves through a vertical semi-circle in as straight a line as possible: the direction of the throw is therefore more important than the distance covered, and a perfectly tossed caber should lie in an exact 'twelve o'clock' line directly in front of the thrower, with its base facing directly away from him.

More than seventy sets of Highland Games are currently held, generally between June and mid-September: and though the majority take place in Highland areas – Perthshire alone boasting at least twelve sets – similar events have become popular throughout Scotland, penetrating even the Lowland and Border counties whose inhabitants, less than two centur-ies ago, would probably have died rather than adopt the customs and dress of 'the barbaric Highlander'.

· Hobby Horse Customs ·

It is probable that men disguised as horses played an important part in pagan rituals, particularly those of the horse-worshipping Anglo-Saxons. No direct link, however, can be established between these pagan beasts and the 'hobby horses' – whose name is derived from a Middle English word for a small riding horse – first recorded during the 15th century in England and Wales: though not in Scotland, where the hobby-horse custom (if it existed) is undocumented. Such animals fall into two categories, the first being the 'Tournament' or 'Horse and Rider' type, where the bearer's head (and sometimes his body) protrudes above the framework of the horse. These, during the 16th and 17th centuries at least, were particularly associated with MORRIS DANC-ING – as at ABBOTS BROMLEY – and in many places this connection has been revived. Similar horses sometimes also accompanied the 'Plough Play' version of the MUMMING PLAY in Lincolnshire and Nottinghamshire: and on MAY DAY famous hobby horses of this kind still appear at MINEHEAD and PADSTOW.

A simpler and therefore perhaps more ancient version of the hobby horse (though none such are certainly recorded before the 18th century) consists of a wooden horse's head – or a real horse's skull – on a pole, whose bearer's body is concealed by a sheet. Almost invariably appearing around CHRISTMAS, these 'Pole' or 'Mast Horses' include the HOODEN HORSE of Kent, the MARI LWYD of South Wales, and the Cheshire SOULING Horse: as well as the 'Old Horse' and the variant 'Old Tup' (or ram) still sporadically active in the Derbyshire-south Yorkshire-Nottinghamshire borderland.

· Hocktide ·
Hungerford, Berkshire: second Tuesday after Easter

The second Monday and Tuesday after EASTER are known as Hocktide – a term of uncertain origin, but perhaps connected with a Germanic word meaning imprisonment or debt, whence the modern slang ex-pression 'in hock' (i.e., 'in pawn'). Certainly the principal custom of these days, during the Middle Ages, was the mock binding or imprisonment of men by women, generally on Hock Monday; and vice versa on Hock Tuesday. As in Easter 'lifting', victims could only obtain their release by paying a ransom, which was usually given to local parish funds (surviving church records, incidentally, show that 'the wyves' always gathered very much more 'Hock-money' than the men). The origins of this mainly southern English practice are also obscure – some maintained that it commemorated a binding or massacre of Danes by Englishwomen, and performed a play on this theme: but, despite the oft-repeated prohibitions of both church and state, it was often accompanied by 'lewd and unhonest sports', including the 'election' of MOCK MAYORS. These also continued for some time after the Reformation, though by then victims were generally trapped with ropes stretched across roads, rather than actually bound.

The old inter-sex jollities, moreover, still play their part in the elaborate Hocktide ceremonies at Hunger-ford in Berkshire, the only ones now surviving: but the main purpose of these relates to the season's more serious role as a QUARTER DAY for the collection of rents and holding of COURTS LEET AND BARON. Until recent local government 'reforms', indeed, the Hungerford Hocktide Court elected the town's administrators for the succeeding year; and it still supervises Hungerford's considerable COMMON LANDS and valuable fishing rights on the River Kennet. These privileges were granted in 1364 by John of Gaunt, within whose vast Duchy of Lancaster estates the town lay – monarchs of Britain, as Dukes of Lancaster, are accordingly still presented with a red rose QUIT RENT whenever they visit – and were confirmed by his gift of an ancient hunting horn (*see* HORNBLOWING, RIPON) which still exists. The horn now used in the Hocktide ceremonies, however, is a replace-ment: donated by a 'Cunstabl' called Jehosaphat Lucas in 1634, its inscription records that 'John a Gaun did

While the bellman blows his horn, Hungerford's 'Tutti Men' – temporarily abandoning their flowered 'tutti poles' – employ a ladder to claim their **Hocktide** kisses from delighted townswomen.

a fee or 'headpenny' from every householder and (by a long tradition, doubtless descended from the old 'binding' custom) to a kiss from every woman they meet. These they now set out to collect, touring houses armed with their ribbon-decked and bouquet-topped 'tutti poles' of office and accompanied by a fantastically dressed 'orange scrambler', who throws fruit to children and offers it to each woman kissed. None may lawfully resist them, and jocular attempts to lock them out are foiled by the use of a long ladder and a window.

More junketings take place after lunch at the Three Swans, where court and Tutti Men gather to throw oranges and hot pennies to children, drink Gaunt's health in 'Plantagenet punch', and 'Shoe the Colts': the colts are visitors or newcomers to Hungerford, and a display is made of driving a nail into their shoe sole until they cry out to 'pay their footing' by ordering more 'punch'. The party then disperses, the Tithingmen to continue their rounds until well into the evening – it being the tradition that they should eventually reach home only in a wheelbarrow – and the commoners to re-assemble on the following Friday for a 'court baron' and 'John of Gaunt's Feast'.

· Hogmanay ·
see NEW YEAR

· Holy Cross Day ·
see PIG FACE SUNDAY

· Holy Innocents' Day ·
see CHRISTMAS

· Holy Thursday ·
see ASCENSION DAY

· Hooden Horse ·
Broadstairs; Canterbury; Charing; Folkestone and elsewhere in East Kent

The Hooden Horse is a native of East Kent, particularly the Isle of Thanet. A close cousin – though geographically far removed – of the Cheshire SOULING Horse and the Welsh MARI LWYD, he consists like them of a horse's head (usually wooden, but sometimes a real skull) with snapping jaws, carried on a stick by a draped man. Unlike them, however, he usually also sports a ribbon-decked mane and a horse-hair tail, and is accompanied by a 'rider' – whom he frequently attempts to buck off – as well as a man-woman 'Mollie' with a besom: instead of MUMMING PLAYS or verse speakers, moreover, he is escorted by handbell ringers, carol singers and (latterly) MORRIS dancers. He formerly came out only during the CHRISTMAS season, when he and his attendants – exclusively farm horsemen in some villages – roamed by night from house to house, seeking alms and hospitality: if admitted, he would prance and snap in a terrifying

give and grant the Riall of Fishing to Hungerford town from Eldren Stub to Irish Stil, excepting som severeal Mill Pound' (ponds).

At 8 a.m. on Hock Tuesday morning, this horn is blown thrice from the town-hall window, summoning the Hungerford 'commoners' – residents of premises to which grazing and fishing rights are attached – to attend their court: a further reminder is then cried by the town bellman, in his scarlet-faced grey coat and gold-laced hat, who walks the streets ringing his bell and collecting penny 'fines' from non-attenders. Those who neither come nor pay will lose all common rights for a year. Once assembled, the court elects various officers, many of whom now have only nominal duties: these include the presiding constable (Hungerford's equivalent of a mayor); portreeve (rent-collector); bailiff (market-toll collector); water bailiffs; ale tasters; commons overseers; 'keepers of the keys of the Common Coffer'; and two of the four 'tithingmen' or 'Tutti Men'.

It is these last who, while the court continues to discuss business, carry out the most famous part of the Hocktide ceremonial. Once responsible for keeping 'watch and ward' over the town, they are still entitled to manner. At genteel Broadstairs, indeed, his sudden appearance frightened a woman to death in 1839, after which local magistrates suppressed the custom.

Elsewhere it died out more gradually during the early 20th century, to be revived on traditional lines during the 1950s. Now the Hooden Horse can be seen not only on Christmas Eve, at Folkestone; but also in Charing during WHITSUN-tide; at the Canterbury 'Hop Hoodening' (first Saturday in September); and even, once again, in Broadstairs (Folk Week, during August).

· Hornblowing ·
Bainbridge, North Yorkshire: 9 p.m. nightly, 27 September until Shrove Tuesday

Each winter evening from 27 September (Old Holy Cross Day) until SHROVE TUESDAY, the 'Forest Horn' is blown on the village green at Bainbridge, in the upper reaches of Wensleydale.

It has been suggested that this custom, unique in Britain, originated as a kind of Last Post for the garrison of Bracchium, the Roman fort still visible above the village. But it is far more likely that it began in the mid-12th century, when Bainbridge became the administrative headquarters of the great Forest of Wensleydale, the wolf-infested hunting preserve of the Earls of Richmond: and that the horncall (audible for miles on a still night) was designed to guide benighted travellers to the only safe harbour in an area so desolate that, even in Elizabeth I's time, strangers were legally obliged to hire a guide 'by reason of the wildness of the same forest and for that the same was not inhabited nor passable' (*see* LOST IN THE DARK BELLS).

Certainly hornblowing was already an immemorial tradition by 1823, the date of the earliest published record. Since then most of the hornblowers have been Metcalfes, descendants of local squires who prospered as henchmen of Richard III and served as Master Foresters under Henry VIII, and who are still the most numerous Bainbridge family. The present incumbent is Alistair Metcalfe, aged ten when he succeeded his great-uncle 'Jammy Jack', who died in 1983 after over thirty years of blowing. His horn, from an African buffalo, was presented to the village in 1864: it replaced two ancient cows' horns, one of which (reputedly dating from 1611) is still to be seen in the Rose and Crown. The new horn also hangs there in summer, but will remain at the hornblower's home during the hornblowing seasons, until he is old enough to enter licensed premises.

· Hornblowing ·
Ripon, North Yorkshire: 9 p.m. nightly

Every night of the year, without exception, the fawn-coated and tricorned hornblower sounds a blast from the four corners of the obelisk (formerly the Market Cross) at the centre of Ripon's main square: he then

Displayed near the motto-emblazoned town hall at a late-Victorian pageant are Ripon's ancient horn (left), on its elaborate baldric: and the later version still used nightly for **Hornblowing**.

blows three times outside the house of the current mayor, to show that his duties are done.

Formerly these were much more demanding: for he is the successor of the Wakeman, who until Ripon elected its first mayor in 1604 was the city's chief law-enforcement officer; and who, having blown the horn

had immediately after to begin his watch and to keep and continue the same until three or four of the clock in the morning. And if it happen any house or houses to be broken into on the Gatesyd [street front] and any goods taken away or withdrawn out of the said houses ... then according to old custom the Wakeman ... shall make good and satisfy unto the party wronged in such manner and to such value as ... he shall be assigned and adjudged.

Ripon Towne Book, 1598

He did, however, have assistants to apprehend 'any well suspected and unruly persons as they shall find in their said watch': and each householder had to pay him 4d a year if their house had two doors, or 2d if it had one. The current salary is £3 a night.

The custom is said to have continued uninterruptedly since Anglo-Saxon times, when Ripon was given a horn in confirmation of its first charter (*see* HOCKTIDE). The present horn dates only from 1865, but the ancient horn still exists, and is carried in procession on 'horn days' (EASTER SUNDAY, WHITSUN, August Bank Holiday, CHRISTMAS DAY and Mayor's Sunday) suspended from a baldric covered with silver symbols of former Wakemen and mayors, ranging from the shears of a medieval tailor to the teapot of a Georgian merchant. Otherwise it is displayed (with another horn of 1690) at the town hall, whose exterior is emblazoned with Ripon's motto: 'Except Ye Lord Keep Ye Cittie, Ye Wakeman Waketh in Vain'. The town also has its Bellman, who rings at 11 a.m. on Thursdays to proclaim the weekly market. (*See also* ST WILFRID'S FEAST)

· Horse Fairs ·

'Do not expect to see swings and roundabouts; bring your wellingtons, and take care of your purses and wallets. Many hotels and guest houses will not accept visitors during Fair Week; certain inns and public houses close down for all or part of this time, and those remaining open are full and overflowing with merrymakers.' These words of warning, taken from a current tourist-board leaflet about the great horse fair at Appleby-in-Westmorland, Cumbria, serve to illustrate the point that these events are not as other modern FAIRS. They are, rather, fairs of the old untidied kind, such as flourished all over Britain before the Victorian revolution that turned all fairs into 'fun fairs': which is to say events where business is as important as pleasure, where pleasure-taking is of a distinctly wild and undisciplined character, and where visitors do well to watch their step as well as their wallet.

There are several reasons why horse fairs have retained this distinctive character. Unlike sheep and cattle, horses are not now numerous enough to be sold at regular auctions, like those which have replaced the old 'beast fairs': and their sale also involves a special kind of person-to-person mystique, which does not flourish well in the commercial auction ring. Above all, however, horse fairs have become very much the preserve of gypsies and other travellers, who take kindly neither to change nor to official prettification.

Appleby Horse Fair, indeed, is certainly by far the largest annual gypsy gathering in Britain, and it also attracts hundreds of 'tinkers', 'potters', 'travelling traders' and other quasi-Romanies. Superseding an April Charter Fair established in 1685, it has been held since 1751 in early June (the big sale day being invariably the second Wednesday in the month) and centres on Fair – or Gallows – Hill outside the town. For weeks and even months beforehand, converging convoys of fair-bound travellers can be seen parked on the roadside verges of northern England and southern Scotland, in vehicles ranging from immense chromium-plated caravans towed by equally showy cars to traditional horsedrawn 'bow-tops' and 'open-lots', generally accompanied by a

Shouting to clear the way, a dealer demonstrates his horse for buyers by running it through the crowds at Appleby Horse Fair.

string of horses and ponies to sell. Seven or eight days before the big sale, they set up camp on the hill, which sprouts all kinds of trading stalls, 'shows' and fortune-tellers' booths. But the number of horses is far too great for the official fair site, so the animals are tethered on any available laneside grazing for miles around, and often demonstrated for buyers by galloping them at full speed along the roads round Fair Hill – even, or indeed especially, if these are crowded with spectators. Until this was very recently prohibited by officialdom, the dealers used to run their horses through the streets of Appleby itself: and the town's bridge over the River Eden still provides a convenient meeting place for communal horse-washing. During the continuous horse-trading of fair week, indeed, the whole town is taken over by gypsies and dealers, for whom the event is an unmissable annual opportunity to renew old friendships – and sometimes to pay off old scores, so that fights are not at all uncommon. When, therefore, the fair disperses after a programme of hair-raising Harness Races on Tuesday and the great final sale on Wednesday, the majority of Appleby's permanent residents heave a collective and entirely understandable sigh of relief.

Though none can compare with Appleby, many more horse fairs exist on a smaller scale – just how many more, however, is difficult to say, for some are almost unadvertised outside the horse-trading fraternity. But in the north of England alone, a travelling dealer leaving Appleby could drop in at Boroughbridge 'Barnaby Fair' (held around 22 June, Old St Barnabas' Day) in North Yorkshire; move on to Brigg Fair in north Lincolnshire (5 August); and return to West Yorkshire for Lee Gap Fair, held in a field between Wakefield and Dewsbury on 24 August: he might then move northward again to Broughbridge Fair (30 September) sited by the A66 eight miles east of Appleby, and finish the season at Yarm October Fair near Middlesborough. Some of these gatherings – like Lee Gap, Boroughbridge and the fairlike horse sales at the Anchor, a lonely pub astride the Welsh border near Bishop's Castle in Shropshire – are 'horse only' events on traditional rural sites: but others, like Yarm and the September three-day sale at Barnet on the northern fringe of London – which dates back seven centuries – take place in conjunction with pleasure fairs. Here and there, too, vestigial one-day sales – 'horse days' – precede otherwise standard fun fairs, as at Bridgwater St Matthew's Fair in Somerset (last Wednesday in September) and, appropriately, at Widecombe Fair in Devon (second Tuesday in September), the goal of Old Uncle Tom Cobley and his cronies on Tom Pearse's borrowed grey mare.

· Horse Races ·

see COMMON RIDINGS; DERBY; FAIRS; GRAND NATIONAL;
HORSE FAIRS; KIPLINGCOTES DERBY; MARYMASS FAIR;
ROYAL ASCOT

· Horseshoe Tax ·
Oakham, Rutland, Leicestershire

All around the interior walls of Oakham Castle hall – which is, incidentally, one of the best-preserved Norman domestic buildings in England – hang more than 200 horseshoes, mostly larger than life iron models inscribed with the name of the donor and the date they were given. These are the gatherings of the ancient 'Horseshoe Tax' custom, whereby every peer visiting the erstwhile county town of Rutland for the first time must give a shoe from one of his horses, or redeem it with a payment of not less than £5. The town authorities claimed the right, if necessary, to stop aristocratic carriages and exact the toll by force: but for many centuries now peers (and monarchs, including Queen Elizabeth II in 1967) have cheerfully handed over either a shoe or, more usually, the redemption money. Its amount dictates the size of the replica erected, and one of the largest shoes was allegedly presented by the first Queen Elizabeth in 1600: the biggest and most ostentatious of all, however, was – characteristically – given

The proceeds of the **Horseshoe Tax**, rows of decorative horseshoes given by passing peers, hang round the walls of Oakham's Norman castle hall.

by the Prince Regent (later George IV), who equally characteristically left his host to pay for it.

The Horseshoe Tax, already well-established by the time of the first known record in 1521, has long been collected by Oakham's Clerk of the Market, and some therefore believe that it is a relic of a medieval market toll on horses sold in the town. But the nature of the custom, the fact that the shoes have always been kept at the castle, and a tradition dating from at least the 17th century all link it instead with the baronial family of Ferrers, lords of the manor of Oakham from before 1130 until 1204 and builders of the castle hall. Taking their name from their ancestral property of Ferrières ('iron-forges') in Normandy, the Ferrers family were hereditary 'premiers barons fossiers' or 'iron founders in chief' of the duchy, and one of their number is said to have served as honorary 'farrier' (shoeing-smith) to the Conqueror at the Battle of Hastings. They bore as their heraldic arms, therefore, six black horseshoes on a silver ground, and it seems very likely indeed that they began the horseshoe toll – or perhaps imported it from Normandy – as a means of reminding their fellow peers of their proud office.

· Hot Cross Buns ·
see GOOD FRIDAY

· Hourglass, Crown and Running Auctions ·

By contrast with CANDLE AUCTIONS, in which the placing of winning bids is largely a matter of chance, some traditional auction customs are specifically designed to allow buyers plentiful opportunity to improve on their 'final' offers – and thus to guarantee the best possible price for the property being sold. At Chard in Somerset, where the right of collecting tolls from FAIRS and market stalls is annually leased on a Thursday in October, this is done by means of an hourglass. The auction begins in the normal way, but when what appears to be the final bid is received, a sandglass is allowed to run out three times in succession, which takes about six minutes. If no other offer is made during this time, the bid succeeds: if a further bid is received, however, the glass is again turned three times, and the lease is not finally sold until the process can be completed without interruption. According to tradition, this custom was devised to give working market-traders at least six minutes' grace – during which they could be serving their customers – to better a bid against them: for the toll rights are well worth having, and winning bids currently average over £3,000.

The custom of 'Selling the Keep of the Wether', held on WHITSUN MONDAY in the Nag's Head at Enderby near Leicester, is conducted along somewhat different lines. The 'Wether' – a pasture presumably once used for 'wethers' or castrated rams – is supposed to have been given to the parish by John of Gaunt, the great Duke of Lancaster who owned much land in the area during the 14th century; and, traditionally by his command, the annual rent of its 'keep' or grazing pays for a feast after the village sports. While this is auctioned, buyers sit in a circle, and pass a silver crown piece from hand to hand: only the person actually holding the crown may bid, and only when the coin has made two complete circuits without further offers being received is the Wether finally declared sold. The proceedings then conclude with a supper of boar's head sandwiches and the smoking of churchwarden pipes.

Perhaps the most extraordinary method of extending bidding time, however, is that employed at the 'Whitebread Meadow Running Auction', which takes place at Bourne in Lincolnshire every EASTER MONDAY. This originated in 1742, when one Matthew Clay bequeathed the parish two pieces of land, whose annual rent was to finance a bread dole to the poor householders of Eastgate Ward. The original lands were enclosed in 1770, but a field called 'Whitebread Meadow' was then substituted – subject to the condition that a thorn at its centre, since twice blown down and replaced, must never be cut or damaged – and this property is still auctioned according to the instructions given in Clay's will.

These require that bids may only be accepted while two boys (or, since 1944, girls) are running up and down a hundred-yard length of road near Queen's Bridge. So long as bids continue to be shouted, they must keep running: for an offer is not declared successful unless a complete out-and-back run can afterwards be performed without any further bids being made. Mischievous buyers, therefore, frequently hold back their bids until the children are nearly 'home', so as to set them running again. When the double 'clear run' has at last been safely made, the winning bidder becomes the tenant of Whitebread Meadow for a year; and until quite recently most of his rent was expended on loaves – 332 at 2d each in 1885, and 380 at 4½d each in 1920. Today, however, increasing costs prohibit such generous distributions: but the £100 or so currently raised still pays for the supper of bread, cheese and spring onions which follows the trustees' meeting in one of the Eastgate pubs, and for the traditional but entirely inadequate reward of one shilling (5p) given to each of the long-suffering runners.

· Housel Cloths ·
see PAX CAKES CEREMONY

· Hubbard's Hymn Charity ·
see GRAVESIDE DOLES

· Hunting the Gowk ·
see APRIL FOOL'S DAY

· Hurling the Silver Ball ·
St Columb and St Ives, Cornwall

Descended from the epic handball matches of Celtic legend, this ancient STREET BALL GAME was once played with almost fanatical enthusiasm throughout western Cornwall, especially at Shrovetide. In its exuberant disdain for fixed rules, indeed, it resembles SHROVETIDE FOOTBALL: but the small silver-coated ball is thrown, passed or 'scrummed' rather than kicked, and at one time (according to Richard Carew's account of 1602) it might even be carried cross-country by bands of whooping horsemen. As 'a play verily both rough and rude … in some sort resembling the feats of warre', however, it suffered the combined onslaught of revivalist Methodism and Victorian propriety, and now survives only in two places.

Apart from the prohibition of horses and the introduction of women into previously all-male teams, the version played at St Columb Major (on Shrove Tuesday and the second Saturday following) most nearly approximates to the Stuart game. Now, as then, 'there is neyther comparing of numbers nor matching of men' between the rival factions from 'Town' – the built-up centre of the parish – and 'Country' – its outlying hamlets: and as many as a thousand players have been known to take part. The apple-wood ball, encased in sterling silver and inscribed:

> Town and Country do your best
> For in this parish I must rest

is ceremonially 'cast up' from a ladder in the market square, either by the winner of the last game or some notable person: whereupon 'that company which can catch and carry it by force, or sleight, to their place assigned, gaineth the ball and victory. Whoever getteth seizure of this ball, findeth himself generally pursued by the adverse party: neither will they leave, till he bee layd flat on God's deare earth, which disableth him from any longer detayning the ball. He therefore throweth the same to some one of his fellows, who maketh away withall in like manner.'

By tradition, play is kept within the town's boarded-up streets for the first hour. But thereafter the hurlers strive to break the silver ball away to their 'place assigned' – for the 'Town', the base of an ancient cross a mile to the south-west; for the 'Country' another such, a similar distance to the north – or else to carry it over the parish boundary at any point. The first to do either wins the game, and the goal-scoring player is carried shoulder-high back to the market square, to pronounce the result. During the evening he will tour St Columb's pubs, consecrating jugs of 'silver beer' by dipping the ball into them: thereafter the ball is his to keep until the next game or, if he chooses to pay the £60 or so for a replacement, as a lifelong trophy.

The St Ives game – formerly contested between a team of 'Toms', 'Wills' and 'Johns' and one of men with other Christian names – is somewhat more restrained. Played on the first Monday after 3 February, the feast day of the town's patroness St Ia (one of a swarm of Dark Age Irish missionaries who crossed to Cornwall in unusual vessels, in her case a miraculously expanding leaf), it begins at 9.30 a.m. with the blessing of the silver ball at her holy well. An hour later, the ball is thrown from the churchyard wall by the mayor, and passed from hand to hand through the streets and along the beach. The goals are two basketball nets, but if no one has scored by noon the player then holding the ball becomes the winner of the 'crown' (25p) prize money.

I

· International Musical Eisteddfod ·
see EISTEDDFODAU

J

· Jankyn Smyth's Charity ·
St Mary's, Bury St Edmunds, Suffolk: Thursday nearest 28 June

An interesting example of a medieval charity which has adapted to the changing times. Jankyn Smyth, a wealthy merchant and great benefactor to Bury St Edmunds, died on 28 June 1481: and, in the usual manner of the day, his will ordered a yearly requiem Mass for his soul on the anniversary of his death. This was to be said at St Mary's church, and was to be attended both by the town councillors and the inmates of the almshouses he had founded, all of whom were afterwards to be regaled with 'cakes and ale'. Less than a century later, however, the Protestant Reformation abolished all requiem Masses as relics of 'superstitious Popery': so the Bury authorities substituted SERMONS and (perhaps in order to further distance it from the 'superstitious' anniversary observance) the service's date was later changed to the Thursday after PLOUGH MONDAY.

In recent years, the ceremony has once again reverted to the Thursday nearest the original date: and councillors and almshouse residents still attend, the latter being presented with their traditional shilling (5p) apiece. But when the company subsequently repair to the Guildhall – built with another of Smyth's benefactions – they no longer consume 'cakes and ale', being treated instead to the more genteel fare of coffee, sherry and fruit cake. (*See also* CHARITIES)

· Jedburgh Ba' Games ·
Jedburgh, Roxburghshire, Borders: 2 February and Fastern's E'en

'Jethart Ba'', the sole survivor in mainland Scotland of the STREET BALL GAMES once widespread throughout Britain, is played on CANDLEMAS DAY and again on 'Fastern's E'en' – locally the first Tuesday after the Candlemas new moon rather than, as elsewhere, necessarily SHROVE TUESDAY. In fact, it was originally a SHROVETIDE FOOTBALL game, allegedly first played with the severed heads of English border raiders: but by 1704 this had become so wild that 'there have been sometymes both old and young near lost their lives thereby', and the burgh authorities prohibited it. The letter of the law, however, forbade only 'the kicking of footballs'. So a handball or 'hurling' game – in which everything *but* kicking was allowed – came to be played instead: and when the local magistrates also attempted to suppress this, in 1848, their ruling was overturned by a traditionalist High Court Judge.

It is, therefore, still waged through the boarded-up and shuttered streets, at Candlemas by the 'Jethart

Fulfilling one of the complex requirements of **John Knill's Charity**, ten white-clad girls dance round 'Knill's Steeple' near St Ives on St James's Day 1926.

Callants' (lads) and on Fastern's E'en between adult 'Uppies' and 'Doonies' born above or below the Mercat Cross. The former attempt to carry, pass or throw the solid wooden ball to Castlehill, and the latter to Townfoot: while on nine years out of ten part of the game is played in the icy River Jed, with both sides endeavouring to manœuvre the ribbon-decked ball into their own 'goal' pool, and liberally 'dooking' each other in the process.

Duns in Berwickshire has revived its traditional 'Hand Ba'' game, once also held on Fastern's E'en but now transferred to the Friday of 'Reiver's Week' (*see* COMMON RIDINGS) in July. Three balls – gold, silver, and coloured – are played in succession, and the burgh's married men compete against its bachelors.

· John Knill's Charity ·
St Ives, Cornwall: 25 July, every fifth year (e.g. 1981, 1986)

John Knill, mayor of the Cornish fishing port of St Ives in 1767, and for many years its customs collector, was clearly determined never to be forgotten there. He began his campaign for remembrance in 1782, by building on the summit of nearby Worvas Hill a fifty-foot-high triangular pyramid – 'Knill's Steeple' – intended to serve both as a sea mark for shipping and, eventually, as his own final resting place. Not content with this, moreover, he devised in 1797 – and tried out in 1801 – what would have been the most elaborate of all GRAVESIDE DOLES, were it not for the fact that Knill's body was never to occupy his towering mausoleum: for difficulties arose over its consecration, and when he died in 1811 he was buried at St Andrew's, Holborn, in faraway London.

The 'Knillian Games' – as the benefaction ceremonies came to be known – had nevertheless been practised at the pyramid before the founder's death, and they have continued to be held there ever since. Every fifth St James's Day (25 July), the mayor and corporation of St Ives, wearing the prescribed white rosettes on their ceremonial robes, lead the procession of beneficiaries up Worvas Hill. There, ten small girls under the age of ten, who must be the daughters of fishermen or tinners, are first required to dance round the 'Steeple' for not less than a quarter of an hour; and must then sing the 'Old Hundredth' Psalm. For this they each receive ten shillings (50p), while the accompanying fiddler is paid £1, and two 'poor widows of sixty-four years and upwards' (whose duty is to see the ceremony properly performed) get £2 apiece.

Nor is this by any means the limit of Knill's posthumous generosity, for many more presentations are yet to be made. The head of the most numerous local family of legitimate children – provided that they have never accepted 'parish relief' and are themselves over sixty – receives £5: and the 'most worthy' girl who has married within the seven months before the Games gets £10 as a MARRIAGE PORTION. The most proficient St Ives net maker, moreover, also receives £5, and so does the best packer of pilchards – though this category has lately been extended to include all kinds of fish packers, for the pilchard industry has much declined since Knill's time, and the pilchard 'follower boys' he also hoped to reward are no more. But the local friendly societies still receive their five-yearly grant, and the trustees still enjoy their 'Knillian dinner'. Thus is John Knill remembered and, as he would surely have wished, thousands of visitors now gather to witness the ceremonies he so carefully planned.

· John Stow Commemoration ·
see COMMEMORATIONS

K

· Kate Kennedy Procession ·
St Andrews, Fife: a Saturday in mid April

'Kate Kennedy' is the heroine of the annual student procession at St Andrews, the oldest of the Scottish universities. Invariably played by a first-year male undergraduate (or 'bejant', from the French *bec jaune* – yellow beak or 'fledgling') in wig and elaborate medieval dress, she rides with her uncle 'Bishop Kennedy' in a horse-drawn carriage, attended by her page, footman and jester and flanked by eight bejants wearing the famous St Andrews red gowns. And before her march or ride a long procession of curiously assorted characters from the history of Scotland and the university, ranging from St Andrew and King Robert Bruce to John Knox, 'the Admirable Crichton', and John Napier, the inventor of logarithms.

Organized by the exclusive 'Kate Kennedy Club' – whose members are mainly the English ex-public school boys so numerous at St Andrews – the ceremony is

believed by some folklorists to be 'a survival of a Celtic spring festival', with Kate taking the place of 'the goddess Brigid'. But the usual explanation is that the first Kate was the beautiful niece of Bishop James Kennedy, who founded St Salvator's College in 1450. Visiting her uncle shortly afterwards, the tale continues, the glamorous lady made such an impression on the undergraduates that they vowed to honour her memory for ever with an annual festival.

The truth of the matter, however, seems to be that the Kate Kennedy custom began in the 1840s as an end-of-term college rag: and that the original Kate was not a person at all, but rather the bell called Katherine which Kennedy presented to his college in 1460. Though this was almost certainly dedicated in reality to Saint Katherine, the Bishop's patroness, the legend had grown up that it was named after his niece, who was thus adopted as the centrepiece of the students' celebration. At first confined to the college, by the 1860s this

During the **Kate Kennedy Procession**, a first-year male undergraduate always takes the part of the probably mythical charmer, seen here with 'her' uncle Bishop Kennedy.

had become a riotous procession through the streets, which was accordingly suppressed as a 'public scandal' in 1874, to be revived in its present pageant form in 1926.

What may well be an older St Andrews custom is that of 'Raisin Monday', generally celebrated about four weeks after the beginning of the university year in October. By long tradition, all new students are assigned a senior undergraduate 'parent', who helps them settle in during the first month of their stay. At the end of that period, the bejant once used to reward his mentor with a gift of raisins, but now he hands over a bottle of wine, for which a receipt must be given in Latin. Since the bejant must carry this receipt with him to lectures throughout the day, however, seniors frequently write it on some curious and unwieldy object, live animals and engineless cars being by no means unknown.

· Key Ceremony, Edinburgh Castle ·
Edinburgh Castle esplanade: approximately every three years (e.g. 1985, 1988)

Edinburgh Castle, whose present structure dates from the 14th century and later but which stands on a towering rock used as a fortress from time immemorial, has never been taken by direct assault: but it has been captured by stealth or treachery almost as often as it has fallen to blockade or bombardment, and this perhaps accounts for the almost paranoid caution still symbolically displayed before handing over its keys to a new governor.

The Key Ceremony – which is said to date back eight centuries, but which was revived in 1936 after a lapse of some eighty years – takes place at three-yearly intervals, on the appointment of a new General Officer Commanding Scotland, who is also automatically Governor of the Castle. Accompanied by the Lord Lyon King of Arms and the other Scots heralds, and by the Scottish state trumpeters, the governor-designate goes in procession to the castle, whose gates are shut fast against him: the trumpeters therefore sound a fanfare, at which the garrison within the fortress raise the alarm, and the garrison commander appears on the battlements with drawn sword in hand. Lord Lyon then approaches, is challenged, and announces that he has come in the sovereign's name to command that the gates be opened for the new governor.

This announcement alone, however, is not sufficient for the garrison commander, who insists on seeing a 'just double' (true copy) of the warrant: which must be passed through a small door in the gate, promptly slammed again until the document has been inspected. Only when it has been carefully examined and found in order are the gates finally opened: the Key of the Castle being then brought under escort to the new governor, who touches it in token of acceptance. (*See also* TOWER OF LONDON)

· Keys, Ceremony of the ·
see TOWER OF LONDON

· King of the Bean ·
see TWELFTH NIGHT

· Kiplingcotes Derby ·
South Dalton, East Yorkshire: third Thursday in March

The Kiplingcotes horse race, held near Market Weighton in East Yorkshire, was first run more than 250 years before the word DERBY entered the racing vocabulary, and it is certainly the oldest race to have written rules and conditions of entry. It was first held in 1519, but was probably not an annual event during its first 100 years. In 1618, a group of Yorkshire hunting men, headed by Lord Burlington, decided that the race was worthy of a permanent place in the calendar. A sum of money was invested to provide for the winner's prize, and it was stipulated that the race will lapse forever if there is a year in which it is not held. In the severe winter of 1947 local farmers led horses around the course to keep the race alive: and on an earlier occasion, when there were no entries, the clerk of the course was obliged to walk the distance leading a cart horse.

The race is held on the third Thursday in March, beginning at noon in the village of South Dalton. The four-mile course takes the competitors through five parishes, finishing near Kipling Cotes Farm in the parish of Middleton-on-the-Wolds. The rules are very strict, even going so far as to state that 'Every rider that layeth hold of any of the other riders, or striketh any of them, shall win no prize.' The most curious condition of the race, however, is that the entry money is paid to the runner-up, the winner receiving only the interest on the original investment. This means that the winner may get only £5 while the second may receive as much as £40. It is believed that the honour of winning is sufficient to ensure that the number of 'non-triers' is kept to a minimum.

· Kirkby Hill Races ·
Kirkby Ravensworth, near Richmond, North Yorkshire: 29 August, every two years

The local nickname for the ceremony of choosing the trustees of Dakyn's Charity, founded in 1555 by Dr John Dakyn, Rector of Kirkby Ravensworth, to endow almshouses for the local poor. On or about the Feast of the Beheading of St John the Baptist (29 August) in every second year, the current vicar and churchwardens select six of 'the gravest and honestest men of the parish' as candidates for the two trusteeships. Following the instructions laid down in the founder's will, each man's name is then publicly written on a slip of paper, which is screwed into a ball, covered in cobbler's wax, and dropped into a jug of water. The senior churchwarden

Past winners of the **Knighthood of Old Green** carefully measure the distance between a contestant's 'wood' and the 'jack'.

now stirs the contents, whereafter the vicar chooses two of the balls 'as chance shall offer them'. The men whose names are written thereon are thus deemed to be 'elected' by divine guidance, and administer the charity's funds for the succeeding two years. (*See also* CHARITIES)

· Kirkwall Ba' Game ·
see SHROVETIDE FOOTBALL

· Kissing Friday ·
see ASH WEDNESDAY

· Knighthood of Old Green ·
Southampton Old Green, Lower Canal Walk, Southampton: usually begins on the first Wednesday in August, and lasts three days

The 'Old Green' at Southampton is said to have been laid down before 1299, and thus claims to be 'the oldest bowling green in the world'. Certainly it is the scene of Britain's longest-established bowling custom, the tournament for the 'Knighthood of Old Green', which has been held there annually since it was initiated by a gentleman named Miller on 1 August 1776. The contestants, members of the Old Green Bowling Club, are known for the occasion as 'gentleman commoners', and the game is supervised by past winners ('Knights') in full regalia of top hat, tail coat, and silver Knight's medal, inscribed 'Win it and wear it'.

The tournament is played according to the original rules, and accompanied by considerable ceremony. Each 'commoner' bowls two 'woods' at the white 'jack', striving to place them as near to it as possible, the Knights then closing round with white rods to measure the intervening distance in secret. At the end of every round a point is given to the commoner whose wood has come nearest, and the first player to gain seven points – a process which usually requires three days of play – is awarded that year's Knighthood, and will in future be addressed as 'Sir' on the Old Green.

L

· Lady Day ·
25 March

Falling exactly nine months before CHRISTMAS, 25 March is celebrated as the Feast of the Annunciation – which is to say the Archangel Gabriel's revelation that the Virgin Mary would bear Christ. As the principal festival of 'Our Lady', the day was held in particular honour by monkish annalists (particularly Cluniacs and Cistercians) and it was probably under their influence that it came by the 12th century to be regarded as the first day of the year, replacing the old Roman NEW YEAR'S DAY on 1 January. This method of dating persisted long in England, and has caused considerable confusion to unwary historians – an event recorded by contemporaries as occurring in January or February 1450, for example, would, according to modern calculations, have taken place in January or February 1451: and though by the 17th century most of Europe (and Calvinist Scotland) had reverted to a January New Year's Day, England did not officially follow suit until the calendar change of 1752. Even then, however, 25 March remained – and still remains – an important QUARTER DAY.

· Lammas ·
1 August

Lammas (Anglo-Saxon: *hlafmasse* – 'loaf mass') was the festival of the beginning of HARVEST, when newly cut corn, or bread made from it, was offered in churches – a medieval custom recently revived in several English parishes. It was also the time when the semi-COMMON LANDS called 'Lammas Lands', used by their owners for crop growing in spring and early summer, were thrown open for common winter grazing.

Further back in time, 1 August was Lughnasad, when FEASTS, gatherings and races were held in honour of the Celtic god Lugh: from these descend the many surviving Scottish Lammas FAIRS, once famous as the time for 'handfast marriages' – trial unions which either party could, without social stigma, agree to end after a year.

· Lanimer Day ·
see COMMON RIDINGS

· Lent ·

Lent, the forty-day period before EASTER, commemorates the forty days of abstinence and meditation which Christ spent in the wilderness before beginning His ministry. For most Christians, therefore, it remains a season of penitence and self-examination: and until the Reformation it was also a strictly kept and legally enforced fast, when no meat, eggs or dairy produce might be eaten (except in dire need or on certain special occasions) and sexual relations were forbidden – hence the belief that Lent WEDDINGS are unlucky. In medieval Britain, moreover, dietary restrictions were almost as much a practical necessity as a religious duty: for Lent (Anglo-Saxon: *lenctene* – spring, when the days 'lengthen') fell at a lean time of the agricultural year, with winter stocks nearly exhausted and harvest still far away.

After the Reformation, however, some Protestants condemned Lenten fasting as a 'Popish superstition', so that the season was little regarded, for instance, in Calvinist Lowland Scotland or Nonconformist areas of Wales: while improved food-storage methods have long since obviated the practical need to cut rations at this time. Yet many people – agnostics as well as Christians – still 'give up something for Lent', frequently alcohol or tobacco: or (perhaps more valuably) make some positive efforts towards self-improvement, in preparation for the season of new life and hope which begins at Easter.

Many of the folk customs and traditions which mark Lent's 'red-letter days' are, indeed, cheerful rather than gloomy ones. Beginning on ASH WEDNESDAY (the day following SHROVE TUESDAY) the season progresses via MOTHERING SUNDAY and Passion or CARLINGS SUNDAY (the fourth and fifth Sundays in Lent) to PALM SUNDAY and its final, climactic Holy Week – when the sombre ceremonies of Maundy Thursday (*see* ROYAL MAUNDY) and GOOD FRIDAY give way to the triumphs of Easter Sunday.

· Letting the Banks ·
see CANDLE AUCTIONS

· Lewes Bonfire Night ·
see GUY FAWKES NIGHT

· Lifting ·
see EASTER

· Lilies and Roses, Ceremony of the ·
see TOWER OF LONDON

· Lion Sermon ·
see SERMONS

· Little Edith's Treat ·
Piddinghoe, near Lewes, East Sussex: 19 July

This touching event perpetuates the memory of 'Little Edith' Croft, who died at the age of only thirteen weeks on 19 July 1868. Her grandmother, Mrs Elizabeth Croft, endowed a fund to pay for an annual 'treat' for Piddinghoe children on her anniversary: and though this no longer covers the cost of the 'tea and sports', local support still maintains them each year.

· Long Rope Day ·
see GOOD FRIDAY

· Longsword Dancing ·
see SWORD DANCING

· Lord Mayor of Kilburn ·
see MOCK MAYORS

· Lord Mayor of London's Installation ·

The ancient and magnificent CIVIC CUSTOMS surrounding the installation of a Lord Mayor of London reflect the great antiquity and prestige of his office: which dates from the 1190s, and which affords its holder not only membership of the Privy Council and the precedence due to an Earl, but also the Admiralty of the Port of London, the Mastership of the Tower, and the privilege of acting as Chief Butler of England at CORONATIONS. Alone among British mayors, moreover, the chief citizen of London is at least nominally chosen, not by his fellow-counsellors, but by the liverymen of the eighty-one City GUILDS.

By long-established custom, the election ceremony takes place on MICHAELMAS DAY at the Guildhall, whose frontage has been barricaded for the occasion by a wooden construction called 'the Wickets', its narrow gates guarded by mace-bearing guild beadles to ensure that none but qualified liverymen may enter. Once these have assembled, the reigning Lord Mayor – preceded by the City Marshal, the swordbearer, and the common cryer – mounts the hall's dais or 'Hustings', which has been strewn with aromatic herbs as a precaution against 'infections and evil smells'. The cryer then orders the liverymen to make their choice, and to guarantee that this is 'free and unfettered', the mayoral party at once withdraws to the Livery Hall, together with those aldermen who have already 'passed the Chair' – or served as Lord Mayor – and are thus no longer eligible. It is they who will make the final choice between the two candidates put forward by the voters.

Such candidates must be aldermen who have already served as sheriff, and invariably the two senior aldermen 'below the Chair' are nominated, the senior of these being always chosen as Lord Mayor. So the result of the election is, in fact, a foregone conclusion: but the voting is nevertheless solemnly carried out, the first-named candidate being greeted with a shout of 'All, All!', the second with 'Next Year', and any others by cries of 'Later On' or 'Another Time'. The nominees' names are then conveyed to the Court of Aldermen in the Livery Hall: who make their foreknown choice behind locked doors, with the City Sword laid upon a bed of rose petals to signify that their decision is made *sub rosa*, which is to say 'in secret'.

Thus is the Lord Mayor elected, but it will be several weeks yet before he takes office, and during this time he is expected to remain unobtrusive, save only when he visits the House of Lords to receive the monarch's consent to his appointment. For that ceremony he wears a 'discreet' violet gown and the sheriff's rather than the mayoral chain, and in this attire he also attends his Admission ceremony at the Guildhall on the second Friday in November – which is known as 'the Silent

Above: The newly elected **Lord Mayor of London** (centre right) stands with his predecessor (with hat) outside the Guildhall, flanked by the State Trumpeters of the Household Cavalry. For election day, the entrance has been barricaded by 'Wickets', bearing the names of the electing guilds and companies. *Right:* During the Lord Mayor's Show, the new chief citizen waves from his State Coach, guarded by a Pikeman of the Honorable Artillery Company.

Change' because, after the Lord Mayor Elect's formal Declaration of Office, the transference of power is effected without a word being spoken. Silently the old and new mayors exchange seats; silently the insignia of office – the Crystal Mace, the Seals and Keys of Mayoralty, the State Sword and the Elizabethan City Purse – are handed to the retiring Lord Mayor; and in silence he passes them to his successor: then, at last, the trumpets sound and the bells of the City's churches ring out.

Even now, however, the installation ceremonies are by no means over, for the day after the Admission – which is to say the second Saturday in November – sees the most famous of them all, the 'Lord Mayor's Show'. This annual pageant originated as the new mayor's ceremonial journey to swear a final oath of allegiance before the Lord Chief Justice: a duty which, by a law of 1215, he is still obliged to undertake. On the morning of the show, therefore, he dons for the first time his fur-trimmed scarlet gown, his 'Cap of Dignity', and his great mayoral chain of office. Over five feet long, this splendid piece of 16th-century regalia is made up of interlinked silver roses, knots and repeated double 'esses' – said to stand for 'Souvent me souviene' (Remember me often) the motto of the royal house of Lancaster – and from it is suspended via a portcullis the Lord Mayor's Badge, a jewelled onyx cameo of the City arms.

Decked in all the insignia of his dignity, the Lord Mayor now watches the show pass from his stand at the Mansion House: and as the long procession of bands and decorated 'floats' (which are supposed to reflect the chosen 'theme' of his year of office) nears its end, he mounts his gilded state coach and takes up his position of honour at the rear. Drawn by six matched shire horses from Whitbread's brewery, the 18th-century coach is preceded by the mounted City Marshal, and around and behind it march the Lord Mayor's bodyguard, the red-coated and armoured pikemen and musketeers of the Honorable Artillery Company. Thus, via Cheapside and Fleet Street, the first citizen and Chief Magistrate of London processes in full state to take his oath at the Law Courts in the Strand, returning later via Victoria Embankment to the Mansion House. His mayoralty has now officially begun: and two days later he will begin his round of engagements by presiding over the Lord Mayor's Inaugural Banquet at the Guildhall, a magnificent occasion which traditionally features a major policy speech by the Prime Minister.

· Lost in the Dark Bells ·

All over Britain, stories are told about lost or benighted travellers who were guided to safety by the sound of church BELLS: and who, in gratitude, left money to ensure the continuation of the ringing for the benefit of others in like case. Such 'Lost in the Dark Bells' are still rung in a few places, of which Newark in Nottingham-

shire perhaps possesses the longest-standing tradition. This relates how a medieval Flemish merchant called Gopher, led out of the autumnal mists of the Trent marshes by the bells of St Mary Magdalen's church, bequeathed 'a certain sum' for the maintenance of ringing during the six weeks ending 'six clear Sundays before the fourth Sunday in ADVENT'. The money has long since disappeared, as has all record of the merchant: but the 'Gopher Ringing' still continues on Sunday evenings in October and November.

A more dramatic tale explains the continuation of curfew bellringing at Burgh-le-Marsh, Lincolnshire, where it takes place at 8 p.m. each weekday evening from 10 October (MICHAELMAS, Old Style) until 7 April (LADY DAY, Old Style). One dark night during the early 17th century, apparently, the captain of a ship negotiating the treacherous sandbanks of the Wash was warned of his dangerous closeness to shore by the sound of the Burgh curfew. Having reached safety, he bought a piece of land in the parish (subsequently called 'Bell String Acre') whose rent was to be used for keeping the curfew bell provided with a silken rope, and to ensure that its ringing would continue 'for ever'.

A Bell String Acre did indeed once pay the curfew ringer's wages, but there is no evidence for the silken rope, and still less for the 'improved' version of the story contained in various modern publications – though it is unknown in Burgh. This provides names both for the captain ('Frohock') and his ship ('Mary Rose') and turns the people of Burgh into wreckers, who refuse to allow the ringing of a warning bell. An aged sexton, however, barricades himself into the belfry and rings until his heart bursts: needless to say, he has a beautiful daughter, and naturally she later marries the gallant sailor her father had preserved.

Traditions along the same general lines account for Lost in the Dark Bells formerly rung throughout the winter in many other places: including Charlton-on-Otmoor, Oxfordshire; Barton-on-Humber, Lincolnshire; St Margaret's at Cliffe, Kent; and Aymestrey, Herefordshire – where it was allegedly funded by a man whom Puck had led in circles all night through nearby Pookhouse Wood. In none of these cases, however, do the original terms of the bequest survive: and it is at least possible that many of the tales grew up to explain ordinary winter ringing to guide wayfarers – whose endowment was a fairly conventional act of medieval piety, not necessarily implying that the donor had ever been benighted himself.

But this is not to deny that some Lost in the Dark Bells – particularly those ordained to be rung commemoratively on a certain specified day – really were financed by grateful travellers. At Twyford in Hampshire, for instance, the bells are pealed at 6.30 a.m. and 7 p.m. on 7 October, after which the ringers and their guests enjoy a feast. This is partly paid for by the successors of William Davies, a Twyford landowner who became lost in a fog while riding on the nearby downs, until the

Even the First World War did not interrupt the ancient **Lot Meadow Custom** at Yarnton, where tenants are seen drawing the named balls from the bag on West Mead in 1917.

church bells made him rein in to get his bearings — whereupon he discovered himself about to plunge into a chalk pit. In gratitude, his surviving will of 1754 provides that a pound be given to the Twyford ringers on each anniversary of his deliverance, 'provided they ring on that day for ever'. A similar adventure accounts for the curfew bellringing at St Mary's, Kidderminster, Worcestershire, on 29 October (Old St Luke's Day); in memory of a certain Pecket, saved by the bell from falling into a chasm while returning from St Luke's Fair at Bridgenorth: and a sadder story for the 'Dead Man's Peal' formerly sounded at Wentnor, Shropshire, on the last Thursday in November, Church Stretton Fair Day. For in this case the homegoing traveller died of cold on the Long Mynd, and the bell was rung to prevent such tragedies occurring again. (*See also* HORNBLOWING; RUSHBEARINGS AND HAYSTREWINGS; SERMONS)

· Lot Meadow Custom ·
Yarnton, Oxfordshire: week after 29 June

The sole surviving example of a practice which dates from the Anglo-Saxon settlement of England during the 6th and 7th centuries, the Yarnton 'lot-meadow' custom is elaborately contrived to ensure the fairest possible distribution of the once-vital village hay-crop. This, in the days before the general enclosure of COMMON LAND, was grown in a large area of open meadow, whose

ownership was shared between the tenants of surrounding farms. But since the land would naturally be boggy in some places and dry elsewhere, the quality of the crop would vary considerably from one part of the meadow to the next: and any permanent division of the field would thus mean that some farmers always got good hay, while others invariably harvested bad. One method of ironing out the inequality, therefore, was to allocate strips of the meadow by an annual lottery, so that a farmer who drew indifferent land in some years could hope for better luck in others: and this system of 'lot-meads' — apparently devised in the Saxon homeland of north-west Germany, where it still flourished during the 19th century — was formerly widespread in parts of southern England. Congresbury and Puxton in Somerset, for instance, once divided their common pasture by some form of lottery, and so too did Wanborough and Sutton Benger in Wiltshire, Southease near Lewes in Sussex and, until late-Victorian times, Aston near Bampton in Oxfordshire.

Though ancient in origin, the Yarnton lot-meadow custom is neither simple in operation nor easy to explain. Basically, Yarnton West Mead — the only survivor of three common pastures in the village — covers an area of eighty-one customary acres, called 'men's mowths' because each comprises the amount of land a single scytheman can mow in a day: and it is divided into fourteen 'lots', one of three customary acres belonging to the church, and thirteen others of six mowths each. To even out the distribution of good and bad hay, however, these lots are not single pieces of land: but are instead parcelled out among the five large 'portions' into which the meadow is sub-divided, so that each lot owner has a strip in every portion. And to make the arrangement more complicated (and fairer) still, the position of the strips within the portion varies from year to year, according to the 'luck of the draw'.

The one constant thing about each lot, indeed, is its traditional name: the church piece being called 'the Tidals' and the rest, respectively, 'Gilbert', 'White', 'Harry', 'Boat', 'Watery Molly', 'Freeman', 'Bolton', 'Rothe', 'Dunn', 'Walter Geoffry', 'Parry', and 'William of Bladon'. These, presumably, fossilize the names of the tenants who shared the meadow at some unknown point in its history: and until quite recently each named lot remained attached to one particular 'common-right' farm in Yarnton, Wolvercote or Begbroke. Currently, however, the lots are sold by auction at the Grapes Inn on the Monday after St Peter's Day (29 June), when a single buyer may purchase several, reducing the number of separate tenants accordingly.

The 'draw' nevertheless takes place in the traditional manner, generally on the day after the sale, when the official called 'the Meadsman' summons the tenants to assemble at one corner of the meadow's first portion. He then produces thirteen ancient cherrywood balls, each with the name of a lot written upon it, and places as many of these as there are tenants in a small bag. (Elsewhere, as at nearby Aston, lots used to be identified instead by a system of simple marks, like 'The Two Uprights' or ' The Frying Pan': and at Congresbury such marks were cut into apples instead of balls.) Putting his hand in the bag, someone next draws a 'mead ball' at random, and the tenant whose lot is named on it claims the first strip in the portion; whereafter the rest claim theirs in the same order as their lots are drawn. Finally, each strip is carefully paced out and delineated with stakes, the new owner's initials being cut into the turf with a knife: and the whole process is repeated in each of the remaining four portions, until all the strips are allocated and every tenant's lot is complete.

Mowing begins soon afterwards, because all the hay must be taken before the meadow is opened for grazing at the end of August. In recent years the cutting has been done with machinery, in the normal course of farm work, but at one time the Yarnton meadow hay-harvest – like similar events in lot meads elsewhere – was 'celebrated yearly with great ceremony'. For the original custom was to mow the entire field in a single day, and teams of scythemen had therefore to be drafted in from miles around. 'Much merriment' ensued, including a plum-pudding feast and a race for the 'Mower's Garland': but so too did deep drinking, wholesale fighting and even a fatality. So in 1817 the mowing period was extended to three days, and after that the festivities gradually petered out.

M

· Maid's Money ·
St Mary's Church House, Reading, Berkshire: around Easter; The Guildhall, Guildford, Surrey: last Thursday in January

'The encouragement of faithful maid servants' – without whom, until very recently, no respectable household could hope to function – was once considered a most worthy and necessary form of charity. Designed to reward long service and 'good character' in domestics (and thus almost as beneficial to employers as to the employed) such foundations were especially frequent in the 17th century, and particularly numerous in the towns along the Thames Valley. Reading alone possessed no less than five of them, the oldest and most elaborate being endowed by John Blagrave in 1611.

A noted mathematician, and the inventor of the 'Geometricall walking staffe', Blagrave willed £10 to the Corporation of Reading each GOOD FRIDAY morning. Of this, 'twenty nobles' (£6 13s 4d) was to be given as a MARRIAGE PORTION to a Reading maid who had served at least five years in the same household 'of good name and fame': and 'to avoid partiality in the choice', three candidates from different parishes were 'to cast and try by lot whose the fortune should be' – or, in other words, to throw dice for it. The winning 'Lucky Maid' then attended an endowed sermon on the duties of servants and masters at St Lawrence's church – where Blagrave's monumental effigy, surrounded by mathematical instruments, is still to be seen. Whereafter a further sum was distributed to the sixty 'poor neighbours' who escorted her home in triumph, while the bells rang a joyful peal.

This very public 'inducement to be industrious, and remain in their places' clearly impressed both the servants and masters of Reading. For during the next two centuries several more Maid's Money CHARITIES were established there, including one to endow a second dicing in August and another which, 'from motives of kindness', furnished consolation prizes for those who had thrown unsuccessfully. United as the Consolidated Charities for Female Servants in 1861, all these foundations continue to operate: but the dicing has ceased, and the reward money is now divided equally among the dwindling and increasingly aged band of 'faithful maidservants' who assemble at EASTER in St Mary's Church House. In 1983 there were nine of them, and each received £60.

On the last Thursday in January, however, two 'unmarried servant maids' – usually well struck in years – still cast dice at Guildford for John How's Charity. Possibly influenced by Blagrave's example (for Reading is not so far distant) in 1674 How bequeathed the annual interest on £400 to be contested between two

'Faithful maid servants' cast dice
for John How's **Maid's Money**
charity at Guildford, 1956

candidates, both of whom must qualify by at least two years' continuous service. Prudently, he also decreed that employees of the corporation members who administer the charity may only throw once every seven years; while those who have worked in alehouses are excluded altogether, unless they have subsequently redeemed themselves by two years' 'respectable' service. Each maid throws her dice on the Guildhall table, and the loser is expected to try again in the following year – unless she loses four times in succession, whereafter she is permanently disqualified, presumably as incurably unlucky or under divine disfavour. Losers, however, now do rather better than winners, for since 1909 they have benefitted from John Parson's Dole: founded in 1702 for apprentices, but scheduled to revert to maidservants if boys ceased to appear, this now produces an annual £12.09 – fifteen pence more than How's bequest.

· Manorial Customs ·

Until comparatively recently, the 'custom of the manor' dominated the lives of a great many of the inhabitants of rural Britain: for, in addition to being bound by the general laws of the whole realm, they were also subject to the particular rules and regulations of the manor in which they dwelt. Varying considerably from place to place, and based on the accumulated precedents of many generations, such customs were enforced by the local COURTS LEET AND BARON: and they regulated not only everyday matters like agricultural practice and the use of COMMON LAND, but also the far more important questions of what payment must be made to the manor

lord for a farm or smallholding, and how property might be passed on to a tenant's descendants.

Under the feudal system which obtained in England, Lowland Scotland and much of Wales during the centuries after the Norman Conquest, the majority of poorer tenants were 'villeins' – which is to say virtually the chattels of the landowner. In return for their smallholdings, they were bound by the custom of the manor to labour for the lord on two or three days in every week, and more often at busy seasons like harvest: and custom also enacted that they must pay 'fines' for permission to marry off a daughter, send a son to school, or even to grind their corn outside the manor. Nor did custom loosen its grip even on their death, for it then decreed that the lord could take their best beast or most valuable possession as a 'heriot'; their widow must pay a fine to avoid forcible remarriage and their heir another before he could inherit the smallholding.

Though most such 'servile customs' had been commuted in exchange for ordinary money rents by the Tudor period, relics of them lingered on in much attenuated form until the present century, and in some places linger still: mainly in the shape of 'social conventions' that the tenant farmers of an estate will provide beaters for a shoot, help cart coal for 'the big house', or paint their doors and windows a uniform colour chosen by the landlord. Until the 1922 and 1925 Property Acts abolished all 'special tenures', moreover, land in some manors continued to be held in return for curious QUIT RENTS – so that a Victorian farmer at Langsett in the West Yorkshire Pennines had to produce a snowball at MIDSUMMER and a rose on CHRISTMAS DAY. Manorial customs also differed considerably in matters of inheritance, for the succession of the eldest son was by no means universal: until the 18th century many Kentish estates ahdered to the ancient local law of 'gavelkind', whereby the land was divided equally between all the sons; while a number of manors preserved the pre-Norman Conquest custom called 'Borough English', whereby the youngest son took over the property, his elder brothers being presumed to have already established themselves before their father's death. In default of sons, some estates allowed the eldest daughter to succeed, but others shared the property between all the daughters, and others again passed it to the nearest male relative.

In some manors, too, custom allowed a widow to keep possession (or 'free bench') of her husband's lands for her lifetime – but only as long as she did not remarry, and 'remained chaste'. A very few places, nevertheless, allowed widows 'detected in incontinency' to retain their rights, provided they performed the extraordinary ceremony of 'riding the black ram'. At Enborne near Newbury in Berkshire, the erring lady had to appear at the Court Leet riding backwards upon the beast, with its tail in her hand, and solemnly repeat the words:

> Here I am
> Riding upon a black ram
> Like a whore as I am
> And for my crincum crancum
> Have lost my bincum bancum
> And for my tail's game
> Am brought to this wordly shame,
> Therefore, good Master Steward,
>   let me have my lands again.

Whereupon the steward was 'bound by the custom of the manor' to re-admit her.

· Marblers' and Stonecutters' Day ·
Corfe Castle, Dorset: Shrove Tuesday

Since at least the 12th century, the many-coloured and fossil-studded Isle of Purbeck marble has been greatly in demand for sculpture and fine decorative building work. In order to protect their monopoly of quarrying and preparing it, local tradesmen therefore formed themselves into an exclusive Guild or Company of Marblers and Stonecutters, which still meets at Corfe Castle each Shrove Tuesday to enforce rules laid down in 1651. The rituals of the day, however, were recorded nearly a century earlier still, and most probably originated in the Guild's medieval heyday.

These begin at noon, when the church's PANCAKE bell summons the Company from the Fox Inn to their meeting in the town hall. There, among other business, they admit new members, who must have served a seven years' apprenticeship, and must pay an entry fee of 6s 8d (33p), a 'penny loaf', and a quart of beer – which they must carry from the Fox, avoiding more or less playful attempts at interception by established Marblers. A shilling (5p) is also levied from each member who has married during the preceding year: except the most recently wed, who is required instead to provide a football for the next part of the ceremony.

Designed to preserve the vital rights of way over which the Purbeck men once transported their quarried marble, this involves a rudimentary game of SHROVETIDE FOOTBALL, played up part of West Street

Old Sam Spooner, champion of the 1880s, 'shoots his tolley' during the revived **Marbles Championships** at Tinsley Green in 1937.

and through a piece of COMMON LAND called 'the Halves'. Once, apparently, the ball was also kicked all along the several miles of road to Owre Quay on Poole Harbour, whence the Company shipped its stone to the workshops of London: and though the quay itself has long since disappeared, the Company still honours its obligation by driving to the site, there to present the ground landowner with the annual pound of pepper – literally a 'peppercorn rent' – which guarantees their right of passage. (*See* GUILDS AND COMPANIES; QUIT RENT CEREMONIES)

· Marbles Championship ·
The Greyhound, Tinsley Green, Sussex: Good Friday

The ancient game of marbles has long been especially popular in Sussex and Surrey, where it was formerly played in LENT, ceasing at noon on 'Marble Day' – GOOD FRIDAY. Both men and boys took the game very seriously, sometimes playing in church porches until service time and resuming immediately afterwards.

Since 1932, a formal championship has been held on Good Friday at Tinsley Green near the Sussex-Surrey border, traditionally the scene of an Elizabethan marbles match between a youth from each county, for the hand of a local girl. Forty-nine marbles are placed on a sanded concrete ring, six feet in diameter, and teams of six men compete in turn to knock as many as possible off, using a 'tolley' or 'shooting marble'. This must be flicked by the thumb only, without any forward movement of the hand, whose index finger is 'knuckled down' to the ring. Afterwards, the highest scorers from each team play individually for the title of 'British Marbles Champion'. Another traditional Sussex match is played outside Battle Abbey, also on Good Friday.

· Marhamchurch Revel ·
see FEASTS, REVELS AND WAKES

· Mari Lwyd ·
Llangynwyd near Maesteg, Glamorgan and elsewhere in South Wales: 24 December – 6 January

The HOBBY HORSE called *Y Mari Lwyd* (which despite other ingenious interpretations, probably means simply 'the grey mare') was once a well-known CHRISTMAS visitor throughout South Wales, but now principally inhabits West Glamorgan and Carmarthenshire (Dyfed). Like her relations, the Kentish HOODEN HORSE and Cheshire SOULING Horse, her essential feature is a decorated head – made either from wood or a real horse's skull – with snapping jaws and bottle-glass eyes: this is carried on a pole by a white-sheeted man, hence her alias of *Y Gynfasfarch* – 'the canvas horse'. Her companions (sometimes formerly called 'Merry [MORRIS?] Dancers') vary in character from place to place: but in Glamorgan they traditionally include a Mare-

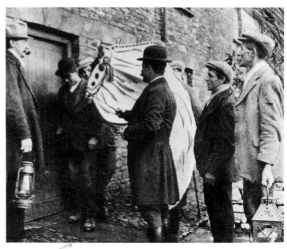

Before being allowed to enter, the Llangynwyd **Mari Lwyd** and her companions must beat the householders in a battle of Welsh verse.

Leader, a Sergeant, a fiddle-playing 'Merryman', and a black-faced Punch and Judy – the last played by the heftiest man available.

Before entering any house, they must conduct a verbal battle of questions and answers, fought exclusively in Welsh verse, against those within; one Glamorgan Mari, for instance, began:

> *Wel, dyma ni'n dwad*
> *Gyfeillion diniwad*
> *I'mofyn am gennad – i ganu*

(Well, here we come, simple friends, to ask permission to sing)

to which the house people replied:

> *Rowch glywed, wŷr doethion*
> *Pa faint ych o ddynion*
> *A pheth yn wych union- ywch enwau.*

(Let us hear, wise men, how many you are, and what exactly are your names)

This can continue for some time, with each side extemporizing more or less uncomplimentary rhymes against the other, until one party 'dries up'. If the insiders fail first, Mari can enter: if the reverse, she must in theory (though rarely in practice) try again elsewhere.

Once within, she rushes about jostling and biting the company: and if Punch and Judy are present, he chases and kisses the women while Judy belabours him with the broom 'she' has used for sweeping the hearth. There may also be carol singing and dancing. Then, after food and drinks supplied by the host and a final verse wishing the house a lucky NEW YEAR, the Mari Lwyd continues her WASSAILING rounds.

· Marriage ·

see WEDDINGS

· Marriage Portion Charities ·

Until comparatively recently, it was customary for every bride to bring her husband a 'marriage portion' of property or money, also called a 'dowry': and he, in return, was expected to 'endow' her with the where-withal (confusingly known as a 'dower') to support herself should she outlive him. Involving very considerable sums of money among the wealthier classes, the dowry custom – which is perpetuated by the convention that brides' fathers pay for WEDDINGS – also applied to poorer brides: some of whom, however, were quite unable to raise even the parson's fees for the ceremony, let alone the small contribution they were expected to make towards the couple's joint finances.

The provision of marriage portions for 'poor and deserving' brides was therefore a popular and useful form of charity bequest. Sometimes the recipients had to be domestic servants of good standing (*see* MAID'S MONEY) and frequently they were required to be residents of a certain district – as in the cases of JOHN KNILL'S CHARITY and of 'Signor Pasquale Favale's Bequest', which is still privately distributed by the town clerk of London every June. Endowed in 1880 by an Italian merchant to commemorate his happy marriage to a London girl, this annually provides dowries for three 'poor and honest' brides between the ages of sixteen and twenty-five, who must either have been born within the City of London or have lived there for seven years.

Probably the most curious conditions attached to a marriage portion charity, however, are those laid down by John Orr, late Paymaster-General of the army in India, for the bequest he made in 1847 to the parish of St Cyrus in Kincardineshire. The annual interest on a legacy of £1000, he decreed, should be divided into five shares: one buys comforts for the local poor, but the other four are distributed respectively to the tallest, shortest, oldest and youngest brides married in the parish during the year. Dates of birth and height measurements are therefore carefully recorded, and at the end of December the gifts are handed out, no candidate being allowed to qualify under more than one heading or receive more than one marriage portion. (*See also* DUNMOW FLITCH; PRETTY MAID'S CHARITY)

· Martinmas ·

11 November

The feast of St Martin of Tours (*c.*315-397) a Roman soldier who turned bishop and was greatly venerated in Britain and France. Once a popular QUARTER DAY for collecting feudal dues (like WROTH SILVER), in Scotland and northern England it remained until the 1920s the high point of the farm-labourer's year. For some, the many hiring FAIRS held now (or at Old Martinmas, 23 November) brought the chance of better employment:

> Good Morning, Mr. Martinmas
> You've come to set me free
> For I don't care for master
> And he don't care for me
> *East Yorkshire*

while all now began their one annual holiday, which often coincided with the spell of fine weather called 'St Martin's Little Summer'. If not, they could console themselves with the belief that a cold snap now presages a mild winter to follow, for:

> If Martlemas ice will bear a duck
> Then look for a winter of mire and muck
> *Leicestershire*

and also with the feasts provided by fellow labourers ('Martinmas Foys' in Scotland) or families – meals copious enough to give Martinmas Sunday the East Yorkshire nickname of 'Rive-kite [split-stomach] Sunday'.

Such feasting was once universal at Martinmas, when in pre-Agricultural Revolution days the majority of farm animals were slaughtered and salted down for lack of winter fodder, and an ancient Celtic tradition decreed that blood must be spilt. Martinmas dinners are still held in some northern farming communities, but elsewhere celebrations have been completely overshadowed by the commemoration of a far greater slaughter – REMEMBRANCE SUNDAY.

· Marvyn Dole ·

Ufton Court, Ufton Nervet, near Reading, Berkshire

Scarcely altered since its foundation in 1581, Dame Elizabeth Marvyn's Charity is still handed out on Maundy Thursday by her successor as Lord of the Manor, from the window of the manor house she herself had built. Anxious that her poorer tenants should be clothed as well as fed after her death, she willed them not only a bread dole (the product of 10 bushels of wheat) but also a yearly gift of '12½ ells of canvas at 1s per ell for shirts and smocks, and 12½ yards of narrow blue cloth at 1s 3d per yard for coats and cassocks' (overcoats). The former now consists of about 150 loaves, anyone who has slept in the village on the previous night being technically eligible for a share: but in practice farm-workers' families receive a loaf per head, and other villagers a loaf per household, which they collect when their names are called by the vicar. Since smocks and cassocks are no longer fashionable, however, the cloth dole now takes the form of nine pairs of bed sheets for local pensioners.

· Mary Gibson's Sermon ·

see SERMONS

· Marymass Fair ·
Irvine, Ayrshire: third or fourth Monday in August

Irvine's ancient Marymass FAIR takes its name from the Feast of the Assumption of the Virgin Mary (15 August) which in Scotland was always 'the Great Feast of Mary', and which – presumably because it coincided with Old LAMMAS – was once also celebrated thereabouts by dancing round blazing hilltop fires. Since 1563, however, when Mary Queen of Scots was escorted through the town by the local Carters' Society – the prime movers of the fair – it has been particularly associated with that misguided and unfortunate monarch: and the Fair Queen ceremonially crowned after a Carters' COMMON RIDING is invariably costumed to represent her. The fair is also famous for the amateur horse races – among them a unique contest for cart horses – which take place on the afternoon of the Riding, and which are said to be even older than the 12th-century fair itself: indeed, they are locally believed to be the oldest horse races in Europe.

· May Bread Charity ·
see BREAD AND BUN DOLES

· May Day ·

The celebration of May Day, the great festival of the coming of summer, has a long and curious history. Originally and essentially a full-blooded pagan rite, it reached an uneasy truce with the Church to flourish throughout the Middle Ages, before falling beneath the ban of post-Reformation Puritanism: subsequently revived as an expression of loyalty to the restored Charles II, May Day festivities again declined during the 18th and early 19th centuries, to rise again – in transmogrified form – on a wave of Victorian enthusiasm for a vanished 'Merrie England'.

In Celtic Britain, the first of May was 'Beltane', the festival when the all-important flocks and herds were turned onto their summer grazing and the gods were invoked for their protection until HALLOWEEN. Though frequently and erroneously connected with Baal, the idol of the biblical Canaanites, the name 'Beltane' seems really to mean 'bright fire' and – like the related MIDSUMMER holy day – it was chiefly celebrated by the lighting of great bonfires on hill-tops: a practice recalled by such place names as Tullybelton ('Beltane Hill') in Perthshire, Tan-y-bryn ('fire hill') in Carmarthenshire, and a number of Tan Hills in northern and western Britain. Beltane fires, moreover, survived in Highland Scotland until about 1830, and in parts of Wales almost into the present century, being surrounded in both places by considerable ritual. Ideally, the wood of nine different types of tree had to be used, and this must be collected by men with no metal whatsoever about their persons: neither might a spark be produced except by rubbing two oaken poles together or drilling a wooden auger into a log – a task traditionally performed in Scotland by nine teams of nine married men, or eighty-one first-born sons. The people then danced sunwise round the flames, and cattle might be driven between two Beltane fires for 'luck' and protection: in times of cattle murrain, too, sick beasts were occasionally 'sacrificed' on the fire, and both Wales and the Highlands long retained a Beltane custom which was presumably a relic of human sacrifice. Cakes, burnt or otherwise marked in one place, were broken into a bag, and the person who drew the marked portion was made to leap three times through the flames, or knocked down and pelted with egg-shells. Finally, brands from the new Beltane fire were distributed to re-kindle the household hearths extinguished before the festival, while ashes of the bonfire itself were kept 'for luck'. In recent centuries, however, Beltane fires were probably kindled less to invoke the gods than 'to burn the witches': for the night before the old pagan festival – which is also a cross QUARTER DAY – was regarded as a particularly uncanny time.

All over the country, nevertheless, young girls ventured out before dawn to wash their faces in May dew – as many still do, particularly along the Welsh borders, in south-western England, and on Arthur's Seat in Edinburgh: this, according to a time-honoured belief, will improve their complexions, 'cure' freckles and – if they wish hard enough while performing the ceremony – perhaps bring them a husband within the year. In some areas, the dew is thought most powerful if collected from hawthorn or ivy, or from beneath an oak: and in others such dew, or that from a new-made grave, was also gathered as a sovereign remedy for a variety of ailments from weak eyes to gout.

Throughout England and Lowland Scotland, however, the central custom of the festival was 'bringing in the May' – whereby much of the night and early morning was spent in the woods and fields, seeking flowering branches to bear home in triumph at sunrise. 'May' can be any kind of tree in bloom by the first, though since the calendar change of 1752 mayers have often been hard put to find any such, save only the 'unlucky' blackthorn: but by Old May Day, eleven or twelve days later, blossom of all sorts is usually plentiful. In most of England, nevertheless, the favourite 'may' is hawthorn, but in Cornwall sycamore is sometimes chosen, while in Scotland, Wales and part of northern and western England 'may' means rowan (or mountain-ash) and birch, both also powerful against witches. Whatever the tree preferred, branches of it were subsequently used to decorate houses, or left on the doorsteps of those favoured by the mayers – who might return later for a tip. More secretive, with good reason, were the 'May Birchers' of 19th-century Cheshire, who employed a rhyming code to proclaim their opinion of the householders within. Hawthorn was a general compliment, and pear was for the fair: but nut was for a slut, plum for the glum, alder ('owler') for a scowler, bramble 'if you ramble', and gorse for the whores.

Frequently, of course, the mayers brought home flowers – particularly the marsh marigold or 'May-flower' – as well as branches, and often these would be woven into elaborate garlands (*see* ABBOTSBURY GARLAND DAY; CASTLETON GARLAND; GARLAND DRESSING). Sometimes twined about two hoops to form a sphere, sometimes crown-shaped, and more rarely pyramidal, such garlands remain popular for primary-school May Day celebrations, and are still occasionally carried about the streets by bands of money-collecting children, especially in the English south Midlands. Very occasionally, too, 'May dolls' – now ordinary dolls, but supposed by folklorists to represent either the Virgin Mary or some goddess of spring – appear within the garlands, or are displayed in flower-lined boxes.

'But the chiefest jewel' the mayers brought from the woods, according to the Elizabethan Puritan Philip Stubbes, 'is their May-pole, which they bring home with great veneration, as thus. They have twentie or fortie yoke of Oxen, every Oxe having a sweet nose-gay of floures placed on the tip of his hornes, and these Oxen drawe home this May-pole (this stinking Idol rather) which is covered all over with floures and herbs bound about with strings ... and sometimes painted with variable colours ... And thus being reared up, with handkerchiefs and flags hovering about the top, they straw the ground round about ... and then fall they to dance about it like as the heathen people did at the dedication of Idols.' Probably of Anglo-Saxon rather than Celtic origin – similar customs still exist in Holland and North Germany – the maypole was generally a fresh cut tree of some straight-growing species like birch or ash: but in towns the same pole might be used year after year, a famous medieval London example being that which annually overshadowed the church of St Andrew 'Undershaft' in Leadenhall Street.

Such maypoles, universal throughout the English-speaking parts of Britain during the Middle Ages, also served as the focus of the MORRIS DANCING, sports, and simple plays known collectively as 'May Games'. These were presided over, not only by a May Queen or May Lady (invariably an adult, and sometimes a man in woman's clothing) but also by a May King, known in many parts of England and Lowland Scotland as 'Robin Hood': an identification which, it has been suggested, connects him with the pagan wood-sprite 'Robin' (alias 'Robin Goodfellow', alias Puck) rather than the legendary outlaw, and which is still remembered in the Helston FURRY DANCE 'Hal-an-Tow' song. English churchwardens, nevertheless, frequently paid for 'Robin Hood' and 'Maid Marion's' costumes, and set them to collect for parish funds; while solid Scots burgesses annually elected one of their number as 'my lord Robene Hude ... to mak sportis and joscositeis in the toun'.

Despite their distinctly dubious origins, indeed, May Day celebrations were tacitly accepted by the medieval church, and enjoyed by every rank of society from royalty downwards. The Protestant Reformation, however, produced a violent reaction against them – at least among the 'stricter sort', who rightly (after their own lights) viewed them as downright paganism. In 1555, therefore, the Calvinist rulers of Scotland prohibited 'the auld wikit maner of Robert Hude ... Queens of May or otherwise', and, despite the ensuing riots, saw the law strictly enforced: while English Puritans like Stubbes inveighed not only against 'idolatrous' maypoles, but also against the immorality attendant upon 'maying' in general, noting that 'of fortie, three score or a hundred maides going to the wood overnight, there have scaresly the third part of them returned home again undefiled'. Finally, in 1644, Parliament banned maypoles altogether, as a 'heathenish vanity, generally abused to superstition and wickedness', and throughout the Commonwealth period all the 'licentious practises' of maying were strongly discouraged.

Maypoles, therefore, became a potent symbol of opposition to 'Godly rule': and when Charles II was restored to the throne on 29 May 1660 a great number were immediately re-erected as a mark of loyalty to the crown. So closely identified were maying and Restoration, indeed, that in many places the May Day festivities were transferred to OAK APPLE DAY, but even where they continued at the original date they probably never regained their former vigour. By the later 18th century, moreover, they were once again declining in favour – except among southern English urban milkmaids, who regularly appeared bearing May Garlands hung about with borrowed silverware; and sweeps in the same area, whose speciality was 'Jack-in-the-Green', a dancing man almost entirely encased in a pyramidal framework of green leaves. And in 1826 a Surrey correspondent to the *Gentleman's Magazine* could lament that 'modern refinement has levelled the Maypole, and forbidden the harmless enjoyment in which our more happy ancestors indulged ... on this day of rustic delight.' 'In the merry days of the Maypole,' he continued, 'we may fairly presume, the young peasant found amusement without resorting to the Public House.'

This Arcadian, rose-tinted, and almost entirely erroneous conception of the 'Olde Englishe' May Day very much appealed to middle-class Victorian sentiment: and by the mid-19th century a revival of the festival – purged, of course, of its 'grosser elements', and decently ordered by squire, parson and school teacher – was in full swing. Maypoles were widely refurbished or newly erected, and round them children were encouraged to dance 'innocent measures' taught by the 'Guild of Merrie England', while carefully supervised child 'garlanders' politely requested donations towards 'a general tea'. For the transmogrified May Day celebration was primarily a 'pretty affair for children': whose central figure – the controversial May King having been quietly forgotten, and the village beauty shunned as 'not

Looking anything but festive, Oxfordshire **May Day** garlanders set out on their rounds at the turn of the century.

quite the thing' – is the tinsel-crowned schoolgirl May Queen.

The great majority of modern 'traditional May Day festivals' date their revival – or indeed their inception – from this Victorian burst of enthusiasm, and share its essential features. Thousands of them are held throughout Britain (generally on the Saturday after May Day, or on some other convenient weekend) and notable among these are the events at Gawthorpe in West Yorkshire, Shoreham in West Sussex, and Ickwell in Bedfordshire (last Saturday in May). Probably the grandest of all, however, is Knutsford in Cheshire's 'Royal May Day', which was begun in 1864 by the Reverend Barnacle and received its proud regal prefix after a royal visit in 1887. Here the usual May Queen's procession, headed by 'Jack-in-the-Green', attains very considerable proportions – a recent show featured four Morris sides and six bands, including the Warrington Scout Band or 'Purple Phantoms': and at its climax, in horse-drawn landaus, ride the schoolgirl Queen and her court, escorted by Robin Hood and his Merry Men and guarded by infant Beefeaters.

Knutsford Royal May Day has also subsumed the ancient and unique local custom of 'sanding' the streets for WEDDINGS, traditionally originated by King Canute (Cnut) in the 11th century. After crossing a nearby ford – which was thereafter known as 'Cnut's Ford' and gave the town its name – the King is said to have scattered the sand from his shoes in the path of a passing wedding party, wishing them happiness and as many children as there were grains of sand. Ever since, patterns and mottoes in brightly coloured sand have been traced on

The 'Olde Englishe' **May Day** as seen through rose-tinted Victorian spectacles: the pagan maypole, the 'stinking Idol' abominated by Puritans, has become the focus of the innocent rustic amusements so much emulated by modern revivals.

the streets for Knutsford brides: and early on May Day morning they are also made outside various public buildings and the homes of the May Queen and her courtiers, the favourite motto being:

Long may they live – happy may they be
Blessed with contentment and from misfortune free.

Despite the overwhelming effect of the Victorian transformation of the festival – another offshoot of which was its adoption as 'Labour Day' – a few more ancient May Day ceremonies nevertheless survive here and there: among these being ABBOTSBURY GARLAND DAY; the FURRY DANCE; GARLAND DRESSING; MAY SINGING; MAYPOLE RAISING; and the MINEHEAD and PADSTOW HOBBY HORSES.

· May Goslings ·
see APRIL FOOLS' DAY

· Mayoring Days ·
see CIVIC CUSTOMS

· Mayor of Ock Street ·
see MOCK MAYORS

· Mayor of Shammickshire's Election ·
see MOCK MAYORS

· Maypole Raising Ceremony ·
Barwick-in-Elmet, West Yorkshire: Easter Monday and Spring Bank Holiday Tuesday, every three years (e.g. 1987, 1990)

Barwick-in-Elmet's eighty-six foot high maypole is said to be the tallest in Britain, and to be the direct successor of poles erected there 'since time immemorial'. Every third Easter Monday, according to long-established custom, it is taken down for refurbishment: and immediately afterwards the villagers assemble at the Market Cross to elect three 'Polemen', who will take full responsibility for it until the next renewal. Their principal task, however, is to oversee its repainting in white with a red and blue spiral, the manufacture of four new flower-and-ribbon garlands to adorn it, and any necessary repairs to the fox-shaped weathervane at its top.

The maypole – made from two larch trees spliced together and completely replaced every fifteen years or so – is then ready for its ceremonial re-raising on Spring Bank Holiday Tuesday, to which the event has recently been transferred from the traditional date of Whitsun Tuesday. After a procession to the bailey of Barwick's Norman castle – where the maypole once used to stand – for the crowning of the 'May Queen', the renewed pole is carefully manœuvred into place in the village centre, using a system of ropes, pulleys and ladders. And finally, to loud cheers, an intrepid volunteer climbs sixty

feet up the pole to release the positioning ropes, continuing to the very summit to triumphantly 'spin the fox' weathervane.

· May Singing ·
Magdalen College tower, Oxford and the Bargate, Southampton: 1 May

At 6 a.m. every MAY DAY morning, the choristers of Magdalen College, Oxford, sing the Latin hymn 'Te Deum Patrem Colimus' from the top of their 140-foot tower: whereafter the college bells sound a joyful peal, and the large audience gathered on Magdalen Bridge set out to follow the MORRIS DANCERS on their May Day rounds of the city.

The origins of this ancient and immensely popular custom are much disputed. Some hold that it originated as part of a May Day requiem Mass for William Lord Berkeley, who in 1491 bequeathed the college the rectory of Slimbridge in Gloucestershire on condition it be carried out: while others derive it from a memorial service for Henry VII, and others again from a thanksgiving for the completion of the tower in 1509. Certainly it was a well-established tradition by the mid-17th century, when it took the form of a concert, wherein 'the choral ministers of this house do according to ancient custom salute Flora every year on the first of May at four in the morning with vocal music of several parts: which, having been well performed, hath given great content to the neighbourhood and the auditors underneath'.

Later on instrumental music was also included in a performance lasting up to two hours, and the current curtailed form of May Singing began almost by accident one very wet May morning during the late 18th century: when, already late in reaching the tower, the choir hurriedly sang the present hymn – which they knew by heart, since it was part of the daily college grace – before once again taking refuge below. Since then, 'Te Deum Patrem Colimus' has invariably been sung, generally accompanied by a suitable madrigal: and the custom of May Singing has spread to a number of other places – notably Southampton, where the choristers of King Edward VI's school sing hymns from the top of the town's ancient Bargate.

· Michaelmas ·
29 September

September the twenty-ninth is the feast of St Michael the Archangel, Captain of the Heavenly Host, who cast the Devil out of Heaven (Revelations 12.7-9) and who is patron saint of soldiers, Normans, horses and high places like St Michael's Mount in Cornwall. It is also a QUARTER DAY and (particularly in the south of England – further north, MARTINMAS was preferred) a 'settling day', when rents and bills were paid, and farm labourers went to hiring FAIRS to seek new masters. Many of these

May Singing on Magdalen College tower, as idealized by the Pre-Raphaelite painter Holman Hunt in 1899.

fairs (like the 'Goose Fairs' at Nottingham and Tavistock, Devon) were also famous for the sale of geese, still a favourite Michaelmas dish. According to one ill-founded legend, this is because Queen Elizabeth was eating goose when she heard of the defeat of the Armada on Michaelmas Day 1588: but the custom is really much older, and based on the practical consideration that geese (especially when fattened on post-harvest stubble) are now at their best. It is very unlucky, however, to eat blackberries at or after Michaelmas (or, some say, after Old Michaelmas, 10 October) because the Devil then spits – or worse – on them, presumably to spite his rival.

· Midsummer ·
23-24 June

The Summer solstice – the longest day, when the sun climbs highest in the sky – actually falls on 21 June: but since early medieval times 'Midsummer Day' has been customarily celebrated on 24 June, the birth Feast of St John the Baptist – who according to St Luke's Gospel (1.36) was born six months before Christ, and hence six months before CHRISTMAS. Despite the Church's success in transferring their date to a Christian anniversary, however, the observances of Midsummer remained as essentially pagan in spirit as those of the other great summer festival, MAY DAY: and the two festivals once had much in common, including 'Robin Hood' games, Maypole (or 'Summer Pole') dancing, and – most notably – the lighting of fires on hilltops.

But while the May fires of Beltane generally burned in Celtic areas, those of Midsummer Eve blazed principally in the parts of Britain settled by Anglo-Saxons and Scandinavians – which is to say most of England, Lowland and eastern Scotland, and the northern Isles of Orkney and Shetland. John Aubrey, writing during the 1680s, reported that: 'still in many places on St. John's night they make Fires on the Hills: but the Civill Warres comeing on have putt all these Rites or customes quite out of fashion': and in much of southern and Midland England Midsummer fires had indeed died out by the 18th century. Further away from the sources of change, nevertheless, they continued to burn well into the Victorian period; especially in parts of Scotland – where, despite the repeated prohibitions of the Kirk, blazing torches from the fire were also carried sunwise round the fields to bless the crops, and, as at Beltane, young men leapt through the flames 'for luck'. At Cairnshee (Gaelic: 'The Fairies' Mound') near Durris in Kincardineshire, moreover, the custom survived until 1945, thanks to a bequest made in 1787 by Alexander Hogg, a wealthy merchant who began life herding cattle at Durris, and who left an annual 10s to the herd boys who made the fire. Here, as elsewhere, each farm in the vicinity had to contribute its share of fuel, or be doomed to ill luck, and the blaze had to be lit just as the sun sank below the horizon.

In northern England, too, Midsummer fires endured until about the 1850s, particularly in Cumbria (where the customary fuel was the magical rowan); Northumberland (where the WHALTON BAAL FIRE still survives); Durham, and Derbyshire. While in westernmost Cornwall, until the 1880s, great bonfires lit up all the hills around Mounts Bay on both Midsummer Eve and the eve of St Peter's Day (28 June): and in Penzance and the neighbouring villages Midsummer revellers carried burning tar-barrels through the streets and swung blazing torches around their heads on chains (*see* SWINGING THE FIREBALLS). Since 1929, moreover, Midsummer Eve fires have again burned on Cornish hilltops from Carn Brea near Redruth to Kit Hill near the Devon boundary: but these were 'revived' by the 'Old Cornwall Society', and they are accompanied by somewhat self-conscious 'Druid' rituals including the burning of 'magic' herbs, of new-cut oaken sickles and of broomsticks and pointed hats – all supposedly designed to 'break the power of the witches'.

There is no doubt, however, that Midsummer Eve and Midsummer night – as witness Shakespeare's play – were once genuinely believed to be particularly uncanny times: or that certain flowers and herbs were gathered as protection against the evil spirits which then walked abroad. Of these safeguards, the most powerful is the yellow 'St John's Wort' – called 'chase-devil' in both French and Latin, and employed in Aubrey's time to exorcise haunted houses – but vervain, yarrow, corn marigold and orpins (or 'Midsummer Men') were also woven into garlands and hung on door lintels or round the necks of farm beasts. Some of them, too, might be used in attempts to divine the future, for which Midsummer Eve (like HALLOWEEN and other 'spirit nights') was an especially auspicious season: if two picked orpins intertwined overnight, matrimony was indicated, but if St John's Wort withered the picker was doomed to disappointment, or even death. A girl bold enough to venture forth at midnight on Midsummer Eve, moreover, could be sure of results if she walked twelve times round the church without stopping, meanwhile scattering hempseed and repeating some such rhyme as:

> Hempseed I sow
> Hempseed I hoe
> Let him that is my true love
> Come after me and mow.

She would then see the phantasm of her destined lover following behind her – or perhaps the lover in person, if she had been careful to publicize her doings in advance.

The gathering of 'fernseed' – which was supposed to appear only at midnight on Midsummer Eve, and to confer the power of becoming invisible on anyone quick enough to collect it – required stronger nerves still, for fairies and witches would do their utmost to prevent mortals sharing their prerogative. And so too did the morbid custom of 'watching the church porch', kept up elsewhere at Halloween or St Mark's Eve (24 April), but on Midsummer Eve in south-western England. There, the spirits of all the living inhabitants of the parish could allegedly be seen entering the church, and those not seen coming out again would certainly die within the year: but should any of the watchers fall asleep during their vigil, they too would die before next Midsummer.

Very few of these customs and beliefs, however, survive in anything like serious form: though 24 June is still marked by several FAIRS, RUSHBEARINGS, COMMON RIDINGS and CIVIC CUSTOMS (including the election of the sheriffs of London), as well as by the rather comical proceedings of the 'Ancient Order of Druids' (founded 1781) at Stonehenge and elsewhere. But Midsummer never enjoyed a Victorian revival like that of May Day, and as a festival it now passes comparatively unhonoured.

· Midsummer Tithes ·
see CANDLE AUCTIONS

· Minehead Hobby Horse ·
Minehead, Somerset: 30 April to 3 May

The May HOBBY HORSES of Minehead in north Somerset – there may sometimes be as many as three of them, 'though the Sailors' Horse is the proper one' – are, unusually, based on a boat-shaped framework seven or eight feet long, carried on the shoulders of a man whose body is entirely hidden by a hanging canvas 'housing' painted all over with circles. A mass of brightly coloured streamers covers the flat top of the horse, and a long rope tail trails behind it: while from its centre protrudes the bearer's head, which is again totally concealed by a tall ribboned cap and a fearsome mask of painted tin.

On the eve of MAY DAY – known as 'Warning Eve' or 'Show Night' – the Sailors' Horse makes its first appearance, touring the Minehead pubs in search of donations and dancing in the streets to the 'Hobby Horse Tune' (alias 'Soldier's Joy') played on drum and melodeons by its attendant 'Sailors': formerly it used also to dart in and out of houses 'for luck', but this is no longer done. Neither is it now blessed by the vicar on May Day morning, when a King and Queen of the May were sometimes elected to accompany it: but at 6 a.m. on that day it still invariably keeps up the ancient custom of walking to Whitecross, a mile west of the town, and there bowing thrice to the rising May sun. Then, on May Day afternoon, the Horse visits the Luttrell family of nearby Dunster Castle, where it is treated to drinks, prances about the Yarn Market, and sometimes skirmishes with a rival 'Dunster Horse': while on the evenings of 2 and 3 May it generally calls on the outlying hamlets of Periton and Cher before finally returning to Minehead for a last dance in the main square.

Everywhere it goes, the Horse chases children, and lashes its tail at passers-by for contributions, which are acknowledged with a courtly triple bow. Until the 1880s, however, its demands were somewhat more forcibly put, for the Horse had a hareskin-covered wooden head, with snapping jaws to catch the unwary, and was preceded by two menacing 'Gullivers' (from Old French: *goulafres*, 'gluttons'?) armed with whips

The essence of a genuine custom: though no-one is there to see, the **Minehead Hobby Horse** dances through the empty streets to its early morning rendezvous with the rising sun.

ible story is that it is merely a copy of the Padstow beast, or indeed the Padstow beast itself, carried off by Minehead raiders: a suggestion indignantly rebuffed by Minehead men, who retort that (if anything) the Padstow custom was pirated from them. Both Horses, however, are credited with frightening away invaders – in Minehead's case the Vikings, who certainly did attack the area in 878 and 1052: while a commentator of 1830 (when the custom had already 'prevailed for ages') believed the Minehead Horse was somehow connected with a ceremony of BEATING THE BOUNDS, a theory given currency by its continuing tour of outlying settlements around the town. Local opinion nevertheless holds that the custom commemorates a shipwreck off Dunster in 1772: when the only thing washed ashore was a dead cow, whose tail was promptly cut off and attached to the Horse – which did, indeed, formerly sport a real cow's tail.

Both of these last 'explanations' may well contain an element of truth: for there is no reason why a Horse with a shipwrecked cow's tail should not have been used for boundary processionings. But however it subsequently fared, it seems most probable that the Minehead Horse – like its Padstow rival and many others long since defunct – originated as a luck-bringing beast of the May Day celebrations.

· Mischief Night ·
Various dates, mainly Halloween or 4 November

All over Britain, children firmly believed themselves entitled to one annual, 'lawless night' of unpunished pranks. In south-western England, 'Nickanan' (Cornwall) or 'Dappy-Door Night' (Devon) was SHROVE Monday, when runaway knocking on closed doors or rubbish thrown into open ones was the rule: but more generally MAY DAY eve or HALLOWEEN – both times when tricks could be blamed on mischievous spirits – was the night for blocking chimneys, whitewashing-over windows, or blowing smoke through keyholes. The Halloween custom, still popular in Scotland, has crossed the Atlantic as 'Trick or Treating'.

In the 20th century, Mischief Night flourishes most strongly in Yorkshire, Lancashire and neighbouring parts of the north Midlands, where it has shifted to 4 November, the eve of GUY FAWKES. The removal and concealment of garden gates is virtually standard practice: and other popular tricks include remote-control tapping on windows with an ingenious arrangement of buttons and string, or pretending to smash them by thumping them with the hand while simultaneously breaking a bottle. Perhaps less humorously, fireworks are pushed through letter boxes, tyres let down, and dog dirt left wrapped in burning paper on a doorstep – so that the householder stamps it out. But as long as the pranks stop short of the downright vandalism they can so easily descend into, people generally tolerate them; because, 'After all, it's Mischief Night'.

and clubs: anyone who steadfastly refused to pay up, moreover, was liable to be held down (or bound with the Horse's tail) and struck ten times with an old boot. According to a firmly believed but unsubstantiated tradition, such practices eventually led to the death of a victim – or even the murder of a policeman – and the consequent abolition of both Gullivers and 'booting'. Token Gullivers have nevertheless lately reappeared with the Alcombe or 'Town Horse': while a nominal 'booting' ceremony sometimes still takes place at Cher, where a volunteer is hoisted by his arms and legs and bumped ten times with the Horse's prow, and then dances round the Horse.

Like the PADSTOW HOBBY HORSE, its better-publicized Cornish relation, the Minehead Horse has prompted much speculation about its origins. The most implaus-

· Mock Mayors ·

The custom of electing 'mock mayors', now enjoyed only in a few places, was once widespread throughout England, being particularly popular in communities which had a large proportion of poor, underprivileged and 'rough' inhabitants. For such highly unofficial goings-on were partly designed to poke none-too-goodnatured fun at the pompous mayor makings of better-off neighbouring towns, or at the aldermanic class in general: and they were frequently rendered all the more odious to the respectable by being held on or near the same date as the genuine ceremonies. Thus the 'elections' at the Lancashire village of Chipping usually coincided with the real mayor making at the nearby borough of Clitheroe, and the 'ceremonies' at Halgaver Moor, Cornwall, with that of Bodmin: while the 'enthronements' of the 'Mayor of Shammickshire' at Bideford, Devon, and of the 'Mayor of the City' at Newbury, Berkshire – where 'a cabbage stalk did duty as a mace' – were held on 9 November, the old date of the London LORD MAYOR'S SHOW.

One of the most famous – or notorious – mock ceremonies, moreover, always coincided with general elections to Parliament. This was the making of the 'Mayor of Garratt' – 'a few straggling cottages near Wandsworth' now represented by the Garratt Lane area of London SW17 – which began as a celebration of a legal victory over would-be enclosers of local COMMON LAND. By the early 19th century (when voters were alleged to qualify by 'having enjoyed a woman in the open air within that district') 'a prodigious concourse of people' flocked from all over London to attend it, 'to the great emolument of the publicans of Wandsworth'. The most important prerequisite of all such elections, indeed, was that everyone present – especially the 'Mayor' and his transvestite 'Lady Mayoress' – should get drunk as quickly as possible, and remain so 'as long as they can get, borrow or steal any ready money'. By late-Victorian times, therefore, the great majority had been forcibly suppressed as an affront to public decency as well as a threat to law and order.

Of the few (considerably toned-down) survivors, perhaps the best known is the election of the 'Mayor of Ock Street', a district of Abingdon, Berkshire, once notorious for its many 'low' inns. This is said to have originated in about 1700, when the Ock Street men, led by one Hemmings, won a fight against the inhabitants of 'the Vineyards' for the horns of a black ox publicly roasted to celebrate the town's Fair Day, the feast of the Translation of St Edmund of Abingdon. Hemmings was thereupon declared 'Mayor' of Ock Street, and the original horns are still carried before his successors, who are annually elected by the current residents of the street on the Saturday nearest 19 June, St Edmund's Day, New Style. Almost invariably a local MORRIS dancer is chosen and, having drunk to his victory from 'the mace' – a 200-year-old wooden bowl – he is invested with sword and sash and chaired up and down Ock Street by his colleagues, who wear the traditional Morris 'whites', top hats, and bells. During the evening the 'mayoral party' tours all the pubs of the district, and dances outside many of them.

The office of 'Lord Mayor of Kilburn', a North Yorkshire village famous for its hillside White Horse, is said by its supporters to be much earlier in origin, though none can say when it began. Enthroned on the final Tuesday evening of a four-day feast (which begins on the Saturday nearest 6 July and thus approximates to MIDSUMMER, Old Style) he is drawn about Kilburn in a handcart, proclaiming his authority for a year and a day and levying arbitrary fines on locals for any 'offences' he can devise, while his 'Lady Mayoress' – a heavily made-up young man – chases and kisses the women. Perhaps intended to guy the proud Lord Mayoral ceremonies of nearby York, the celebrations continue at the Forester's Arms, whose landlord is sometimes fined a barrel of beer; and end with the singing of a curious song about 'Old Grimy', a character improbably identified with 'Grim', alias the Norse god Odin.

Another famous mock mayor ceremony, abandoned because of 'extreme rowdyism' in 1893, has now happily been revived at Randwick, near Stroud, Gloucestershire, a village once mainly populated by impoverished weavers. This is Randwick 'Wap', a word which defies interpretation – though in the local dialect 'wap-eyed' meant 'bleary' and 'wappered' conveyed 'worn out', conditions surely familiar to the participants in the old Wap: a drinking bout of truly heroic proportions, beginning with the 'chusing in' of the 'Mayor' on HOCKTIDE MONDAY and often lasting for a full week. Already recorded as well established in 1703, its origins are as usual uncertain: but one village tradition traces it to a medieval feast celebrating the completion of the parish church, after which the master mason fell drunkenly into a pond; while another maintains it was once a real election, held under a mysterious and now unfindable royal charter.

The present ceremony, re-started in 1972, is markedly different from its predecessor in many ways. It is now held on the second Saturday in May, in order to fit in with the once separate but perhaps still more ancient village custom of CHEESE ROLLING. A 'Wap Queen' and carnival parade have moreover been added, and the mayor is now 'chus'd in' well beforehand by a 'franchise' widened to include anyone willing to register and pay a nominal fee. But the old Wap delicacy of *wiput* (a kind of bread-pudding) is again on sale: and above all the Mayor's Procession, the essential part of the custom, keeps faith with the original.

With his 'Mopman' to clear the way, and accompanied by his 'High Sheriff', his 'Sword Bearer' and a bevy of 'Flag Boys', 'Wand Carriers' and 'Cheese Bearers', the 'Mayor' is carried on a chair from the site of the old stocks to the Mayor's Pool. Then, in the proper and time-honoured fashion, His Worship's

Bearing his sword and drinking-bowl 'mace' of office, the **Mock Mayor** of Ock Street, Abingdon, is chaired along the street by his morris-dancer colleagues.

bearers carry him straight into the water, to dump him, chair and all, in the middle: whereupon the Mayor's Song is sung amid much splashing. Its words, extolling the virtues of the 'peaceful trade of weaving', have however been somewhat pruned to exclude 'improper' verses: and it is now sung, not to the previous 'unsuitable' tune of the 'Old Hundredth Psalm', but to the innocuous 'Greensleeves'.

· Morris Dancing ·

With their fluttering handkerchiefs and jingling bells, 'the Morris Dancers' are now once again a familiar sight at summer festivals: and the revival of this form of ceremonial dance is one of the most remarkable phenomena of British 20th-century culture. It was, largely, the work of the folk-song collector Cecil Sharp, who in 1899 happened upon a performance by one of the few surviving teams of the Cotswold region: thus inspired to set about the recording of extinct or remembered dances, he then began to teach them to folklore enthusiasts – his very first pupils being (ironically enough, in view of the contempt for female dancers affected by subsequent all-male revival groups) the members of a 'working girls' club'. Officially recommended to schoolteachers in 1909, morris dancing thereafter went on from strength to strength: and though its following (reverting to type) is now mainly composed of robust and somewhat beery young men rather than earnest intellectuals, enthusiasm has steadily continued to grow, so that hundreds of active 'sides' now flourish throughout the country.

Due to the circumstances of the revival, 'morris' has become virtually synonymous with the particular type of dance Sharp collected and extolled: the six-man stick-clashing or handkerchief-waving dances of the south-west Midlands, performed on a set dancing-ground by two ranks of white-clad dancers decked with ribbons, cross-belts and bells. And though attempts to re-establish more appropriate local dance traditions are now gathering strength, this specifically regional form has, regrettably, spread far beyond its original Cotswold and Thames Valley heartland to become the standard 'revival morris'. Formerly, however, the word 'morris' had a far broader meaning: for it was not only used to describe all kinds of British ceremonial (as opposed to social) group dancing – including the distinctive SWORD dances of north-eastern England – but also applied to MUMMING PLAYS, many of which include no dancing at all. All these rituals share the common factor of having been performed by more or less 'disguised' men – though the degree of disguise varies from the vestigial ribbons and rosettes of Cotswold morris dancers to the elaborate hats,. suits of tatters and blackened faces retained both by dancers from other regions and by mummers: and herein, perhaps, lies the best clue to the vexed problems of the origins of 'morris' and the meaning of its name.

Almost certainly derived from 'Moorish', the dance's title has (since at least the 17th century) been taken to indicate that it originated either in North Africa or in Moorish medieval Spain: whence it was supposed to have been introduced into Britain either by the followers of Queen Eleanor of Castile, wife of Edward I, or by the English soldiers who fought in the Spanish campaigns of the 14th century. This theory (allegedly corroborated by the blackening of performers' faces to represent Moors) can however be dismissed on a number of grounds. For nothing like the English dance has ever been discovered in the Moorish lands, though somewhat similar performances do or did exist – with titles such as *mooriske*, *moriskentanz* and *danse moresque* – in many parts of northern Europe. Given the inherent improbability of an imported custom penetrating so deeply and widely into medieval folk culture, it therefore seems likely that the dance was really an ancient native ceremony, whose exponents disguised themselves by the cheap, easy and remarkably effective method of face-blacking: and that it subsequently acquired its title from this practice. Thus, in the words of E.K. Chambers (1903): 'the faces were not blackened because the dancers represented Moors, but rather the dancers were thought to represent Moors, because their faces were blackened.' Moors, of course, were the only black race familiar to medieval Europeans: and it is worth remarking that by the early 20th century, when 'nigger minstrel' bands had replaced moors as the negro stereotype, the black-faced dancers-cum-mummers of the Welsh borders referred to their activities as 'niggering'.

In all probability, then, the dance is older than its name: the latter being clearly well established in England by the time of its earliest known mention in 1458, when Alice de Wetenhalle (a London widow with Suffolk connections) bequeathed a silver cup engraved 'cum moreys dance'. Just how old the dance is, however, cannot be even approximately estimated: though current thinking leans towards the view that – like the other form of 'morris', the mumming play – the dance originated as a pre-Christian fertility or luck-bringing ceremony, and it is even possible that the name 'moorish' once alluded to its pagan rather than its black-faced associations. A very great deal of unfounded nonsense, nevertheless, has been written about morris's alleged 'pagan fertility rite' element: and all that is certain is that, by the time it is first recorded in the early Tudor period, the dance had joined such associated (and equally dubious) activities as MAY DAY 'Robin Hood Games', maypoles and HOBBY HORSES in being subsumed into the fabric of Christian parish life. Churchwardens' accounts from the Thames Valley area, indeed, show that money collected by dancers at EASTER, May Day, WHITSUN and other parish FEASTS was customarily devoted to church funds: while the 'Mores dawnsars' costumes and accoutrements – which at Kingston-upon-Thames, between 1507 and 1538, included four 'coats of white fustian spangled', two of 'green satin', and one 'dysard's' (Fool's) coat, along with 'silver paper', 'gold skins', 'double-soled shoon' and 'garters with bells' – were both provided by the church and kept there between outings.

Neither did the link between morris and churches wholly disappear at the Protestant Reformation – in 1612, for example, the churchwardens of Great Marlow in Buckinghamshire were still hiring out their parish 'coats and bells' to nearby Bisham, for a fee of half-a-crown – much to the disgust of Puritans like Philip Stubbes, who wrote the following account of the dance in 1583. Its performers, he begins, wear liveries of 'green, yellow or some other light wanton colour'

... and as though they were not gawdy enough ... they bedecke themselves with scarffes, ribbons and laces, hanged all over with golde rings, precious stones and other jewelles. This done they tie about either leg 20 or 40 belles, with rich handkerchiefs in their hands ... borrowed for the most part of their Mopsies and loving Bessies for bussing them in the dark. Thus, all things set in order, they have their hobbie horses, dragons and other antiques, and thundering drummers to strike up the devil's dance withal. Then march this heathen company towards the church and churchyard, their pipers pipying, their drummers thundering, their stumps daunsing, their belles jingling, their handkerchiefs fluttering about their heads, their hobbie horses and other monsters skarmyshing among the throng like madmen; and in this sort they go to the church (tho' the minister be at prayer or preaching) dancing and swinging their handkerchiefs over their heades in the church like devils incarnate, with such a confused noise that no man can heare his own voice.... Then after this about the church they go again and again, and so forth into the churchyard ... wherein they daunce all that day and (peradventure) all that night too. And thus these terrestriall furies spend the Sabbath-day.

By this time, then, the morris had already acquired all its familiar trappings: the bright colours, the ribbons, the handkerchiefs, the shining trinkets – to 'deflect away evil', or perhaps just to reflect the sun – and the jingling bells to emphasize the step: indeed, a 17th-century 'morris' costume in Perth Museum, probably worn for the Glover's Guild dance recorded in 1633, is set with no less than 252 bells, carefully tuned in twenty-one harmonizing sets of twelve.

During the 16th and 17th centuries, moreover, morris dancing was by no means confined to the countryside. For it was also danced (as at Perth) by town guildsmen, and at princely courts – the earliest Scots record, in a poem written by William Dunbar before 1513, refers to the court of James IV, where

> Sum singis, sum dances, sum tellis storyis
> Sum lait at even bringis in the moryis

- as well as in masques and on the London stage. Literary references to it abound during this period, though many of these adopt a somewhat condescending tone towards the 'rustique sport':

> Where every younker shaked his bells
> Till sweating feete gave fohing smells
> *Cobbe's Prophecies, 1614*

so it seems that fashionable interest in the dance was already on the wane by the time it was included among the 'abuses' legally prohibited by a Cromwellian ordinance of 1654. And though the ban was lifted at the Restoration, during the next 200 years the morris never really recovered either its official links with the church or its upper-class patronage.

Early 17th-century morris dancing near Richmond Palace, on the banks of the Thames in Surrey. Decked in the familiar bells and ribbons, the dancers include a 'man-woman', a hobby horse, and a fool with collecting ladle.

Yet it still continued to be danced at all manner of rural festivals and special occasions: as well as being performed as a money-raiser at slack seasons or when times were hard. The masons of north Herefordshire and the boatmen of the Severn, for example, both habitually toured their dances when severe frosts prevented them from plying their trades: while many Cotswold sides not only perambulated the neighbouring villages during the week after Whitsun, but also regularly ventured as far as London – where the Abingdon men were noticed in 1783, and a large number of teams performed during Queen Victoria's CORONATION celebrations in 1837 – generally making more money by dancing there than they earned as an itinerant haymaking or harvest gang on the way home. But by the mid-19th century the morris was – like so many other British customs – beginning to decline in many parts of its range, and in some it had already disappeared altogether.

From such records as have come to light (and there are doubtless many more awaiting discovery amid unpublished churchwardens' accounts and rural newspaper archives) it is nevertheless possible to gain some idea of the various regional dance traditions which once existed. Best known of these, as we have seen, is the 'Cotswold' morris which flourished originally in Oxfordshire, Gloucestershire, north Berkshire, and adjacent parts of Buckinghamshire, Bedfordshire, Northamptonshire and Warwickshire: but whose epicentre was apparently the area north of Oxford, where the annual Whitsuntide 'Lamb Ale' festival at Kirtlington

(suppressed in 1858) regularly attracted many visiting teams. Whitsun, indeed, was the usual time for performing this style of morris, which (apart from its solo 'jigs') was invariably danced by 'sides' of six white-clad men, generally accompanied by a fantastically dressed 'Fool' (also called 'the Squire' and usually the leader and best dancer) and sometimes by a 'cake bearer', who carried a cake impaled on a sword and distributed pieces of it to spectators 'for luck'. Well over a hundred Cotswold teams are known to have existed after 1800: and a dozen of them survived long enough to allow Cecil Sharp to record some sixty of their dances, which thus became the basis of the modern Cotswold repertoire.

The side from Bampton near Witney (or rather the sides, since the disagreements which notoriously plague both original and revival morris have produced three rival teams) still dances there annually on Spring Bank Holiday Monday, as it has danced around Whitsun without a break – except during the First World War – 'since time immemorial'. And though it cannot claim quite so unbroken a tradition, the team from Headington near Oxford is equally famous: for its musician William Kimber was Sharp's first teacher, and it has contributed more dances than any other side to the morris canon. Other renowned Cotswold teams, moreover, exist or existed at Adderbury, Brackley, Bucknell, Burford, Ducklington and Eynsham, all in Oxfordshire; at Abingdon, Berkshire (see MOCK MAYORS); Ilmington in Warwickshire; Badby in Northamptonshire; and Bledington, Chipping Campden and Longborough in Gloucestershire.

But if the Cotswold morris is generally recognized as the most highly developed and sophisticated form of the dance, it is also regarded as the furthest removed from the original ethos of the 'disguised ritual'. Closer to this, most probably, were the less complex morris dances of Derbyshire: which were generally performed in June by teams of up to twenty-four ribboned and white-clad men who (though they rarely wore bells) traditionally 'disguised' themselves with flowered hats. At Winster near Matlock, moreover, the sixteen-strong team was divided into 'men's' and 'women's' sides, the latter being played by men in particularly elaborate headgear: and here too the dance retained a whole range of extra 'characters' more usually associated with mumming plays – a King and (male) 'Queen', a Fool, a Hobby Horse, and a black-faced 'Witch' who cleared the dancing place with her broom. Associated at Tideswell with the dressing of WELLS, and at Castleton with the CASTLETON GARLAND, the Derbyshire dances (by contrast with the 'stationary' Cotswold convention) were all 'processionals', which continually progressed forward as the team made its rounds of the village, stopping from time to time to perform a simple 'partners meet-and-cross'.

In this they resemble both the highly ritualized ABBOTS BROMLEY HORN DANCE (performed not far from the Derbyshire boundary) and the 'North Western Processional Morris' of nearby Lancashire and Cheshire. Closely connected with the processional RUSHBEARINGS so popular in the north-west, the latter was again often danced by very large teams, notable among these being those from Lymm and Stalybridge in Cheshire, of Royton in Lancashire, and the well-known revival team from Garstang in the same county. Like the Derbyshire dancers, too, the Lancashire and Cheshire men wore very elaborate flowered and ribboned hats, but instead of handkerchiefs they either flourished two short ribboned sticks, rhythmically swung 'slings' (elongated cotton-filled bags, weighted at one end) or, alternatively, carried 'garlands', semi-circular flowered hoops held rigidly with both hands. As they pranced beside their rushcarts, moreover, their dance steps were emphasized by the clash of their iron-shod and belled clogs: while one famous surviving team, the Britannia Coconut Dancers of Bacup in Lancashire, also strikes together 'nuts' made from cotton-bobbin tops, which are attached to their hands, thighs and waist.

Formed in 1857 from workers in the nearby Royal Brittania Cotton Mills, this unique eight-man team appears in the streets of Bacup every Easter Saturday with completely blackened faces, wearing an extraordinary costume of black jerseys and breeches, short red-and-white tiered skirts, white stockings and 'turbans', and black clogs. Accompanied by the town's brass band, they perform two alternate dances, one with garlands and the other the 'coconut dance', a 'stepping' and leaping measure punctuated by the rippling clatter of the hand discs on those of the thighs and waist. These dances, like their costume and black faces, are supposedly derived from 'Moorish pirate dances' which somehow found their way to Cornwall, and were brought thence to Lancashire by itinerant miners.

Be that as it may (and it almost certainly may not) black faces and skirts or other female costumes were certainly an ancient form of morris 'disguise', which was retained longest by the dancers of the Welsh border counties of Shropshire, Herefordshire and parts of Worcestershire. These, unusually, performed their simple stick-clashing dances mainly during the Christmas season: and at Broseley near Much Wenlock in Shropshire the black-faced 'women's side' of the twelve-man team wore petticoats, while the 'men' (here and throughout the middle-March region also black-faced) wore mummer-like suits of 'tatters' made from cloth or paper strips – as do the 'Shropshire Bedlams' from Bishop's Castle, the leading 'Border Morris' revival team. What little we know of Welsh morris proper, suggests that (in north-east Wales at least) some of the dancers associated with the May Day custom of carrying round the ribbon-decked 'cangen haf' ('summer branch') also blacked their faces and wore short skirts over their breeches, while their leader and money-collector was a black-faced and petticoated 'man-woman' called the 'Cadi Ha''. The dance they performed, nevertheless, seems to have been a handkerchief-waving version of the 'north-western processional' borrowed from neighbouring Lancashire and Cheshire.

On the other side of those counties – in Yorkshire, Northumberland and Durham – the morris dance proper gives way altogether (and apparently without any overlapping of the customs) to the quite different sword dance. This was, however, also sometimes known as 'morris', and may perhaps have been what was meant by that term in Scotland, where the 17th-century 'morris dancers' of Perth were certainly armed with 'rapperis'. The north-eastern sword dance likewise shares its traditional PLOUGH MONDAY date with the primitive morris or 'Molly Dance' of East Anglia and the south-east Midlands: whose performers, wearing tall ribboned hats and led by a man-woman 'Molly', danced the simplest of all English dances around their ploughs.

Comparatively little has so far been discovered about the regional styles of other areas – though a pamphlet of 1609 recommends 'western men for gambols, Middlesex men for tricks above ground, Essex men for the hey, Lancashire for hornpipes … but Herefordshire for a morris dance': and, unless the Cornish FURRY DANCE can be accepted as a kind of processional, there is scarcely any record at all of morris dancing anywhere in the extreme south of England. The chief strongholds of the custom, therefore, would appear to have been the English Midlands, and particularly the western side of them: and it may well be that, thanks to the extraordinary success of the 20th-century revival, morris dancing is more widespread now than ever it was in the past.

Bampton, the longest-established 'Cotswold' **morris dancing** side, performing a six-man handkerchief dance on the squire's lawn. The fiddler here is the renowned eighty-year-old William Wells, whose family accompanied the side for more than two centuries.

A specialized version of 'Lancashire Processional' **morris dancing,** the Garland Dance, performed by the Britannia Coconut Dancers of Bacup: note the iron-shod clogs and cotton-bobbin 'nuts' on hands, waist and thighs.

The team that sparked off the great 20th-century **morris dancing** revival: the famous Headington side, whose predecessors first fired Cecil Sharp with enthusiasm, perform a Cotswold stick dance.

· Mothering Sunday ·

The fourth Sunday in LENT, also called 'Mid-Lent' and 'Refreshment Sunday' – because some relaxation of Lenten abstinence was then allowed, in honour of the Feeding of the Five Thousand, the day's Gospel reading – is best known as Mothering Sunday. Its link with motherhood is alleged – without much firm evidence – to stem either from a medieval practice of visiting cathedrals and other 'mother churches' on this day, or from its frequently occurring proximity to LADY DAY, the principal commemoration of the Mother of God. As a celebration of human motherhood, however, it is not recorded until the mid-17th century, 'when all the children and grandchildren' were said 'to meet at the head and chiefe of the family, and have a feast'.

This was at Worcester, the centre of the western region – stretching from Lancashire to Devon, with a concentration along both sides of the Welsh border – where the old form of 'mothering' was always most popular, and where it may indeed have originated. Children living away from home – including servants and apprentices, who expected a holiday for the purpose – flocked to their parents' houses, often making long journeys on foot: and the re-united family would then perhaps attend church together before sharing a meal of some traditional dish, lamb and veal (recalling the Prodigal Son's 'fatted calf'?) being understandably considered appropriate in most places.

But the main purpose of the visit was to present 'mother' with 'a small sum of money, a trinket, or some nice eatable': and the most favoured 'nice eatable' was – as it still is in some families – the 'simnel cake'. The name of this confection, according to one legend, derived from a contentious couple called Simon and Nell, who quarrelled over whether to bake or boil it and eventually did both; and according to another from the rebel Lambert Simnel, who worked in Henry VII's kitchen after his defeat in 1487: in fact, it descends from the medieval Latin word (*simnellus*) for the fine wheaten loaves baked on special occasions since Edward the Confessor's reign. All the modern variants of the simnel cake, however, are much more elaborate. The Shrewsbury version (which claims to be the original) encases a rich fruit mixture in a glazed saffron-bread crust: while the Devizes simnel is star-shaped and crustless; that from Bury in Lancashire saucer-like and stuffed with spiced currants; and the Yorkshire form (also sold throughout the winter) resembles a Christmas cake with a layer of almond paste.

Though simnel cakes never lost their appeal, the observance of Mothering Sunday (having reached a zenith during mid-Victorian times) was said to be 'declining' even in its Herefordshire heartland by 1912, and to be 'virtually extinct' by 1935. Since the Second World War, however, it has enjoyed an extraordinary and still-increasing revival of popularity throughout Britain, largely due to a transfusion from (and confusion

with) the entirely separate American festival of Mother's Day. Conceived as recently as 1907 by a Miss Anna Jarvis of Philadelphia, and celebrated on the second Sunday in May (the anniversary of her mother's death) this crossed the Atlantic with hundreds of homesick GIs in 1944, and at once hybridized with the waning native custom. To it we owe the cards, the rise in florists' prices, and even the name (Mother's Day) generally if wrongly associated with the modern British festival: yet this nevertheless remains firmly attached to its old mid-Lent date, when special Mothering Sunday children's services are held in many churches.

· Mumming Plays ·
Halloween – Easter, but mainly around Christmas

'Mumming' may be derived from the Germanic *mummen* – a mask; or the French *momer* – to act in a dumb show. Either is appropriate, for mummers still conceal their identity (in Scotland and northern England, indeed, they may be called 'guisers') while many of their activities were conducted in silent mime. In 1377, for example, a 'mummerie' of masked and elaborately costumed Londoners diced, danced and feasted with King Richard II, all apparently without uttering a word. Such elaborate CHRISTMAS 'disguisings', recorded at English and Scots royal courts throughout the later Middle Ages, were merely the aristocratic version of the ancient and widespread custom of luck- or fertility-bringing midwinter visits by supposedly unidentifiable 'beings' (*see* HOODEN HORSE; MARI LWYD). And though 'Persones wyth Vysoures ... disgysed or apparelde as Mommers' were suppressed by law in 1511 (allegedly because criminals used the custom as a cloak for 'murders, felonies and rapes') mumming persisted at a popular level long after its abandonment by the great. Latterly, no doubt, this was because it provided a welcome opportunity for collecting alms; and it may have been the need to combine an ancient ritual with a largesse-generating 'good show' that gave birth to the 'mumming play'.

When this originated is uncertain, but by the 18th century it had assumed roughly its present form – which is basically as follows. A group of men (only very recently have women participated) enter the place of performance, and stand 'mum' in a semi-circle. Possibly because the anti-mask law remained in force until 1829, they are disguised instead by 'blacking-up'; by character costume; or by strips of cloth or paper sewn over their clothes, and perhaps also hanging from elaborate hats to conceal their faces – this being the oldest surviving type of mummer's dress, retained longest in southern England. Starting with the 'letter-in' (usually a 'Clown' or Old Father Christmas) they step forward in turn to deliver their speeches, traditionally without much acting, and then return to their places.

The central (and clearly the most essential) part of the ritual begins when the hero – often Saint or 'King'

Left: One of the combatants is slain during the Marshfield 'Paper Boys' **mumming play.** He carefully falls onto a mat, designed to protect his 'disguise' of newspaper strips sewn to a 'cowgown'. *Below:* While Father Christmas looks on, the Doctor prepares to revive a pair of 'corpses' in the Crookham mumming play: here the 'disguise' is made from strips of wallpaper.

George but sometimes a more localized figure like the Scottish William Wallace – fights an opposing champion, or occasionally a whole succession of enemies: these have names like 'Bold Slasher', 'The Black Prince of Paradine', or 'The Turkish Knight' – known to one company of Sussex 'Tipteerers' as 'Turkey Snipe'. After a spirited battle, one of the combatants (not always the 'villain') is slain. But a Doctor appears, who boasts lengthily and nonsensically of his skill and travels, and then miraculously revives the dead man.

This enactment of death and resurrection over, several apparently irrelevant comic characters step forward. Their number varies with the availability of performers, and their identity with regional tradition, but Beelzebub and a hefty male 'Lady' are widely popular. Full of local and topical allusion – whose 'broadness' may be tailored to the audience – the principal purpose of their speeches is to encourage generous giving to the collection which invariably ends the performance.

Such is the most widespread type of mumming play, known to folklorists as the 'Hero-Combat'. It was once performed from the Channel to the Scottish Lowlands – with the apparent exception of East Anglia, Kent and most of Wales – but was most common in south-central and south-Midland England, where a number of long-established groups remain active. Most notable are the Mummers of Bampton and Headington, Oxfordshire; the famous 'Paper Boys' of Marshfield, Gloucestershire, with their newspaper-strip costumes; and the wallpaper-

tatter clad Hampshire mummers of Crookham (where the play has been performed for at least a century) and of Andover, with their splendidly decorated hats. All these, together with hundreds of revived groups all over England, appear around Christmas. But in the Cheshire area, the mummers traditionally go SOULING at HAL-LOWEEN: while in Cumbria, Lancashire and West Yorkshire (where the play is influenced by printed 'chap-book' versions) the 'Pace-egging' mummers perform at EASTER.

Two regional variants on the Hero-Combat play also exist. In the Lincolnshire, Leicestershire and Nottinghamshire 'Plough play', a Fool character woos and wins a Young Lady – played, of course by a man – but is accused of fathering an Old Woman's bastard baby: the action thereafter proceeds normally. Since it features marriage and birth as well as death and resurrection – the whole life cycle – this may well be the oldest type of mumming play. Having died out (largely because of its 'impropriety') it has now been revived in its native area, usually on its traditional date of PLOUGH MONDAY.

Around this time, too, the SWORD dance play is still occasionally performed in Yorkshire, Durham and Northumberland. Instead of a stylized combat, its hallmark is the ritual beheading of a victim, who at the culmination of an intricate dance is caught in a star-shaped 'knot' of interlinked swords. He is then miraculously revived, thus completing the symbolism of midwinter death and new life which is central to all the 900 or so known versions of the British mumming play.

N

· National Eisteddfod ·
see EISTEDDFODAU

· Neville's Cross Commemoration ·
Durham Cathedral: Saturday nearest 29 May

After evensong on the Saturday nearest 29 May, Durham Cathedral choir sing anthems from the south, east and north sides of the great central tower – but not, for some reason now uncertain, from the western side.

The origin of this custom is equally obscure: and though it coincides with OAK APPLE DAY, it apparently has nothing to do with Charles II. It is usually said, rather, to commemorate the battle of Neville's Cross, fought near the city on 17 October 1346, when an English force routed King David II's invading Scots army. Some of the Durham monks were anxiously watching the struggle from the predecessor of the present tower – curiously enough, they must have done so from its western side – and when they saw the Scots turn to flee, they raised a joyful 'Te Deum': rejoicing the more, reported one contemporary, because the victory saved them a £1000 ransom demanded by the invaders. The monks and their Anglican successors have since continued the thanksgiving with few lapses: one of these, during the Civil War, was ended by the Restoration, when the celebration was transferred from the battle anniversary to that of the king's return.

That, at least, is one story. But some authorities plausibly prefer to trace the custom to the magnificent GUILDS procession that used to take place on 29 May, in connection with which 'the singing boys sang an anthem from the top of the steeple': and others again to a 'Te Deum' sung to celebrate the extinguishing of the great fire of 25 May 1429, which destroyed the original tower but spared the remainder of the cathedral.

· New Forest Customs ·
see FOREST CUSTOMS

· New Year ·
31 December – 1 January

The welcoming of the New Year remains the greatest of all annual festivals in Scotland, where it is often called 'Hogmanay' – a word whose meaning has never been satisfactorily established, though it has variously been derived from the Anglo-Saxon *Haleg Monath* (Holy Month), the Gaelic *oge maidne* (new morning) and, improbably, the French *au gui mener* (lead to the mistletoe). What seems certain, however, is that its Scottish importance was partly gained at the expense of

the CHRISTMAS celebrations suppressed as 'popish and superstitious' by the Kirk, so that midwinter festivities assumed a more secular (though in some ways more pagan) date and character.

In the northernmost parts of England, too, New Year celebrations are both general and enthusiastic, but towards the south and east they are progressively more and more overshadowed by Christmas. Even there, however, they appear to be growing in popularity, particularly among those who object to the cosiness of the 'family Christmas', or for whom Christ's Nativity allegedly has no meaning: and a widespread custom among younger people is to spend Christmas with kin, but New Year with friends.

New Year jollifications have long been louder and more communal than those of Christmas. Vast public gatherings – notably at Edinburgh's Tron Kirk, Glasgow's George Square and London's Trafalgar Square – greet the New Year with the linked-arm singing of 'Auld Lang Syne', the kissing of total strangers, and a cheerful cacophony from all manner of hooters and other noise-making engines: while countless churches, having tolled out the Old with muffled BELLS, remove the muffles to ring in the New with joyous peals. In Scotland and the Borders, too, a number of places hold communal BURNING THE OLD YEAR OUT ceremonies with bonfires and torchlight processions (*see* ALLENDALE TAR BARRELS; BURNING THE CLAVIE; SWINGING THE FIREBALLS; UP-HELLY-AA).

Such celebrations are encouraged by the firmly held belief that the coming year must begin happily, luckily, and after a clean break with the past: hence the universal addiction to New Year's resolutions (all too often the product of over-indulgence, and lasting only as long as its aftermath) and the still common dislike of carrying over into the new year any task left unfinished in the old. Hence, too, the once general custom of giving and receiving New Year's gifts – which until the 18th century far outshone Christmas presents in number and splendour, and which in northern and western Britain survived until very recently in the tokens (called hogmanays in Scotland) given by or to 'new year's gifting' children. In Wales and the Marches, for instance, where they sang songs like:

> We wish you a merry Christmas, a Happy New Year
> A pocket full of money and a cellar full of beer
> A good fat pig to last you all the year
> Please to give us a New Year's Gift
>
> *Radnorshire*

these carried a *callenig* (Welsh: New Year), an apple decorated with nuts or stuck with grain; in eastern Scotland, they brought red herrings; while in parts of England they would expect to receive (especially from godparents) confections like Suffolk 'kitchel-cakes', Coventry 'God-cakes', or St Albans 'popladys'.

All these things symbolize plenty in the coming year, to be further courted by allowing nothing whatever to be taken out of the house on New Year's Day. Thus normally generous people would flatly refuse to lend anything then, especially a light to re-kindle a neighbour's ominously extinguished fire: while usually house-proud matrons would keep even dust, slops, and peelings indoors until 2 January. In fact, everything done or not done on the opening day of the year would influence the succeeding twelve months: and, above all, it was and is vital to ensure that its first visitor should be a propitious one.

Throughout Scotland and northern England, therefore, midnight on 31 December finds first footers poised to bring in the New Year luck. There are many local variants on the rules governing their appearance and behaviour, but nearly everywhere men are preferred (in most parts of England and Wales, indeed, a female caller at *any* time on New Year's Day was once an unmitigated disaster) and the darker they are, the better. In some areas of eastern Scotland, East Yorkshire and Lincolnshire, however, fair men are the favourites; while around Bradford in West Yorkshire (as in parts of Aberdeenshire) 'Lucky Birds' with red hair are actively encouraged, despite the horror – based either on Judas's allegedly red hair or some more ancient taboo – this colouring evokes elsewhere.

Tall, good-looking and well-made first footers are invariably hoped for, though some regions prefer bachelors and others married men. Appropriately, the shape of their feet is also important, a high instep 'that water will run under' being particularly desirable in Scotland. Flat-footed people are therefore very unlucky, as are those with any kind of lameness, squint, or natural blemish, or whose eyebrows meet in the middle: so too are people dressed in black or mourning clothes, carrying knives or pointed tools, or known for stinginess. An empty-handed visitor was so badly omened that he might be suspected of deliberately ill-wishing the house.

What he should bring also changes somewhat from area to area (a branch of living evergreen in Yorkshire, a sheaf of corn or a herring in parts of Scotland). But his usual gifts are a piece of coal or other firing; a loaf; and a bottle of whisky. On entering, he must place the fuel on the fire (and sometimes stir it), put the loaf on the table, and pour a glass for the head of the house, all normally without speaking or being spoken to until he wishes everyone 'A Happy New Year'. He must, of course, enter by the front door, and if possible leave by the back. Similarly, in Wales and the Marches, the back door releases the Old Year at the first stroke of midnight: it is then locked 'to keep the luck in', and at the last stroke the New Year is let in at the front.

In those regions, too, the ancient customs of 'Creaming the Well' is remembered, if not still occasionally practised. The 'cream' is the first water from any well or spring – best of all from a holy or curative one – on New Year's Day. Since this could be drawn only once, people often raced to get it: especially young women, for its

New Year first footing in Scotland, from an engraving of 1882.

possession brought marriage within the year, or at the very least luck and beauty. Mercenary, married or determinedly independent girls might alternatively sell the water to their mistress, and in the 1950s new year's gifting Pembrokeshire children still offered it to householders. In parts of Scotland, however, the 'Flower of the Well' was used to wash dairy utensils and given to cows, to increase milk production: and in the Highlands (where water was taken instead from a 'living and dead ford', crossed both by ordinary traffic and funerals), it was drunk by all in the house, which was then fumigated with burning juniper.

Finally, the New Year is a favoured time for looking into the future, when newspaper 'astrologers' are busier than ever. More old-fashioned people, however, may prefer random 'dipping' into a bible and noting the first verse their eye falls on: or observing the direction of the wind:

> If New Year's Eve night wind blow south
> That betokeneth warmth and growth
> If west, much milk and fish in the sea
> If north, much cold and storms will be
> If east, the trees will bear much fruit
> If north-east – flee it, man and brute

For whatever happens at this prophetic season is sure to influence the course of the coming year.

O

· Oak Apple Day ·
29 May

On 29 May 1660 (his thirtieth birthday) King Charles II made his triumphal entry into London, thereby ending both his long exile and the English Republic created after the Civil War: and soon afterwards Parliament ordered this 'Happy Restoration' of the monarchy to be annually commemorated with church services, bellringing and bonfires. From the very beginning, however, the essential elements of the celebration were bunches or boughs of oak leaves (if possible including the fly-generated growths called oak apples). Officially, these recalled the oak in which Charles had hidden from Parliamentary troops after his defeat at Worcester (1651), but they may also have perpetuated a far older pagan festival honouring the most sacred of trees. At any rate, Oak Apple Day soon became so popular – especially in the Royalist north and west of England – that it absorbed many MAY DAY and other customs (see GROVELY RIGHTS DAY; NEVILLE'S CROSS COMMEMORATION): and until late-Victorian times churches, houses, farm horses and even railway engines were regularly decked with oak. People who failed to wear oaken sprigs, moreover, risked being stung with nettles, pelted with eggs, kicked or (especially in Sussex, where the anniversary was called 'Pinch Bum Day') pinched as 'Roundheads' – a custom still perhaps maintained by children in a few places.

Though general adult observation of the day has almost died out, more formal celebrations continue here and there. On or near it, the Chelsea Pensioners of Charles II's Royal Hospital honour their founder by parading with oak sprigs, decking his statue with oak, and consuming beer and plum pudding: and their fellow veterans at Lord Leycester's Hospital, Warwick, keep up similar customs. At Worcester (the 'loyal city' whence Charles fled to his oak) the Guildhall gates are hung with boughs, and a commemorative service is held: while at Northampton (which the King gave a thousand tons of oak to rebuild, after a disastrous fire) the mayor and corporation process with gilded oak sprays to the oak-wreathed royal statue at All Saints' church. Related festivities occur on the day itself at Aston-on-Clun, Shropshire (ARBOR DAY) and Castleton, Derbyshire (CASTLETON GARLAND) and on the nearest Saturday at Fownhope near Hereford, where the local 'Hearts of Oak' friendly society parades with oak-apple-decked staffs.

· The Oaks ·
see THE DERBY

· Old Man's Day ·
Braughing, near Bishop's Stortford, Hertfordshire: 2 October

One of the most curious of all British customs, this cheerful GRAVESIDE DOLE is said to commemorate an equally extraordinary event. As the coffined body of Matthew Wall, an Elizabethan Braughing farmer, was being carried from his home in Fleece Lane to the churchyard, the bearers slipped on some dead leaves and dropped it. Whereupon, to the amazement of the funeral party, the coffin opened and out stepped the 'corpse', revived by the jolt and so perfectly restored to health that he married in the following year and lived on to a ripe old age. In gratitude for his providential escape from being buried alive, the 'Old Man's' will of 1595 made a number of charitable bequests to the parish, all of which were to be distributed on 21 September, the feast of St Matthew – though it is not quite clear whether this was the anniversary of Wall's revival or simply his 'name day'.

At any rate, Old Man's Day is still celebrated at Braughing on 2 October – which is to say St Matthew's Day, Old Style. Gathering at the top of Fleece Lane, the rector and the village children – twenty of whom receive four old pence each from the bequest – follow the coffin's route to the churchyard, while the bells toll as if for a funeral. As they go, they sweep up the dead leaves along the path: another requirement of the will, but one which seems odd if it really was leaves that saved Matthew's life. The party then gather round the Old Man's grave – which is supposed to be dressed annually with brambles to keep off sheep – while the rector reminds them of the story and prays both for Wall and for the parish: and finally the church bells change their funereal tolling to a joyful wedding peal, in honour of the Old Man's 'resurrection' and his subsequent marriage.

· Opening of the General Assembly ·
Assembly Hall, Edinburgh: May

The General Assembly of the Scottish Kirk, which originated as a gathering of Protestant lords, commoners and clergy in 1560 but became a council of ministers and church elders in 1578, was for long periods of its early history the real government of Scotland. Seeking to set the 'rule of God's Word' above the rule of Parliament, to impose strict Presbyterian morality and doctrine on the whole nation, and to resist by force the interference of Stuart Kings and Cromwellian generals, it was twice suppressed, but eventually emerged triumphant in 1690. After the abolition of the separate Scots parliament by the Act of Union with England in 1707, moreover, it became the nearest thing Scotland possessed to a national assembly: and though its influence was impaired by the split or 'Disruption' in its ranks in 1843, and latterly by the general decline in religious belief, it still remains a powerful factor in Scottish life.

This importance is reflected by its annual opening ceremony in May, which is occasionally attended by the monarch of Great Britain in person, but more often by a Lord High Commissioner specially appointed for the event: who, as the sovereign's direct representative, lives throughout Assembly Week at the Royal Palace of Holyroodhouse and is accorded all princely honours, including a twenty-one-gun ROYAL SALUTE. The procession to the Assembly, moreover, is led by the Scottish heralds in their elaborately embroidered tabards, and includes such officials as the Hereditary Bearers of St Andrew's Flag and of the Royal Banner of Scotland, with the Hereditary Lord High Constable and the Hereditary Master of the Household for Scotland. But despite all this attendant pomp, the Lord High Commissioner – having made a formal Speech from the Throne – takes no part in the Assembly's actual deliberations: for, as centuries of struggle have proved, 'it is God, not Kings, that is the real Head of the Kirk'.

· Orange-giving Ceremony ·
Sileby, Leicestershire: a Sunday in May

A curious example of a 'custom' manufactured by the Press, and subsequently provided with an exceedingly dubious pedigree. The ceremony of giving oranges to children in Sileby churchyard (now performed on the Sunday-school anniversary in May) is frequently declared to be a commemoration of the Battle of Waterloo. In fact, its origins can be precisely dated to a newspaper article of the late 1950s, written after a reporter had visited Sileby in search of 'a story about life in the past'. He was accordingly introduced to the then churchwarden, eighty-nine-year-old Mr Charles Hudson, who recalled a childhood memory of hearing old villagers speak about a day, in their own youth, when oranges were distributed to children under the churchyard elm. This had been a once-only event, presumably marking some special occasion: but what the occasion was had passed beyond recall.

The resulting newspaper article, however, reported the 'Orange-Giving Ceremony' as 'an ancient village tradition', which had regrettably been allowed to lapse: and a few days later a public-spirited local businessman asked if he might 'revive the custom' with a yearly gift of oranges for distribution on the Sunday-school anniversary. Arrangements to do so were therefore put in hand: and the attendant publicity provoked speculation about the 'original' presentation. The old people Mr Hudson recalled, it was estimated, must have been children during the first two decades of the 19th century, when the principal public events were the British victories at Trafalgar (1805) and Waterloo (1815). Trafalgar celebrations, however, would have been tempered by mourning for Nelson: whereas Waterloo was an absolute victory, and one which occurred in June, an ideal season for open-air distributions – though not, incidentally, for oranges, which at

that time would have been obtainable only during the winter months! Given that the ceremony did mark a national event (and not, as is perhaps more likely, a purely local occasion) Waterloo therefore seemed to the speculators the most likely candidate.

Though founded on such slender 'evidence', the Waterloo theory was soon being reported as a fact: and before long – despite the protests of the Sileby church authorities, who knew the truth of the matter – the 'traditional custom' begun by the 1950s newspaper had become 'a revived commemoration of the Battle of Waterloo'.

· Oranges and Lemons Service ·
St Clement Danes, the Strand, London WC2: a weekday in late March

'Oranges and Lemons', say the bells of St Clemen's
'You owe me five farthings', say the bells of St Martin's.

Thus runs the famous nursery rhyme, which is usually associated with St Clement 'Danes' church, in the Strand: much controversy, however, surrounds both this church's 'surname' and its connection with citrus fruits. According to some, the former derives either from the burial there of Harold Harefoot (d.1040), son of King Canute, or from a nearby massacre of Vikings: but the most probable explanation is that the church once served a Danish merchant community settled just outside London's walls, who naturally chose St Clement, patron of sailors, as its dedication. Its 'oranges and lemons' link, traditionally, sprang from the landing of these imported fruits at a Thames wharf adjacent to the old churchyard – whereafter they had to pay a toll to pass through the lawyers' colony of Clements Inn. Certainly the Inn porters, until relatively recently, presented an orange and a lemon to each of its tenants on NEW YEAR'S DAY, collecting a half-crown in return: but whether this custom originated or merely perpetuated the citrus connection remains unclear. It is even possible that the song refers to another London St Clement's, in Eastcheap: or that it arose simply because 'lemons' provides a rare rhyme with 'Clement's'.

Amid all this speculation, it is gratifying to report that the modern Oranges and Lemons service has a clear-cut origin. In 1920, accepting the church's associations without question, the then vicar installed a carillon of bells to play the nursery-rhyme tune: and on 31 March of that year its first ringing was celebrated with a children's service, followed by a distribution of appropriate fruit donated by Danes living in London. This ceremony continued annually until the Second World War, when St Clement's was virtually destroyed by bombs – as if to further 'confirm' the rhyme, five farthings were found among the ruins, and duly handed over to St Martin's-in-the-Fields. By 1957, however, church and carillon – which rings the tune daily at 9 a.m., noon, 3 p.m. and 6 p.m. – had been

After the annual **Oranges and Lemons Service** at St Clement Danes in 1967, the appropriate fruit is handed out to local schoolchildren.

restored as an RAF memorial, and the service was then resumed. Today it is attended by the children of St Clement Danes primary school, who read the lessons, recite the rhyme, and sometimes play it on handbells, before each receiving an orange and a lemon from the piled tables arranged – if dry – outside the church.

· Orders of Chivalry ·

The idea of orders of chivalry – groups of knights banded together under particular rules, with special insignia or badges, and an avowed common purpose – originated with the multi-national 'military orders of religion', half monk and half soldier, which sprang up during the Crusades. By the 14th century, however, crusading enthusiasm had given way to fascination with the romances and ideals of chivalry, and particularly with the legends of King Arthur's Round Table: while attempts to unite all Christendom against the heathen, increasingly seen as an unattainable aspiration, gave place to the growing nationalist ambitions of rival kings. It was against this background that 'secular orders of chivalry' developed in most European countries: the oldest and longest-lasting of them all being the English Order of the Garter.

This was founded by Edward III in 1348, at a high point of English success in the Hundred Years War with France. Placed under the special patronage of St George, its establishment (then as now) was the sovereign and twenty-five knights, the great majority of whom were the King's leading field commanders: a military tradition which has been maintained throughout much of the order's history. It is probable, too, that the blue and gold colours of the famous 'Garter' worn below the left knee (being the hues of the arms of France) alluded to Edward's alleged rights to the French crown: while the Order's motto, 'Honi Soit Qui Mal y Pense' – 'Shame to him who thinks ill of it' – may well have been directed at critics of the King's claims to the French throne.

According to a tradition first recorded by Tudor chroniclers, however, both Garter and motto originated from an incident which occurred at a feast celebrating the capture of Calais in 1347: when the King's mistress the Countess of Salisbury was mocked by courtiers for shedding her garter during a dance. But Edward at once stepped forward and tied the blue ribbon round his own knee, sternly uttering the motto as a rebuke to the mockers and declaring that the Garter would soon be held in the highest esteem. This story does indeed appear to have some historical foundation: and it has also given rise to an ingenious if decidedly implausible theory about the Garter's original significance, canvassed by those who believe that an underground pagan witch-cult persisted in high places long after the official adoption of Christianity. Pointing to the 'fact' that the order's twenty-six members constitute a 'double royal coven' of twice thirteen, while its earliest official robes were decorated with 169 (or thirteen times thirteen) embroidered garters, these suggest that the Countess's concealed garter was really the symbol of the secret cult, to which the King gave open support by his words and actions.

Though this outrageous fantasy can safely be dismissed – if only because the Order's earliest rules insisted that any knight who strayed from religious orthodoxy must be expelled – the Garter's full membership has certainly always been kept down to twenty-six: an exclusiveness which greatly enhanced its prestige over that of many European orders, whose membership proliferated into hundreds. From its first foundation, however, a very few foreign princes and rulers – generally those with whom the monarchs of England wished to cement a useful alliance – have been admitted as additional 'Stranger Knights': while the further twenty-six 'Poor Knights' envisaged by the founder – deserving veterans of gentle birth, maintained by the Crown and now called 'Military Knights' – still reside permanently at Windsor and attend daily services at the Order's own Chapel of St George within the castle precincts. In this vast and splendid church, rebuilt by Edward IV in 1475, the banners and crested helmets of current knights hang permanently above their stalls, while the generations of long-dead members who have sat in their places are commemorated by engraved heraldic 'stall-plates': and it is here, in the burial place of most English monarchs since Henry VIII, that the annual Garter Service takes place.

This ceremony (which is held in June, generally on the Monday of ROYAL ASCOT WEEK, the date nearest ST GEORGE'S DAY when the sovereign is sure to be in residence at Windsor) is private to the Order: but the

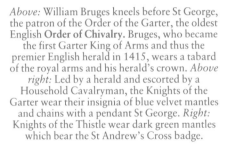

Above: William Bruges kneels before St George, the patron of the Order of the Garter, the oldest English **Order of Chivalry**. Bruges, who became the first Garter King of Arms and thus the premier English herald in 1415, wears a tabard of the royal arms and his herald's crown. *Above right:* Led by a herald and escorted by a Household Cavalryman, the Knights of the Garter wear their insignia of blue velvet mantles and chains with a pendant St George. *Right:* Knights of the Thistle wear dark green mantles which bear the St Andrew's Cross badge.

public may apply for tickets to view the procession from the royal apartments (where the investiture of any new knights is performed) to the chapel. Revived in 1948 after a lapse of a century, the procession's route is guarded by lines of dismounted Household Cavalrymen: at its head walks the Constable of the Castle, followed by the Military Knights in their scarlet tunics and white sashes, and the heralds and pursuivants of the College of Arms in their richly embroidered tabards. Then come the knights themselves, in their blue velvet mantles emblazoned on the shoulder with gartered crosses of St George, their plumed Tudor bonnets and their great gold and enamelled collars, with the pendant image of the saint fighting the dragon. These are followed by the royal princes and the Queen Mother, and finally by the Sovereign's Procession – the Prelate, Chancellor and Register of the Order, Garter King at

Arms (the senior English herald) and the Gentleman Usher of the Black Rod, leading the Queen and Prince Philip: while an escort of Yeomen of the Guard brings up the rear.

Next in seniority among British orders of chivalry – which all follow the pattern of Garter insignia and ceremonial – is the Scottish Order of the Thistle. If its own mythology is to be believed, this 'Most Ancient and Noble Order' owes its inception to a probably fictitious King Achaius, who established it during the 8th century to commemorate a victory over the Saxons: but its true ancestor seems to be the Order of St Andrew founded in about 1540 by James V. When that ill-starred monarch died two years later, however, it fell into abeyance; and though the equally unlucky James VII and II attempted to revive it under its present title in 1687, this too proved a false start, so that the Thistle dates its continuous existence only from 1703. What it lacks in antiquity, nevertheless, the Order makes up in exclusiveness, for its membership is confined to sixteen 'Knights Companions', plus a handful of Royal and of Extra (i.e. foreign) Knights. These wear mantles of dark green velvet with a St Andrew's Cross badge, elaborate collars of golden thistles and rue-sprigs, and plumed bonnets: and once a year (generally on or about ST ANDREWS DAY, 30 November) they process across Edinburgh's Parliament Square for a service (including an installation ceremony if necessary) in the Thistle Chapel, specially built onto St Giles's Cathedral in 1911. The Lord Lyon King at Arms, the Scottish heralds and pursuivants, and the Royal Company of Archers also take part: and if the Queen is present she is preceded by the senior Scottish earl, bearing James IV's Sword of State.

The Order of the Bath – the next in precedence, now that the Irish Order of St Patrick (like the Orders of the Star of India and the Indian Empire) is no longer awarded – derives its title from the ritual bath taken by medieval knights before their dubbing, and by monarchs on the eve of their CORONATIONS. From at least the Coronation of Henry IV in 1399, it was the custom for a number of especially favoured candidates for knighthood to undergo this purifying ceremony at the same time as the king, and to be thereafter knighted by him: but though these 'Knights of the Bath' consequently enjoyed added prestige, and also wore distinctive crimson robes on state occasions, they do not seem to have been organized into a formal body. This was the work of George I, who in 1725 'revived' the order – albeit without its original coronation or ablutionary connections – as a reward for distinguished soldiers and sailors. Greatly expanded after the Battle of Waterloo in 1815, the Bath's comparatively large membership (which also includes leading civil servants) is now divided into three classes: Knights Grand Cross (GCB), Knights Commanders (KB) and Companions (CB). The Knights Grand Cross alone, however, are privileged to hang their banners above their stalls in King Henry VII's Chapel in Westminster Abbey: and they alone wear the Order's crimson mantle to attend the installation ceremonies held there at approximately four-yearly intervals.

Two other orders of chivalry also hold ceremonial services, both of them at St Paul's Cathedral in London. The senior of these is the Order of St Michael and St George, founded in 1818 to honour diplomats and officials of the Foreign Service: this again is divided into Knights Grand Cross (GCMG), Knights Commander (KCMG) and Companions (CMG) – the initials being irreverently alleged to stand for 'Call Me God', 'Kindly Call Me God', and 'God Calls Me God'. Again, too, only the uppermost grade wears the Order's light-blue silk mantle to the annual services held in a special chapel in the cathedral. This rule also applies to the rose-pink mantle of the most recently founded and much the largest order of chivalry, that of the British Empire.

Established in 1917 to reward services to the Empire and Commonwealth, at home or abroad, its 100,000 or so members become Knights (or Dames) Grand Cross (GCBE); Knights (or Dames) Commander (KBE or DBE); officers (OBE); or Members (MBE): and at least some of them attend three- or four-yearly services in the main body of St Paul's Cathedral.

· Orr Bequest ·
see MARRIAGE PORTION CHARITIES

· The Oxford and Cambridge Boat Race ·
River Thames, Putney to Mortlake, London: a Saturday in March or April

It seems somewhat extraordinary that this rowing match between two crews of university undergraduates, not necessarily better oarsmen than those of any other boat club, should have achieved such enduring fame and popularity. A few years ago, public interest in the event seemed on the wane, but there has since been a resurgence of enthusiasm, and the Oxford and Cambridge Boat Race is again one of London's premier spring attractions.

The first inter-university race was held at Henley in 1829, the brain-child of Christopher Wordsworth of Trinity College, Cambridge – nephew of the poet, and subsequently Bishop of Lincoln – and his Oxford friend Charles Merivale. It became an annual event in 1839, but was not transferred to its present Putney to Mortlake course until 1845. So far, Cambridge has scored marginally more wins than Oxford, and has also achieved the longest unbroken run of victories, during the thirteen years between 1924 and 1936. The history of the race has also been packed with incident: oarsmen collapsing; revolts by crews; a dead heat; and numerous sinkings – for instance in 1978, when Cambridge foundered at Barnes Bridge. The frequency of waterlogging is largely due to the fact that the contest is rowed along the Tideway, a tidal stretch of river which contains several reaches particularly hazardous in squally spring weather. It may be that university teams are not often up to Olympic standard (and there has been much debate about this) but there can be no doubt that a crew capable of covering this four-and-a-quarter-mile course in seventeen or eighteen minutes must be extremely strong, fit and well disciplined.

At the turn of the century, when the event was at the height of its popularity, a great fleet of pleasure craft followed the contesting boats, 'all bumping and jostling and fouling each other in frantic style': and race officials had some trouble in maintaining order. Today, television probably affords the best opportunity of seeing the whole contest: but the spirit of the Victorian races continues among the crews and their vociferous supporters, and the course includes several miles of excellent vantage points.

The Cambridge boat founders at Barnes Bridge during the **Oxford and Cambridge Boat Race** of 1978.

P

· Pace Egging ·
see EASTER

· Padstow Hobby Horse ·
Padstow, Cornwall: 1 May

Like its relation and rival from MINEHEAD, the Padstow HOBBY HORSE is a beast of MAY DAY, but at Padstow it has retained more of the old 'Maying' associations, and the ceremonies surrounding it are somewhat more complex. These begin as the clock strikes midnight on May morning, when the singers gathered outside the Golden Lion Inn strike up the first verse of the 'Night Song', in honour of the landlord and his wife:

Rise up Mr. __, and joy to you betide
For summer is acome unto today [a-coming in today]
And bright is your bride, that lays down by your side
In the merry morning of May.

They then move off round the town, serenading local personalities or special friends with suitable verses, like:

Rise up Miss __, all in your smock of silk
And all your body under as white as any milk

or, to a wealthy man:

Rise up Mr. __, I know you well afine
You have a shilling in your purse and I wish it was in mine

and continuing until the person named does 'rise up' and come to the window to greet them. This 'night-singing' continues until about 2 a.m., when the 'Mayers' temporarily disband, to rest before the coming of the 'Obby Oss' and the festivities of May Day proper.

The first horse to appear, outside the Padstow Institute at 10 a.m., is the 'Blue Ribbon', 'Temperance', or 'Peace Oss': which, as its names indicate, was introduced by some of the soberer inhabitants of Padstow during the 1890s, and revived after the First World War. This is, however, merely an imitation of the real and original 'Old Oss', which emerges from the Golden Lion an hour later, accompanied by its band of

Lured on by its club-bearing Teaser, the **Padstow Hobby Horse** cavorts through the crowded streets: around it stand some of the white-clad and be-sashed mayers called 'Pairs'.

white-clad 'Mayers', its toppered 'master of ceremonies' and, most important, by its fantastically dressed 'Teaser' with his padded club.

The Oss itself is a fearsome creature, based on a six-foot-diameter hoop covered by a long-skirted black tarpaulin which hides the body of the bearer. Attached to its front is a small wooden horse's head with snapping jaws and a fringe of hair, but its most terrifying attribute is the beaked, fur-tufted and gaping mask — allegedly brought either from Africa or 'the South Seas' during the 1860s — that conceals the bearer's head at the centre of the round body. Above it rises a tall conical cap, painted with the mystic letters 'O.B.': which are supposed by some to represent 'Obby', but said by others to be the initials of a famous former carrier, one Oswald Brenton.

After dancing about with his Teaser, the Oss capers off on its rounds of the town, alternately beckoned and

threatened by passes of the high-stepping Teaser's club: while behind it come the mayers (or 'Pairs') performing a curious twisting and diving dance. From time to time the crowd challenge it to charge with a shout of 'Oss, Oss, we Oss', and charge it does, its chief aim being to corner a young girl, envelop her with its skirts, and pinch her. This is believed to be very 'lucky' for the victim, guaranteeing her a husband or a baby within the year, according to circumstances: and until the early part of this century her luck was plain to all, proclaimed by the marks of the grease and blacklead with which the inside of the Oss's tarpaulin used to be smeared.

All this while, the attendant mayers — and many of the spectators — are singing verses of the 'Night Song', among them:

Unite and unite and let us unite
For Summer is acome unto day
And whither we are going we will all unite
On the merry morning of May.
The young men of Padstow, they might if they would
They might have built a ship and gilded her with gold
The maidens of Padstow, they might if they would
They might have made a garland of the
    white rose and the red
On the merry morning of May.

But at intervals they change over to the slower and more melancholy 'Day Song', with its single verse:

O where is St. George, o where is he – O
He's out in his long boat, all on the salt sea-O
Up flies the kite, down falls the lark-O
Aunt Ursula Birdhood she had an old yowe [ewe]
And she died in her own park-O.

At this point the Oss sinks to the ground as if dying, while the Teaser squats beside it and strokes it gently with his club, and young children venture out to touch it: then, to a sudden burst of drumming, it bounds to its feet again and dances furiously, as the crowd take up the 'Night Song' once more:

Up Merry Spring and up the merry ring
For Summer is acome unto day
How happy are the little birds that merrily do sing
On the merry morning of May.

And so the 'Old Oss' gambols on until the early evening, at last meeting the 'Blue Ribbon Oss' — which until now has politely pursued a different route — in Broad Street, where the two end the celebrations by dancing together round a giant maypole.

Even within living memory, however, the Oss's habits have altered somewhat. The twelve little girls in white which formerly accompanied it do not now appear, and 'All-Sorts', the traditional man-woman of its retinue, is not always present. Neither is it any longer led down to the sea at 'Obby Oss' slipway, and since 1930 it has ceased its once invariable visits to Treator Pool, where it 'drank' and splashed the spectators with water: a ritual which, like the discontinued blacking of the girls, was believed to bring luck to all those wetted.

No doubt other changes have occurred over the centuries; for though documentary record of the Padstow Oss stretches back only until the early 1800s, the custom is almost undoubtedly of far more ancient origin. And though the Oss is clearly one of those luck-bringing beasts which used to appear all over the country on May Day, Padstow people like to believe that it is unique to them. Contemptuously sweeping aside the slander that it was simply copied from Minehead, some assert that the custom honours the town's patron, St Petroc, who during the 6th century crossed from West Wales to found the monastery of 'Petrokestowe', later Padstow. The Oss, they believe, represents a fearsome local dragon which the saint – represented by the Teaser – eventually bound with his girdle and led out to sea, whence the former visits to Obby Oss slipway.

Certainly a legend about Petroc and the dragon was current by the Middle Ages, and there is nothing in this theory to conflict with the tradition that, during the Hundred Years War, the Padstow Obby Oss scared off a French raiding fleet which appeared off Stepper Point. Since 'the young men of Padstow' (as in the song) had built a ship and sailed away in it to join King Edward III, the town's women brought out the Oss and (led, some say, by 'Aunt Ursula Birdhood') marched behind it along the cliff tops in their red cloaks: whereupon the Frenchmen hurriedly made off, believing them to be an English army with the Devil himself at its head. And while the 'red cloaks' element is most probably borrowed from a Napoleonic incident at Fishguard in Pembrokeshire (where Welsh women thus attired contributed to the defeat of a French 'invasion') there is no reason to discount the Padstow tale altogether: for the port did historically send ships to aid Edward III, and French raiders undoubtedly did threaten Cornwall, notably in 1337 and 1378.

· Palm Sunday ·

The Sunday before EASTER, when the Church commemorates Christ's triumphant entry into Jerusalem before His Crucifixion: when traditional Palm Sunday hymns are sung – notably 'All glory, laud and honour' and 'Ride on, ride on in majesty' – and crosses made from palm leaves are blessed, distributed, and often carried in procession during the service. Established by at least the 5th century, this last custom was discontinued as 'idolatrous' in Protestant churches after the Reformation, and only generally revived under 'High Church' influence during Victorian times. Until the present century, moreover, the branches which the Jerusalem crowd strewed in Christ's path were only rarely symbolized in Britain by real (and necessarily imported) palm: instead, almost any kind of native greenery

available in early springtime was pressed into service, though the favourite was the early-flowering willow (*salix caprea*) known as 'English palm'.

It was this tree that was sought by the young people who never ceased to go 'a-palming', even during the centuries when festival services were banished from the church, setting out into the countryside long before dawn and returning with catkin-decked hats and 'palm' crosses to keep 'for luck' throughout the year. This custom, however, has now virtually died out, and so too have most of the local traditions – many of them pagan in feeling, if not in origin – once associated with it. On Pontesbury Hill in Shropshire, for instance, 'palmers' also sought a mysterious 'Golden Arrow', and competed to cut the first lucky sprig from a haunted yew: while in parts of the English Midlands and North they made gifts to certain holy WELLS, whose water was then ceremonially drunk, shaken up with liquorice root ('Spanish') or sugar – hence the day's local nicknames of 'Shaking', 'Spanish', or 'Sugar-Cup Sunday'.

Other alternative titles include 'Fig Sunday', from the now almost extinct Midlands custom of eating fig pies or 'figgy puddings', ostensibly in memory of the barren fig tree cursed by Christ: and the Welsh *Dydd Sul y Blodau* (Flowering Sunday) from the floral decoration of family graves still carried on in urban South Wales – though this is now more usually transferred to Easter itself. (*See also* PAX CAKES)

· Pancake Bells ·

In medieval times, all churches rang BELLS on SHROVE TUESDAY morning, in order to remind parishioners to come to confession ('shriving') before LENT began. Confession went out with the Reformation, but the pre-Lenten carnival atmosphere of the day continued, as did the custom of eating pancakes and, in many cases, the bellringing – eagerly awaited by apprentices and schoolchildren as a signal to begin their holiday. Now the holiday too has disappeared, but a dwindling number of churches keep up the ringing 'to remind housewives to put their pancakes on the stove'.

Among places where this is still done are Berwick-upon-Tweed, Northumberland; Richmond, North Yorkshire, and Scarborough in the same county, where the Pancake Bell – formerly that of St Thomas's Hospital – is rung in the town museum at the conventional hour of noon. At Burgh-le-Marsh, Lincolnshire, however, it tolls for the hour after ten o'clock; and at Newark, Nottinghamshire, it is sounded at eleven by the youngest ringer – a reminder of the days when apprentices claimed the right to ring the Pancake Bell themselves. Something of the old holiday atmosphere also survives at Toddington, Bedfordshire, where the bell releases schoolchildren to run up nearby Conger Hill: there, if they set their ears to the ground, they can hear 'the Pancake Witch' sizzling her pan of subterranean fritters.

· Pancake Day ·
see SHROVE TUESDAY

· Pancake Races ·
see SHROVE TUESDAY

· Parliament ·

During its seven centuries or so of existence, the 'Mother of Parliaments' has developed an intricate and complex structure of customs and ceremonies – more, indeed, than any other British institution,save only the monarchy. Many of these, however, are of a private and internal nature, inaccessible to the general public: and as such they can only be summarized here.

Easily the most splendid is the State Opening of Parliament, which generally occurs in October or early November, after a recess intended to allow members to get in their harvests. On the evening before it (or the morning of the opening) the cellars of the Palace of Westminster are ceremonially but thoroughly searched by Yeomen of the Guard, carrying candle lanterns despite the modern electric lighting. This custom is generally believed to date from (and commemorate) the Gunpowder Plot of 1605, when such a search discovered and arrested GUY FAWKES: but may in fact have originated during the 'Popish Plot' scare of 1678.

This done, two processions set out from Buckingham Palace, each with a mounted escort of Household Cavalry: the first conveys the crown, carried in its own coach and guarded by Royal Watermen; and the second, the Queen and her family. Arriving at Westminster at 11 a.m., the monarch processes in crown and full 'parliament robes' to the House of Lords, the senior and Upper House: and when she has assumed the Throne there, her messenger – known as 'Black Rod' – sets off to summon the members of the House of Commons. Since Charles I's disastrous and ill-advised attempt to arrest the 'Five Members' in 1641, no monarch has entered that Lower Chamber in person: and the Parliamentary privilege won during the Civil War years that followed is still symbolically asserted by the closing of the Commons' doors against the royal emissary. Only after he has knocked upon them three times with his black rod, and politely requested admittance, may he convey his message: and the MPs then process to the Lords for the 'Queen's Most Gracious Speech' – which, though read by the monarch, is in reality an announcement of the government's political programme.

Both Houses of Parliament also observe a great deal of ceremony at ordinary times. For the Lords, each day begins with the processional entry of the Lord Chancellor, preceded by his mace bearer and the custodian of the Purse which once contained the Great Seal for the authentication of state documents – formerly an essen-

Left: On the night before the State Opening of **Parliament**, Yeomen of the Guard set off to search the Palace of Westminster's cellars for gunpowder plotters and other seditious persons. *Above:* The Speaker's mace-bearer heads the procession from the House of Commons to the House of Lords in 1977. Behind him is the be-wigged Speaker and Black Rod with his staff of office, then Prime Minister Jim Callaghan and the Leader of the Opposition.

tial part of the Chancellor's office. Nowadays, he combines membership of the Cabinet and headship of the Judiciary with the task of representing the government from his seat on 'the Woolsack' – whose contents represent the source of England's medieval prosperity – though he has no power to direct the debates of his fellow peers.

The Speaker of the Commons, by contrast, does both keep order and control debates there – though he never participates himself, and only votes in the very unusual event of a deadlock: his office (which dates from 1376) is thus effectively a non-political one, and his seat in Parliament is by convention never contested. Without his presence, no business may be conducted, for none other has the power to invite members to speak: the rarely occurring election of a new Speaker, indeed, must be carried out by an elaborate mime. Each Commons sitting therefore opens with his ceremonial entry, accompanied by the mace-bearing Serjeant-at-Arms (who is responsible for executing his disciplinary orders), his train-bearer, and his chaplain – who conducts the inaugural prayer 'that Members shall lay aside all private interests, prejudices and partial affections, in order that the public wealth, peace and tranquility of the Realm may be maintained'.

While pursuing these laudable ends, MPs must also take heed of a host of minor customs, many of considerable antiquity. On entering and leaving the House, for instance, they must bow towards the Speaker – but not *to* him, for they are honouring the altar that stood behind his throne in the days when Parliament was held in St Stephen's Chapel. They must not, however, step over the red lines painted on the floor in front of the Government and Opposition benches, nor cross the carpet separating them – precautions designed to prevent rival members running each other through with their swords during stormy debates.

Neither may they smoke, though they may take snuff from the House of Commons snuff box, which is kept by the Principal Door-Keeper and made of wood taken from the chamber destroyed by bombs in 1941: and they may also drink alcohol at unusual hours of the day and night – for the Commons bars, being technically in a royal palace, are not governed by any licensing laws. By the terms of an Act guaranteeing them free access at all times, moreover, members have the right to stop all traffic while crossing the road to enter the House: while at the end of each session the cry of 'Who goes home?' echoes round its corridors, a relic of the days when members banded together under armed guard before setting forth into the footpad-haunted night.

· Passing Bells ·

Passing BELLS proper were originally rung to solicit prayers for a dying person, to summon the priest to his bedside with the Last Rites and (it was popularly believed) to scare off demons lying in wait for his departing spirit. In most cases, they would shortly be followed by the tolling of a 'Death Knell', announcing his death and encouraging prayers for his soul: and though this last practice was condemned by Protestant reformers – who regarded prayers for the dead as 'vain and superstitious' – it is this which has now survived (albeit in a rapidly dwindling number of places) and which is now called 'the Passing Bell'.

Almost always, this indicates the age and sex of the dead by the number and arrangement of bell strokes: but the exact method of doing so varies greatly from parish to parish, and in 1900 there were over seventy variations within a single county. That still used at Burgh-le-Marsh, Lincolnshire (if any of the old local families request it) begins with single strokes on the tenor bell, three times three for a man and three times two for a woman: these are called 'tellers' or 'tailors', hence the proverb 'Nine Tailors make a Man' and the title of Dorothy Sayers' famous novel. The bell is then tolled for a period long enough to recite Psalm 130 ('Out of the deep have I called unto Thee') whereafter the tellers are repeated, and the age of the departed is rung in tens. For a small child the treble is used instead of the tenor bell, and the tolling is omitted.

In other parishes, tolling may continue for over an hour, and a much more precise system of tellers is used, ranging from nine strokes for a husband, through a diminishing number for bachelor, matron, spinster and boy, to three for a girl. Everywhere, however, passing bells are quite distinct from those later tolled at FUNERALS.

· Passion Sunday ·
see CARLINGS SUNDAY

· Pax Cakes Ceremony ·
Hentland-with-Hoarwithy; King's Caple; and Sellack, Herefordshire: Palm Sunday

After the PALM SUNDAY service in the south Herefordshire parishes of Hentland-with-Hoarwithy, King's Caple, and Sellack, round biscuits called 'Pax Cakes' are distributed to every member of the congregation: as each is handed over, the words 'Peace and Good Neighbourhood' are repeated, and this admirable sentiment is also stamped on the cakes, surrounding an image of the Lamb of God. This distribution is now usually done outside the church door, but in bad weather the cakes may be both given out and eaten inside: this was once the invariable custom; and at Hentland (if not in the other two villages) each bun – formerly more substantial than at present – was shared between groups of three or four parishioners. In all three places, moreover, each used to be washed down with a cup of free beer or cider: but towards the end of the 19th century this part of the ceremony faded away, the victim of rising prices and Victorian notions of 'decorum'.

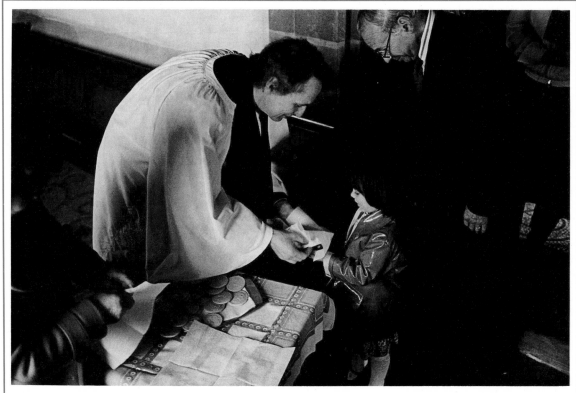

The vicar of Hentland-with-Hoarwithy hands over a Palm Sunday **Pax Cake** to a small parishioner, in token of 'Peace and Good Neighbourhood'.

Betokening the reconciliation of all local feuds and animosities, in preparation for the coming EASTER festival, this laudable custom is of considerable antiquity. It is generally held to have been originated, in about 1670, by Lady Jane Scudamore – who certainly did leave an annual endowment of 5s 10d from her Sellack estates 'for the Pax Gift of Pastry Cakes and Ale on Palm Sunday': this was continued until 1942, since when the ceremonies have been financed by parish funds. The Hentland churchwardens' accounts, however, show that Lady Jane was merely continuing 'cakes and ale' payments made since at least 1630 by her father-in-law, John Lord Scudamore: and that the custom was already regarded as 'ancient' even in his time.

A 'High Church' Anglican, Scudamore was famous alike for his development of the Herefordshire cider apple, his lavish refurbishing of local churches, and his encouragement of the medieval religious observances which lingered long after the Reformation in this remote corner of England: it was probably due to him, for instance, that 'housel cloths' (a species of bib, worn to catch crumbs of the consecrated Host) survived at Sellack and (perhaps uniquely in Britain) survive there still, though they are now simply hung over the altar rail during Communion services. It is likely, therefore, that the Pax Cake ceremony was another such pre-Reformation custom, perpetuated rather than founded by the traditionalist Scudamores: and that it was, in fact, originally a medieval PEACE AND GOOD NEIGHBOUR-HOOD FEAST.

· Peace and Good Neighbourhood Feasts ·

'It was the manner in times past, upon Festival evens, for Parishioners to meet in their Church-Houses or Church-yards, and there to have a drinking fitt for the time. Here they used to end many quarrels between neighbour and neighbour.' Thus wrote John Aubrey in the 1690s when such 'peace and good neighbourhood feasts' – widely popular during the later Middle Ages, when they were often held in the church itself – were already fast declining: which is a pity, for many a bitter local feud was ended under the influence of their copious 'cakes and ale', and the opportunity they provided of 'begetting better neighbourhood and brotherly love' would not come amiss in many modern communities.

A handful, however, still survive, mainly due to bequests by CHARITIES for their perpetuation: and perhaps the nearest to the spirit of the originals is that held annually in Church Street, Kidderminster, Worcestershire, on MIDSUMMER EVE. This stems from a gift of £2, invested by an unknown maiden lady on condition that the interest arising should provide a 'farthing loaf' on 23 June for every child in the street: and that on the same day all its male inhabitants should meet 'to reconcile and compose any differences between them'. The date of this legacy is uncertain: but 'a certain society for the promotion of friendly intercourse among the inhabitants of Church Street' had already existed 'since time immemorial' in 1776, when a wealthy local bachelor named John Brecknell gave it fresh impetus. Increasing its endowment by £150, he stipulated that every child or unmarried person should be given a 'twopenny plumb-cake' as well as a farthing loaf, and that 'pipes, tobacco and ale' be provided for the reconciliation meeting.

Though these bequests have long since become insufficient to meet its costs, Church Street's modern 'residents' – the shopkeepers and businessmen who have premises there – still enthusiastically maintain the custom, taking turns to act as host: and have added several touches of their own. In recent years, for instance, the small cottage loaves and 'plumb cakes' – a type of Eccles cake, supplied by the same local firm for over a century and a half – have been distributed to all Church Street workers, sometimes by girls in the costume of John Brecknell's day. A full-scale dinner, moreover, now precedes the smoking of the long churchwarden 'pipes of peace' and the chairman's ceremonial offer to mediate in any disputes: whereafter, most appropriately, a collection is taken to provide comforts for elderly Church Street people in homes or hospitals.

The Midsummer date of the Kidderminster custom is somewhat unusual: for Peace and Good Neighbourhood Feasts were more often arranged during LENT, so that no lingering dispute should mar the EASTER festival. Thus that of the London Stationers' Company falls on ASH WEDNESDAY, when guild members attend SERMONS in St Faith's Chapel of St Paul's Cathedral, and subsequently return to their Hall for 'cakes and ale' endowed in 1612 by a stationer named Norton: while the Herefordshire PAX CAKES CEREMONY falls on PALM SUNDAY, and the Wicken 'Love Feast' used to be observed on Maundy Thursday.

Now held on the last Thursday in May, the Wicken feast commemorates the union (in 1587) of the two tiny parishes of Wick Dyve and Wick Hamon, near the Northamptonshire border with Buckinghamshire. According to tradition, the two communities had been constantly at feud, so their amalgamation into 'Wicken' was cemented by a feast of ale and cakes – for which, in the 18th century, the rector provided 'three bushels of flour; six pounds of butter; six pounds of currants and three shillings' worth of spice and caraway seeds'. Rather less now suffices, but the Love Feast is still eaten – after morning service and the singing of the hundredth Psalm – beneath the ancient 'Gospel Elm' once featured in BEATING THE BOUNDS of the parish.

Watched by a younger generation of his family, Mr Hutton of Harton House Farm plants the 1983 **Penny Hedge** in Whitby harbour sands: while Mr Belchamber, bailiff of the Fyling court leet, sounds the traditional horn call.

· Penny Hedge ·
Whitby, North Yorkshire: annually, day preceding Ascension Day

At 9 a.m. on the eve of ASCENSION DAY, a number of stakes are driven with an ancient mallet into a muddy beach near Boyes Staithe in Whitby harbour, and osiers are then woven among them to form a 'hedge' strong enough to withstand three tides. This done, the bailiff of the COURT LEET of Fyling causes a horn to be blown, and shouts 'Out upon ye, [Shame on you] out upon ye'.

The accepted explanation of this custom is most circumstantial. On 16 October 1159, it relates, the lords of three nearby manors hunted a wild boar into the chapel of Eskdaleside, then occupied by a hermit monk of Whitby Abbey. The hermit, however, shut the doors against their pursuing hounds, whereupon the thwarted sportsmen mortally wounded him with their boar spears. On his deathbed, nevertheless, the monk begged his abbot to forgive the murderers, provided they performed a certain penance. In future they and their descendants were to hold their lands as tenants of the Abbey, and each Ascension Eve they were to cut ('with a

Knife of a Penny Price') a specific number of stakes and osiers in Strayhead Wood, under the supervision of the Abbey bailiff; they were then to carry these on their backs to the waterside, and there build a 'Penance Hedge' while the bailiff reminded onlookers of their crime.

This splendid story, unfortunately, is demonstrably untrue: it was probably concocted at the time of Henry VIII's Dissolution of the Monasteries, to explain a custom whose real origin was forgotten, but whose performance would secure tenants' lands under the new régime. In fact, as records show, the hedge is the last vestige of a much longer 'Horngarth' (intended for some such practical purpose as to contain the Abbey's cattle or protect its landing place) which Whitby tenants were once required to build annually as part of their rent. The bailiff's supervision of their woodcutting also had a prosaic origin – to prevent them from taking and selling surplus timber. The custom, moreover, certainly dates from long before the hermit's alleged murder, and may even stem from Saxon practice.

So the Penny Hedge is that rare phenomenon, a ceremony even older than it claims to be: perhaps, indeed, the oldest surviving MANORIAL custom in Britain. Only one set of tenants now perform it: and since 1888 the Hutton family of Harton House Farm, Fylingdales, have built their horngarth so efficiently that it has never once failed to withstand three tides. If it fell, they believe, they could forfeit three acres of farmland.

· Peppercorn Rents ·
see MARBLERS AND STONECUTTERS DAY;
QUIT RENT CEREMONIES

· Pepys Commemoration ·
see COMMEMORATIONS

· Piepowder Courts ·
see FAIRS

· Pig-Face Sunday ·
Avening, near Stroud, Gloucestershire:
Sunday after 14 September

The village festival of Avening in Gloucestershire – held on the Sunday after the Feast of the Exaltation of the Holy Cross (14 September) – is locally known as 'Pig-Face Sunday', and after evensong on that day pig's cheek or 'pork-chap' sandwiches are served in the parish hall, being also available in some local pubs. Until quite recently, moreover, whole pigs' heads were prominently displayed around the village, and afterwards eaten with apple dumplings.

Though many other Gloucestershire communities once marked their FEASTS with such traditional dishes – at neighbouring Nymphsfield, for instance, the special-ity was 'heg-peg-dump' (wild-plum pudding) and Woodchester also favoured pigs' cheeks – Avening claims that its custom is unique: and two quite different stories are told to account for it. According to one, the dish commemorates the capture of an exceptionally troublesome wild boar, which had long plagued the surrounding woodlands: instead of being slaughtered in the usual way, therefore, the beast was ceremonially hanged from an oak in the village centre, and afterwards eaten amid much rejoicing.

The rival legend, however, relates that the pig-faces were first served at a banquet attended by Queen Matilda, wife of William the Conqueror, to celebrate her foundation of Avening parish church in about 1080. That she did indeed found the church is not impossible, since it later passed to her favourite 'Abbaye-aux-Dames' at Caen in Normandy: but the tradition that she did so as an act of repentance for her part in the death of Brihtric, the Saxon owner of Avening before the Norman Conquest, is altogether less plausible. This is based on a sensational tale, already current by the 12th century, which tells how Brihtric once journeyed as an ambassador to the court of Matilda's father, the Count of Flanders: there the young Matilda fell in love with him, but he rejected her advances, whereupon she married the Conqueror in a fit of pique. Yet she did not forget the slight, and when England fell into her husband's power she avenged it by engineering Brih-tric's downfall, seizing all his lands and leaving him to die in a Winchester dungeon.

The legend of Matilda and Brihtric, however, is almost certainly fabulous: and in any case it seems to have been attached to Avening only in comparatively recent years, as a means of lending individuality to what was probably a perfectly ordinary village celebration. (*See also* COW HEAD WAKES)

· Pinch Bum Day ·
see OAK APPLE DAY

· Pipe Walk ·
From St Mary Redcliffe to Knowle, Bristol: a Saturday
afternoon in September

This specialized form of BEATING THE BOUNDS commemorates a gift of piped spring water to the parish of St Mary Redcliffe, traditionally made by Robert de Berkeley when he succeeded as Lord of the Manor of Redcliffe in 1190. Beginning at St Mary's – which Queen Elizabeth I called 'the fairest, goodliest and most famous parish church in England' – the vicar and parishioners assert their ownership of the pipe by walking its two-and-a-half-mile course to the source of the spring near St Barnabas church at Knowle. Members of the party are sometimes 'bumped' on one or more of the fourteen stones which mark the underground passage of the water, and at another point a manhole cover is lifted so that the pipe itself can be inspected. No longer, however, do the processioners follow the exact line of the pipe across a railway track, as they did until the 1930s; instead, they now make a detour by the road.

· Plague Sunday ·
Eyam, Derbyshire: last Sunday in August

On the last Sunday afternoon in August, Anglican and Nonconformist clergy lead a procession from the parish church of Eyam, in the Peak District of Derbyshire, to a natural amphitheatre called Cucklet Delf, where a memorial service is held. This commemorates the heroism of the villagers during the Eyam plague, which began when a box of infected clothes from London – then in the grip of the Great Plague – arrived there in late August 1665. Soon the deadly disease was spreading rapidly throughout the village, and the inhabitants prepared to flee, thus carrying it into the surrounding countryside. But the new vicar, William Mompesson, backed by his wife Catherine and his predecessor Thomas Stanley (a Puritan ejected after the Restoration) persuaded them to stay, promising to remain and minister to them and arranging for food to be brought to certain places on the edge of the village, where money was left in running water. One of these, called Mompesson's Well, is still to be seen, as is Mompesson's Chair in the church.

For more than a year the plague raged, carrying off about 260 of Eyam's 350 people, including Catherine Mompesson. Thanks to their self-sacrifice, however, the neighbouring communities remained virtually untouched: a fact annually remembered at the remote spot where, after Eyam church had been closed for fear of infection, Mompesson preached every Sunday to his dwindling congregation. (*See also* WELLS AND WELL DRESSING)

· Plough Monday ·
Early January

The Monday after TWELFTH NIGHT, when farm work began again – usually with spring ploughing – after the CHRISTMAS holidays. On this day, in medieval times, real or symbolic ploughs were blessed and incensed by parish priests: and money was collected to maintain the 'Plough Light', kept burning before some saint's image to ensure year-long good fortune for local GUILDS of farm workers. Lights, images and guilds were all swept away by the Protestant Reformation, but the plough-blessing ceremony itself was too deeply rooted in the agricultural calendar to disappear altogether, and in some areas it lingered on just long enough to merge with the revivals which became popular during and after the Second World War.

Generally centring on an old-fashioned horse plough (which, following a long-standing tradition, may be kept permanently in church) such services now usually occur on the Plough Sunday before the old festival. Congregations pray:

Early 19th-century **Plough Monday** festivities.

God speed the plough,
the plough and the ploughman,
the farm and the farmer,
machine and beast and man

and ask a blessing, not merely on ploughing, but on all the farming operations of the coming year. Among many other places, plough blessings are held annually at Exeter Cathedral and Bratton Fleming, Devon; Cottered and Flamsteed, Hertfordshire; Cawston, Norfolk; Hambridge, Somerset; Chichester Cathedral, Sussex; at Newchurch in the Isle of Wight; and at Bolton Percy, Goathland, Knaresborough and Long Marston in Yorkshire.

Here and there, too, folklore enthusiasts have revived a less hallowed but perhaps still more ancient Plough Monday custom, which was once widespread throughout the corn-growing eastern English counties from Essex to Northumberland. There, bands of young farm labourers, fantastically dressed in tatters or ribboned and rosetted shirts, would haul a decorated plough about their villages, demanding largesse from all they met: and, in many cases, ploughing up the pavements, dunghills or gardens outside houses which declined to pay up.

In Yorkshire and the north-east, where they were called 'Plough Stots' (bullocks) because they acted as draught beasts, they were (and at Goathland near Whitby still are) accompanied by SWORD DANCING. Further south, the 'Plough Jags' or 'Plough Bullocks' of Leicestershire, Nottinghamshire and Lincolnshire (where the tradition survived into the 1930s) performed a 'Plough play', a version of the MUMMING play: while the 'Plough Witches' of the Fenlands took with them a STRAW BEAR and those of East Anglia performed simple MORRIS dances. Others merely cracked whips and shouted, but even these generally ran to a Fool and a 'Betty' – a man in women's clothes. All of which suggests that, though the custom may once have been used to collect Plough Light funds (as it was certainly later done simply 'to get money for drink'), its origins may well go back to pre-Christian times.

· Plygain Services ·
see CHRISTMAS

· Preston Guild Merchants ·
Preston, Lancashire: week beginning on the Monday after 29 August, every twenty years (e.g. 1972, 1992)

In the north-west of England, rare or doubtful happenings are sometimes said to occur 'once every Preston Guild'. The scepticism implied, however, is quite unfounded: for, with one single exception (the wartime event of 1942, which was postponed for a decade and thus altered the sequence) meetings of the Preston Guild Merchant have been held with unfailing regularity every twenty years since 1562. Irregular meetings, moreover,

are recorded over two centuries earlier, and have probably been held ever since the Guild was confirmed by a charter of Henry II in 1179.

In Preston, as in other 'chartered boroughs', the grant of a Guild Merchant gave the wealthier inhabitants the freedom to choose their own local government officials, administer their own justice, and maintain a tight control on the town's trade. For, except during FAIRS, none but Guild Freemen could buy or sell in the borough and none but the sons or time-served apprentices of Guild members could become Freemen. At one time, indeed, outsiders were not permitted even to live in the town if the Guild disapproved of them, and a host of Guild regulations governed every aspect of Preston life, from the suppression of murderous brawls to the price of beer and the control of straying pigs.

From time to time, therefore, the Guild needed to hold full 'Courts', at which its royal charters were read and confirmed, its rules and bye-laws reviewed or added to, and its roll-call of members checked. In 1562 – except in cases of 'distress to our franchise' – these were fixed at twenty-year intervals, when they were to be held on the Monday following the Feast of the Beheading of St John the Baptist (29 August) the town's patron: and the chief ceremonial event of the Guild Merchant proceedings is still the Court, which every Freeman Burgess must attend in person or by proxy, there to renew his 'freedom' at a cost of 3½p and enrol any sons born since the last Guild, for a due of a shilling (5p) each.

The real powers and privileges of freemen, however, have long since passed away: and the fact that Preston (alone among chartered boroughs) continues to celebrate its Guild's foundation may well be due to the very infrequency of the attendant festivities, and the consequent enthusiasm with which these have always been pursued. At one time, indeed, the junketings continued for a full six weeks of hearty feasting and deep drinking; and though the Guild was curtailed to a week in 1842, and greatly sobered down under Victorian Nonconformist influence, it is still conducted on a generous scale. There are no less than nine major processions – four civic ones to the parish church, including one for women headed by the lady mayoress; one each by Roman Catholics, Anglicans, Nonconformists and the town's friendly societies; and a torchlight parade: and the festival week's other attractions include a pleasure fair, dances, concerts, sports and special exhibitions – one of which, in 1972, featured 'an exact replica of Coronation Street's "Rover's Return"'. (*See also* GUILDS AND COMPANIES)

· Pretty Maid's Charity ·
Holsworthy, Devon: second Wednesday in July

At the first stroke of noon on the second Wednesday in July – the opening day of St Peter's Fair – a young woman emerges from the tower door of Holsworthy parish church: her identity has hitherto been kept a close secret, but now she is revealed to the waiting crowd as the chosen recipient of that year's 'Pretty Maid's Charity'. As such, she will receive about £3.50, the annual interest on a legacy bequeathed in 1841 by the Reverend Thomas Meyrick of Cartamartha, whose brother was once Rector of Holsworthy. With the admirable motive of promoting 'peace on earth and goodwill among men', Meyrick directed its payment 'to the young single woman resident in Holsworthy, under thirty years of age, who is generally esteemed by the young as the most deserving, the most handsome, and the most noted for her quietness and attendance at church'. 'May this well-meant example,' the donor somewhat optimistically added, 'lead rulers to see and know that subjects are better directed and led by harmless amusement, and by judicious reward, than by the fear of punishment.'

· Proclamation Ceremony ·
see CORONATIONS

· Punky Night ·
Around Hinton St George, Somerset: last week in October

A 'punky' – derived either from 'pumpkin' or 'punk' (tinder) – is a lantern made from a hollowed-out mangel-wurzel containing a candle, whose light shines through a design etched into the outer skin. On the last Thursday night in October, the children of Hinton St George, near Yeovil, carry these round the village boundary and through the streets, collecting money and chanting:

> It's Punky Night tonight
> It's Punky Night tonight
> Give us a candle, give us a light
> It's Punky Night tonight

or some variant like:

> Adam and Eve wouldn't believe
> It's Punky Night tonight.

In recent years, they have then gone to the Victory Hall for the judging of the best punky design (it might be a face, an animal, or a flower pattern) and the crowning of the Punky King and Queen – the children who have collected most for charity.

Though a somewhat similar custom is widespread on HALLOWEEN, a few nights later, the people of Hinton insist on a quite different origin for theirs. 'Long ago', it seems, the village menfolk went to Chiselborough Fair (formerly held on 29 October) and got too drunk on cider to find their way home: so their wives made punkies, and set off in a body to gather them in. Nearby Lopen – which tells the same story and also claims to have begun the custom, each village asserting that the other 'stole it' – holds its own punky on a variable night in the same week: and lately other south Somerset villages have followed suit.

Q

· Quarter Days ·

Quarter or term days, falling at three-monthly intervals, are days when quarterly payments and rents are traditionally due, and agricultural tenancies are begun or ended. At present they are fixed at CHRISTMAS (or NEW YEAR); LADY DAY (25 March); MIDSUMMER (24 June) and MICHAELMAS (29 September): but formerly their usual dates varied from area to area, and included EASTER; HOCKTIDE; MARTINMAS and ST ANDREWS DAY

'Cross-quarter days' (CANDLEMAS; MAY DAY; LAMMAS and HALLOWEEN) which fall midway between two quarter days, were sometimes regarded as unlucky or uncanny – doubtless because they all coincided with pagan festivals.

· Quit Rent Ceremonies ·

Quit rents originated during the Middle Ages, as purely nominal and symbolic rents paid for certain lands or properties – especially those originally granted to a favourite of the landowner, or for some special piece of good service. Designed to preserve the overlord's technical title to the property, they also served as a public reminder that the tenant did not own it absolutely, and it was perhaps for this reason that they often took picturesque or curious forms. One Oxfordshire knight, for example, held his estates in return for delivering a roast pork dinner whenever the king hunted in Wychwood; while the tenant of Petticoat Hole Field, at Stockton-on-the-Forest, near York had (until the 19th century) to provide a yearly petticoat to some poor village woman. Among the most popular and widespread types of quit rent, however, were those paid either in peppercorns (hence 'peppercorns rents', as on MARBLERS' AND STONECUTTERS' DAY) or in red roses.

One such 'Red Rose Rent' is rendered, on MIDSUMMER DAY, to the Lord Mayor of London. Various alluringly circumstantial – if entirely apocryphal – tales are told to account for this. But the truth seems to be that it originated as an ordinary quit rent for a *hautpas* (or footbridge) linking two houses which formerly stood on either side of Seething Lane, in the parish of All Hallows, Barking-by-the-Tower: these were owned by the famous soldier Sir Robert Knollys, whose leading part in defending London against Wat Tyler's rebels in 1381 probably explains the purely honorific nature of the payment. The ceremonies surrounding it – revived in 1924, after a long lapse, by the Reverend 'Tubby' Clayton, Vicar of All Hallows, and continued since his death by the London Company of Watermen and

Above: The Lord Mayor of London accepts his annual red rose, the **quit rent** for Sir Robert Knollys' long-vanished footbridge, from the Verger of All Hallows-by-the-Tower. *Right:* London's City Solicitor ceremonially smashes a bundle of hazel sticks with a hatchet, thus performing the quit rent for property granted seven centuries ago by King John.

Lightermen – are, however, picturesque enough. For on Midsummer morning the Verger of All Hallows, heading a procession of vicar, parishioners and watermen, carries a perfect red rose (generally grown in a Seething Lane garden) to the Mansion House: there, in the presence of a guard of honour of liveried DOGGETT'S COAT AND BADGE winners, it is presented on a blue altar cushion to the Lord Mayor, as rent for the long-vanished *hautpas*. It was no doubt this ceremony that inspired another red rose rent, instituted only in 1955 and paid annually to the Duke of Northumberland for a playing field at Newburn, Northumberland.

The two quit rents rendered each October at the Law Courts in the Strand, by contrast, have been paid continuously for over seven centuries, except for a brief hiatus during the Commonwealth. The first, now called the 'Faggot Service', apparently originated in 1211, when King John granted a piece of 'waste land' called 'the Moors', at Eardington in Shropshire, for a quit rent of 'two knives'. Perhaps some long-forgotten joke or comic incident was thus commemorated, for the King (who was certainly campaigning in Shropshire during 1211) was notorious for his odd sense of humour: and such might well explain the baffling stipulation (recorded later in the 13th century) that one knife should

be 'good enough to cut a hazel rod' but the other so 'bad' that it would 'bend in green cheese'.

At any rate, by the time the property passed to the City of London in 1521, it had become customary to test both knives by publicly cutting – or failing to cut – a hazel stick in the Court of Exchequer: and at some subsequent date, a hatchet and blunt billhook replaced the 'good' and 'bad' knives. At the command of the Queen's Remembrancer, therefore, the City Solicitor of London still ceremonially produces the billhook, and makes scant impression on a 'faggot' of hazel sticks, laid on a block in the Quadrangle Court. He then takes up the hatchet and smashes the twigs to fragments, whereupon the Remembrancer pronounces 'Good Service' and the quit rent is complete.

For the second payment, the Solicitor solemnly counts out six ancient horseshoes and sixty-one horseshoe nails, holding up each for the Remembrancer's inspection until 'Good Number' is declared. This is the altogether more logical quit rent for 'a certain tenement called the Forge' – long since covered by Australia House – in the parish of St Clement Danes': and it has been paid since at least 1235. (*See also* BREAD AND CHEESE DOLE; CORONATIONS; HAXEY HOOD GAME; MANORIAL CUSTOMS; PENNY HEDGE; RED HOSE RACE)

R

· Raisin Monday ·
see KATE KENNEDY PROCESSION

· Ram Roasting ·
Kingsteignton, near Newton Abbot, Devon: Spring Bank Holiday Monday

On Spring Bank Holiday Monday, the flower and ribbon-decked carcase of a ram lamb is ceremonially borne through the village of Kingsteignton, and then spit roasted over an open fire. A programme of sports and dancing continues while it is being cooked, and when it is done slices are distributed to as many people as possible – or at least to those with 'lucky' programme numbers. Until recently, this custom was observed on WHITSUN MONDAY, and previously to that the roasting itself took place on Whitsun Tuesday – the Monday being devoted (before 1885) to a procession in which the doomed but still living lamb was drawn round the parish in a cart covered with garlands of flowers. Further back still, 'it is said', the roasting was done in the bed of the village's Fairwater stream, which was temporarily diverted during the festival.

According to legend, this custom originated in 'early British times', when the stream – Kingsteington's main water supply until 1895 – dried up during a catastrophic drought. The local pagan priests therefore advised the villagers to sacrifice a ram lamb, either to reinforce their prayers for water or, according to another version, as a thanksgiving when those prayers were answered. At any rate, the Fairwater resumed its flow, and since that time (once more 'according to tradition') it has never again failed, however hot the summer: perhaps because the Kingsteignton folk have religiously practised their ceremony annually (except for a brief lapse during the Second World War) even though they had to substitute a deer for a lamb during the meat-rationing years between 1946 and 1954.

So, at least, runs the story, and it would perhaps be churlish to doubt it: but it seems at least possible that the Kingsteignton legend simply provides a local gloss on what was once a fairly widespread Devon custom. For at least two neighbouring parishes, Buckland-in-the-Moor and Holne, once also held annual ram roastings – albeit at MIDSUMMER: and although both these have likewise been associated (on highly suspect evidence) with 'pagan survivals', a spitted lamb would be the obvious choice as a centrepiece for ordinary village festivals in this predominantly sheep-raising area. Whatever their 'pagan' significance, moreover, ram lambs are also easily the most expendable members of the flock.

· Randwick Wap ·
see CHEESE ROLLING; MOCK MAYORS

· Rapper Dancing ·
see SWORD DANCING

· Red Hose Race ·
Carnwath, near Lanark, Strathclyde: third or fourth Thursday in August

Said to be the oldest surviving running race in Britain, and certainly the only one whose terms are prescribed by royal charter, the Red Hose Race has its origins in the curious QUIT RENT or *blenche ferme* by which the Barony of Carnwath is held from the Crown. According to a grant made by King James IV to the third Lord Somerville in 1508, its owners must annually pay: 'One pair of hose containing half an English bluecloth ... at the Feast of Saint John called Midsummer, to any person running most quickly from the eastern end of the town of Carnwath to the cross called Cawlo Cross.' The original distance run thus seems to have been about three miles: and the custom is supposedly connected with the Lord of Carnwath's practice of training messengers to give warning of border raids – though these would surely have been more efficient had they ridden horses. It is perhaps more likely, indeed, that the quit rent perpetuated a traditional MIDSUMMER race which was already in existence; and even possible that it was merely devised to amuse the third Lord Somerville, whom contemporaries described as 'ane simpletoune, altogither unfitt to mannadge or direct his own privat affairs'.

However this may be, the race has always been taken seriously, since any lapse in the quit rent would technically incur the forfeiture of the estate. Until the late 18th century, therefore, the Barons of Carnwath used each year to despatch a certificate of its performance to the Lord Advocate in Edinburgh, where the winner's name was announced at the Mercat Cross: and royal permission had to be obtained before the race could be suspended during the First World War years. Over the centuries, nevertheless, the details of the custom have changed considerably: for the race is now run, not at the Midsummer Fair, but as part of the sports at the August Agricultural Show, and the distance now covered has been reduced to a mile. Instead of the waist-length blue cloth hose originally stipulated, moreover, the prize is now a pair of locally knitted woollen stockings; and these, by long tradition, are always coloured red.

· Red Rose Rents ·
see QUIT RENT CEREMONIES

· Refreshment Sunday ·
see MOTHERING SUNDAY

· Remembrance Sunday ·
Sunday following 11 November

At 11 a.m. on 11 November 1918 – 'the eleventh hour of the eleventh day of the eleventh month' – an armistice brought to an effective end the Great War of 1914-18, in which Britain alone lost nearly a million men. This day (which is also MARTINMAS, the feast of a soldier saint and the traditional time of blood-letting) and this hour were therefore chosen to remember them, with a Two-Minute Silence that until recent decades brought towns, factories and homes to a complete standstill.

Today, when the dead of World War II and of subsequent campaigns are also commemorated, Armistice Day itself is less significant, and most ceremonies take place on the following Remembrance Sunday. Artificial poppies, sold in aid of ex-Service charities and recalling flowers which grew among the trenches and graves of Flanders, are almost universally worn: and parades headed by bemedalled veterans march from churches to place wreaths of them on war memorials, from the London Cenotaph (where the Queen and political leaders participate) to those of the tiniest villages. But the bands, uniforms and patriotic speeches about heroism have less to say about the real meaning of the day than the small wooden crosses placed privately in 'Gardens of Remembrance', with their tales of individual loss and suffering.

· Riding the Black Ram ·
see MANORIAL CUSTOMS

· Rive-kite Sunday ·
see MARTINMAS

· Rogationtide ·
see BEATING THE BOUNDS

· Rough Music ·
see TIN CAN BAND

· Royal and Ancient Golf Club Customs ·
St Andrews, Fife

The origins of golf are obscure: all that is certain is that by 1458 the game had become well enough established in Scotland to constitute a major distraction from the serious business of archery practice, and was thus ordered to be 'utterly criyt doune and nocht usyt'. In 1491, however, it had to be forbidden again as 'unproffitable': and a few years later, in 1507, one Alexander Meill of Brechin became the first recorded victim of a course dispute when John Thowles 'suddenly struck him dead with a staff called a golf club'. But despite these dangers and prohibitions, Stuart monarchs from James IV onwards all appear to have played –

Royal and Ancient Golf Club customs lay down that each new Captain must attach a new silver ball to these already encrusted silver clubs.

including Mary Queen of Scots, who excited public disapproval by golfing within a week of her husband Darnley's murder: and it was probably King James VI and I who introduced the game to England in 1603.

Scotland, nevertheless, long remained the chief stronghold of the sport: and though the oldest Scots club is the Honourable Company of Edinburgh Golfers (founded 1744), the paramount society is the Royal and Ancient Golf Club of St Andrews, which except in the USA is recognized throughout the world as the foremost authority on the rules of the game. St Andrews, whose 'Old Course' is said to be the most formidable in Britain, had been called 'the metropolis of golf' as early as 1691: and there, in 1754, twenty-two 'Noblemen and Gentlemen' founded the club which became 'the Royal and Ancient' in 1834. Its title was granted by King William IV (one of whose own titles had been Duke of St Andrews) who three years later presented the 'Gold Medal with the Green Ribbon' which is still the principal trophy of the Autumn Meeting in September, as the 'Silver Cross of St Andrew' is that of the Spring Meeting in May. On ceremonial occasions, moreover, Captains and past Captains assume coats in the royal livery colours of red with a blue velvet collar: and at the Autumn Meeting Dinner the Captain also wears the gold medal donated in 1839 by William IV's widow Queen Adelaide, while past Captains wear replicas.

The annual captaincy of the Royal and Ancient, which is decided in secret by a jury of past Captains, is the highest honour in the world of golf: but distinguished golfers are not always chosen, and Kings Edward VII, Edward VIII and George VI have all been Captains. Whatever his status, however, the new Captain must ceremonially 'play himself in' with a single shot at the Autumn Meeting: at the very instant after he does so a cannon is fired, and the caddies stationed on the fairway race to recover the golf ball, the winner being rewarded with a gold sovereign or its considerably greater cash value. Every Captain must also attach a new silver ball to the Silver Club which was the society's first trophy (each of the twenty-two founders contributing five shillings towards it) and whose winner, in the days before 'nomination', was also awarded the captaincy. So many Captains have now added their tributes that second and third Silver Clubs have become necessary: but new members still solemnly kiss the original at their first Autumn Meeting Dinner.

· Royal Ascot ·
Ascot, Berkshire: four days in mid-June

Racing on Ascot Heath has enjoyed royal patronage from the beginning, for Queen Anne is said to have personally chosen the course, and certainly attended the first meeting there in 1711. After her death, however, the royal family appears to have forgotten the place for a couple of generations: and it was not until the 1760s that the Duke of Cumberland – the victor of Culloden, and variously known as 'Sweet William' or 'Stinking Billy' – really got the event going. Later in the same century, the Prince Regent and his circle gave the meeting the social cachet it has enjoyed ever since, and it was he – as George IV – who began the continuing tradition of the royal procession to the course. This now begins by car at Windsor Castle, but transfers into open horse-drawn landaus, escorted by scarlet-coated outriders in gold-laced top hats, to drive down the Straight Mile at the start of each afternoon's racing. Its destination is the Royal Box, before which stretches the sacrosanct Queen's Lawn – admittance only by personal invitation from the monarch – and the somewhat less

King George VI and Queen Elizabeth open the 1949 **Royal Ascot** meeting by driving down the course in a landau drawn by the famous 'Windsor Greys'.

exclusive Royal Ascot enclosure, restricted to 3000 spectators with the appropriate social qualifications and the 'correct' form of dress.

Royal Ascot, however, is not merely a fashion-show-cum-garden-party, the principal outdoor event of the London season. For the racing itself is a focus of international attention, with prize money high enough to attract good horses from all over Europe, so that winning at Ascot carries more than just social significance. The principal race is for the Ascot Gold Cup, presented by George III in 1807, this being one of the longest flat-races in the calendar: then there are the King Edward VII stakes, often called the 'Ascot Derby'; the Prince of Wales Stakes; the Coventry Stakes for two-year-olds; and the Hardwicke Stakes, which is usually contested by the previous season's 'classic' winners.

· Royal Ceremonies ·

Since the sovereign is the head both of the State and of the Church, most British official ceremonies are in some sense 'royal': but the events mentioned here are those in which the monarch is personally involved. The greatest of these, of course, are CORONATIONS, held since 1066 in Westminster Abbey – for though since 1603 the monarch has been the ruler of Scotland as well as England, Wales and Northern Ireland, no separate Scots coronation has taken place since Charles II was crowned at Scone in 1651. But the ancient Scots coronation regalia called 'the Honours of Scotland' is still kept at Edinburgh Castle – notable among it being the 'Crown of Robert Bruce', the Sword of State presented to James IV by the Pope in 1507, and the Sceptre of James V – and this was borne before Queen Elizabeth during her post-Coronation Progress through Edinburgh in 1953. The sovereign also has a separate 'Bodyguard for Scotland', the Royal Company of Archers (see SILVER ARROW CONTESTS), which is the Scots counterpart of the English Yeomen of the Guard, and which attends her throughout all state visits to Scotland. During these she generally stays at the Palace of Holyroodhouse in Edinburgh, her official rather than her private Scottish residence – which is Balmoral in Aberdeenshire, beloved of Queen Victoria.

The great majority of royal ceremonies, however, take place in and around London: the most splendid being the annual State Opening of PARLIAMENT, held in late October or early November. Of colourful military occasions, the best known is TROOPING THE COLOUR, which the sovereign invariably attends: and she or another member of the royal family is frequently also present at the ceremony of 'Beating Retreat', a display of marching and counter-marching and of massed bands held in Horse Guards' Parade on several evenings in late May or early June. Generally performed by the Foot Guards regiments, but sometimes by other units (particularly the Royal Marines), this originated in the practice of beating drums as a signal for troops to

'retreat' to their camp at nightfall, and it closes with the playing of the Evening Hymn and the sounding of the Last Post. In some years, too, a member of the royal family attends the Founder's Day parade at Chelsea Hospital on OAK APPLE DAY: while the sovereign always takes the leading part in that reminder of the other face of war, the REMEMBRANCE SUNDAY service at the Whitehall Cenotaph. Other church services regularly attended by the Queen include those of the ORDERS OF CHIVALRY and the annual presentation of the ROYAL MAUNDY: and the EPIPHANY GIFTS CEREMONY also remains officially a royal occasion, though the monarch is rarely present in person.

There are also a number of 'royal events' which have no long-established ritual or ceremonial and which are observed with varying degrees of formality. In June, for example, the Queen traditionally attends the racing at ROYAL ASCOT: and, surrounded by considerably less state, she frequently patronizes the DERBY, the Badminton Horse Trials in April, and almost invariably the HIGHLAND GAMES at Braemar. In most years, too, she visits the Chelsea Flower Show for a private view on the day before its opening (generally in late May): and, more publicly, attends the Royal Film Performance at the Odeon, Leicester Square in March, and the Royal Command Performance at Drury Lane Theatre or the London Palladium in November. Every year, moreover, at least some of the approximately 8000 guests who attend one of the royal garden parties – generally three at Buckingham Palace and one at Holyroodhouse – have an opportunity of meeting the sovereign or her family.

· Royal Company of Archers ·
see ROYAL CEREMONIES; SILVER ARROW CONTESTS

· Royal Maundy ·
Maundy Thursday

At the Last Supper on the first Maundy Thursday Christ washed the feet of His disciples, enjoining them thereafter to 'wash one another's feet' in token of mutual love and humility: and later the same evening he pronounced: 'A new commandment I give unto you, That ye love one another; as I have loved you; (John 13. 4-15, 34). From the 13th century at least, English monarchs symbolically obeyed this commandment (Latin: *mandatum*, hence 'Maundy') by washing the feet of their poorest subjects on the day before GOOD FRIDAY; presenting them at the same time with gifts of food, clothes and money.

This ceremony attained its greatest elaboration under the Tudors, by which time it was customary to include as many paupers as the monarch then had years, plus one for the 'year of grace' until the next Maundy Thursday: and to give each of them a like number of pennies. They also received a lenten meal of fish and bread; a bowl of wine; material for new clothes; and

Clad in all their sombre finery, recipients of the 1926 **Royal Maundy** display their alms-purses and specially minted 'Maundy Money' outside Westminster Abbey.

shoes and stockings: while the poorest of them all was subsequently presented with the robe or dress the monarch wore during the distribution. Queen Elizabeth I, however – either because of her notorious unwillingness to part with any of her gowns or from more practical considerations – substituted for the last an extra gift to each pauper.

She did, nevertheless, continue to wash their feet in person, and even to kiss these afterwards: though she sensibly refrained from doing so until the feet had already been cleansed in turn by a laundress, the Royal Sub-Almoner and the Lord High Almoner. This practice, indeed, endured for some time after 1698, when the ceremony-hating William III ended royal participation in the distribution: and is still commemorated by the linen towels worn by Almonry officers during present-day Maundies, as well as by nosegays of strongly scented flowers – originally intended to neutralize the smell of unwashed pauper feet – still carried by principal participants.

For over two centuries, the ceremony of the Royal Maundy was continued without a break by the Almonry staff. Then, in 1932, George V revived the custom of distributing it in person, and since 1944 this has become regular: at present, it is observed every fourth year at Westminster Abbey, and in the intervening three at various provincial cathedrals and major churches. It begins with the ceremonial entry of two processions: the Queen's, including the local choir and clergy and her own choir of the Chapel Royal (*see* EPIPHANY GIFTS);

and the Almonry's, escorted by Yeomen of the Guard – one of whom carries on his flat-topped Tudor hat a great silver dish piled with purses. Already seated in the choir are one more man and one more woman than Her Majesty has years, all over sixty-five and selected for their long service to Church and community.

After prayers and a reading of the relevant St John's Gospel passage, the Queen first presents each of these with £3 in normal currency: this replaces the old clothing gift, and is contained in purses of green leather for women and of white leather for men – the colours of the Tudor royal livery. Then, following a lesson from Christ's Sermon on the Mount (Matthew 25. 31-45), she again passes up the line of women and down that of the men to make the second distribution, this time of red and white purses: the first contains £1 and £1.50 in ordinary currency, representing the 'Robe Money' and the food allowance; and the second holds the 'Maundy Money' itself.

This specially minted silver coinage consists of four-penny, threepenny, twopenny and penny pieces, one complete set being given for each decade of the sovereign's age and the balance made up from single coins: and though it is strictly legal tender, it is rarely spent as such. Maundy Money is also received by the four nosegay-bearing Children of the Royal Almonry, chosen annually either from orphanages, or from disadvantaged families: and in the spirit of this ancient ceremony's first Founder, these are also given more concrete financial support.

· Royal Salutes ·

Guns appear to have been fired to honour kings and other great personages since artillery was first introduced into Britain in the mid-14th century: though on one occasion the custom proved fatal to the monarch so honoured. For during a royal salute at Roxburgh in 1460, King James II of Scotland ('mair curieous nor becam him or the majestie of ane king') incautiously stood too close to the chancily constructed cannon, and 'was unhappely slane with ane gun, the quhilk brak in the fyring'. On this occasion the guns seem to have been loaded, and such was certainly the case when 'Mons Meg', the massive 'bombard' still to be seen at Edinburgh Castle, was fired in 1558 to celebrate the wedding of Mary Queen of Scots, propelling a half-ton ball more than a mile and a half: Meg herself, moreover, eventually burst while firing a birthday salute to the Duke of York, later James VII and II.

Present-day salutes are fired with more reliable weapons – which are, of course, never loaded with live shell. They take place annually on the anniversary of the Queen's accession (6 February); the Queen's birthday (12 April); Coronation Day (2 June); The Duke of Edinburgh's birthday (10 June); the Queen's official birthday (second Saturday in June, *see* TROOPING THE COLOUR); and the Queen Mother's birthday (5 August): and certainly the most spectacular salutes are those fired in Hyde Park by the King's Troop of the Royal Horse Artillery. Honoured with that title by George VI in 1947, and privileged to retain their Victorian uniform of blue jacket frogged in yellow, red-striped breeches and fur busbies with red 'bags' and white plumes, the troop is equipped with thirteen-pounder guns of First World War vintage, each pulled by six horses. Shortly before noon on saluting days, six of these are brought at full gallop onto the park's exercise grounds, where they are swiftly and expertly made ready, and fire a total of forty-one rounds – twenty-one being the usual number of a royal salute, plus another twenty because the park is Crown property – at ten-second intervals.

At the TOWER OF LONDON, however, salutes of sixty-two guns are fired: the usual twenty-one, plus twenty because the Tower is a royal palace, plus another twenty-one as a compliment from the City of London. Here the weapons used are twenty-five-pounder howitzers, the favourite gun of the Second World War, and the operating unit is the City's own territorial regiment, the Honourable Artillery Company. The senior British volunteer unit, the company originated as a body of

The thirteen-pounder guns of the King's Troop, Royal Horse Artillery, fire an Accession Day **royal salute** in Hyde Park.

medieval London archers called the Guild of St George. Granted a royal charter in 1537 as the Fraternity of Longbows, Crossbows and Handguns, it later became the 'Artillery Company': and though its members officered the London Trained Bands for Parliament during the Civil War, since the Restoration its 'Captain-General' has always been a member of the royal family, the current title-holder being the Queen. Being still composed of part-time soldiers, moreover, its salutes are not fired at noon, but at the more convenient time of 1p.m. On the Queen's official birthday, however, salutes at both Hyde Park and the Tower are fired at 11a.m., thus coinciding exactly with the sovereign's entry into Horse Guards' Parade for the ceremony of Trooping the Colour.

A salute is also fired at this hour, in Hyde Park only, to mark the Queen's arrival at the House of Lords for the State Opening of PARLIAMENT; and on REMEMBRANCE SUNDAY a single gun is fired at Horse Guards' Parade to indicate the beginning of the 'Two-Minute Silence' at 11 a.m., another being shot to signal its end; while for state visits full salutes are fired at both Tower and park, at the precise moment (generally around 12.30 p.m.) when the visitor steps onto the platform of Victoria Station. They are also fired in honour of special events like royal weddings, births and funerals: and at CORONATIONS exceptional 101-gun salutes begin as the crown is placed on the sovereign's head.

On these and the six usual occasions, royal salutes are also fired in various places outside London: including Edinburgh Castle (41 guns); Windsor (only 21, since the saluting area is outside the royal park); and a number of provincial garrison towns such as York, where 21-gun salutes are fired in the Museum Gardens.

Returning heroes celebrate Armistice Day 1918 with an out-of-season **rushbearing** at Greenfield, near Oldham, Lancashire: as was customary in that area, its centrepiece was the towering mitre-shaped rush-cart, decked with flags and greenery.

· Running Races, Traditional ·

see HAT AND RIBBON RACE; HOURGLASS, CROWN AND RUNNING AUCTIONS; RED HOSE RACE; ST BARTHOLOMEW'S BUN RACE; WEDDINGS

· Rushbearings and Haystrewings ·

The customs of rushbearing and haystrewing – despite other ingenious but far-fetched explanations advanced by folklorists – clearly stem from the practical need to provide a cheap and easily obtainable covering for the earthen or stone floors of early buildings. Churches and houses alike were therefore strewn with rushes, hay or straw (depending on local availability and the season of the year) which furnished both covering and rudimentary insulation, as well as cushioning the knees of worshippers and pleasantly scenting the building – at least when they were freshly cut and regularly changed. Churches, accordingly, were newly strewn before great festivals like EASTER, CHRISTMAS, and particularly, WHITSUN: or on the feast day of their patron saint, especially if this fell during the summer months, when rushes and

hay are at their best. Associated as they thus already were with special services, by the later Middle Ages strewing days had developed a ceremonial of their own, centring on the rushbearing procession to the church: and in some areas these processions became so dominant a feature of the parish wake that neither post-Reformation Puritan disapproval nor even the advent of boarded floors and kneelers – which did away with the need for rushes – could diminish their popularity.

In north-western England – Cumbria, Lancashire, Cheshire, and the adjacent parts of Yorkshire and Derbyshire – rushbearings were indeed the greatest events of the year, reaching a pinnacle of splendour in the early 19th century. Their focus was the rushcart, with its towering load of green rushes skilfully piled in a pyramid or mitre shape: secured by flower-woven rush ropes, topped by oaken boughs and worked with patriotic slogans, these were often also hung about with all manner of glittering silverware – a display intended to show off the wealth of the community and (so folklorists declare) to 'reflect away' ill luck. Among the populous valleys of industrial south-east Lancashire, the

The famous Cumbrian **rushbearing** procession at Grasmere focusses on this hand-woven linen 'rush-sheet', borne by green-clad girls.

cradle of the rushcart tradition, as many as ten might appear in one procession, each hauled by a small army of men or a team of decorated horses: before them marched brass bands, and around them capered MORRIS dancers, whose 'North-western Processional' style evolved from such parades. Not infrequently, moreover, the proceedings were further enlivened by fights between rival bands of rushcarters: and it was partly due to such 'rowdiness' that, like so many other similar customs, rushbearings went into a sharp decline during the late-Victorian period.

Rushcarts still appear, however, at Saddleworth and other places in the Oldham-Bury-Rochdale area of south-east Lancashire, generally during August: and the rushcart tradition has also been revived at Sowerby Bridge, just over the West Yorkshire border (first Saturday and Sunday in September) where token bunches of rushes are presented to each church along the lengthy processional route; while another revived West Yorkshire rushbearing, at Haworth (on a Sunday in June) culminates in the traditional manner with the scattering of rushes along the aisles of the parish church. At Macclesfield Forest Chapel in Cheshire, where the revived service takes place on the nearest Sunday to 12 August — because that was the date when the Earl of Derby arrived for the grouse shooting — rushes plaited with flowers cover the entire floor: while at Lymm, near Stockport in the same county (second Monday in August) a civic procession — though now bereft of its once-renowned rushcart, drawn by six 'Old Lymm Greys' — carries bunches to church and lays them on the

chancel steps. Near the Cheshire border with Wales, moreover, Farndon (2nd Sunday in July) and Tarvin (a Sunday in July) maintain the local custom of rush-decking (or 'hilling') graves and tombstones as well as the church gate and porch: and at Bishop's Castle in Shropshire a newly established rushbearing — complete with rushcart procession, morris dancers and church strewing — is held on the Sunday nearest the patronal festival of St John the Baptist, which is also MIDSUMMER DAY.

In Cumbria, rushes are now neither carried on carts nor strewn, but instead plaited into elaborate emblems called 'bearings', which are borne in procession and then used to decorate the church. Probably the best-known of the Cumbrian ceremonies — which invariably coincide with dedication festivals — is that of Grasmere, held on the Saturday nearest St Oswald's Day (5 August) and much patronized during its history by luminaries like Wordsworth and Ruskin. Headed by a band playing the 18th-century 'Jimmy Dawson's March', the procession's centrepiece (a Ruskinian addition) is the hand-woven linen 'rush sheet' carried by six green-and-white-clad schoolgirls: during the service a special rushbearing hymn (of 1835) is sung, and afterwards 'Grasmere gingerbread' marked with St Oswald's emblem is distributed to the children. A similar ceremony, with its own local hymn and gingerbread distribution, takes place at neighbouring Amble-side on the Saturday nearest the Visitation of the Blessed Virgin (2 July), when over 300 bearings, of every conceivable shape, are carried. On the eastern edge of the county, however, at Warcop (St Peter's Day, 29 June) and Musgrave (first Saturday in July) bearings always take the form of crosses tied with red ribbon: and at Warcop, where the custom is said to have continued without a break since the church's 13th-century foundation, these hang in the porch throughout the year. While at Urswick in Furness (Sunday nearest MICHAELMAS) the pride of the procession is the Rush Queen's banner of St Michael and the Dragon, carried since the ancient ceremony was revived in 1905.

Rushbearings, however, are not and never have been confined to north-western England. Records show that the custom once also flourished from Kent to Lincolnshire and from Somerset to Norfolk, and the oldest surviving ceremony which can be traced with certainty takes place at St Mary Redcliffe, Bristol, on Whit Sunday. This is the 'Rush Sunday' service, instituted in 1493 to commemorate William Canynges, merchant adventurer and five times mayor of Bristol, who largely rebuilt the magnificent church before retiring from the world as a simple priest, and who celebrated his first Mass there on Whit Sunday 1468 – a traditional season for rushbearing. Rushes from Somerset, therefore, are still strewn for the occasion, which is attended by the Lord Mayor in full state, accompanied by his sword-bearer, the eight city maces, and scarlet-gowned councillors carrying posies of spring flowers. Farnborough, on the Kentish fringe of Greater London, also has commemorative 'Rush SERMONS', endowed by one George Dalton in 1566 and held on the Sunday nearest St Peter's Day (29 June), though the church's patron is St Giles. Rushes are then strewn in the chancel, and the sermon's subject – the transitory nature of human life – is said to have been inspired by the drowning of a benighted drunkard in a reed bed near Dalton's house: according to another version, however, the donor himself narrowly escaped death in a swamp, and endowed the ceremony in thanksgiving.

Similar apocryphal tales (much resembling those associated with LOST IN THE DARK BELLS, but here 'explaining' bequests of hay meadows) and a like attachment to St Peter's Day also characterize the once very numerous haystrewing customs of the south-east Midlands: whose comparative obscurity – and accelerating decline – is doubtless due to their lack of accompanying ceremony. At Langham in Rutland, for instance, the hay spread without ritual on the 'Feast Sunday' following Petertide formerly came from 'Bell Acre', allegedly the gift of a blizzard-bound lady saved by the sound of Langham bells: and though neither ceremony nor legend attaches to the Petertide rushes strewn at nearby Barrowden, these are still always cut in the same field – doubtless also a bequest to the parish. At St Peter's, Braunstone, Leicestershire, moreover, the relevant hay meadow – now covered by a gasworks, which pays the church £1.50 rent each year – is said to have been donated by another benighted lady, this time rescued by the parish clerk: the custom, nevertheless, seems to have been transferred from neighbouring Glenfield where strewing has now ceased but where a 15th-century effigy is still identified as the lady herself.

Nothing is remembered about the originator of 'grass-strewing' at Odell, Bedfordshire – practised on the second Saturday in July (i.e. Petertide Old Style): but the hay donor at Old Weston, Huntingdonshire was allegedly motivated only by a determination to muffle the clattering of farm-labourers' boots during the 'Feast Sunday' service after St Swithin's Day (15 July). Elizabeth Theed, who gave the original hay meadow at Wingrave, Buckinghamshire in 1786, is credited with the same noise-abating motive, though 'benighted traveller' tales are also told of her: there, rushes instead of grass are now strewn on the Saturday after St Peter's Day, when a morris dancers' procession and special service also take place. Closest of all to the old spirit of the custom, however, is the long-established haystrewing at Shenington in north Oxfordshire, where grass mown in the churchyard is spread on Whit Sunday and renewed on the two Saturdays following: on the Monday after the second strewing, moreover, a CLUB WALK tours the village behind an enormous banner, whereafter beer and buns are consumed in the village hall.

· Rushbearing Sermon ·
see SERMONS

S

· St Andrew's Day ·
30 November

St Andrew, one of Christ's twelve Apostles, is the patron saint of Scotland: some of his bones are said to have been brought to what is now St Andrews in Fife during the 4th century, and since medieval times the X-shaped saltire cross upon which he was supposedly crucified has been the Scottish national symbol. His day, therefore, is a patriotic festival: and though now overshadowed in Scotland itself by BURNS NIGHT, it is much celebrated by Scots expatriates, who mark it with ceilidhs, piping, and dinners of such traditional dishes as singed sheep's head, haggis and whisky. The Royal Scots Corporation in London also display 'the Scots Box', given in 1611 to contain a fund for poor Scotsmen who came south with King James VI and I: this still helps needy Scots in the London area.

In England, the day is now little regarded: but Old St Andrew's Day (11 December) was once celebrated 'to a riotous extent' by the Midlands lace makers who also claimed him as their patron, and a relic of this may survive in the TIN CAN BAND.

Distributing currant buns to children after
St Bartholomew's Bun Race.

· St Bartholomew's Bun Race ·
St Bartholomew's Hospital, Sandwich, Kent: 24 August

The Hospital (or almshouse) of St Bartholomew, just outside the ancient CINQUE PORT of Sandwich, is said to have been founded with the booty of the great sea fight on St Bartholomew's Day 1217, when the ships of the Cinque Ports routed a French invasion fleet commanded by the pirate-sorcerer Eustace the Monk. It may, in fact, be even older; and it has certainly maintained its medieval traditions in remarkably unaltered form. For its sixteen elderly 'brothers and sisters' still inhabit separate cottages, grouped about a 13th-century chapel and surrounded by the hospital's own farmland: and every St Bartholomew's Day (24 August) the Mayor of Sandwich still makes his ceremonial visitation, to attend a memorial service for the hospital's founders and witness the selection – traditionally carried out by 'pricking' a name on the list of residents – of its 'Master' for the coming year.

The ceremonies then conclude in livelier fashion, with local children racing round the chapel for a reward of a currant bun apiece, while every adult present receives a 'St Bart's biscuit' bearing a representation of the hospital's ancient seal. Just how and when this custom originated is uncertain, but it seems likely to be less than a century old, and to have replaced the 'St Bartholomew's Dole' of bread, cheese and beer given to children on earlier visitation days. And that, in turn, perpetuated the still older tradition of offering a regular WAYFARERS' DOLE to the hundreds of poor pilgrims and other travellers who – in the days when Sandwich was among the greatest ports in the land – passed by the hospital on their way to the holy shrine of St Thomas of Canterbury.

· St Bartholomew's Day ·
see ABBOTS BROMLEY HORN DANCE; BURNING BARTLE;
COW HEAD WAKES

· St Blaise's Day ·
see BLESSING THE THROATS

· St David's Day ·
1 March

Saint David, Dafydd or Dewi (*c*.520-588), the founder and first abbot-bishop of Menevia (now St David's, Dyfed), has been venerated since the early Middle Ages as the patron of Wales. The Welsh custom of wearing leeks on his feast day is, however, of uncertain origin. It is generally said to commemorate a victory over the English, when the Welsh – commanded either by Cadwallawn (d. 634) or by St David himself – wore leeks as a recognition device: but Shakespeare's *Henry V* and other authorities connect it with the battle of Crecy (1346), when the Black Prince's Welsh bowmen allegedly 'did good service in a garden where leeks did grow'. Alternatively, the leek may have been chosen because its colours – green over white – echo the ancient Welsh standard; or simply because it was apparently a favourite Welsh food: while yet another explanation makes it the symbol of the saint himself, recalling the vegetarian asceticism which won him the title 'Aquaticus' (The Water Drinker).

Whatever the reason, this supposedly 'blood-cleansing' vegetable continues to be worn by patriotic Welsh people – including, by long tradition and official order, all members of Welsh regiments, whose newest recruits may also be required to eat a whole one raw, to the ceremonial beat of the drum. Some more smell-sensitive Cambrians, however, prefer to remember the saint's day with a daffodil, just possibly because its country nickname of 'daffy' somewhat resembles 'Dafydd' – and hence, 'Taffy'.

In parts of western England, 1 March has altogether less pious and nationalistic associations: for it was traditionally the day when fleas awoke from winter slumber and invaded houses, so that doors and windows were fastened 'to keep out the black soldiers'. On the other side of the country, and particularly in East Anglia, it also inaugurates a season when wild and windy weather can be expected:

> First comes David,
> Then comes Chad
> Then comes Winnold, roaring like mad

St Chad (feast day 2 March) being the patron of Lichfield and St Winnold (or Winwaloe, 3 March) a Breton abbot venerated both in Norfolk and Cornwall. If, on the other hand, March 'comes in like a lamb', it wil infallibly 'go out like a lion': or, of course, vice versa.

· St George's Day ·
23 April

The patron saint of England – as well as of Greece, Portugal and Aragon, of soldiers and of boy scouts – Saint George was traditionally a Christian centurion martyred at Lydda in Palestine during the late 3rd or early 4th century: his dragon-slaying exploits, however, are not heard of until the later Middle Ages. Though honoured in England by Anglo-Saxon times, he did not supersede St Edmund of East Anglia and St Edward the Confessor as the national saint until the 13th century, his promotion being mainly due to his popularity among returning English crusaders. But thereafter his cult grew apace, for he was made patron of Edward III's Order of the Garter in 1348, and his name was shouted as a battle-cry by the English soldiers who fought beneath his red-cross banner during the Hundred Years War. In thanksgiving for his part in the victory of Agincourt, moreover, his feast day was in 1415 declared a national religious festival of the highest rank.

During the late medieval period, therefore, 23 April was widely celebrated – notably at London, Norwich, Chester, Leicester and York – with civic processions, pageants of the saint slaying the dragon, and displays of his statue on horseback: it was also a favourite time for FAIRS and horse races, and Lichfield in Staffordshire still holds COURTS LEET on this date. After the Reformation, however, such festivities progressively declined in popularity, and a rhyme recorded by John Aubrey in the 1680s indicates a growing scepticism about the saint's very existence:

> To save a Mayd, St George the Dragon slew
> A pretty tale, if all is told be true
> Most say there are no Dragons; and tis sayd
> There was no George; pray God there was a Mayd.

Saint George nevertheless remains the principal hero of MUMMING PLAYS, and his feast enjoyed a revival of popularity with the upsurge of 'Empire' patriotism which reached its height in 1914; being marked by half-holidays for schoolchildren, special church services, and the wearing of red 'English' roses. In recent years, however, it has been comparatively little observed – except at Stratford-upon-Avon, where it coincides with Shakespeare's birthday COMMEMORATIONS – and the saint's prestige suffered a setback in 1960, when the Roman church effectively demoted him from its calendar. But since the thirty-sixth of the Anglican Thirty-Nine Articles decrees that 'The Bishop of Rome hath no jurisdiction in this Realm of England', this high-handed action need not be regarded: and on 23 April (as on other great religious and national festivals) the red cross of St George still flies above every English parish church.

· St James's Day ·
see BLESSING THE SEAS AND FISHERIES

· St Nicholas's Day ·
see ADVENT; CHRISTMAS

· St Peter's Day ·
see RUSHBEARINGS

· St Swithin's Day ·
see FAIRS

· St Thomas's Day ·
see ADVENT

· St Wilfrid's Feast Procession ·
Ripon, North Yorkshire: Saturday before the first Monday in August

This ancient procession marks the beginning of Ripon's annual fair, originally held – by a royal charter dating from 1108 – around the April feast day of St Wilfrid (c.634-c.710), but subsequently transferred to the LAMMAS anniversary of the saint's triumphant return from exile in 686. Wilfrid, a forceful and turbulent character,

An appropriately formidable-looking figure impersonates Ripon's forceful patron in the St Wilfrid's Feast Procession.

was nevertheless much revered in Ripon, whose Minster he founded: and during the Middle Ages an effigy of him used to be ceremonially borne through the streets on the opening day of the fair. At the Protestant Reformation, however, this custom was condemned as 'idolatrous': and since then the saint's part has been played by a local man in full bishop's robes, who rides a white horse at the head of a procession of decorated 'floats'. The parade ends with a short service of thanksgiving at the Minster – where the Anglo-Saxon crypt of Wilfrid's building is still to be seen – and inaugurates a fortnight-long programme of celebrations, concerts and sports.

· Sayer's Charity ·
see BREAD AND BUN DOLES

· Selling the Keep of the Wether ·
see HOURGLASS, CROWN AND RUNNING AUCTIONS

· Sermons ·

On the second Wednesday after EASTER, the Lord Mayor, sheriffs and aldermen of London process in full state from the Guildhall to the nearby church of St Lawrence Jewry in Gresham Street, EC2, there to hear a sermon on Christ's Resurrection. This custom dates, with one short break, from the Middle Ages; when the civic dignitaries of London were wont to attend a series of Easter sermons, preached on the Monday, Tuesday and Wednesday after the feast from the open-air pulpit outside St Mary's almshouse or 'spital' (i.e. hospital), in what is now 'Spitalfields'. Discontinued when the pulpit was demolished by Puritans in 1642, the 'Spital Sermon' was revived after the return of Charles II in 1660, and was thereafter preached annually in various City churches before reaching its present home during the 1940s.

The Spital Sermon, however, is most unusual in its medieval origins. For the commemorative sermon is essentially a Protestant and post-Reformation institution, and the endowment of such annual feasts of spiritual uplift – often supplemented by temporal nourishment in the form of BREAD AND BUN DOLES, presumably designed to ensure a full congregation – was a particularly popular form of CHARITY during the 17th and 18th centuries. The anniversaries of Protestant triumphs, notably those of the defeat of the Spanish Armada on 29 July 1588 and the capture of GUY FAWKES on 5 November 1605, were therefore favourite dates for commemoration: and the Sundays nearest to them are still marked by 'Armada' and 'Gunpowder Plot' sermons (both endowed by Luke Jackson in 1630) at St Peter's church in Nottingham – where a ST GEORGE'S DAY sermon, founded as recently as the 1950s, is also preached. The 'Handy Sermon', preached at St Giles's, Oxford on or about 10 March, was intended as a more personal declaration of loyalty to the Reformed religion: for its founder, William Handy, was presumably a

convert from Catholicism, and his will of 1622 ordained that the anniversary of his death be commemorated by a sermon giving thanks to God for delivering the nation from 'Popery and Idolatry', and 'bringing the giver the light and truth of the Gospel'. Ironically, however, St Giles's is now exceptionally 'High': so the sermon currently deals with 'some aspect of divergence between the Anglican and Roman Churches', being 'couched in instructional rather than controversial terms'.

Other providential escapes, though from earthly rather than spiritual perils, are also commemorated annually by sermons at London and Newark. The 'Lion Sermon', preached on or about 16 October at St Katharine Cree, Leadenhall Street, London EC3, was endowed in 1649 by Sir John Gayer, Lord Mayor of London and a leading light of the East India Company. During one of his trading ventures to Arabia, Sir John somehow became separated from his companions, and suddenly found himself face to face with a desert lion. Alone and unarmed as he was, he remembered the story of Daniel in the lions' den and fell to his prayers: whereupon the savage beast, after prowling around him for a while, stalked off and left him untouched. In gratitude, therefore, his will bequeathed much of his fortune to charity, and endowed a sermon in his home parish on the anniversary of his deliverance: this invariably includes both a re-telling of Sir John's adventure and a text from the Book of Daniel.

Still more miraculous, perhaps, was the escape of Hercules Clay, Mayor of Newark in Nottinghamshire at the time when that town was beleaguered by Parliamentary forces during the Civil War. On the night of 11 March 1644, Clay dreamt three times that his house was on fire. Twice he arose from his bed, found nothing amiss, and went back to sleep: but after the third warning he hustled his family into the street, and minutes later an exploding 'grenadoe' from a besieging battery struck and demolished the house. Clay's will accordingly bequeathed £200 to Newark corporation, half the interest of which was to pay for an appropriate anniversary sermon, and half to endow a commemorative distribution of 'penny loaves' to the local poor. The latter part of the custom has recently been discontinued, but a 'Bombshell Sermon' is still preached annually at Newark parish church on or about 11 March, the lesson being read from a bible which belonged to Hercules Clay himself.

Some sermon donors chose rather to rebuke a particular vice, or advocate a particular view of life. Mrs Susannah Cocks Nanfan, who in 1745 founded the annual sermon against 'the Bloody Sin of Duelling' at Berrow in Worcestershire, is said to have been motivated by the death of one of her family in such an encounter: a sermon is still preached on the Sunday nearest 5 February, but though its endowment continues to derive from the rent of the 'Bloody Meadow' where the fatal fight occurred, the 'folly of duelling' is no longer prevalent enough to provide its regular theme.

St Paul's Cross, outside old St Paul's Cathedral, was a favourite venue for London civic **sermons** in Jacobean times: covered galleries were provided for dignitaries.

The 'abominable vice of drunkenness', however, is still specifically attacked by the 'Michael Solomon Sermon' which is 'very occasionally' preached on a Sunday in May at St Wulfram's church, Grantham, Lincolnshire: originally endowed in 1706 as an annual event 'on the Sunday next after the Alderman's choice' (election) this may perhaps have been intended as a warning against excessive civic junketings, but curiously enough its funding comes from the rent of the famous Angel and Royal Inn on Grantham High Street.

The transitory nature of mortal existence, appropriately, is also a favourite subject for memorial sermons. Thus the members of the London Stationers' Company who process to St Martin's-within-Ludgate for the 'Bubble Sermon' on the first Tuesday in June are annually reminded that 'Life is but a bubble' – such being the will of Richard Johnson, an 18th-century benefactor to the company: and the frailty of life is likewise the theme of the Rushbearing Sermon at Farnborough in Kent, endowed in 1566 and preached on the Sunday nearest 29 June. 'Mary Gibson's Sermon' at Sutton in Surrey, however, represents an attempt to defy the ravages of time: preached on 12 June, the anniversary of her death in 1772, its performance is one of a series of conditions this wealthy widow attached to a considerable bequest she made to Christ's Hospital School. In return, the school's governors must also carefully inspect the Gibson family vault beneath the church on sermon day, and ensure that any necessary repairs are carried out: for if either inspection or sermon are ever neglected, the whole legacy will pass to another institution.

· Shakespeare's Birthday Ceremony ·
see COMMEMORATIONS

· Shaking Sunday ·
see PALM SUNDAY

· Shepway, Court of ·
see CINQUE PORTS CUSTOMS

· Sheriff's Ride, Lichfield ·
see BEATING THE BOUNDS

· Shrovetide Football ·

Once an essential feature of SHROVE TUESDAY celebrations in many British towns and villages, STREET BALL GAMES now survive only in a handful of places. These may take the form of HURLING or 'football', but the latter bears only a passing resemblance to the highly formalized modern game, being a mass free-for-all played with a minimum of rules by a virtually unlimited number of participants.

Perhaps the oldest established game, at Atherstone near the Warwickshire border with Leicestershire, is said to have originated during King John's reign as an inter-county struggle for a bag of gold. Locally recruited teams replaced those from the rival shires at the turn of the century, but the object of the game is still to gain and keep possession of the large football thrown from an upper window of the Three Tuns at 3 p.m. on Shrove Tuesday. Thereafter the battle rages along the boarded-up main street, and at one time it was also traditional to play the ball into the workhouse yard, so that the inmates 'could have a kick or two'. Once, too, the game continued until nightfall, but it now ends at 5 p.m., when the team holding the ball is awarded it as a trophy. In recent years – after one team 'captured' it at the outset by kicking it to a fast runner, who promptly disappeared with it – the ball's mobility has been decreased by filling it with water. After 4.30 p.m. however, it may still be deflated and hidden – thus avoiding the fierce concluding scrum which, in 1979, the police only managed to disentangle after a full half hour.

Most Shrovetide football games, however, involve the scoring of goals at sites fixed by ancient tradition. At Sedgefield, County Durham, for instance, these are a pond and a stream 500 yards apart, and the match ends when one side touches down at the other's base. But at Workington, Cumbria – whose game, played since at least 1779, now takes place on GOOD FRIDAY, Easter Tuesday and the following Saturday – the rival teams of 'Uppies' and 'Doonies' must carry the ball to their *own*

Much of Ashbourne's free-for-all **Shrovetide Football** game takes place in the Henmore stream which intersects the two-mile-long pitch: somewhere in the middle of this 'Hug' is the ball.

slow, laborious and gloriously muddy – three goals in one day being a rarely attained record.

On Alnwick in Northumberland's quarter-mile-long pitch, however, teams from the rival parishes of St Michael and St Paul must score three goals (called 'hales') to win. Here, too, the game has been exiled from the town centre to a water meadow: but the ball is still piped from Alnwick Castle by the Duke of Northumberland's personal piper, and at the end of play it still becomes the trophy of whoever can carry it off the field – which is generally possible only by swimming the River Aln. Kirkwall, Orkney also plays a street football game, but on CHRISTMAS DAY and NEW YEAR'S DAY: on each occasion a Boys' Game occurs in the morning, but the real business of the day is the five-hour Men's Game – once again between Uppies and Doonies – in the afternoon.

Shrovetide football games were also formerly played (among many other places) at Derby (where over a thousand regularly took part); Scone, Perthshire (whose bachelors played its married men); Musselburgh near Edinburgh (where unmarried women played matrons, and the latter always won); Chester-le-Street, Durham (whose game was suppressed in the 1930s); and Dorking, Surrey, where the balls were inscribed:

> Kick away, both Whig and Tory
> Wind and water, Dorking's glory.

(*See also* BOTTLE KICKING; HAXEY HOOD GAME; HURLING THE SILVER BALL; JEDBURGH BA' GAME; MARBLERS' AND STONECUTTERS' DAY)

· Shrove Tuesday ·

The Tuesday forty-one days before EASTER is the eve of the Lenten fast, which begins on the succeeding ASH WEDNESDAY: hence its old Scots and northern English name of 'Fassens' or 'Fastern's E'en', and its Welsh one of *Nos Ynyd* – the night of the beginning (Latin: *initium*). On this day, in medieval and earlier times, all Christians made their compulsory pre-LENT confessions, or 'shrifts' – whence 'Shrove' Tuesday – and seized their last opportunity to eat the meat, eggs, butter and other 'luxury' foods prohibited during the coming season of privation. Thus fried rashers ('collops') of meat were the traditional dish on the previous 'Collop Monday': and on Tuesday all eggs, butter and fat remaining in the house were made into pancakes – hence the festival's usual nickname of Pancake Day.

For though the strict observance of Lent is now rare, there are few households which go without Shrove Tuesday pancakes, and many which make a ritual of turning them over by tossing them from the frying pan. So too do many schools, colleges and other institutions – notably Westminster School, whose 'Pancake Greeze' dates from at least the early 18th century. Having been ceremonially led in by a mace-bearing beadle, the school cook must toss his pancake over a beam sixteen feet

goals, respectively the wall of Workington Hall and a harbour capstan. Formerly drawn from colliers and steelworkers, Uppies are now simply dwellers in Workington's Upper Town: while Doonies (once sailors and dockers) live by the waterfront.

Ashbourne in Derbyshire's Royal Shrovetide Football Game is also contested – on ASH WEDNESDAY as well as Shrove Tuesday – between 'Up'ards' and 'Down'ards', born north or south of the Henmore stream which intersects both town and pitch. First recorded in 1682 (but certainly older) it has been played every year since then, despite repeated attempts to suppress it. These culminated, in 1891, with the drafting in of police reinforcements to prevent the game starting: but a local woman managed to smuggle in a ball under her long skirt, and thereafter the magistrates capitulated, insisting only that the match be transferred from its traditional town-centre site to Shawcroft meadow.

Apart from this, it remains perhaps the least 'tidied' of all Shrovetide football games. Starting at 2 p.m. with the throwing in of a hand-made and elaborately painted ball by some celebrity (in 1928 it was the Prince of Wales, hence the 'Royal' prefix) it may continue for up to eight hours – that is, until long after dark. Though it may be kicked, carried, thrown, or indeed conveyed in any way (except by car) the ball generally travels via a series of hard-fought scrimmages or 'Hugs': and since the pitch separating the watermill 'goals' is over two miles long (and also crossed by a number of streams) progress is

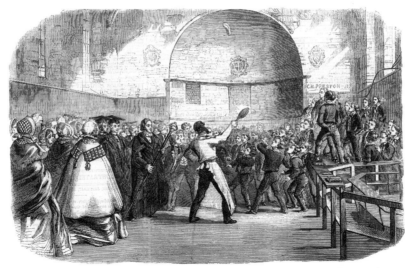

A Victorian **Shrove Tuesday** 'Pancake Greeze' at Westminster School: at the time the whole school scrambled for the pancake, but on this particular occasion the cook failed to toss it over the bar.

above ground. Once, every Westminster boy scrambled for it as it fell; but now only a single representative of each form does so, latterly in fancy dress. Even so the scrum is a fierce one, for he who gains the largest part (formerly it had to be the whole pancake, which must never touch the ground) also claims a guinea prize.

Pancake tossing – which gave the dish its Scottish name of 'sauty [French: *sauté*] bannocks' – is also an essential part of the increasingly popular pancake races. The oldest and most famous, held at Olney, Buckinghamshire, is somewhat dubiously alleged to have begun in 1455, when an absent-minded housewife ran to church with pancake pan still in hand. Revived after a lapse in 1947, it is run over 415 yards by women over sixteen, who must have lived in Olney for three months, wear cap and apron, and toss their pancakes at least three times during the race. The winner receives a kiss from the PANCAKE BELL ringer and a prayer book from the vicar: and since 1949 Olney has competed for the fastest winning time with Liberal, Kansas, USA, which runs a simultaneous race over a similar course. Winster in Derbyshire's race – for men, women and children – is also well established, having begun in 1870: while contests of more recent origin are run in at least a dozen other places, including Lincoln's Inn Fields, London; Liverpool; Ely in Cambridgeshire; and Bodiam, Sussex.

But Shrove Tuesday falls at a lean time in the agricultural year, and in past centuries not everyone could afford even the simple ingredients of a pancake – or of such local Shrovetide delicacies as 'Baldock doughnuts' and the spiced buns called 'Norwich hot coquilles'. Poorer folk therefore claimed the right to go 'Shroving' or 'Gooding', begging for pancakes, food or money with some traditional verse like:

Lard's scarce and flour's dear
That's what makes me come shroving here.
Sunningwell, Berkshire

By Edwardian times, however, this custom was left to children: who still practise it (albeit in a highly formalized and supervised manner) in a few places like Gittisham, Devon, where it is called 'Tip-Toeing' from the rhyme:

Tip, tip, toe
Please for a penny, then we will go.

Elsewhere, particularly in Wales and south-western England, refusal would mean a shower of stones or broken pottery against the door – a custom called 'Lent-Crocking' or 'Lent-Sharding', which purportedly symbolized the fact that cooking pots would not be needed until the fast was over. Sometimes, moreover, the crocks were (and still occasionally are) thrown 'just for fun', whereafter the 'crockers' ran off as quickly as possible: for, if caught, they would have their faces blackened, or be made to clean every shoe in the house. And in parts of Devon and Cornwall, the 'Dappy-Doorers' and 'Nickanans' kept Shrove Monday and Tuesday evenings as MISCHIEF NIGHTS.

Such licensed lawlessness was, until quite recently, an essential element in the celebration of Shrove Tuesday. For it was universally regarded as a time of carnival – a word, indeed, derived directly from its Latin title of *carnelevarium* (putting meat aside) – when normal rules were suspended in a last outburst of exuberance before penitential Lent: and as such it was, save Christmas, perhaps the most popular festival of the whole year. Even now, it is still an official half-holiday in some British schools: and it has long since been an unofficial

Scarborough always celebrates **Shrove Tuesday** with mass skipping on Foreshore Road.

one, obtained by ritualized tricks like 'barring-out' the teacher or – with a show of reluctance – after conventional rhymed appeals:

> Pancake day is a very happy day
> If you don't give us a holiday
> We'll all run away.
> *Saltfleetby, Lincolnshire, 1920s*

Servants, workmen and apprentices, too, eagerly await-ed the pancake bells which released them to join in the day's manifold disports. Often these were free-for-all events involving the entire community, like the Shrove Tuesday skipping which still continues at Scarborough, North Yorkshire. Between noon and 5 p.m., nearly a mile of Foreshore Road is closed to traffic, and thousands of people – children, adults, residents and strangers alike – skip five or ten abreast over ropes stretched across it. Mass STREET BALL GAMES (*see* HURLING THE SILVER BALL; SHROVETIDE FOOTBALL) also survive in a few places: but by and large the excitement of Shrove Tuesday has departed, and it is now merely Pancake Day.

· Signor Pasquale Favale's Bequest ·
see MARRIAGE PORTION CHARITIES

· Silver Arrow Contests ·

Silver arrows were frequently given as prizes in medieval archery contests, and two ancient examples are still competed for. Probably the oldest – and, it is claimed, the oldest British sporting trophy still awarded – is the Musselburgh Silver Arrow: whose exact origins are unknown, but which has been annually shot for at Musselburgh near Edinburgh since at least 1603, the date of the earliest survivor of the named medals presented to the town each year by the Arrow's winners. These, incidentally, also enjoy the right to graze one goose on Musselburgh Common for twelve months after their victory.

Since 1676, the competitors have been members of the 'Society of Archers' formed in that year from 'gentlemen bowmen residing in Edinburgh'. Incorp-orated by royal charter in 1703 – in return for a 'reddendo' (or QUIT RENT) of three silver-barbed arrows every WHITSUN – the society was accepted as a ceremon-ial royal bodyguard during that extraordinary outburst of 'Tartan Romanticism', George IV's visit to Scotland in 1822: and has since been known as the 'Royal Company of Archers, the King's (or Queen's) Body-guard for Scotland'. It thus claims spiritual descent from the guard of bowmen established by Mary Queen of Scots in 1561 – itself an offshoot of the 'Garde Ecossais du Corps du Roi', the Scots archer bodyguard employed by French Kings from the 15th century until the Revolution: and its 500 or so members, in their dark-green uniforms and eagle-feathered bonnets, play a prominent part in all Scottish ROYAL CEREMONIES. For all its competitions (including those for the Musselburgh Arrow and for the Queen's Prize, contested at Holy-roodhouse each June) the company favours the ancient practice of 'clout-shooting': whereby the arrow is shot high into the air, and aimed to drop onto a target lying on the ground some 180 yards from the bowman – a distance almost twice as great as that customary for the normal mode of target shooting, as used by their rivals the Scorton Archers.

These Scorton Archers, named after a village near Richmond in North Yorkshire, dispute not only the Royal Company's claim to be the oldest surviving British archery club, but also its claim to possess the oldest trophy. Their challenge to the former is undoubtedly valid, since the Scorton association was founded in 1673, three years before its Scots rival: but the age of the Scorton Silver Arrow for which it competes cannot be so firmly established. There seems little doubt, however, that the Yorkshire trophy existed before 1673, and tradition relates that it was originally awarded by Queen Elizabeth to a group of Oxford bowmen, being subsequently brought to Scorton by the famous Roger Ascham (1515-68), author of the archery treatise *Toxophilus* and the Queen's favourite tutor. But though Ascham's family certainly lived near Scorton, and he is known to have attended meetings of Yorkshire

bowmen, firm evidence for his connection with the Arrow is lacking – as is any foundation for the tale that it was left at Scorton by an Oxford undergraduate who eloped with a local chambermaid.

The Scorton Silver Arrow, at any rate, is still shot for every June at a venue somewhere in Yorkshire or south Durham, though 'gentleman archers' (or amateurs) from any area or nation may compete. The winner of the Arrow, the first bowman to score a central 'gold' on the target, also becomes the year's Captain of the Scorton Archers: the first to score an 'inner' or 'red' being awarded a silver bugle-horn (dating from 1834) and the title of Lieutenant. A second silver bugle is presented to the Yorkshire-born archer who achieves the largest number of hits of any kind during the contest: while the bowman who scores the 'worst white' by placing his shaft nearest the edge of the target (a very difficult shot, if intended) receives the 'Ancient Horn Spoon', said to be as old as the Arrow itself. Should any unlucky archer 'curse or swear within the hearing of any of the company', however, he is fined a shilling for every oath, 'to the use of the poor of that place or township where they shoot'. (*See also* WOODMEN OF ARDEN)

Members of the Royal Company of Archers, the Queen's Bodyguard for Scotland, who compete annually for the Musselburgh **Silver Arrow**, said to be Britain's oldest sporting trophy.

The famous Wild Horse, star attraction of the Antrobus **Souling** play and a suitably sinister creature for his Halloween appearances, poses with his Driver and their accompanying mummers.

· Souling ·

Antrobus, Cheshire, and elsewhere: first two weeks in November

All Saints' and All Souls' Days, the first two days in November, are the Christian successors of the pagan Feast of the Dead (*see* HALLOWEEN). In the Middle Ages, special prayers were then said for souls suffering in purgatory, and though the Protestant Reformation officially abolished this practice, poor people still went begging for the spiced 'soul-cakes' which were given either as payment for prayers or (especially in Wales) as a direct offering to the departed. By Victoria's reign, however, the 'souling gifts' themselves had become all-important, so that farm labourers sang:

All that we soul for is ale and strong beer

while the few children who now keep up the custom in Shropshire and Cheshire, where they sing:

Soul, soul, for a souling cake
I pray, good missus, a souling cake
Apple or pear, plum or cherry
Anything good to make us merry

or who go 'Caking' around Dungworth near Sheffield, do so mainly to collect money for fireworks.

In north-western Cheshire, where adult souling survived longest, gangs of soulers also performed a MUMMING PLAY, and were accompanied – as nowhere else – by a HOBBY HORSE or 'Old Hob', a horse's skull carried on a pole by a sheeted man (*see* HOODEN HORSE; MARI LWYD). One such, the famous Wild Horse of Antrobus, is still the star attraction of a souling play revived in the 1920s after a short lapse, and now performed in country pubs during the first two weeks of November. Though he prances, snaps his jaws, and generally terrorizes the audience, his Driver (who is dressed as a huntsman, and tries to sell him) admits that he is very old – and so he is, for he was captured over a century ago, in a fight with soulers from a rival village.

· Spanish Sunday ·
see PALM SUNDAY

· Spital Sermon ·
see SERMONS

Despite harrassment by some extraordinarily depraved-looking children, a Victorian cook prepares the Christmas pudding on **Stir-up Sunday**.

· Stir-up Sunday ·
Sunday before Advent Sunday

The Sunday before ADVENT, when the Church of England collect begins; 'Stir up, we beseech thee, O Lord, the wills of thy faithful people: that they, plenteously bringing forth the fruit of good works.' Irreverent choirboys parodied this with:

> Stir up, we beseech thee
> The pudding in the pot
> And when we do get home tonight
> We'll eat it up all hot

while housewives took the prayer as a reminder to stir up less spiritual fruit – the mixture for CHRISTMAS puddings and mince pies, in order to give these time to mature before the great day.

The custom is still kept up in many households, the rule being that all present must take part: mother; father; children in order of age, including babies; and any visitors or servants. A wooden spoon (in honour of Christ's wooden crib) must be used, and stirring must be done in the lucky sunwise or clockwise direction, with the eyes shut, and while making a secret wish.

· Stow Commemoration ·
see COMMEMORATIONS

· Straw Bear Day ·
Whittlesey, Cambridgeshire: Saturday before Plough Monday

Since 1980, the 'Straw Bear' has again made his appearance at Whittlesey, near Peterborough. Played by a man wrapped from head to foot in tightly twisted straw bands (which envelop him so completely that one of his predecessors had to be hastily unstrawed 'when he were took short') with a long straw tail and a conical

The nightmarish figure of the **Straw Bear** once again walks the streets of Whittlesey: but he now appears in broad daylight, to the amusement of a small spectator.

straw helmet covering his face, he dances about the town collecting money for charity.

This revival now takes place on the Saturday before PLOUGH MONDAY: but up until about 1909 – whereafter the custom was suppressed as a form of begging – the Straw Bear accompanied the Plough Monday 'Witches' either on the day itself, or on the following 'Straw Bear Tuesday'. He came, moreover, by night, when he was led chained from house to house, going down on all fours to growl and caper as the door was opened.

In his heyday, the principal prowling grounds of this somewhat sinister midwinter beast (*see* HOODEN HORSE, MARI LWYD) were the Fenland villages between Peterborough and Huntingdon: but he also operated much further north, around Holton-le-Clay near Grimsby in Lincolnshire – where he was carried bodily about his round ('though he had to be a big man') and performed part of a play. His origins are obscure. He may be very ancient, and related to the ritual straw bears which once appeared in places as far away (and as far apart) as Germany and Andorra: or he may have derived his name, though presumably not his form, from the performing bears that toured English villages until well within the present century.

'Nothing but beastly fury and extreme violence': scenes like this, from the Kirkwall New Year game in Orkney, make it easy to understand why officialdom has always frowned on **street ball games**.

· Street Ball Games ·

From Orkney to Cornwall, mass ball games are still played annually through the streets of a few British towns and villages, often on SHROVE TUESDAY. The ball may be a 'football', like that used in SHROVETIDE FOOTBALL or on MARBLERS' AND STONECUTTERS' DAY; a solid wooden 'handball', as in the HURLING games of Cornwall or the JEDBURGH BA' GAME; or some other object, as in BOTTLE KICKING and the HAXEY HOOD GAME. It may be thrown, kicked, carried or 'scrummed' – in the now extinct mass games of Scots 'gowff' and English 'bandy' or 'hoky', moreover, it might also be propelled with curved clubs – or, most frequently, any or all of these methods may be used. For the common feature of these games is an almost complete lack of set rules, and a total disregard for the size or equality of the two teams. All that is necessary is that the ball – having been played, in the words of a 17th-century Cornish account, 'over hilles, dales, hedges, ditches; yea, and thorow bushes, briers, mires, plashes and rivers whatsoever' – shall be touched down at one of two traditionally fixed goals, which may be several miles apart.

The current games also share the common distinction of having survived centuries of official disapproval and attempts at forcible suppression, to which similar matches in hundreds of other places have long since

fallen victim. Almost all the early references to mass 'ball-plays', indeed, occur in prohibitions of them – like the London edict against 'certain tumults arising from great footballings' (1314); the Scots declaration 'that the fut ball ande the golf be utterly criyt doune and nocht usyt' (1458); or the Manchester by-law against 'companies of lewd and disordered persons ... playing with the ffotebale in the streets' (1608). These were prompted in part by the belief that such games distracted men from militarily useful sports like archery: but more by the well-founded view that they were 'nothing but beastly fury and extreme violence, whereof proceedeth hurt' (1531).

This was largely because they were (and still are) invariably contested between potentially antagonistic groups from rival villages, districts of towns, or GUILDS. So they not infrequently degenerated into mass brawls, during which serious injuries or even deaths sometimes occurred: or (what was infinitely worse for the authorities) into full-scale riots – the Peasants' Revolt of 1381, for instance, was commonly nicknamed 'the Hurling Time'. As late as 1930, the six-centuries-old game at Chester-le-Street, County Durham, was finally suppressed by the police: and those that have continued have done so only because of a general improvement in behaviour, and after a curtailment of their duration or an enforced move from their traditional town-centre pitches to a park or recreation ground. But survive they have, a relic of the days when people preferred playing themselves to watching professionals, and when they worked out their aggressions on the pitch rather than in the streets surrounding the stadium.

· Sugar-cup Sunday ·
see PALM SUNDAY

· Swainmote and Attachment, Court of ·
see FOREST CUSTOMS

· Swan Upping ·
The River Thames, between Sunbury-on-Thames, Surrey and Pangbourne, Berkshire: third full week in July, Monday to Thursday

The swan, the largest and most impressive of British birds, has been one of the badges of the English royal house since the 14th century: and since at least that time swans have been regarded as royal birds, whose ownership was the carefully guarded prerogative of the crown. Even as late as 1895, therefore, the unlicensed killing of a swan was punishable by seven weeks' hard labour, and until recently the keeping of the birds on private lakes required special royal permission, while all swans on open waters are still automatically the property of the monarch. The only exception to this rule is that a certain number of Thames swans have belonged

since about the 1470s to the London GUILDS of the Vintners and the Dyers, who are the last survivors of the various bodies once entitled by royal grant to 'swan-rights' on the river.

From the days of the first Queen Elizabeth, therefore, the two companies have organized an annual 'Swan Voyage' along the Thames, at the time when the new broods of cygnets are about two months old: and in the course of this all the swan families encountered are 'upped' from the water, the adults being examined for the beak marks which distinguish the companies' swans from the unmarked royal birds, and the cygnets being marked according to parentage and ownership. During the 17th and 18th centuries, when the Vintners and Dyers still possessed magnificent state barges, the 'upping' was accompanied by much feasting and ceremonial; and though much of this has now ceased, the Swan Voyage is still a colourful sight. Leading the procession of six rowing boats (which until recently started in the City of London, but now begins well up-river at Sunbury) is the craft containing the Queen's Swanherd, flying a banner with the Queen's crowned initials at the prow and another depicting a swan at the stern: this, like the second royal boat, is rowed by men in jerseys of red, the royal livery colour also worn by the Swanherd. The Vintners' two craft follow, commanded by the company's Swan Marker in his green livery and each flying a single flag with the company's arms and a swan badge: and behind these come the two boats of the blue-liveried Dyers, flying similar flags.

Striped-shirted Vintners' men mark a brood of cygnets during an Edwardian **Swan Upping** voyage, while the swan-wardens of the Crown and the Dyers look on.

All three sets of uppers, however, co-operate closely throughout their four days of river work, adroitly manoeuvring their craft to entrap the swimming birds and employing still greater skill (for an angry swan is not to be trifled with) in swiftly 'upping' both adults and cygnets into the boats, where their legs are tied together. The young then have their wings 'pinioned' (or clipped) so that they cannot fly too far away from the Thames, and the beaks of the parents are inspected. If both prove to be unmarked 'Queen's swans', the whole family is at once freed and returned to the water: but if their beaks bear either the single nick which identifies Dyers' birds or the double nick of the Vintners – whence 'The Swan with Two Necks' (or 'nicks'), a fairly common inn-sign – the cygnets are marked in a similar way before release. Often, of course, the young are the product of a 'mixed marriage', and in such cases half the brood are marked (or left unmarked) like the 'cob' (male swan) and half like the 'pen' (female), odd cygnets being awarded to the cob. And so the Swan Voyage slowly proceeds up to Pangbourne, stopping at a different place each night and not forgetting, as Windsor Castle first comes into view, to stand and salute 'Her Majesty the Queen, Seigneur of the Swans'.

For the royal Swanherd and the two company wardens the work does not end at Pangbourne, since they share between them the duty of caring for all Thames swans throughout the year – no light task in largely urban Thames-side, especially now that so many birds are being poisoned by fishermen's lead weights. It should not be forgotten, however, that one of the principal reasons why Crown and companies originally preserved swans was in order to eat them at banquets, and this both Vintners and Dyers still do once a year,

nine-month old cygnets being served as preferable to the somewhat tough and muddy-tasting adults. Both companies' dinners involve elaborate ceremonial, and that of the Vintners is sometimes called the Five Kings' Feast, thus commemorating an occasion during the 14th century when Henry Picard, Vintner and Lord Mayor of London, entertained five monarchs at a single banquet – probably the Kings of England, France, Scotland, Denmark and Cyprus, the second and third being prisoners of the first. The toast of the Vintners' Company, therefore, is 'may it flourish, root and branch, for ever with Five and the Master', and this is always followed by 'five cheers'.

· Swearing on the Horns ·
Ye Old Wrestlers Tavern, North Rd, Highgate, London N6: 8 p.m. – midnight; Wednesday before Spring Bank Holiday and Wednesday nine days after Summer Bank Holiday

It's a custom at Highgate that all who go through,
Must be sworn on the horns, Sir, and so, Sir, must you.

Highgate stands astride the ancient road into London from the north, and the custom of making travellers 'swear on the horns' there may have originated with northern cattle drovers. It may, however, have been a burlesque CIVIC ceremony (*see* MOCK MAYORS) or simply a local joke – a version of the once endlessly repeated chestnut about the horns supposedly sprouted by deceived husbands – kept up by publicans to encourage trade. Certainly the latter was true by the mid-18th century, when most Highgate inns 'kept a pair of horns fastened to a stick, in order to administer a ludicrous oath to all travellers of the middle rank' – of whom

A gullible 'traveller of the middle rank' **Swearing on the Horns** before an apronned Highgate landlord: from a Cruikshank engraving of 1796.

eighty stage-coach-loads a day might pass through the Red Lion alone.

The custom faded with the coming of railways, but was revived early this century at the Wrestlers: where, twice yearly, a wigged and gowned 'judge' administers the 1796 version of the oath: 'You swear ... that you will not eat Brown Bread when you can have white ... that you will not drink Small Beer when you can get Strong (except you like them better); but you will kiss the Maid in preference to the Mistress, if you like the Maid better – So help you Billy Bodkin.' The applicant then kisses the horns presented by the 'clerk', and so becomes a 'Freeman of Highgate' – entitled, if he wants a rest there, to kick any pig out of a ditch and take her place: 'but if you see three lying together, you must only kick out the middle one and lie between the other two.' All this is set down on a certificate, and a fee is exacted – not, as formerly, for the judge's beer-money, but for a local charity.

· Swinging the Fireballs ·
Stonehaven, Kincardineshire: 31 December

At the stroke of midnight on NEW YEAR'S EVE, the north-eastern Scottish port of Stonehaven ignites fireballs for its BURNING THE OLD YEAR OUT ceremony. These wire-netting globes, packed with rags and other paraffin-soaked combustibles, are attached to long wire ropes and swung blazing round the heads of local young people, who parade their fiery arcs up and down the High Street of the Old Town. Great skill and dexterity is needed to perform this exciting spectacle without accidents either to the swinger or the crowd, but such are almost unknown.

Said to ward off evil spirits and witches – for whom this area used to be notorious – as well as to ensure prosperity in the coming year, the custom of swinging fireballs was once widespread: something similar, for instance, was done in Cornish fishing ports on MIDSUMMER EVE. In Stonehaven, however, it began only in the mid-19th century, when it was brought by immigrant fishermen from outlying villages: and as the town's fisheries declined, so too did the ceremony. But efforts were made to keep it going, and it is now once again popular.

· Sword Dancing ·

The linked-sword dances of north-eastern England (which are not to be confused with the solo sword dancing of the Scottish Highlands) are performed by five, six or eight men: traditionally they appear only during the CHRISTMAS season, particularly on PLOUGH MONDAY.

The ceremony begins with the dancers walking round in a circle, in some versions clashing their swords together: then they place these over their shoulders, each man grasping the point of the sword in front of him with one hand, while keeping hold of his own hilt with the other. Next, the swords are lowered to waist-level, so that the dancers form a ring, linked 'hilt and point' by their weapons. This link is normally maintained throughout the dance; and though some versions include figures which involve breaking it, these are regarded as comparatively recent additions.

Always maintaining their grip on their own and their neighbour's swords, the dancers then perform a series of complicated figures. Each following the other, they jump over and pass under the weapons, either singly or in pairs, so that the whole set turns itself inside-out and right-way-about many times. As a culmination, the swords are ingeniously woven together into a pentagonal, hexagonal or octagonal star (variously called the Lock, Rose, Knot or Nut) which is held aloft for display.

Both forms of sword dance share these basic characteristics: but otherwise they differ in many respects. The 'Longsword dances' of Yorkshire are performed by six or eight men, who use semi-rigid swords made from wood or metal, about three feet long, with a simple hilt at one end. After the Lock has been made – and sometimes passed from hand to hand round the marching ring of dancers – it is dropped over the head of a 'Fool' or similar character, so that it rests about his neck. Then, at a given signal, the dancers suddenly and simultaneously withdraw their swords, whereupon the 'victim' falls 'dead' to the ground.

This dramatic feature is not, however, now included in the 'Rapper dances' of Northumberland and Durham. For these five-man dances are performed with short two-foot 'rappers' of flexible sprung steel, having both a fixed hilt and a swivelling point-guard: and their pentangular Nut is therefore so small and sharp-edged that sudden withdrawal might well result in a genuine beheading. So the Nut may be either symbolically rested round the victim's neck, or used to knock off his hat: but more often it is simply held up while the team clog-dance in line, sometimes also performing athletic feats like back-somersaults over the swords.

With their quick, elaborate 'stepping' (far more complicated than the longsword men's 'running lope') and their tight, intricate figures (impossible with rigid longswords) the rapper dances are indeed much the showier of the two types: perhaps because, being frequently performed by miners to raise money during periods of unemployment, they were therefore continually polished and improved. Certainly they are the more modern variant, for the technology necessary to produce flexible rappers did not develop until after 1740, by which time the rigid longsword dance was already well established.

Exactly how, when, and where the sword dance originated are, however, exceedingly vexed questions. Because of its survival in Yorkshire, a county heavily settled by Scandinavians, it is frequently but unfoundedly alleged to have been 'brought over by the Vikings'. Yet it is also widespread throughout Northumberland

Top: Many Yorkshire longsword teams, like this one from Handsworth near Sheffield, have adopted quasi-military uniforms. *Above:* The Grenoside **sword dancing** team from South Yorkshire place the 'Lock' round their fur-hatted captain's neck.

The greater flexibility of the two-handled 'rappers' of Northumberland and Durham allows very tight and intricate **sword dancing** figures to be made by teams like Earsdon, who wear the pitman's costume typical of rapper men.

That **sword dancing** is essentially a midwinter custom is demonstrated by the York Gentleman's longsword team, here performing the Kirkby Malzeard dance in a January blizzard.

and Durham, whose Norse immigrants were few: while the earliest known accounts of British linked-sword dances (which date from the second quarter of the 17th century) show that their range then extended as far outside the Danelaw as Perth and Elgin in Scotland. In such Viking-infested counties as Leicestershire and Nottinghamshire, moreover, there is no record of the custom whatever.

Nor, significantly, is there any evidence for its existence in Norway, and very little for Denmark: though a document of 1550 reports something very like the English dance in Sweden. The custom was, however, clearly far more popular in the Low Countries (where it was depicted by Peter Brueghel in about 1600, and still survives around Brussels) as well as in Germany and Austria: and linked-sword dances featuring Locks are or were also performed in parts of France, Italy, Spain, Portugal, Czechoslovakia and Yugoslavia.

This universality suggests that sword dancing long pre-dates the present racial structure of Europe: and attempts have been made to associate it with a prehistoric priesthood of smiths or ironworkers. The MUMMING PLAYS associated with many versions of the dance, however, may provide a better clue to its origins. In all surviving examples, each dancer vigorously denies responsibility for the killing of the victim:

> I'm sure it's none of I, that did this bloody act
> It's he that follows me, that did it, for a fact

and so on round the circle, until the 'dead man' is revived by a 'Doctor' or similar character.

It is possible, therefore, that the dance originally represented the sacrifice of either a man or a totem beast – in some places, 'victims' still wear animal-skin caps – whose death and symbolic resurrection were somehow vital to the community. So that no single person should bear the blame for this necessary but 'bloody act', the dancers (like a firing squad) performed it collectively: and it was perhaps as a further precaution against human or divine retribution that they first assumed the disguises – suits of tatters, elaborate hats, or coloured woollen beards, worn so that 'no-one might know them' – which many dancers retained until the late 19th century. By then, however, the ritual had long since lost its original significance, and generally also its associated drama: and had become merely an attractive display, performed for 'luck' or for money. So neater and 'more suitable' costume was adopted – pseudo-military dress for longsword dancers, and stylized 'pitman's' shirt, sash and breeches for rapper men – and such is still worn by most traditional teams active today.

Among the longsword dancers, perhaps the best known are the 'Plough Stots' of Goathland, near Whitby, where two men's and a boys' team perform on Plough Monday, dressed in pink or blue 'uniforms' with military caps. A number of other teams, including those of Redcar and Loftus, also operate in the same north-east Yorkshire area, where annual contests are held at Whitby. While at the opposite corner of the county, around Sheffield, the long-established eight-man teams of Handsworth and Grenoside both dance on Boxing Day – the former in 'hussar-style' dress and the latter less martially clad in paisley tunics, with a rabbit-skin hat for their leader. And among the seventy or so other versions of the longsword dance known to have once existed in Yorkshire, those of Ampleforth; Escrick; Flamborough; Kirkby Malzeard; Kirby Moorside; Poppleton and Sleights are also sometimes performed – though not always by teams from their native villages. For interest in longsword dancing is growing rapidly, and it may eventually oust the MORRIS DANCING which has lately infiltrated its home area from the Midlands and the South.

Across the border into Durham, Greatham near Hartlepool has revived not only its dance – a blend of longsword and rapper traditions – but also, unusually, its associated play, performed together on Boxing Day. While in the rapper country proper, and especially round Newcastle – where the custom never died out – many teams still perform their spectacular dances, popular versions being those from Amble, Earsdon and North Walbottle, Northumberland; and High Spen, Swalwell and Winlaton in County Durham.

T

· Taily Day ·
see APRIL FOOLS' DAY

· Tandering ·
see TIN CAN BAND

· Tar-Barrel Rolling ·
see GUY FAWKES NIGHT

· Tayler's Bun Service ·
see BREAD AND BUN DOLES

· Test Matches ·

'Test matches', the high point of the cricketing season, are played between England and national sides from the West Indies, New Zealand, India, Pakistan and, above all, between England and Australia. The very first Test match was contested between those two countries, at Melbourne in 1877; and so also was the first English Test, at Kennington Oval, London, in September 1880: and since then the four-yearly Anglo-Australian Tests have always been the most keenly contested. These are known as the 'battle for the Ashes', a legendary trophy first heard of after England's defeat by Australia in

The **Tichbourne Dole** of 1670 is distributed by Lady Mabella's heirs, in front of the manor house which collapsed beneath her curse when the charity was temporarily and disastrously discontinued.

1882: on the morning following the match, an 'obituary' in the *Sporting Times* stated that English cricket had 'died at the Oval', and that 'The body will be cremated, and the Ashes taken to Australia'. When a touring team restored England's honour by winning the next year's Test, therefore, some Australian ladies presented its captain with an urn containing 'the Ashes' of a burnt cricket stump, and this now occupies a place of honour in the famous M.C.C. pavilion at Lord's cricket ground in north London. Lord's and the Oval remain the venues for the principal matches in any Test series, but matches are also played at Headingley (Leeds, Yorkshire); Old Trafford (Manchester); Trent Bridge (Nottingham); and sometimes Edgbaston (Birmingham).

· Tichborne Dole ·
Tichborne, Hampshire: 25 March

Though probably the oldest of all surviving British CHARITIES, the Tichborne Dole is perhaps best known for the dramatic working-out of the curse attached to it, and for its link with the famous Victorian fraud case of the 'Tichborne Claimant'. Its beginnings, too, were by all accounts sensational enough. During the 12th century, as the crippled Lady Mabella de Tichborne lay mortally sick, she begged her husband to provide for the village poor after her death: whereupon the hard-bitten Sir Roger, pulling a flaming torch from the fire, cynically promised to give them the yield of all the land she could encircle before it burnt out. To his amazement, however, the dying woman at once struggled from her sickbed, and succeeded (some say with divine aid) in dragging herself on all fours round an area of no less than twenty-three acres, still called 'the Crawls'. The crop from this land, she then demanded, must be annually given to the poor each LADY DAY: if this benefaction were ever discontinued, moreover, a terrible curse would fall on Sir Roger's descendants. First seven sons would be born to the family, but these would be followed by a generation of seven daughters, whereafter the name of Tichborne would die out and the ancient Tichborne manor house would fall to ruin.

Heeding Lady Mabella's warning, for 600 years the Tichbornes faithfully distributed a dole of bread made from Crawls-grown corn; and during this time the family – though staunch Catholics – held on to their estates through all the vicissitudes of civil war and religious upheaval. By the end of the 18th century, however, the charity had become so widely known that flocks of vagrants came annually to Tichborne Park, and in 1794 the local magistrates prevailed upon Sir Henry (who should have known better, since he already had seven sons) to suppress it.

Almost at once, the Tichbornes began to pay the penalty – with interest. Sir Henry himself was imprisoned by Napoleon for eleven years, and during his absence part of the house collapsed, the remainder being demolished. Five of his sons, moreover, died young or without male issue – though the eldest, true to the prophecy, produced seven daughters: while Edward, the next heir, was first persuaded by a much-needed legacy to change his name from Tichborne to Doughty, and then lost his own only son in infancy.

In 1835, therefore, Edward capitulated to Lady Mabella and restored the dole – but too late to avoid the final stroke of vengeance. For Roger, his eldest nephew and heir, born under the curse, was drowned at sea in 1859: and yet more disastrously, was subsequently impersonated by an Australian who laid claim to the family estates. This gave rise to seven years of very public controversy, including the longest civil action and the most protracted criminal case on record: and by the time the Tichborne Claimant was finally unmasked in 1874, the rightful heirs – descended from a child born after the lifting of the curse – had been forced to spend more than £100,000 on defending their heritage.

Not surprisingly, then, the dole has never again been allowed to lapse – though in 1948 it very nearly fell victim to 'Austerity' bread-rationing rules: but a public outcry resulted (during which Sir Anthony Tichborne was offered gifts of over 5000 private bread coupons) and eventually the Ministry gave way. Currently, however, one-and-a-half tons of flour (still made from wheat grown on Lady Mabella's Crawls) is distributed instead of loaves; and every adult parishioner of Tichborne and Cheriton is entitled to a gallon apiece, while children receive a half-gallon, the maximum dole being four gallons a household. As Lady Mabella directed, this is still dispersed from the steps of Tichborne House on Lady Day (25 March), after a blessing by a Catholic priest and prayers for the heroic foundress's soul.

· Tin Can Band ·
Broughton, Northamptonshire: second Sunday in December

Having gathered at midnight outside St Andrew's parish church, a large crowd of young men and boys march about the village for about an hour, banging on dustbin lids, watering cans and other metal 'instruments', and generally producing as loud a cacophony as possible.

This noisy custom (which has survived several moves to suppress it) is said locally to have begun either as an attempt to frighten away the gypsies who used to camp nearby, or to shame a gypsy girl who had given birth to an illegitimate baby – which is likely enough, since communities all over England once used similar 'rough music' parades to advertise their disapproval of adulterers, wife-beaters and other erring or unpopular people. Yet the timing of the celebration – on the night before the village feast and thus around Old ST ANDREW'S DAY

– also suggests a survival of the old Northamptonshire custom of 'Tandering', whereby the patron saint of the many local lace makers (and of Broughton church) was honoured with MUMMING, 'masquerading processions' and the drinking of hot elderberry wine 'to a riotous extent'.

· Tolling the Devil's Knell ·
All Saints' church, Dewsbury, West Yorkshire: 24 December

Many churches ring their BELLS on CHRISTMAS EVE, and not a few still toll 'PASSING BELLS' to indicate the age and sex of a dead parishioner: but All Saints', Dewsbury, is the only church 'whose Christmas bells, ring the Devil's knell'. Beginning at about 10 p.m., the tenor bell sounds as many strokes as there are years since Christ's Nativity, the last timed exactly to coincide with the first chime of midnight, when Jesus was born and Satan died. (Formerly the tolling started after midnight, and was preceded by five times five rings to identify the deceased – four fours being the announcement of a man's death and three threes of a woman's.) Each year, unfortunately, the Devil bounces back, and another stroke must be added to his knell: if this is not done, some say he will be free to trouble the parish in the succeeding twelve months.

The custom's origin is unrecorded: but it certainly dates from well before 1828, when it was revived 'after a lapse of some years'. Local opinion, indeed, makes it as old as the tenor bell (now recast) on which it is rung. Known as 'Black Tom of Soothill', this was traditionally given in medieval times by a prominent local landowner named Sir Thomas Southill – perhaps the historical personage who died in 1535 – to expiate the murder of a boy he threw into a smith's furnace (or, alternatively, a dam). It is possible, therefore, that he also instituted the knell, as an annual reminder of his crime.

Eighteenth-century ringers prepare for **Tolling the Devil's Knell**: from a chap-book.

· Tossing the Caber ·
see HIGHLAND GAMES

· Tower of London ·

Castle and palace, treasury, armoury and prison, the Tower of London was begun during the reign of William the Conqueror, and the most famous of its customs perhaps originated not much later. This is the Ceremony of the Keys, intended both to secure the fortress against surprise attack and to prevent the escape of its often illustrious prisoners. Shortly before 10 p.m. on every night of the year, the Chief Yeoman Warder proceeds to the Tower's outermost gate, escorted by four dress-uniformed soldiers of the Tower Guard: one of them carries a lantern, but their principal purpose is to protect the Keys from seizure by lurking enemies of the state. While they present arms in salute, the warder then locks in succession the three gates controlling the causeway over the moat. Before he can enter the fortress proper, however, he is challenged by the sentry at the Bloody Tower arch:

> 'Who goes there?'
> 'The Keys'
> 'Whose Keys?'
> 'Queen Elizabeth's Keys'
> 'Pass, Queen Elizabeth's Keys.'

The party now march into the courtyard, where the Keys are saluted by the Main Guard, drawn up on the

'God Preserve Queen Elizabeth!': the chief Yeoman Warder concludes the nightly Ceremony of the Keys at the Tower of London.

Jewel House steps: then, as the bugler sounds the Last Post and the clock strikes ten, the warder cries 'God Preserve Queen Elizabeth', to which the guard reply 'Amen'. Finally, the Keys are taken to the Governor's House for overnight custody. Admission to this ceremony must be arranged well in advance.

The Tower's celebrated Yeoman Warders (who except in the presence of royalty, normally wear blue undress uniform) regularly appear in their scarlet Tudor splendour three times a year: when, led by the Chief Warder with his ceremonial mace and the Yeoman Gaoler with his formidable axe, they escort their governor to CHRISTMAS, EASTER and WHITSUN services at the Tower's chapel of St Peter-ad-Vincula. They also wear 'state dress' on ASCENSION DAY every third year (e.g. in 1984), to accompany the choirboys and other children who then perform a BEATING OF THE BOUNDS ceremony of the Tower's former 'Liberty', or administrative jurisdiction outside its walls. At each of the thirty-one boundary stones, the chaplain declaims 'Cursed is he that removeth his neighbour's landmark', and the children obey the order to 'Whack it, boys, whack it!' with their willow wands.

Other public events at the Tower include CHANGING THE GUARD: and the firing of ROYAL SALUTES, not only on the usual occasions but also to honour visiting heads of state, whose forty-one gun salutes begin – by radio co-ordination – as they step onto the platform of Victoria station. Many of its observances are, however, private, including the Ceremony of the Lilies and Roses on the anniversary of Henry VI's murder on 21 May 1471: these emblematic flowers are then laid at the traditional scene of the crime – in the oratory of the Wakefield Tower – by representatives of Henry's two foundations, Eton and King's College, Cambridge.

· Travice Dole ·
see GRAVESIDE DOLES

· Trooping the Colour ·
Horse Guards' Parade, London: 11 a.m. on a Saturday (normally the second Saturday) in June

In the days (ending with the Crimean War) when British regiments still followed their flags into battle, and rallied round them if the fighting grew desperate, it was essential for soldiers to recognize the 'Colours' of their own unit. Thus originated the practice of 'Trooping the Colour', once done to display it to new recruits, but since 1805 carried on ceremonially to celebrate the sovereign's 'official birthday' – which is fixed at a Saturday in early June, in the hope of good weather. All seven regiments of the Household Division take part, but only one Colour is trooped each year, being provided in turn by one of the five regiments – Grenadiers, Coldstreamers, Scots, Irish and Welsh – of Foot Guards. What results is easily the most impressive of all regular ROYAL CEREMONIES.

The Grenadier Guards march past the young Queen Elizabeth II during the 1956 **Trooping the Colour** ceremony.

Wearing the uniform of the appropriate regiment, the Queen leaves Buckingham Palace and rides down the Mall, accompanied by a sovereign's escort from the two Household Cavalry units – the Life Guards and the Blues and Royals – with their gold-coated mounted band. Arriving at the Horse Guards' Parade shortly before 11 a.m., she finds drawn up there some 500 guardsmen, whom she proceeds to inspect. She then moves to the Archway, where she will remain motionless on her horse for the next hour and a half.

Now the 360-strong massed bands of the Foot Guards perform, marching and countermarching in slow and then in quick time, all without misplacing a note or a step. Next, as they play the relevant regimental slow march, the Colour is trooped by being carried along the motionless ranks of guardsmen, a process which ends exactly on the stroke of 11.30 a.m. This done, the Colour party leads the guards (now formed into eight units) past Her Majesty and round the four

sides of the Parade, first at a slow and then a quick march. And finally the Household Cavalry follow suit, at a walk and then a trot, while their own band plays.

But the spectacle is not yet over. Riding now at the head of her Foot Guards, the Queen returns down the Mall to Buckingham Palace, where she takes the salute not only of all the Household units which attended her birthday parade, but also of the Royal Horse Artillery who (at 11 a.m.) have fired a ROYAL SALUTE in Hyde Park. Then (after a private ceremony in the inner courtyard, where carrots are presented on silver salvers to the escort horses) the royal family appears on the palace balcony, there to acknowledge the RAF's 1 p.m. fly-past and greet the cheering crowds.

Tickets for Trooping the Colour (allotted strictly by ballot, and by the Brigade Major H.Q. Household Division) are few in number, and much in demand. But a good view of the procession along the Mall can be obtained by anyone who arrives there sufficiently early.

· Turning the Devil's Stone ·
Shebbear, near Holsworthy, Devon: 5 November

During the evening of 5 November each year, the ringers of Shebbear in north Devon sound a discordant jangle on the bells of St Michael's church: then, arming themselves with ropes and crowbars, they laboriously turn over a massive boulder which lies outside the eastern gate of the churchyard. If this is not done, they believe, some calamity will overtake Shebbear in the coming year: and when the ceremony was omitted on one occasion during the First World War, the following twelve months brought misfortune both to the village and its surrounding farms.

How and when this observance began are unknown, but it clearly has nothing to do with GUY FAWKES NIGHT: and it may originally have been performed a few days earlier – at HALLOWEEN, when the forces of evil are strongest. For the stone is said to belong to the Devil himself, and the jangling bells are designed to frighten him off before his power is defied by the turning. Some declare that he dropped it (or threw it at the church) when he was cast out of Heaven by St Michael (*see* FURRY DANCE) and others that he lies beneath it: while an alternative legend asserts that it was first quarried as the foundation stone of a church at nearby Henscott, but was persistently moved by supernatural means to Shebbear whenever the builders tried to use it.

Certainly the boulder – a lump of quartz conglomerate six feet long and four feet wide, weighing almost a ton – is not geologically native to Shebbear, nor indeed to anywhere else in south-western England: neither can it have been deposited by a retreating glacier, since the glacial ice did not penetrate so far south. At one time it

By **Turning the Devil's Stone**, the parishioners of Shebbear defy Satan's power and preserve their village from misfortune for another year.

was probably used as the 'moot' (or meeting) stone of the Anglo-Saxon administrative 'Hundred' centred on Shebbear: but the stories surrounding it, and its position due east of the church, beneath an ancient oak, suggest strongly that it also figured in some pagan ritual. It was possibly in an attempt to neutralize the boulder's power, therefore, that the early Christians of Shebbear decided to raise their church nearby, and to dedicate the building to St Michael the Archangel, mightiest of all the Devil's opponents and the usual patron of churches on pagan sites. If so, they seem not to have been entirely successful, for the Exeter Bishops' registers record that in 1454 the church was 'burnt by a fire from Hell': perhaps the stone had not been turned that year.

· Tweedmouth Feast ·
see FEASTS, REVELS AND WAKES

· Twelfth Night ·
5-6 January

The Twelfth Night (5 January) and Twelfth Day (6 January) after CHRISTMAS – called in Scotland 'Uphalie-day', the 'ending of the holy days' (*see* UP-HELLY-AA) – mark the conclusion of the traditional Christmas season. Their celebrations, a last fling before the return to workaday life on PLOUGH MONDAY, were once almost as enthusiastic as those of Christmas itself. After the 1752 calendar change had 'lost' twelve days of the year, moreover, conservative rural folk long persisted in keeping this season as 'the real Christmas': and ancient Christmas customs like the MARI LWYD; MUMMING PLAYS; SWORD DANCING and WASSAILING still centre upon it.

Twelfth Night proper, however, was a time for indoor revelry, games of forfeit, 'disguisings' and plays – like Shakespeare's eponymous comedy, probably written for a court celebration in 1601: all this being presided over by a 'Lord of Misrule' or 'King of the Bean', the guest served (theoretically by chance) with the slice of Twelfth Cake containing a bean, coin or other concealed 'charm'. This custom began its decline in the 18th century, when the lucky charms migrated into Christmas puddings: but the Twelfth Cake itself, growing ever larger and more elaborately iced, continued popular until late Victorian times – after which its descendants diminished into Christmas cakes. One of very few still to appear on the traditional date is the famous Baddeley Cake. Endowed by the will of Robert Baddeley, a pastry-cook turned actor who 'died in harness' in 1794, this Twelfth Cake has since then been annually served to the company performing at London's Theatre Royal, Drury Lane on 6 January.

Though secular Twelfth Night festivities have faded almost to vanishing point, 6 January has retained its ancient religious significance. For it is also the Feast of the Epiphany (Greek: *epiphaneia* – manifestation)

Laurence Harvey, heading the cast of *Camelot*, cuts the traditional **Twelfth Night** 'Baddeley Cake' at the Theatre Royal, Drury Lane.

which commemorates the manifestation of the infant Christ to the Three Kings and hence, by extension, to the whole non-Jewish world. Observed by the early church even before the institution of Christmas and long regarded (as it still is by Eastern Orthodox communities) as the more important festival, Epiphany continues to be widely celebrated with special services, sometimes including gift-bearing processions representing the journey of the Magi. (*See* EPIPHANY GIFTS CEREMONY)

· Twopenny Starvers ·
see BREAD AND BUN DOLES

· Tynwald Ceremony ·
Tynwald Hill, St Johns, Isle of Man: 5 July, or if 5 July falls on Saturday or Sunday, the Monday following

Exactly half-way between St Bees Head in Cumbria and Strangford Lough in northern Ireland, and a mere sixteen miles from Burrow Head in Scots Galloway, the Isle of Man has been ruled in turn by Norwegian Vikings from Ireland (*c.*900-1266); by the Kings of Scotland (1266-1333); by a series of English baronial families, notably the Stanley Earls of Derby; and, since 1765, by the British Crown. Throughout the centuries, however, it has always contrived to maintain some degree of independence from its greater neighbours: and it continues to make its own laws, levy its own taxes, and control its own internal expenditure, all via the ancient institution called 'Tynwald'.

With its upper and lower Houses – the Legislative Council and the 'House of Keys' – under the Queen's Lieutenant-Governor, Tynwald now functions in much the same way as the Westminster PARLIAMENT, making laws and submitting them to the monarch for the royal assent: and its business is done during normal sessions at Douglas, the capital of Man. Originally, however, Tynwald was a great open-air assembly of all the freemen of the island, held once a year to hear the laws recited and to apply them to the settlement of the various disputes and blood feuds which had arisen in Man's six 'sheadings' (Old Norse: *settungr*, 'sixings') – the ancient territorial divisions which each had to provide a fully-equipped warship for the use of the Kings of Man. Its name is derived from the Norwegian *Thingvollr*, the field of the 'Thing' or assembly: and though the precise date of its origin is unknown, there is no doubt that it began during the period of Viking occupation, most probably during the reign of King Godfred Crovan – popularly known as 'King Orry' – the Norse adventurer who fought beside Harold Hardrada at Stamford Bridge before becoming the first independent ruler of Man in 1079. At that time 'Things' were both the usual means of preserving the peace and the great social events of the year throughout all the Scandinavian lands – the Sagas, for instance, are full of the doings at the Icelandic 'Allthing' at Thingvellir – and this extraordinarily democratic method of 'government' was doubtless the only one acceptable to Orry's independently minded followers.

Once a year, moreover, the Manx Tynwald reverts to its original form: or rather to the form of the earliest recorded ceremony in 1417, by which time much of the free-speech element beloved of the Vikings had already been feudalized away. The ceremony, nevertheless, still takes place at the old Norse 'field of assembly' at St Johns, near the centre of the island and not far from the boundary between its major 'Northside' and 'Southside' divisions. There stands the ancient circular Tynwald Hill, twelve feet high and terraced round with four concentric steps or platforms. According to an unproven but plausible tradition, it is said to have been constructed with soil brought from all sixteen of the island's parishes, thus rendering it both 'no man's land' and 'every man's land': and certainly it was raised over a prehistoric burial mound, so that it was perhaps a place of Celtic gatherings even before the Norsemen came. The MIDSUMMER date of the assembly – which since the 1752 calendar change has been held on or about 5 July, Old Midsummer Day – and the great fair which used to accompany it are also alleged to point to a pagan Celtic ancestry: but in fact most Scandinavian Things were

Ranged round the ancient step-mound on the old Norse 'field of assembly', **Tynwald** listens while the Chief Coroner demands peace and order during the reading of the year's Manx laws.

accompanied by much trading and held on the Midsummer date later called St John's Day – whence the dedication of the nearby St John's Chapel.

From this chapel, after a short service, the Queen's Lieutenant-Governor leads the Tynwald's procession to the hill. Before him is borne the medieval Sword of State, emblazoned with the island's famous badge of three conjoined legs in armour, which is apparently based on a symbol used by the Norse Kings of Dublin and which illustrates the Manx motto, 'Whichever way you throw it, it will stand': and his path from chapel to mound is strewn with green rushes, more probably a relic of St John's Day RUSHBEARINGS than 'a survival of offerings to the sea-god Manannan'. When he reaches the hill, the Queen's representative assumes the eastward-facing seat of the Norse Kings on its uppermost platform, and beside him sits the Bishop of Sodor and Man, thus exercising his right both as the last survivor of the Manx 'barons' and as the successor of Odin's chief priest: while around them stand the members of the Legislative Council, including Man's two 'Deemsters' or judges. Once known as 'Lawmen', these are the longest-established and historically the most important of Tynwald's officials, whose duty is not only to pronounce 'doom' or judgment but also to make the laws known to King and people: until 1422, moreover, Manx laws were oral 'breast-laws' rather than written 'book-laws', and the Deemsters were therefore required to know them all by heart.

On the next platform down stand the members of the 'House of Keys': whose title is an Anglicization of the Manx *Kiare-as-feed* ('Four and twenty') and whose number has remained constant since the Norse period when sixteen of them represented Man and the remaining eight came from the long-lost Manx dominions in the 'Out Isles' or Hebrides. Nowadays all twenty-four are elected by Manx constituencies, but formerly 'the Keys' were a self-perpetuating council of powerful landowners, whose task was to assist the Deemsters with the remembrance and interpretation of the laws. Then the vicars of the island parishes, the parish 'captains' nominally responsible for local defence, and other minor officials take up position on the lowest steps of the hill; the 'commons' range themselves round about it; and 'the holding of Tynwald' is ready to begin.

Before this can be done, however, the assembly must be 'fenced' by the Chief Coroner, who is also the Coroner of Glenfaba sheading in which Tynwald Hill stands: repeating an ancient formula, he orders that none present shall 'quarrel, brawl or make disturbance' while Tynwald is in session – a very necessary prohibition when rival parties to blood feuds came there for judgment, and had to be deterred from taking matters into their own hands by threats of hanging, drawing and quartering if they did so. This done, the real business of the day proceeds with the reading out (in Manx and English) of summaries of all the laws passed on the island since the last assembly. Before 1866, the full text of all enactments was repeated in both languages, and until about 1914 no law was considered effective until it had received the approval of the whole gathering: which was (and is still) signified by three rousing cheers for the monarch of Great Britain at the end of the reading. Even now, moreover, the Lieutenant-Governor must wait for this shout of public assent before signing the new laws: and thus is maintained at least the spirit of the Norse assemblies which began on Tynwald Hill nearly a thousand years ago.

U

· Up-Helly-Aa ·
Lerwick, Shetland: last Tuesday in January

Very much nearer to Norway than to Edinburgh, the Shetlands are the northernmost of the British Isles, and the latest to become British: for until 1469 they remained subject to the Danish crown. Indeed, many Scandinavian customs still persist there, including the month-long celebration of Yule (a very necessary antidote to the cold, dark, northern winter). This continues until twenty-four days after CHRISTMAS, Old Style, when the Shetland capital of Lerwick marks 'Up-Helly-Aa' (the ending of the holy days) with one of the most spectacular of all fire festivals.

The Burning of the Ship and Torchlight Procession, its principal attractions, are nevertheless of comparatively recent origin. Formerly, Lerwick held a BURNING THE OLD YEAR OUT ceremony with sledges of blazing tar barrels, dragged through its streets by hornblowing gangs of fantastically dressed 'guizers'. Like many other 'rowdy' customs throughout Britain, this was officially suppressed in late-Victorian times. But the guizers were not to be thwarted: and having organized themselves more formally, they introduced first the procession and then, in 1889, a thirty-foot Viking longship to lead it.

Preparations begin months in advance, under the overall direction of an elected 'Guizer Jarl'. Dragon-prowed and hung with shields, the elaborate ship is built entirely by voluntary labour, with materials purchased from donations. Meanwhile the 500 or more guizers, splitting into ten-man squads, are secretly devising their respective costumes and 'acts': except to the Jarl, the nature of these must not be divulged until the great day.

Since 1931, this has begun with the posting at the Mercat Cross of the ten-foot high 'Bill' or 'Guizer Jarl's proclamation' – a satirical review of the year's local events, not lacking in personal references. Next, at 10 a.m., the Jarl and his own team of guizers, all in full Viking costume, escort the wheel-mounted ship to the seafront, where it remains on display until, at 6.45 p.m., it is dragged to the starting point of the procession. Soon afterwards, the Jarl takes his stand at its helm, his Viking bodyguard about him: and behind it range two long columns of multifariously clad guizers, each bearing a five-foot blazing torch. Then, to the music of

The Guizer Jarl's Viking ship, soon to go up in flames, is an appropriate centrepiece for the Norse Shetlands' great midwinter festival of **Up-helly-aa**.

pipe and brass bands and the singing of the Up-Helly-Aa song, the procession moves off.

When it reaches the burning site near the town centre, the torchbearers form a great circle about the ship, which the Vikings now desert: at a bugle call, all the brands are flung onto it at once and, while the guizers raise 'The Norseman's Home', it blazes swiftly to its fiery end.

For the guizers, however, the night's celebrations are only just beginning: each of the fifty or so squads considers it a point of honour to visit, in rotation, every one of Lerwick's thirteen halls – there to play their 'acts', dance, and take copious refreshment. Few, therefore, reach home before the appearance of the late Shetland dawn.

· Uppies and Doonies ·

see JEDBURGH BA' GAMES; SHROVETIDE FOOTBALL

V

· Valentine's Day ·
14 February

The origins of this famous lovers' festival are entirely obscure. Apart from sharing their feast day, it has no connection whatever with the two shadowy (if not completely fictitious) martyrs called Saint Valentine: and there is no real evidence to link it with the Roman fertility rites of Lupercalia, which fell at about the same season. Its source, rather, may have been the medieval legend (itself of uncertain derivation) that birds meet on 14 February to choose mates for the coming spring. Certainly the earliest known 'valentines' are poems (like Chaucer's 'Parliament of Fowls') on this theme, composed for the Valentine's Day festivals of 'joyous recreation and conversation about love' held at the courts of late-14th-century England and France.

There, probably, also began the custom of drawing lots for valentines: an excellent method of overcoming shyness which was enthusiastically carried on all over Britain until very recently, and may still continue in a few places. Usually, girls' names were written on slips of paper and drawn by boys, but often each girl also drew a boy's name, so that everyone had a pair of valentines to choose between. Alternatively, names were picked out in couples: and on the Scottish Borders slips were drawn thrice and returned after the first two occasions, a name drawn three times in succession being 'infallibly that of a future spouse'. Whatever the version, 'these little sports often ended in love' – if this did not already exist, for such lotteries could easily be 'fixed' in advance.

So, too, can the apparently much more risky and haphazard custom of taking as a valentine the first person of the opposite sex (excluding your own family) seen on 14 February. Mrs Pepys, for instance, shaded her eyes all the festival morning in 1662, 'that she might not see the paynters … gilding [the] chimney-piece', until Will Bowyer came to be her valentine: and children still have themselves led about with tight-shut eyes until the 'right' valentine is at hand.

Whether the valentine be selected by lot, chance, or deliberate decision, it was (and is again becoming) customary to present them with a gift. In the past, this might range from the opulent jewellery showered on royal mistresses, via the conventional gloves or (more daringly) garters, to the ploughboy's love-knot of plaited straw: while purple-wrapped chocolate hearts and pink fluffy teddy bears are much favoured currently. Until recently, moreover, East Anglian children expected presents of sweets or pennies from *all* the adult 'valentines' they could 'catch' by repeating (before they themselves could be spoken to) some such rhyme as:

> Good morning to you, Valentine
> Curl your locks as I do mine
> Two in front and two behind
> Good morning to you, Valentine.

By the mid-18th century, however, costly valentine gifts were being replaced by elaborate versions of the written love messages customary since the festival's beginnings. Ideally, these should be poetic compositions by the sender in person: but as early as 1669 a published *Valentine Writer* was available to the unimaginative, who could also employ formulae like the modern:

> Postie, postie, dinna fa' [fail]
> If Pam's no' in, gi' it ţae her Ma
> *Kincardineshire, 1960s*

or

> Wayne is ace
> Wayne is cool
> Wayne and Shaz will always rule.
> *York, 1983*

While the artistic frequently exercised their talents for painting, lace edging and other kinds of embellishment: and the malicious misused the custom by despatching 'humorous' greetings, often really and intentionally cruel, to the ill-favoured, deformed or long-unmarried. In this they were protected by the firm convention (partly intended to increase the receiver's excitement and, partly, perhaps, to foil inquisitive and disapproving parents) that valentines must be sent anonymously.

Commercially printed valentine cards (already being produced in tens of thousands well before the appearance of the CHRISTMAS card in 1846) rapidly superseded such home-made offerings: and reached their zenith of popularity during the 1870s and 80s. By then, the sentimental type was featuring birds made with real feathers, posies of dried flowers and spun-glass hearts, all trimmed with ribbon and gold lace: while the 'vulgar' sort – which specialized in figures with removable hair, teeth and even legs – had grown coarser than ever. Perhaps because of a general improvement in taste, valentine-sending markedly decreased towards the end of Victoria's reign, and was reported to be 'dying out' by the 1920s: but since the Second World War it has again become increasingly general, 'naughty' or 'daring' cards being much in vogue. The latest in the long succession of Valentine's Day fashions, however, is that of addressing painful intimacies to curiously nicknamed lovers via the advertisement columns of newspapers.

· Verderers' Courts ·
see FOREST CUSTOMS

· Virgins' Crowns ·
see FUNERALS

W

· Wakes ·
see FEASTS, REVELS AND WAKES; FUNERALS

· Walking Days ·
see FEASTS, REVELS AND WAKES

· Wassailing ·
24 December-6 January

Now kept up only in a very few places (such as Grampound in Cornwall) this ancient and cheerful CHRISTMAS practice was once widespread throughout Britain. *Waes Heil*, the favourite Anglo-Saxon toast, translates literally as 'be whole', 'be healthy' (more freely 'Here's to you', or even 'Cheers!') and the essence of the custom is the drinking of mutual healths from a large communal 'wassail bowl', usually turned from ash or maple and often richly decorated with ribbons. This can be passed round a private party: but it was more frequently borne from house to house by 'wassailers' who filled it (or expected it to *be* filled) with some such heady concoction as 'Lamb's Wool' – hot ale, nutmeg and sugar, with toast and roasted crab-apples.

They might come on Christmas Eve, NEW YEAR'S EVE or TWELFTH NIGHT, according to local custom: but, like other Yuletide 'processioners' (*see* HOODEN HORSE; MARI LWYD; MUMMING PLAYS; SWORD DANCING) they invariably announced their presence with a 'letting-in song':

> Here we come a-wassailing
> Among the leaves so green
> Here we come a-wassailing
> So fair to be seen
> *Yorkshire*

Be here any maids? I suppose there be some
Sure they will not let young men stand on the
　cold stone
Sing hey all you maids, come draw back the pin
For to let we jolly wassailers in.
> *Gloucestershire*

The wassailing proper then took place:

> Good master and mistress, here's a health
> 　to you we give
> And sing jolly wassail as long as we live
> And if we do live, 'til another New Year
> Then perhaps we may call, and see who
> 　do live here
> *Gower, South Wales*

and since the singers were usually the 'poor folk of the parish', they rarely failed to ask (or get) a reward of food or drink:

> Come butler come bring us a bowl of the best
> I hope your soul in Heaven do rest
> But if you do bring us a bowl of the small
> Then down fall butler, bowl and all
> *Gloucestershire*

or money:

> Now neighbours and strangers we always do find
> And hope we shall be courteous, obliging and kind
> And hope your civility to us will be proved
> As a piece of small silver in token of love.
> *Grampound, Cornwall*

· Wassailing the Apple Trees ·
Carhampton, Somerset: 17 January;
Henfield, West Sussex: 6 January

Until quite recently the healths of farm animals, beehives and even field crops as well as of humans, were ceremonially drunk during the WASSAILING in the CHRISTMAS season. So too, in the cider-making regions of southern and western England, were those of apple orchards: and a few such rituals still continue in Somerset and Devon, notably at Carhampton near Minehead. There, on TWELFTH NIGHT, Old Style, was-sailers gather round a big old tree chosen to represent its fellows, and sing:

> Old apple tree, we wassail thee, and hoping thou
> 　wilt bear
> For the Lord doth know where we shall be, till
> 　apples come another year
> To bear well and bloom well so merry let us be
> Let every man take off his hat and shout to the old
> 　apple tree
> Old apple tree, we wassail thee, and hoping thou
> 　wilt bear
> Hat-fulls, cap-fulls, three-bushel bagfulls
> And a little heap under the stairs
> Hip! Hip! Hooray!

Shotguns are then fired through its branches ('to scare off evil spirits') and the tree's health is drunk in warm cider afloat with toast, passed round in a bucket: some of this is also poured over its roots, and cider-soaked toast left on its boughs – ostensibly for the birds, but perhaps originally for some guardian godling.

A very similar custom – known as 'Apple Howling' (from 'Yuling'?) and performed on 'new' Twelfth Night – has been revived at Gill Orchard, Henfield, West Sussex. But here, following local tradition, the ceremonies also include the blowing of horns; the thrashing of the tree 'to make him bear'; a different incantation:

> Stand fast root, bear well top
> God send us a good howling crop
> Every twig, apples big! Every bough, apples enow!

and a final cacophonous howling, 'to wake him up'.

· Wayfarers' Doles ·
St Cross Hospital, Winchester, Hampshire: every weekday

During the Middle Ages, the provision of 'wayfarers' doles' – food and sometimes accommodation for pilgrims and other needy travellers – was largely the responsibility of the Church, and particularly of the monasteries. When these last were swept away by the Reformation, therefore, impoverished wayfarers suffered accordingly, and a number of CHARITIES were established to assist them. Like Richard Watt's still-active foundation at Rochester in Kent – endowed in 1579 to give shelter to 'six poor travellers, not being rogues or proctors' (professional beggars) – most of these were nevertheless careful to limit the scope of their relief: and (lest wandering paupers become a charge on the parish) to stipulate that it could be given on one occasion only.

One medieval establishment, however, continues – at least symbolically – to dispense charity to all comers. This is the Hospital of St Cross at Winchester: founded in 1136 by the great Bishop Henry de Blois, the hospital still supports the thirteen poor men ordained by its original charter, who wear on their black gowns the silver cross of the Knights Hospitallers: as well as a smaller number of Brothers in red gowns with the badge of the Cardinal's Hat, members of the 'Order of Noble Poverty' which Cardinal Henry Beaufort attached to the foundation in 1446. In addition, St Cross for many centuries provided a substantial daily meal for no less than a hundred paupers – who each received three pounds of bread, a bowl of soup, a 'mess' of fish, cheese or eggs and three quarts of small beer, and were allowed to carry home what they could not eat: fifty 'out-pensioners' are now maintained instead. And throughout its long and chequered history (which incidentally included the Victorian scandal that inspired Trollope's 'Barchester' novel, *The Warden*) it has also furnished a daily dole to travellers.

On every weekday of the year, two large loaves and two gallons of beer are divided into thirty-two small portions: the bread being served on a wooden platter and the drink in an ancient horn cup bearing the hospital's silver cross. A share is then given, without question or condition, to the first thirty-two applicants who knock at the porter's lodge and request their wayfarers' dole.

Wearing the silver badge of the Knights Hospitallers, a Brother of Winchester's ancient St Cross Hospital dispenses the centuries-old **Wayfarers' Dole** of bread and beer to two Edwardian travellers.

· Weddings ·

'Marriage', proverbially, 'is a lottery'; and even in these days of experimental 'living together' and easy divorce, it remains the greatest gamble most people ever take. So it is scarcely surprising that weddings are still compassed about with a host of customs, rituals and superstitions: their meaning may be largely forgotten, but the luck their observance brings cannot be dispensed with.

Unless you believe that:

> To change the name and not the letter
> Is change for worse and not for better

surviving custom admittedly provides scant guidance in choosing a partner. But once the decision to wed has been taken, prudent couples will begin by consulting the traditional rules for fixing the date. Several of these are rooted in the Church's former ban on sexual relations during certain penitential seasons, so that:

> Advent marriage doth deny
> But Hilary [13 Jan] gives thee liberty
> Septuagesima says thee nay
> Eight days after Easter says you may
> Rogation bids thee to contain
> 'Til Trinity sets thee free again

and many still hold that those who:

> Marry in Lent
> Live to repent

(*see* ADVENT; ROGATION DAY; LENT). Others (following ancient pagan custom) hold May an unlucky month — especially now that no tax advantages accrue from marrying then. June weddings should be fortunate, but delay until the busy time of haytime and harvest is perilous, for

> They that wive
> 'Twixt sickle and scythe
> Shall never thrive.

The safest season to marry, indeed, is between HARVEST and CHRISTMAS — when supplies for wedding feasts were once most plentiful.

> Marry in September's shine
> Your living will be rich and fine
> If in October you do marry
> Love will come but riches tarry
> If you wed in bleak November
> Only joy will come, remember
> When December's showers fall fast
> Marry and true love will last.

Even then, however, care must be taken with the phase of the moon (which should be waxing, or full) and the day of the week — Sunday, of course, being out of the question:

> Monday for wealth
> Tuesday for health
> Wednesday the best day of all
> Thursday for crosses
> Friday for losses
> Saturday, no luck at all.

If the wedding is to be in church, the next hurdle is the calling of the banns on the three Sundays beforehand — in many parts of Britain, it is thought most unlucky for the couple to be present. Neither must the bride allow her married name to be used, even jokingly, before the marriage, or this may never take place.

By now the wedding dress will be well under way, though the bride must not make it herself, nor try it on complete before the ceremony — a stitch is usually added at the last moment, and only then must the veil be put on. Often this is an heirloom, the 'something old' traditionally worn with

> …something new
> Something borrowed, something blue
> And a sixpence in your shoe.

Today, virginal white 'gowns' are almost universal, though these are considered unsuitable for divorcees or widows (who used sometimes to marry in only their undershifts or 'smocks', thus symbolically repudiating former husbands' debts). Some thrifty brides, moreover, prefer the older tradition of a wedding dress they can subsequently 'wear for best': but if so, they must carefully consider its colour.

> Marry in white, you have chosen right
> Marry in green, ashamed to be seen
> Marry in grey, you'll go far away
> Marry in brown, never live in a town
> Marry in blue, love ever true
> Marry in red, wish yourself dead
> Marry in yellow, ashamed of your fellow
> Marry in black, wish yourself back
> Marry in pink, of you he'll aye think
> [or more ominously, Your fortunes will sink].

It is not clear whether these warnings also apply to the dresses of bridesmaids, but no girl who hopes for marriage should fill that role more than twice.

Next, the pitfalls of the day itself must be avoided. The bride should not, of course, see the groom before she meets him in church, nor look back on her way there: while encounters with funerals, mourning women or open graves are all downright catastrophic. Sweeps, however, are extremely lucky, as are grey or white horses — hence those used for royal wedding coaches and, by extension, the white cars provided by some taxi firms.

Having arrived safely (but traditionally a little late) the bride should avoid stumbling when walking up the aisle: nor should the groom turn to watch her, though his best man may do so. In more exciting times, it was the best man's duty to guard against rivals' last-minute attempts to kidnap her or, conversely, to help the groom snatch her from her unwilling parents – practices still occasionally recalled by the young men's running races at weddings in northern Britain. Now the best man guards only the ring, which is traditionally plain gold and invariably worn on the third finger of the left hand, whence a vein was once supposed to flow direct to the heart: to drop it in church is a dire omen, and it must never afterwards be mislaid or tried on by another.

The ceremony over, the newly-weds are greeted by pealing BELLS – to scare off evil spirits – and sometimes pass into marriage through an arch of appropriate objects (swords for servicemen, pitchforks for farmers or, not unusually, bedpans for nurses) held aloft by a guard of honour. Confetti is now thrown over them, though the litter-conscious prefer more traditional fertility symbols like rice or grain: and at Knutsford in Cheshire their path may be decorated with lucky sand patterns (*see* MAY DAY). In parts of Wales, north-eastern and south-western England, however, the churchyard gates will be tied against them, to be opened only after the village children have been bribed with a shower of coins.

The far greater expense of the subsequent wedding reception is conventionally borne by the bride's father, a memory of the dowry or MARRIAGE PORTION he once paid the groom's family. Its centrepiece, the lucky white-iced wedding cake, should be cut by bride and groom together, as their first joint task in life. A more difficult one may be concealing the honeymoon destination, once designed to foil the irate parents of runaways but now to baulk pranksters, from whom the going-away car also needs protection – the boots and shoes traditionally attached to it are lucky, but I once had to remove a litter of piglets from a farming couple's vehicle. Modern newly-weds, however, are at least spared the old ceremony of being 'bedded-down' by the entire wedding party.

Only one danger now remains, the cantankerous spirits of the threshold: to avoid them, the groom must carry his bride into their new home. Thereafter, it is to be hoped, the couple will qualify for the DUNMOW FLITCH, and go on to celebrate their twenty-fifth (Silver); fiftieth (Gold) and sixtieth (Diamond) wedding anniversaries.

· Weighing the Mayor ·
The Guildhall, High Wycombe, Buckinghamshire: an evening in late May

Though the jocular custom of 'Weighing the Mayor' is sometimes alleged to have stemmed from a pointed remark made by Queen Elizabeth I about the corpulence

This smiling Mayor of High Wycombe evidently believes she has lost some bulk since the previous **Weighing the Mayor** ceremony.

of High Wycombe's civic dignitaries, its recorded history dates back no further than late-Victorian times. Since then, the town's incoming and outgoing mayors have been publicly weighed – by means of a curious tripod-mounted chair – on the evening of election day: and so too (if they wish it) are the new and old lady mayoresses, with any other councillors or corporation officials who care to participate.

Their weights are recorded by the Chief Inspector of Weights and Measures, and called out by the bellringing beadle: but in the case of the retiring mayor, only the previous year's figure is declared. Should he have lost weight since the last ceremony, the beadle then adds 'And *no* more': an announcement always greeted by cheers, since he is supposed to have worked off the surplus pounds by hard work while in office. If the ex-mayor has gained in substance, however, the beadle admits the old weight 'And *a bit* more': whereupon the crowd barrack him for paying more attention to civic jollifications than to mayoral labours.

· Wells and Well-dressings ·

The custom of honouring certain wells and springs undoubtedly dates from pre-Roman times, when these vital sources of water were believed to be the dwelling places of powerful deities, generally goddesses. Particularly revered were wells whose mineral-rich waters possess curative powers – like those of Bath in Somerset or Buxton in Derbyshire, which were dedicated respectively to the Romano-British goddesses Sulis and Arnemetia. Nor did such magical springs lose their popularity with the arrival of Christianity, though they were then (at least nominally) re-consecrated to more respectable patrons, the pagan 'Lady of the Well' becoming 'Our Lady' and Arnemetia of Buxton being transmogrified into 'Saint Anne'. Despite the sporadic disapproval of the medieval Church, moreover, and the total condemnation of Protestant reformers, reverence for 'holy wells' has survived in various attenuated forms until the present day.

Quite apart from those 'medicinal springs' which became the centrepieces of fashionable spas, a number of curative wells – notably St Winifred's Well at Holywell in Flintshire – continue to attract considerable numbers of hopeful pilgrims: while water from now-neglected springs like that at Pilleth in Radnorshire – dedicated to St Mary, but reputedly haunted by a stag-headed former tenant – is still occasionally sought as a remedy for sore eyes or skin complaints. Such water was thought more potent if drawn on a particular day – usually NEW YEAR'S DAY, PALM SUNDAY or ASCENSION DAY – when children in many parts of the country drank it mixed with sugar or liquorice. Other wells, not necessarily curative, were and perhaps still are credited with the power of foretelling the future, which they did by rising or sinking to presage disasters, or by reacting in some particular manner when objects were cast into

them: and others again – the ubiquitous 'wishing wells' – are still half-believed to grant secret desires in return for a present of a pin or a piece of money. The habit of making gifts to wells, attested by archaeological evidence since prehistoric times, seems indeed to be quite ineradicable even in these supposedly rational times: one recently revealed well in the undercroft of York Minster, for example, had acquired a lining of coins within weeks of the area being opened to visitors.

An alternative method of honouring and rewarding holy wells is to 'dress' or decorate their exterior. This could be done by tying a 'clout' or rag (often red) to the well's surrounding trees whenever a visit was made or a cure performed: and evidence that this practice continues can still be seen at a few 'Rag' or 'Cloutie' wells, particularly in the Scottish Highlands. More often, however, the well would be ceremonially decked with flowers and green branches on some special day in the year, generally either the feast of its patron saint or one of the great springtime festivals like WHITSUN or Ascension Day. Widespread throughout Britain during the Middle Ages, this form of well-dressing thereafter went into a gradual decline under Puritan influence: though in some places it was incorporated into BEATING THE BOUNDS and in others it died very hard. John Aubrey, for example, tells how the inhabitants of Droitwich in Worcestershire were persuaded to abandon their decking custom at the time of the Civil War: but when their saline spring promptly reacted by drying up, they determined to revive it – 'and notwithstanding the power of the Parliament ... the Minister there and also the Soldiers, they did and will dress it, and the salt-water returned again.'

Well-dressing now continues mainly in Derbyshire and the immediately adjacent parts of the surrounding counties, but even there long-established ceremonies are greatly outnumbered by revived or entirely new customs, many of them (curiously enough) established under the auspices of the Church. Great care is taken, however, to divorce the current observances from any taint of paganism: for they are invariably declared to be 'symbols of Thanksgiving to the Almighty for the precious gift of drinking water', and the subjects of the elaborate dressings are nearly always biblical scenes.

These dressings, a far cry from the haphazard collection of boughs, garlands and ribbons once used to deck wells, appear to have developed in Derbyshire during the first quarter of the 19th century – at the very time when the revival of well dressing was gathering strength. Their basis is a shallow wooden tray, thickly covered with moist clay, upon which a mosaic picture is inlaid with flower petals, leaves, pine cones, pebbles and other natural materials. The complex design – perhaps Moses striking water from a rock, or Jesus at Jacob's Well – is first sketched on a sheet of paper, and then pricked through onto the clay: items like roads and walls are made first, from long-lasting bark, moss or cones; next, outlines are boldened with seeds and

Above: The longest-established and probably the most famous **well-dressing** ceremony is that of Tissington in Derbyshire, where this elaborate and determinedly Christian dressing was erected in 1899.
Left: Seeds, petals and all manner of other natural materials are carefully pressed onto a wet clay base.

berries; and finally (often on the night before the ceremony) the perishable flower and petal elements of the picture are added, the petals being generally overlapped scale-wise in order to shed rain. When complete, the whole dressing – which may be as much as twelve-feet high, and mounted in an architectural surround, also elaborately dressed – is carefully erected over the well: kept sprayed with water, it will perhaps survive for ten days.

Many Derbyshire communities, moreover, produce several of these lovingly and artistically made pieces of ephemera every year, one for each of their wells. Among them is Tissington, where the longest established of the well-dressing ceremonies takes place on Ascension Day. According to one local tradition, this originated in 1350, in thanksgiving for the purity of the water supply which had saved the village from the Black Death: while another declares that it began in 1615, after the never-failing Tissington wells had succoured the whole surrounding area through a terrible drought. Probably much older than either event, the ceremony had certainly assumed roughly its present form by the 1790s. All five village wells are dressed, a special church service is held in the morning, and during the evening a procession of clergy, choir and congregation visits and blesses each in turn.

Barlow, on the opposite side of the county, also claims a 17th-century origin for its ceremony, held on the Wednesday after the patronal festival of St Lawrence (10 August). Here, however, a pump and basin were erected over the well in 1840, and it is this that is now dressed, with a triptych picture made exclusively from whole flowers. Youlgreave, too, dresses five public taps on the Saturday nearest MIDSUMMER DAY; and at Wirksworth, where the taps which replaced the wells have in turn disappeared, the dressings are set up on their sites during the fourth week in May. Here the ceremonies are accompanied by the crowning of a 'Queen of the Wells' and a week-long festival, and so too is the dressing of St Anne's Well at Buxton in late July. In its present form, the Buxton custom dates only from about 1840, but the well and its successive guardians – Arnemetia and 'St Anne' – were attracting pilgrims throughout the Roman and medieval periods: while at Bradwell (where the dressing is now held in early August) the 'Lady of the Well' once had to be offered new pins on Palm Sunday before she would grant children clean water at Easter.

Across the Staffordshire border, Endon also has a well-dressing ceremony, which dates from at least 1845 and is now held over Spring Bank Holiday weekend: and so, much further afield, has Bisley in Gloucestershire, where the Ascensiontide custom of decorating seven springs was begun in 1863 by the High Church rector Thomas Keble. New or revived ceremonies also take place during May in the Derbyshire villages of Ashford-in-the-Water, Etwall, Middleton, and Monyash, and at Newborough in Staffordshire; during

June in Bakewell, Hope, Edlaston, Litton, Rowsley, Tideswell and Wyaston; in July at Glapwell, Heath, Holmewood, Pilsley, Stoney Middleton and Whitwell, as well as at Dore in West Yorkshire and Headon in Nottinghamshire; in August at Bonsall, Eyam (see PLAGUE SUNDAY) and Wormhill; and in September at Hartington.

· Westminster Pancake Greeze ·
see SHROVE TUESDAY

· Whalton Baal Fire ·
Whalton, near Bedlington, Northumberland: 4 July

Burned on Old Midsummer Eve, the Whalton 'Baal' Fire is probably the only genuine survivor of the MIDSUMMER bonfires which once blazed in many parts of Britain, Northumberland being one of their last strongholds. Its name, moreover, has nothing to do with Baal, the sun god of the Old Testament Canaanites, but is derived either from the Celtic word *bel* ('bright') or, more likely, from the Anglo-Saxon *bael*, meaning simply 'a fire' (cf. 'Beltane' OR MAY DAY).

Undoubtedly originating before the calendar change of 1752, the Whalton custom is said to 'date from time immemorial', and to have taken place on the present site – near the village pub in the main street – for at least two centuries. Until about 1914, moreover, considerable ritual attended the building of the fire: and tradition dictated that the cart of gorse and other fuel might be drawn by horses only as far as the township boundary, whereafter it had to be hauled into the village by hand, with much shouting and blowing of horns. The whole community then turned out to watch the fire being stacked, and before it was lit children joined hands and danced about it, scrambling afterwards for sweets and pennies. Towards evening the blaze was set afire, while beer contributed by local gentry and farmers was consumed by the bucketful: and as the flames died down young couples leapt through the embers 'for luck'.

The children still get their sweets, and 'Whalton Baal' is still toasted with drinks from the village inn: but the fire-building ceremony has ceased, few couples now appear to dance round the blaze, and it seems possible that the last British Midsummer fire custom may soon die out altogether.

· Whitebread Meadow Running Auction ·
see HOURGLASS, CROWN AND RUNNING AUCTIONS

· Whitsun ·

Whit Sunday is the English name for the Feast of Pentecost, when the Holy Spirit descended in tongues of flame on the assembled Apostles, thereby miraculously endowing them with understanding of the work they were to do. Thus its title has sometimes been derived from 'wit' – in the old sense of 'wisdom' – but it is virtually certain that Whit Sunday (Old English:*hwitan Sunnandaeg*) was originally 'White Sunday', probably referring to the white garments worn by the pagan converts traditionally baptized then. Falling as it does fifty days (Greek: *pentikosti*) after EASTER, Whitsun is a 'movable feast': and one of the greatest in the Christian calendar, celebrated with peals of BELLS, the floral decoration of churches, and the singing of seasonal anthems like 'Come, Holy Ghost'. In recent years, it has become more specifically Christian than ever: for the many more or less secular spring festivities that once centred upon Whit Sunday and Monday have generally now been transferred to the 'fixed' Spring Bank Holiday – which is, however, still commonly known as 'Whit' – on the last weekend in May.

The popularity of Whitsun as a season for communal celebrations is due in part to the fact that it is a less solemn time than Easter, a less disreputably pagan feast than MAY DAY, and normally a better bet for good weather than either. For its observances are almost invariably cheerful and frequently outdoor affairs, many of them sprung from the Whitsun 'Church ales' once held throughout England, Wales and (until the Reformation) Lowland Scotland. These combinations of

PEACE AND GOOD NEIGHBOURHOOD FEASTS, fund-raising events and sports days, often accompanied by MORRIS DANCING and other shows, are extinct as such: but some of their spirit survives in localized customs like BREAD AND CHEESE THROWING; CHEESE ROLLING; the COTS-WOLD OLYMPICK GAMES; the COURT OF ARRAY; the DUNMOW FLITCH; the Kingsteignton RAM ROASTING; and the directly descended Walking Days: and even – though much diluted – in the sedate village fêtes everywhere seen at Whitsun or its modern substitute. Once marked by meals of seasonal dishes like Sussex roast veal and gooseberry tart, Cornish pigeon-squab pie or Yorkshire cheesecakes, this joyful festival was also – and still is – a favourite time for FAIRS, and for community ceremonies like BEATING THE BOUNDS, RUSH-BEARINGS and dressing WELLS.

· Whuppity Stourie ·
Lanark, Strathclyde: 1 March

'Whuppity Stourie' (now more often 'Whuppity Scoorie') is a custom of obscure origin, peculiar to the ancient Royal Burgh of Lanark. It takes place at the parish kirk, whose BELLS, silent from October to

Whirling their paper balls, children run round Lanark Kirk on **Whuppity Stourie** night.

February, resume their nightly ringing at 6 p.m. on 1 March. At the first stroke, local primary schoolchildren set off to run three times round the church in a sunwise direction, whirling about their heads paper balls tied to strings and belabouring each other with these as they go. When the bells have ceased ringing, the first boy and girl to complete three circuits are given money prizes – a comparatively recent feature, introducing a hitherto unknown 'racing' element – while the remaining children scramble for a shower of coins thrown by the Provost.

Until the turn of the century, Whuppity Stourie was a much more boisterous occasion. For young men also took part, caps rather than paper balls were whirled, and participants tried to 'buff' the burgh bellman as well as each other. Thereafter they marched in a body to fight a 'stringed-bonnet' battle with the lads of New Lanark: and whichever side won paraded the streets shouting a victory song.

The fight was suppressed by the magistrates, and even striking with paper balls is now discouraged – albeit unsuccessfully. But the sunwise running and the whirling – probably the essential elements of the custom – survive, a happy hunting ground for folklore theorists. Some claim that they originated in the whipping of penitents round the church; others that they were some kind of ritual to welcome spring; and others again that they were designed to exorcize evil spirits who travelled about in clouds of *stour* (dust). Certainly Whuppity Stourie was the name of a bad fairy who, according to a Lanarkshire version of the Rumplestiltskin story, could only be foiled by guessing her name. Whether tale or custom came first, however, is another matter for debate.

Perpetuating a bereaved mother's devotion, a sailor adds the annual Good Friday offering to the **Widow's Bun** collection.

· Wicken Love Feast ·
see PEACE AND GOOD NEIGHBOURHOOD FEASTS

· Widow's Bun Ceremony ·
The Widow's Son Inn, 75 Devons Rd, London E3:
Good Friday

Each GOOD FRIDAY, a sailor or 'Wren' ceremonially adds a newly made 'hot cross bun' to the netted cluster which hangs permanently from the ceiling of the Widow's Son pub at Bromley-by-Bow, in London's East End. Thus is commemorated the poor widow whose cottage stood on this site during the early 19th century: and who, expecting her only son home from the sea one EASTER, baked a bun to greet him – perhaps because, among their many other semi-magical properties, such buns were believed to be a charm against shipwreck. But the charm apparently came too late, for the seaman never returned: yet his loss remained unconfirmed and, refusing to abandon hope, his mother continued to bake and keep a bun for him on every Good Friday until her own death.

Thereafter the custom was faithfully kept up by subsequent residents of her cottage, by then famous as 'the Bun House'. And when a pub rose in its stead, this was named 'the Widow's Son', a condition of its tenancy being that a sailor must perpetuate the old lady's devotion each year, and be paid a pint of beer for his trouble. Buns are also occasionally added to mark special events – such as Mafeking Night and the Coronation of Queen Elizabeth II – and more than 200 now hang in the net.

· Wild Horse of Antrobus ·
see SOULING

· William Wallace Commemoration ·
see COMMEMORATIONS

· Woodmen of Arden's Grand Wardmote ·
Meriden, Warwickshire: first week in August

The eighty-strong company of archers called the Wood-men of Arden was founded in 1785, but claims spiritual descent from the medieval bands of bowmen which ranged the Forest of Arden when it covered half of Warwickshire. Its meetings, therefore, display a curious amalgam of medieval and 18th-century styles. Called 'wardmotes', after the ancient forest court assemblies, they take place at Meriden, a village which is said to be the exact centre of England and (still more dubiously) to have once hosted an archery contest attended by Robin Hood himself: and the greatest of them is the Grand Wardmote in August, which features a four-day shoot-ing match. For this members use six-foot yew bows of medieval pattern, and arrows stamped (according to medieval custom) with their equivalent weight in silver: but their costume is of the 18th century – a green frock-coat and buff waistcoat, with the gilt buttons of the society; white trousers; and a wide-brimmed green shooting hat. (*See* SILVER ARROW CONTESTS)

· Wrestling, Cornish and Cumberland ·

The origins of wrestling are lost in the vastness of prehistory, but as an organized sport it was certainly flourishing in Britain by Roman times. It remained popular during the Middle Ages, when it was regarded as an important part of military training: and the Elizabethan schoolmaster Roger Ascham also recom-mended it as an essential element of boys' education. In the early 18th century, moreover, it was promoted as 'indispensable to fencers and duellists' – notably by the eccentric Nottinghamshire baronet Sir Thomas Parkyns, who frequently hurled 'creditors and other contentious persons' over his head, and whose effigy in wrestling posture can still be seen in Bunny church.

Only traditionally patterned longbows and wooden arrows may be used during the **Woodmen of Arden's Grand Wardmote.** The archer aims to drop his arrow onto a 'clout' (like the one by his feet) some 180 yards away.

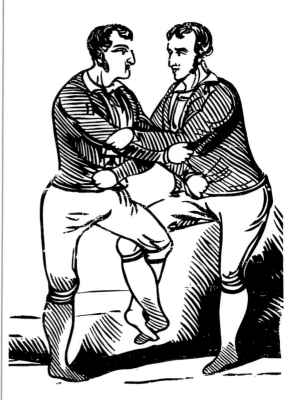

The costume and grip customary in Cornish **wrestling** are seen in this printer's block of the 1820s, used for posters to advertise matches in the Liskeard area.

The approved form of the sport at this time was Cornish wrestling, which continues to thrive in the North Cornwall villages of St Columb Major, St Merryn, St Wenn and Perranporth, and which is now enjoying something of a revival thoughout the Duchy. Wrestlers wear specially made sailcloth jackets, and their feet must be bare. The object is to throw an opponent squarely onto the ground: and while neither handholds below the belt nor kicking are allowed, the sides of the feet may be used to unbalance him.

The chief difference between Cornish and Cumberland wrestling – which is probably quite as ancient a sport – is in the method of holding. In the Cornish style the contestants stand apart at the beginning of the bout, only clasping each other when the match begins. But in Cumberland wrestling the competitors begin with hands clasped behind each other's backs, with one arm over the shoulder and one under, and this hold is maintained until a throw is accomplished.

Probably the best-known gathering of Cumberland and Westmorland wrestlers is at Grasmere Sports, held on the third Thursday after the first Monday in August: but the sport is also enthusiastically carried on at Ambleside Sports (Thursday before first Monday in August); Cockermouth Show (Saturday before first Monday in August); Keswick Show (late Summer Bank Holiday); Westmorland County Show, Kendal (second Thursday in September); and at Wasdale Head Show (second Saturday in October).

· Wroth Silver ·
Knightlow Hill, near Dunchurch, Warwickshire:
11 November

Before sunrise on MARTINMAS DAY, the representatives of certain parishes in the Knightlow Hundred division of Warwickshire gather at the ancient Hundred meeting place on Knightlow Hill. Here the agent of the Lord of

The grip demonstrated by these splendid gentlemen is maintained throughout Cumberland **wrestling** matches.

the Hundred – the Duke of Buccleuch – awaits them: and when he has read the Charter of Assembly he calls upon them to pay their 'Wroth Silver'. Each man then places a prescribed sum of money – which varies from parish to parish, and ranges from ½p to 11½p – in a hollow in the stone base which is all that remains of Knightlow Cross, repeating the words 'Wroth Silver' as he does so. Thus he avoids a penalty of £1 for every penny unpaid, or of a white bull with a red nose and red ears – 'whichever the Lord's steward chooses to demand'. The ceremony completed, the whole company go to the Dun Cow Inn at Dunchurch, where they are treated to breakfast at the Duke's expense, and drink his health in hot rum and milk.

One of the oldest continuously performed customs in Britain, the collection of Wroth Silver was well established in Knightlow Hundred by 1236, and probably began a century or so earlier. Formerly called 'warth-penny' or 'ward-money', the tax originally bought exemption from the duty of keeping 'watch and ward' against rebels and law breakers: but local tradition insists that its real purpose was to guarantee villagers' rights to drive cattle across the Lord's lands, a belief lent weight by the customary forfeit of the white bull with red points – the type of beast most valued in the early medieval period. The bull forfeit, conversely, may have given rise to the cattle-driving story: for a mere wayleave due seems unlikely to have been enforced so strictly, or in such exact terms, as the collection of Wroth Silver has apparently always been. During the mid-19th century, in fact, a bull was actually demanded from a defaulter: and though the total sum now levied amounts to less than fifty pence, the money must still unfailingly be paid before dawn breaks.

Y

· Yule Logs ·
24 December

Once general throughout Britain (particularly the English northern and western counties, and Scotland) this ancient CHRISTMAS custom is now practised only in a few traditionalist homes and pubs. On Christmas Eve a large log, sometimes decorated with seasonal evergreens, is ceremonially brought in: it must never be purchased, but should either be got from the householder's land or garden; 'found' elsewhere; or given. It is then lit with a fragment of last year's log (also kept to preserve the house from fire and lightning) and should burn continuously for at least twelve hours. In the days of more generously sized hearths, when whole tree stumps were used, it might be kept alight throughout the Twelve Days of Christmas; and in any case it must not go out until deliberately extinguished, or a year's bad luck will follow.

Oak is the favoured timber for Scots Yule Logs: but English 'Christmas Blocks', 'Brands' or 'Clogs' are usually of fruit-tree or ash wood. In Somerset and Devon, indeed, an 'Ashen Faggot' – a bundle of green ash sticks – is preferred to a log: this is tied with a large number of twisted-bark 'binders', and as each burns through and bursts the company is traditionally entitled to a round of drinks.

Bringing in the **yule log** for Victorian Christmas festivities.

Select Bibliography

General

D. Attwater *The Penguin Dictionary of Saints* Harmondsworth 1965

John Aubrey *Three Prose Works (1688-97)* (ed. J. Buchanan-Brown) Fontwell Sussex 1972

M.M. Banks (ed.) *British Calendar Customs (Scotland)* London and Glasgow 1939

T. Blount *Fragmenta Antiquitatis or Jocular Tenures* London 1815

J. Brand *Observations on the Popular Antiquities of Great Britain* London 1848-9

British Tourist Authority *Britain: Customs and Folklore* London 1983

B. Bushaway *By Rite – Custom, Ceremony and Community in Britain 1700-1880* London 1982

H. Edwards *A Collection of Old English Customs* London 1842

M. Gascoigne *Discovering English Customs and Folklore* Aylesbury 1980

G.L Gomme (ed.) *The Gentleman's Magazine Library*, Vols. 1 (Manners and Customs) and 3 (Popular Superstitions) London 1883-4

G. Grigson *The Englishman's Flora* St Albans 1975

C. Hole *A Dictionary of British Folk Customs* London 1978

W. Hone *The Every-Day Book* London 1838

A. Howard *Endless Cavalcade* London 1964

F.M. McNeill *The Silver Bough: National and Local Festivals of Scotland* Glasgow 1959-68

I. and P. Opie *The Lore and Language of Schoolchildren* Oxford 1959

Reader's Digest *Folklore, Myths and Legends of Britain* London 1973

H. Sykes *Once a Year: Some Traditional British Customs* London 1977

A.R. Wright and T.E. Lones (eds.) *British Calendar Customs (England)* London 1936-9

Regional

W. Boase *The Folklore of Hampshire and the Isle of Wight* London 1976

M. Brentnall *The Old Customs and Ceremonies of London* London 1975

K.M. Briggs *The Folklore of the Cotswolds* London 1974

T. Deane and T. Shaw *The Folklore of Cornwall* London 1975

E. Hasted *History and Topographical Survey of Kent* Canterbury 1798

D. Jones-Baker *The Folklore of Hertfordshire* London 1977

E.M. Leather *The Folklore of Herefordshire* (reprint) Wakefield 1973

T.M. Owen *Welsh Folk Customs* Cardiff 1959

K. Palmer *The Folklore of Somerset* London 1976

R. Palmer *The Folklore of Warwickshire* London 1976

E. Porter *The Folklore of East Anglia* London 1974

J. Raven *The Folklore of Staffordshire* London 1978

M. Rowling *The Folklore of the Lake District* London 1976

E.H. Rudkin *Lincolnshire Folklore* (reprint) Wakefield 1973

J. Simpson *The Folklore of Sussex* London 1973

J. Simpson *The Folklore of the Welsh Border* London 1976

R. Whitlock *The Folklore of Devon* London 1977

R. Whitlock *The Folklore of Wiltshire* London 1976

Some special subjects

H.B. Walters *The Church Bells of England* Oxford 1912

J.A.R. Pimlott *The Englishman's Christmas* Hassocks, Sussex 1978

L.G.W. Legg *English Coronation Records* London 1901

H. Schramm *A History of the English Coronation* Oxford 1937

I. Starsmore *English Fairs* London 1975

E.C. Cawte *Ritual Animal Disguise* Cambridge 1978

C. Sharp and H.C. Macilwaine *The Morris Book (1912-24) (reprint)* Wakefield 1974-5

A. Helm *The English Mummers' Play* Woodbridge, Suffolk, 1981

A. Burton *Rush Bearing* Manchester 1891

C.Sharp *The Sword Dances of Northern England (1913) (reprint)* Wakefield 1977

SCOTLAND

Northumberland

Cumberland

Durham

Westmorland

Yorks

Lancs

Lincoln

Cheshire Derby

Nottingham

WALES

Salop

Stafford

Leicester Rut-
land

Norfolk

Cambridge

Warwick

Northampton

Hunts

Suffolk

Hereford

Worcester

Bed-
ford

Gloucester

Oxford

Buckingham

Hertford

Essex

Berks.

London

Wilts.

Surrey

Kent

Somerset

Hants.

Sussex

Devon

Dorset

Cornwall

0   20   40   60   80   100 mls.

0   50   100   150 kms.

Regional Gazetteer

Within the regions, customs and ceremonies are listed alphabetically under the names of the places where they occur. Normally the custom is cited by the title of entry in which it is described (e.g. Rushbearings): but where this is not appropriate the title of the entry appears in small capitals (e.g. Hay Strewing *see* RUSHBEARINGS). Dates of occurrence are given, except where the custom takes place at irregular or uncertain intervals.

DEVON AND CORNWALL

Ashburton, Devon
Courts Leet: *July and November*
Barnstaple, Devon
Fairs
The Glove is Up: *Wednesday nearest 17 October*
Bideford, Devon
Courts Leet: *Easter*
Bratton Fleming, Devon
Plough Blessing *see* PLOUGH MONDAY
Brixham, Devon
Blessing the Sea: *Rogationtide*
Burrator Reservoir, nr Plymouth, Devon
Burrator Reservoir Ceremony: *July*
Chawleigh, Devon
Club Walk: *1st Saturday in June*
Dartmouth and Kingswear, Devon
Blessing the Sea: *Rogationtide*
Dunstone, Devon
Courts Leet
Exeter, Devon
The Glove is Up: *Tuesday before 1st Wednesday in July*
Plough Blessing *see* PLOUGH MONDAY
Gittisham, Devon
Tip Toeing *see* SHROVE TUESDAY

Hatherleigh, Devon
Fire Festival: *Wednesday after 5 November see* GUY FAWKES NIGHT
Helston, Cornwall
Furry Dance: *8 May*
Holsworthy, Devon
Pretty Maid's Charity: *2nd Wednesday in July*
Honiton, Devon
The Glove is Up: *1st Tuesday after 19 July*
Iddesleigh, Devon
Club Walk: *Saturday nearest May Day*
Kingsbridge, Devon
The Glove is Up: *late July*
Kingsteignton, Devon
Ram Roasting Ceremony: *Spring Bank Holiday Monday*
Marhamchurch, Cornwall
Marhamchurch Revel: *Monday after 12 August see* FEASTS, REVELS AND WAKES
Marldon, Devon
Apple Pie Fair: *August Bank Holiday Saturday see* FAIRS
Newton Abbot, Devon
Cheese and Onion Fair: *Wednesday nearest 21 August see* FAIRS

Ottery St Mary, Devon
Guy Fawkes Night: *5 November*
Padstow, Cornwall
Padstow Hobby Horse: *1 May*
Perranporth, Cornwall
Wrestling, Cornish
St Columb, Cornwall
Hurling the Silver Ball: *Shrove Tuesday and second Saturday following*
St Ives, Cornwall
Hurling the Silver Ball: *Monday after 3 February*
St Merryn, Cornwall
Wrestling, Cornish
St Wenn, Cornwall
Wrestling, Cornish
Shebbear, Devon
Turning the Devil's Stone: *5 November*
Sidmouth, Devon
Hot Cross Buns *see* GOOD FRIDAY
Spitchwick, Devon
Courts Leet
Tavistock, Devon
Goosey Fair: *early October see* FAIRS
Widecombe, Devon
Horse Fair: *2nd Tuesday in September*

WESSEX
(DORSET, HAMPSHIRE, ISLE OF WIGHT, SOMERSET, WILTSHIRE)

Abbotsbury, Dorset
Abbotsbury Garland Day: *13 May*
Andover, Hampshire
Mumming Play: *Christmas*
Bridgwater, Somerset
Guy Fawkes Night: *5 November*
Horse Fair: *last Wednesday in September*

Carhampton, Somerset
Wassailing the Apple Trees: *17 January*
Chard, Somerset
Hourglass Auction: *1st Thursday in October*
Chedzoy, Somerset
Candle Auction

Corfe Castle, Dorset
Marblers' and Stonecutters' Day: *Shrove Tuesday*
Cricklade, Wiltshire
Courts Leet
Crookham, Hampshire
Mumming Play: *Christmas*

Hambridge, Somerset
Plough Blessing *see* PLOUGH MONDAY
Keevil, Wiltshire
Bread and Bun Dole: *a Sunday after Easter*
Langport, Somerset
Club Walk: *Saturday nearest 29 May*
Leigh, nr Sherborne, Dorset
Candle Auction
Long Sutton, Somerset
Club Walk
Lyndhurst, Hampshire
Verderers' Court: *3rd Monday in every second month, beginning in January see* FOREST CUSTOMS
Marlborough, Wiltshire
Mop Fair: *29 September see* FAIRS
Minehead, Somerset
Minehead Hobby Horse: *30 April – 3 May*

Mudeford, Hampshire
Blessing the Sea: *Rogationtide*
Harvest of the Sea *see* HARVEST FESTIVALS
Newchurch, Isle of Wight
Plough Blessing *see* PLOUGH MONDAY
Poole, Dorset
Beating the Bounds
Portland, Dorset
Beating the Bounds
Courts Leet
Priddy, Somerset
Fairs: *Wednesday nearest 21 August*
Salisbury, Wiltshire
Grovely Rights Day: *29 May*
Southampton, Hampshire
Blessing the Sea: *Rogationtide*
Courts Leet: *October*
Knighthood of Old Green: *early August*
May Singing: *1 May*

Stockbridge, Hampshire
Courts Leet
Tatworth, Somerset
Candle Auction
Tichborne, Hampshire
The Tichborne Dole: *25 March*
Twyford, Hampshire
Lost in the Dark Bells: *7 October*
Wareham, Dorset
Courts Leet: *November*
Winchester, Hampshire
Wayfarers' Dole: *every weekday*
Wishford, Wiltshire
Candle Auction: *Rogationtide*
Grovely Rights Day: *29 May*

SOUTH-EAST ENGLAND
(KENT, SURREY, SUSSEX)

Alciston, Sussex
Good Friday Skipping
Biddenden, Kent
Biddenden Maids' Charity: *Easter Monday*
Bodiam, Sussex
Pancake Race *see* SHROVE TUESDAY
Broadstairs, Kent
Blessing the Sea: *4th week in August*
Hooden Horse: *August*
Canterbury, Kent
Civic Ceremonies
Hooden Horse: *1st Saturday in September*
Charing, Kent
Hooden Horse: *Whitsun*
Chertsey, Surrey
Black Cherry Fair: *2nd Saturday in July see* FAIRS
Chichester, Sussex
Plough Blessing *see* PLOUGH MONDAY
Croydon, Surrey
Founder's Day: *around 22 March*
Ebernoe, Sussex
Ebernoe Horn Fair: *25 July*
Epsom, Surrey
The Derby: *1st Wednesday in June*
Farnborough, Kent
Rushbearings: *Sunday nearest 29 June*

Findon, Sussex
Fairs: *September*
Folkestone, Kent
Blessing the Sea: *July*
Hooden Horse: *Christmas Eve*
Guildford, Surrey
Maids' Money: *last Thursday in January*
Hartfield, Sussex
Graveside Dole: *Good Friday*
Hastings, Sussex
Blessing the Sea
Clipping the Church: *Mothering Sunday*
Henfield, Sussex
Wassailing the Apple Trees: *6 January*
Hythe, Kent
Cinque Ports Ceremonies
Lewes, Sussex
Guy Fawkes Night: *5 November*
Margate, Kent
Blessing the Sea: *January*
Newington-by-Sittingbourne, Kent
Blessing the Cherry Orchards: *May see* BEATING THE BOUNDS
Piddinghoe, Sussex
Little Edith's Treat: *19 July*

Rochester, Kent
Admiralty Court: *1st or 2nd Saturday in July*
Beating the Bounds
Romney, Kent
Cinque Ports Ceremonies
Rye, Sussex
Civic Ceremonies
Sandwich, Kent
Cinque Ports Ceremonies
Civic Ceremonies
St Bartholomew's Bun Race: *around 24 August*
Shoreham, Sussex
May Day
South Heighton, Sussex
Good Friday Skipping
Sunbury-on-Thames, Surrey
Swan Upping: *3rd week in July*
Sutton, Surrey
Mary Gibson's Legacy: *12 June see* SERMONS
Tinsley Green, Sussex
Marbles Championship: *Good Friday*
Whitstable, Kent
Blessing the Sea: *around 25 July*
Wolton, Surrey
Forty Shilling Day: *around 2 February*

CHANNEL ISLANDS AND ISLE OF MAN

Channel Islands
La Clameur de Haro

St John's, Isle of Man
Tynwald Ceremony *5 July*

LONDON
(INCLUDING MIDDLESEX)

Barnet
Horse Fair: *September*
Buckingham Palace
Changing the Guard: *daily in summer, alternate days in winter*
Chelsea
Flower Show, Floral Hall: *late May* see ROYAL CEREMONIES
Oak Apple Day, Royal Hospital: *around 29 May*
Dalston, E8
Holy Trinity Church, Clown Service: *February or March see* COMMEMORATIONS
Drury Lane, Theatre Royal
Baddeley Cake see TWELFTH NIGHT
Fern Street Settlement, E3
Farthing Bundles: *monthly*
Guildhall
Election of Sheriffs: *Midsummer Day* see CIVIC CUSTOMS
Lord Mayor of London's Installation Ceremonies: *Michaelmas and 2nd Friday in November*
Harlington, Middlesex
Bells and Bellringing: *5 November*
Highgate
Swearing on the Horns: *Spring and August Bank Holidays*
Horse Guards Parade
Beating Retreat: *late May or June see* ROYAL CEREMONIES
Royal Salutes
Trooping the Colour: *a Saturday in early June*
Houses of Parliament
see PARLIAMENT
Cromwell Commemoration: *around 3 September see* COMMEMORATIONS
Hyde Park
Royal Salutes
Law Courts, Strand
Faggot Service: *October see* QUIT RENTS
Lincoln's Inn Fields
Pancake Race see SHROVE TUESDAY
Lord's Cricket Ground
Test Matches
Manor of the Savoy, Strand
Beating the Bounds: *Ascensiontide, five-yearly*
Mansion House
Civic Ceremonies
Guilds and Companies
Lord Mayor of London's Installation Ceremonies
Quit Rent Ceremonies

River Thames
Doggett's Coat and Badge Race: London Bridge to Cadogan Pier: *July*
Oxford and Cambridge Boat Race: Putney to Mortlake: *a Saturday in March or April*
St James's Palace
Epiphany Gifts Ceremony: *6 January*
Changing the Guard: *daily in summer, alternate days in winter*
St Paul's Cathedral
Stationers' Service: *Ash Wednesday* see GUILDS AND COMPANIES
Orders of Chivalry Ceremonies
Tower of London
see TOWER OF LONDON
Changing the Guard: *daily in summer, alternate days in winter*
Royal Salutes
Trafalgar Square
New Year's Eve celebrations
Wembley Stadium
Cup Final: *Saturday in early May*
Westminster Abbey
Coronations
Florence Nightingale Commemoration: *around 12 May* see COMMEMORATIONS
Orders of Chivalry ceremonies
Westminster School
Pancake Greeze see SHROVE TUESDAY
Whitehall
Changing the Guard: *daily*
Charles I Commemoration: *30 January see* COMMEMORATIONS
Remembrance Sunday, at Cenotaph
Widow's Son Inn, Devons Road, E3
Widow's Bun Ceremony: *Good Friday*

CEREMONIES AND EVENTS IN CITY CHURCHES

All Hallows-by-the-Tower
Beating the Bounds: *Ascensiontide*
Knollys Rose: *June see* QUIT RENT CEREMONIES
St Andrew Undershaft, Leadenhall Street
Stow Commemoration: *around 5 April see* COMMEMORATIONS
St Bartholomew the Great, Smithfield
Graveside Dole: *Good Friday*

St Botolph's-without-Aldgate
Sir John Cass Commemoration: *around 20 March see* FOUNDERS' DAYS
St Bride's, Fleet Street
Bridewell Service: *2nd Tuesday in March see* FOUNDERS' DAYS
St Clement Danes
Beating the Bounds: *Ascensiontide*
Oranges and Lemons Service: *late March*
St Etheldreda's, Ely Place
Blessing the Throats: *3 February*
St James, Garlickhythe
Vintners' Procession: *2nd Thursday in July see* GUILDS AND COMPANIES
St Katherine Cree, Leadenhall Street
Lion Sermon: *around 16 October see* SERMONS
St Lawrence Jewry
Spital Sermon: *2nd Wednesday after Easter see* SERMONS
St Margaret Pattens, Eastcheap
Basketmakers' Service: *last Wednesday in October see* GUILDS AND COMPANIES
St Martin's-in-the-Fields
Costermongers' Harvest Service: *1st Sunday in October see* HARVEST FESTIVALS
St Martin's-within-Ludgate
Bubble Sermon: *1st Tuesday in June* see SERMONS
St Mary Aldermary
Skinners' Procession: *2nd Thursday after Whitsun see* GUILDS AND COMPANIES
St Mary-at-Hill
Harvest of the Sea service: *October* see HARVEST FESTIVALS
St Olave's, Hart Street
Pepys Commemoration: *around 26 May see* COMMEMORATIONS
St Sepulchre's-within-Newgate
Christ's Hospital Service: *around 21 September see* FOUNDERS' DAYS
see also CHARITIES
St Stephen Wallbrook
Grocers' Procession: *10 July see* GUILDS AND COMPANIES

THAMES VALLEY AND COTSWOLDS
(BERKSHIRE, BUCKINGHAMSHIRE, GLOUCESTERSHIRE, OXFORDSHIRE)

Throughout region:
Morris Dancing

Abingdon, Berkshire
Mayor of Ock Street: *Saturday nearest 19 June see* MOCK MAYORS

Aldermaston, Berkshire
Candle Auction: *December, every three years*

Ascot, Berkshire
Royal Ascot: *mid June*

Avening, Gloucestershire
Pig Face Sunday: *Sunday after 14 September*

Bampton, Oxfordshire
Morris Dancing: *Spring Bank Holiday*
Mumming Play: *Christmas*

Bisley, Gloucestershire
Wells and Well-dressing: *Ascensiontide*

Bristol
Bread and Bun Dole, St Michael's-on-the-Mount: *Easter Tuesday*
Civic Ceremonies
Fairs
Pipe Walk, St Mary Redcliffe: *September*
Rushbearings, St Mary Redcliffe: *Whit Sunday*

Bucklebury, Berkshire
Courts Leet

Charlton-on-Otmoor, Oxfordshire
Garland Dressing: *May Day*

Chipping Campden, Gloucestershire
Cotswold Olympick Games: *Friday and Saturday after Spring Bank Holiday*

Cirencester, Gloucestershire
Fairs: *around 10 October*

Cooper's Hill, Brockworth, Gloucestershire
Cheese Rolling: *Spring Bank Holiday Monday*

Dorney-with-Boveney, Buckinghamshire
Courts Leet

Fenny Stratford, Buckinghamshire
Fenny Poppers: *11 November*

Forest of Dean, Gloucestershire
Verderers' Court *see* FOREST CUSTOMS

Headington, Oxfordshire
Morris Dancing
Mumming Play: *Christmas*

Henley, Oxfordshire
Henley Royal Regatta: *early June*

High Wycombe, Buckinghamshire
Weighing the Mayor: *late May*

Hungerford, Berkshire
Hocktide: *2nd Tuesday after Easter*

Marshfield, Gloucestershire
Mumming Play: *Christmas*

Olney, Buckinghamshire
Pancake Race *see* SHROVE TUESDAY

Oxford
Beating the Bounds, St Michael at the Northgate
Handy Sermon, St Giles Church: *around 10 March see* SERMONS
May singing
St Giles Fair: *Monday and Tuesday after 1st Sunday after 1 September see* FAIRS

Painswick, Gloucestershire
Clipping the Church: *Sunday after 19 September*

Pangbourne, Berkshire
Swan Upping: *3rd week in July*

Radley, Oxfordshire
Clipping the Church: *Easter*

Randwick, Gloucestershire
Cheese Rolling: *1st Sunday in May*
Randwick Wap: *2nd Saturday in May see* MOCK MAYORS

Reading, Berkshire
Maids' Money: *Easter*

St Briavels, Gloucestershire
Bread and Cheese Throwing: *Whit Sunday*

Shenington, Oxfordshire
Hay Strewing: *Whit Saturday and two Saturdays following see* RUSHBEARINGS

Tewkesbury, Gloucestershire
Fairs: *around 10 October*

Ufton Nervet, Berkshire
The Marvyn Dole: *Maundy Thursday*

Wallingford, Berkshire
Bells and Bellringing

Windsor, Berkshire
Changing the Guard
Garter Ceremony: *June see* ORDERS OF CHIVALRY

Wingrave, Buckinghamshire
Rushbearings: *Saturday after 29 June*

Yarnton, Oxfordshire
Lot Meadow Custom: *week after 29 June*

EASTERN ENGLAND
(BEDFORDSHIRE, CAMBRIDGESHIRE, ESSEX, HERTFORDSHIRE, HUNTINGDONSHIRE, NORFOLK, NORTHAMPTONSHIRE, SUFFOLK)

Braughing, Hertfordshire
Old Man's Day: *2 October*

Broughton, Northamptonshire
Tin Can Band: *2nd Sunday in December*

Bury St Edmunds, Suffolk
Jankyn Smith's Charity: *Thursday nearest 28 June*

Cambridge, Cambridgeshire
Ascension Day Singing, St John's College
Fairs: *Midsummer*

Cawston, Norfolk
Plough Blessing *see* PLOUGH MONDAY

Colchester, Essex
Colchester Oyster Ceremonies: *September and October*

Corby, Northamptonshire
Corby Pole Fair: *Whit Monday, twenty-yearly*

Cottered, Hertfordshire
Plough Blessing *see* PLOUGH MONDAY

Dunmow, Essex
Dunmow Flitch: *June, leap years*

East Horndon, Essex
Courts Leet

Ellington, Huntingdonshire
Bread and Bun Dole: *Good Friday*

Ely, Cambridgeshire
Pancake Race *see* SHROVE TUESDAY

Epping Forest, Essex
Verderers' Court *see* FOREST CUSTOMS

Flamsteed, Hertfordshire
Plough Blessing *see* PLOUGH MONDAY

Geddington, Northamptonshire
Bread and Bun Dole: *May Day*

Horning, Norfolk
Blessing the Broads: *1st Sunday in August see* BLESSING THE SEA
Ickwell, Bedfordshire
May Day: *1st Saturday in May*
King's Lynn, Norfolk
Fairs: *fortnight after 14 February*
Odell, Bedfordshire
Hay Strewing: *2nd Saturday in July see* RUSHBEARINGS
Old Weston, Huntingdonshire
Hay Strewing: *Sunday after 15 July see* RUSHBEARINGS

St Ives, Huntingdonshire
Dicing for Bibles: *Whit Sunday*
Southwold, Suffolk
Fairs: *2nd Monday after Whitsun*
Toddington, Bedfordshire
Pancake Bells
Whittlesey, Cambridgeshire
Straw Bear Day: *Saturday before Plough Monday*
Wicken, Northamptonshire
Peace and Good Neighbourhood Feast: *last Thursday in May*

Wisbech, Cambridgeshire
Fairs: *late July*
Wiveton Green, Norfolk
Bread and Bun Dole: *monthly*
Woodbridge, Suffolk
Bread and Bun Dole: *weekly*
Graveside Dole: *2 February*
Yarmouth, Norfolk
Harvest of the Sea service: *October see* HARVEST FESTIVALS

WEST MIDLANDS AND WELSH BORDERS
(HEREFORDSHIRE, SHROPSHIRE, STAFFORDSHIRE, WARWICKSHIRE, WORCESTERSHIRE)

Abbots Bromley, Staffordshire
Abbots Bromley Horn Dance: *Monday after Sunday following 4 September*
Alcester, Warwickshire
Courts Leet: *June*
Aston-on-Clun, Shropshire
Arbor Day: *29 May*
Atherstone, Warwickshire
Shrovetide Football
Berrow, Worcestershire
Duelling Sermon: *Sunday nearest 5 February see* SERMONS
Bishops Castle, Shropshire
Morris Dancing
Rushbearings: *Sunday after 24 June*
Bromsgrove, Worcestershire
Courts Leet
Fairs: *Midsummer*
Ascension Day Singing
Coventry, Warwickshire
Fairs: *29 May – 4 June*
Dunchurch, Warwickshire
Wroth Silver: *11 November*
Endon, Staffordshire
Wells and Well-dressing: *Spring Bank Holiday weekend*

Evesham, Worcestershire
Ascension Day Singing
Fownhope, Herefordshire
Club Walk: *29 May*
Henley-in-Arden, Warwickshire
Courts Leet
Hoarwithy, Herefordshire
Pax Cakes: *Palm Sunday*
Kidderminster, Worcestershire
Lost in the Dark Bells: *29 October*
Peace and Good Neighbourhood Feast: *Midsummer*
King's Caple, Herefordshire
Pax Cakes: *Palm Sunday*
Lichfield, Staffordshire
Beating the Bounds: *Ascension Day and around 8 September*
Court of Array: *Spring Bank Holiday Monday*
Courts Leet: *23 April*
Dr Johnson Commemoration: *Saturday nearest 18 September see* COMMEMORATIONS
Fairs
Guilds and Companies Ceremonies
Malvern, Worcestershire
Ascension Day Singing

Meriden, Warwickshire
Woodmen of Arden's Grand Wardmote: *1st week in August*
Newborough, Staffordshire
Wells and Well-dressing: *May*
Sellack, Herefordshire
Pax Cakes: *Palm Sunday*
Stratford-upon-Avon, Warwickshire
Shakespeare Commemoration: *23 April see* COMMEMORATIONS
Uttoxeter, Staffordshire
Dr Johnson Commemoration: *Monday after 18 September see* COMMEMORATIONS
Warwick, Warwickshire
Courts Leet
Fairs: *around 10 October*
Ascension Day Singing
Worcester, Worcestershire
Oak Apple Day: *29 May*
Wroxall, Warwickshire
Ascension Day Singing

WALES

Throughout region:
Eisteddfodau;
St David's Day: *1 March*

Cardigan, Cardiganshire
Eisteddfod: *early July*
Cilgerran, Cardiganshire
Coracle Racing: *August*
Hay-on-Wye, Breconshire
Fairs: *May*

Knighton, Radnorshire
Fairs: *May*
Lampeter, Cardiganshire
Eisteddfod: *early August*
Laugharne, Carmarthenshire
Beating the Bounds: *Spring Bank Holiday Monday*
Civic Customs
Llanfair Caereinion, Montgomeryshire
Beating the Bounds

Llanfihangel-yng-Ngwynfa, Montgomeryshire
Plygain service *see* CHRISTMAS
Llangollen, Denbighshire
Eisteddfod: *early July*
Llangynwyd, Glamorgan
Mari Lwyd: *Christmas*
Mynachlogddu, Pembrokeshire
Courts Leet
Newport, Pembrokeshire
Beating the Bounds

NORTH MIDLANDS
(DERBYSHIRE, LEICESTERSHIRE, LINCOLNSHIRE, NOTTINGHAMSHIRE, RUTLAND)

Ashbourne, Derbyshire
Shrovetide Football
Barlow, Derbyshire
Wells and Well-dressing: *Wednesday after 10 August*
Barrowden, Rutland
Rushbearings: *Sunday after 29 June*
Blidworth, Nottinghamshire
Cradle Rocking: *Sunday nearest 2 February see* CANDLEMAS
Bourne, Lincolnshire
Running Auction: *Easter Monday see* HOURGLASS, CROWN AND RUNNING AUCTIONS
Bradwell, Derbyshire
Wells and Well-dressing: *early August*
Braunstone, Leicestershire
Hay Strewing: *around 29 June see* RUSHBEARINGS
Brigg, Lincolnshire
Horse Fair: *5 August*
Burbage, Derbyshire
Clipping the Church: *July*
Burgh-le-Marsh, Lincolnshire
Lost in the Dark Bells: *weekdays 10 October – 7 April*
Pancake Bells: *Shrove Tuesday*
Passing Bells
Buxton, Derbyshire
Wells and Well-dressing: *late July*
Castleton, Derbyshire
Castleton Garland: *29 May*
Croyland, Lincolnshire
Courts Leet

Derby, Derbyshire
Egg Rolling see EASTER
Edwinstowe, Nottinghamshire
Boy Bishop see ADVENT
Enderby, Leicestershire
Selling the Keep of the Wether: *Whit Monday see* HOURGLASS, CROWN AND RUNNING AUCTIONS
Eton-cum-Stockdales, Leicestershire
Courts Leet
Eyam, Derbyshire
Plague Sunday: *last Sunday in August*
Wells and Well-dressing: *August*
Grantham, Lincolnshire
Drunkenness Sermon: *a Sunday in May see* SERMONS
Hallaton, Leicestershire
Bottle Kicking and Hare Pie Scramble: *Easter Monday*
Haxey, Lincolnshire
Haxey Hood Game: *6 January*
Headon, Nottinghamshire
Wells and Well-dressing: *July*
Langham, Rutland
Hay Strewing: *Sunday after 29 June see* RUSHBEARINGS
Laxton, Nottinghamshire
Courts Leet: *December*
Market Harborough, Leicestershire
Graveside Dole: *Easter Saturday*
Newark, Nottinghamshire
Bombshell Sermon: *around 11 March see* SERMONS
Lost in the Dark Bells: *October and November*
Pancake Bells: *Shrove Tuesday*

Nottingham
Goose Fair: *begins 1st Thursday in October see* FAIRS
Armada, Gunpowder Plot and St George's Day Sermons see SERMONS
Oakham, Rutland
Horseshoe Tax
Old Bolingbroke, Lincolnshire
Candle Auction: *4th week in March*
Sileby, Leicestershire
Orange-giving Ceremony: *a Sunday in May*
Tissington, Derbyshire
Wells and Well-dressing: *Ascension Day*
Whissendine, Rutland
Candle Auction: *3rd week in March*
Winster, Derbyshire
Pancake Race see SHROVE TUESDAY
Wirksworth, Derbyshire
Wells and Well-dressing: *4th week in May*
Youlgreave, Derbyshire
Wells and Well-dressing: *Saturday nearest Midsummer*

Other Derbyshire Well-dressing ceremonies at:
Ashford-in-the Water, Etwall, Middleton, Monyash: *in May*;
Bakewell, Edlaston, Hope, Litton, Rowsley, Tideswell: *June*;
Glapwell, Heath, Holmewood, Pilsley, Stoney Middleton, Whitwell: *July*;
Bonsall, Wormhill: *August*;
Hartington: *September*

YORKSHIRE
(EAST YORKSHIRE (E), NORTH YORKSHIRE (N), WEST YORKSHIRE (W))

Askrigg (N)
Club Walk: *1st Thursday in June*
Bainbridge (N)
Hornblowing: *nightly, 27 September – Shrove Tuesday*
Barwick-in-Elmet (W)
Maypole Raising: *Spring Bank Holiday, three-yearly*
Bolton Percy (N)
Plough Blessing see PLOUGH MONDAY
Boroughbridge (W)
Horse Fair: *around 22 June*
Brighouse (W)
Pace Egg Play *see* EASTER

Clifton (York)
Courts Leet: *October*
Danby (N)
Courts Leet: *October*
Denby Dale (W)
Denby Dale Pie
Dewsbury (W)
Tolling the Devil's Knell: *24 December*
Dore (W)
Wells and Well-dressing: *July*
Dungworth (W)
Local carols see CHRISTMAS
Souling

Ecclesfield (W)
Local carols see CHRISTMAS
Flamborough (E)
Harvest of the Sea service: *October see* HARVEST FESTIVALS
Fyling (N)
Courts Leet
Gawthorpe (W)
May Day
Goathland (N)
Plough Monday
Sword Dancing
Grenoside (W)
Sword Dancing: *Boxing Day*

Guiseley (W)
Clipping the Church: *5 August*

Handsworth (W)
Sword Dancing: *Boxing Day*

Haworth (W)
Rushbearings: *June*

Hubberholme (N)
Candle Auction: *1st Monday in January*

Ingbirchworth (W)
Local carols *see* CHRISTMAS

Kilburn (N)
Mock Mayors: *Saturday nearest 6 July*

Kirkby Ravensworth (N)
Kirkby Hill Races: *29 August, alternate years*

Knaresborough (N)
Plough Blessing *see* PLOUGH MONDAY

Lee Gap (W)
Horse Fair: *around 24 August*

Long Marston (W)
Plough Blessing *see* PLOUGH MONDAY

Midgley (W)
Pace Egg Play *see* EASTER

Mytholmroyd (W)
Pace Egg Play *see* EASTER

Richmond (N)
Beating the Bounds: *September, seven-yearly*
Bells and Bellringing
Harvest Festivals: *a Saturday in September*
Pancake Bells: *Shrove Tuesday*

Ripon (N)
Hornblowing: *nightly*
St Wilfrid's Feast Procession: *Saturday before 1st Monday in August*

Scarborough (N)
Pancake Bells
Skipping *see* SHROVE TUESDAY

Scorton (N)
Silver Arrow Contests

Seamer (N)
Fairs: *15 July*

South Dalton (E)
Kiplingcotes Derby: *3rd Thursday in March*

Sowerby Bridge (W)
Rushbearings: *1st Saturday and Sunday in September*

West Witton (N)
Burning Bartle: *Saturday after 24 August*

Whitby (N)
Blessing the Sea: *Rogationtide*
Penny Hedge: *day before Ascension Day*

Yarm (N)
Horse Fair: *October*

York
Civic Ceremonies
Guilds and Companies Ceremonies
Royal Salutes

NORTH WEST ENGLAND
(CHESHIRE, CUMBERLAND, LANCASHIRE, WESTMORLAND)

Throughout area:
Rushbearings;
Lancashire and Cheshire 'North-Western Processional Morris' *see* MORRIS DANCING

Aintree, Liverpool
Grand National: *1st Saturday in April*

Ambleside, Westmorland
Rushbearings: *Saturday nearest 2 July*
Wrestling, Cumberland: *Thursday after 1st Monday in August*

Antrobus, Cheshire
Souling: *1st two weeks in November*

Appleby, Westmorland
Horse Fair: *early June*

Appleton Thorn, Cheshire
Bawming the Thorn: *late June*

Bacup, Lancashire
Britannia Coconut Dancers: *Easter Saturday see* MORRIS DANCING

Bolton, Lancashire
New Year Fair *see* FAIRS
Rivington Pike Fair: *Good Friday see* FAIRS

Brough, Westmorland
Horse Fair: *30 September*

Cockermouth, Cumberland
Wrestling, Cumberland: *Saturday before 1st Monday in August*

Egremont, Cumberland
Crabapple Fair: *Saturday nearest 18 October*

Farndon, Cheshire
Rushbearings: *2nd Sunday in July*

Grasmere, Westmorland
Rushbearings: *Saturday nearest 5 August*
Wrestling, Cumberland: *Thursday after 1st Monday in August*

Kendal, Westmorland
Wrestling, Cumberland: *2nd Thursday in September*

Keswick, Cumberland
Wrestling, Cumberland: *August Bank Holiday*

Knutsford, Cheshire
Knutsford Royal May Day *see* MAY DAY

Lancaster, Lancashire
Beating the Bounds: *Wednesday after Spring Bank Holiday, seven-yearly*

Leigh, Lancashire
Travice Dole: *Maundy Thursday see* GRAVESIDE DOLES

Lymm, Cheshire
Rushbearings: *2nd Monday in August*

Macclesfield Forest Chapel, Cheshire
Rushbearings: *Sunday nearest 12 August*

Manchester, Lancashire
Whit Walks: *Spring Bank Holiday Monday see* FEASTS, REVELS, AND WAKES

Musgrave, Westmorland
Rushbearings: *1st Saturday in July*

Neston, Cheshire
Club Walk: *1st Thursday in June*

Penrith, Cumberland
Egg Rolling *see* EASTER

Preston, Lancashire
Egg Rolling *see* EASTER
Fairs: *last week in August*
Preston Guild: *twenty-yearly*

Saddleworth, Lancashire
Rushbearings: *August*

Tarvin, Cheshire
Rushbearings: *July*

Urswick, Lancashire
Rushbearings: *Sunday nearest Michaelmas*

Warcop, Westmorland
Rushbearings: *29 June*

Warrington, Cheshire
Walking Day: *Friday nearest 30 June see* FEASTS, REVELS, AND WAKES

Wasdale Head, Cumberland
Wrestling, Cumberland: *2nd Saturday in October*

Westhoughton, Lancashire
Cow Head Wakes: *August*

Workington, Cumberland
Shrovetide Football: *Good Friday and Easter*

NORTH-EAST ENGLAND
(DURHAM AND NORTHUMBERLAND)

Throughout area:
Carlings Sunday;
New Year's Eve First Footing;
Sword Dancing

Allendale Town, Northumberland
Allendale Tar Barrels: *31 December*
Alnwick, Northumberland
Shrovetide Football
Berwick-upon-Tweed, Northumberland
Beating the Bounds: *May Day*
Bells and Bellringing
Fairs: *last Friday in May*
Pancake Bells
Bowes, Durham
Courts Leet
Cullercoats, Northumberland
Blessing the Sea: *Rogationtide*

Durham
Civic Ceremonies
Durham Miners' Gala: *2nd Saturday in July*
Neville's Cross Commemoration: *29 May*
Greatham, Durham
Sword Dancing: *Boxing Day*
Mickley, Northumberland
Courts Leet
Morpeth, Northumberland
Beating the Bounds
Bells and Bellringing
Newbiggin-by-Sea, Northumberland
Beating the Bounds: *Wednesday nearest 18 May*
Newburn, Northumberland
Quit Rent Ceremony

Newcastle-upon-Tyne, Northumberland
Fairs
Sword Dancing
Norham, Northumberland
Blessing the Tweed: *Rogationtide see* BLESSING THE SEA
North Shields, Northumberland
Blessing the Sea: *Rogationtide*
Sedgefield, Durham
Shrovetide Football
Tweedmouth, Northumberland
Tweedmouth Feast: *begins Sunday after 18 July see* FEASTS, REVELS AND WAKES
Whalton, Northumberland
Whalton Baal Fire: *4 July*

SCOTLAND

Throughout country:
New Year celebrations;
Burns Night: *25 January*;
Highland Games;
Common Ridings, especially Borders;
St Andrews's Day: *30 November*

Aberdeen, Aberdeenshire
Common Riding: *mid-June*
Annan, Dumfriesshire
Common Riding: *1st Saturday in July*
Biggar, Lanarkshire
Burning the Old Year Out: *31 December*
Braemar, Aberdeenshire
Highland Games: *early September*
Burghead, Morayshire
Burning the Clavie: *31 December*
Carnwath, Lanarkshire
Red Hose Race: *3rd or 4th Thursday in August*
Coldstream, Berwickshire
Common Riding: *1st Thursday in August*
Comrie, Perthshire
Burning the Old Year Out: *31 December*
Cowal, Argyllshire
Highland Games: *mid-August*
Dumfries, Dumfriesshire
Common Riding: *last week in June*
Duns, Berwickshire
Ball Game: *July see* JEDBURGH BA' GAME
Common Riding: *first week in July*
Eaglesham, Renfrewshire
Kilmarnock Bonnet Race: *mid-May, alternate years see* FAIRS

Edinburgh
Egg Rolling *see* EASTER
Key Ceremony, Edinburgh Castle
May Day
New Year celebration, Tron Kirk
Opening of the General Assembly: *May*
Orders of Chivalry ceremonies: *November*
Royal Salutes
Elderslie, Lanarkshire
Wallace Commemoration: *around 23 August see* COMMEMORATIONS
Fort William, Invernesshire
Highland Games: *mid-July*
Galashiels, Selkirkshire
Common Riding: *last week in June*
Glasgow
New Year celebrations, George Square
Hawick, Roxburghshire
Common Riding: *early June*
Inverkeithing, Fife
Hat and Ribbon Race: *1st Thursday in August*
Irvine, Ayrshire
Marymass Fair: *3rd or 4th Monday in August*
Jedburgh, Roxburghshire
Common Riding: *early July*
Jedburgh Ba' Game: *2 February*
Kelso, Roxburghshire
Common Riding: *early July*
Kirkwall, Orkney
Shrovetide Football: *Christmas*
Lanark, Lanarkshire
Common Riding: *mid-June*
Whuppity Stourie: *1 March*

Langholm, Dumfriesshire
Common Riding: *last Friday in July*
Lauder, Berwickshire
Common Riding: *first Saturday in August*
Lerwick, Shetland
Up-Helly-Aa: *last Thursday in January*
Linlithgow, West Lothian
Common Riding: *Tuesday after 2nd Thursday in June*
Lockerbie, Dumfriesshire
Common Riding: *2nd Saturday in June*
Melrose, Roxburghshire
Common Riding: *last week in June*
Musselburgh, Midlothian
Common Riding: *mid-July*
Silver Arrow Contests
Peebles, Peeblesshire
Common Riding: *Midsummer Eve*
Penicuik, Midlothian
Common Riding: *2nd week in June*
St Andrews, Fife
Kate Kennedy Procession: *mid-April*
Royal and Ancient Golf Club Ceremonies
St Cyrus, Kincardineshire
Marriage Portion Charity
Selkirk, Selkirkshire
Common Riding: *Friday after 2nd Monday in June*
South Queensferry, West Lothian
The Burry Man: *2nd Friday in August*
South Ronaldsay, Orkney
Boys' Ploughing Match: *mid-August*
Wick, Caithness
Burning the Old Year Out: *31 December*